STUDY GUIDE TO ACCOMPANY
RUSSELL · GENERAL CHEMISTRY

D1450447

STUDY GUIDE TO ACCOMPANY
RUSSELL · GENERAL CHEMISTRY

NORMAN EATOUGH

Professor of Chemistry
California Polytechnic State University
at San Luis Obispo

McGraw-Hill Book Company

New York   St. Louis   San Francisco   Auckland   Bogotá   Hamburg   Johannesburg   London
Madrid   Mexico   Montreal   New Delhi   Panama   Paris   São Paulo   Singapore   Sydney
Tokyo   Toronto

Study Guide to Accompany RUSSELL: GENERAL CHEMISTRY

Copyright © 1980 by McGraw-Hill, Inc. All rights reserved.
Printed in the United States of America. No part of this publication
may be reproduced, stored in a retrieval system, or transmitted, in any
form or by any means, electronic, mechanical, photocopying, recording,
or otherwise, without the prior written permission of the publisher.

ISBN 0-07-054311-9

567890 DODO 89876

This book was set in Times Roman with Univers by Automated Composition
Service, Inc. The editors were Anne T. Vinnicombe and Scott Amerman;
the designer was Hermann Strohbach; the production supervisor was
Charles Hess.
R. R. Donnelley & Sons Company was printer and binder.

Cover: Photomicrograph of a crystal of sodium chloride grown by
evaporation of an aqueous solution of table salt to dryness.
Magnification: ×270. (*Photomicrograph by Eric V. Gravé.*)

CONTENTS

CONTENTS

TO THE STUDENT

This *Study Guide* is intended to help you understand the many principles, concepts, and calculations in a general chemistry course. It is written to accompany John B. Russell's *General Chemistry* and is organized just like the text with a section in the *Study Guide* corresponding to each section in the text. This makes it very easy to locate the examples and explanations in the *Study Guide* that correspond to specific areas in the text.

The *Study Guide* is written to accompany the text, not to replace it. It should be used side by side with the text as you study. The *Study Guide* is designed to guide you through your study of the text by helping to organize the concepts and correlating Learning Objectives with worked examples and homework problems in the text. Additional examples and explanations are given to parallel all new mathematical operations and difficult concepts in the text.

Each chapter in the *Study Guide* includes an overview of the text chapter, a summary of key equations when mathematical concepts are presented, an extensive list of learning objectives, an explanation of new skills that includes worked examples, and a self test.

I Chapter overview   Chapter overviews are designed to explain what each chapter is all about and to help you identify the most important concepts discussed. Brief explanations of more difficult areas and applications are given. The chapter overviews should be read before you read the corresponding text chapter.

II Key equations   The most important equations of the chapter are summarized and keyed to the text section. Brief explanations of the variables in the equations are included.

III Learning objectives   This is a comprehensive list of the concepts and operations presented in the chapter which you should learn. The objectives are keyed to text sections and homework problems and to the *Study Guide* New Skills section and Self Test problems. You can get maximum benefit from this section by using it to find examples and problems that apply to the specific learning objectives emphasized by your instructor.

IV New skills   Explanations and worked problems are presented to reinforce and supplement the examples and discussions in the text each time a new skill is presented. The *Study*

Guide often approaches a given concept in a manner somewhat different from the text presentation. Getting a slightly different view of a concept sometimes makes it easier to understand. Whenever a new skill is introduced, the first example is worked in step-by-step detailed procedure. When this skill is used in following examples, there will be a less detailed explanation and you will be expected to supply some steps yourself. When the explanations seem to leave out some steps, you should refer back to earlier examples involving the same skill for a more detailed presentation.

V Self tests Each chapter has true-false, completion, and multiple-choice questions. They are designed to test your mastery of the learning objectives. Answers for all self test questions and solutions to mathematical problems are provided at the end of the *Study Guide*. Make an honest effort to work all the problems before looking at the solutions. Even if you are wrong or could not work the problem all the way through, you may be able to see where you made the error and what you should have done. You can then try a similar problem and apply what you have learned. This technique will pay off in rapid improvement of your ability to set up and solve problems.

If this approach still does not work, or if you do not understand where the error is, reread the text and *Study Guide* sections pertaining to that area, rework the example problems, and then try the problem again. If you are still unable to solve the problem, discuss your approach to it with your instructor.

Effective study habits The text and *Study Guide* are designed to present concepts and problems in a logical manner, but they must be integrated into an effective total study pattern that correlates text, *Study Guide,* classroom lectures, and problem sessions to give you the maximum benefit for time spent.

I Your effort Getting an A in chemistry is not impossible, but unless you are a gifted genius it will take considerable time and effort. You are the one who has to decide to put forth the effort. This *Guide* is designed to give you the maximum benefit for your time. The key is to learn to study *efficiently* so you do not waste time. A routine study schedule will help immensely, but this requires much self discipline.

II Preparation before lectures Read the *Study Guide* and text material rapidly the night before your lecture. Examine the tables, graphs, and figures so you know what will be covered in lecture. Do not try to understand all the details and problems at this time, but prepare so you know why your instructor is covering a given topic and concentrate on how the concepts are approached and what points are emphasized. This will make the lectures more understandable. The text, the *Study Guide,* and your instructor should complement each other by presenting different views of the same material.

III During lecture Attend regularly and take concise notes, preferably in outline form. Your preparation before lecture will help you recognize the important points and examples as your instructor presents them.

IV After lecture Review your notes as soon as possible, preferably the same day. If your notes seem sketchy, spend some time soon, that evening if possible, clarifying points, adding ideas, and correcting errors. This serves the dual purpose of reinforcing concepts in your mind and providing meaningful review material to use in preparing for exams.

V Homework problems

Often homework is not required or graded in college chemistry courses, but the types of problems suggested provide a valuable clue to what your instructor thinks is important.

The more homework problems you do, the easier it will be to work similar problems on exams. Use the worked examples in the text and *Study Guide*. They are designed to help you work the problems at the end of the chapter, and they reinforce the concepts being studied.

VI Preparing for exams

Review every few days. Short periods of time spent in frequent reviews are much more effective than the same amount of time spent cramming the night before an exam. You learn effectively by repetition and identifying problem areas while there is still time to do something about them before exams.

VII Taking exams

Often your grade will depend entirely on one or two exams, so they are important. Start early to review your notes, homework problems, and examples. Try to anticipate the types of problems you are likely to encounter and work some like them. The problems you work in class or discussion sections should be a clue to what to expect on exams.

The presence of mind that comes from being well prepared can often help you over rough spots during an exam.

Problem solving

Many homework and exam problems will require mathematical operations. Usually the mathematics itself is not the major stumbling block and high-school algebra should provide sufficient background. The major challenge is in transforming word problems into a solution. The best help in this area is practice. Learning by doing is the best way to develop the skills necessary to solve problems. A major purpose of the course, your text, and this *Study Guide* is to help you become proficient in solving problems.

I Read the problem

Sometimes it is necessary to determine what is given in a problem because it is not stated explicitly. You will need to extract the data needed. Sometimes it helps to write the data in a table when you start the problem. Determine what is wanted or expected for the solution. Look for the *find . . . , how much . . . ,* and *what is . . .* phrases to determine what the problem is asking you to do. Be sure you understand all the terms used in the problem; use the text glossary whenever needed.

II Plan your solution

When you know what is given and what is wanted in a problem, you can often use the unit factor method to transform the data into an answer. This method is discussed in Section 1-7 of the text and *Study Guide*. You should not be worrying about plugging in numbers at this stage. Concentrate on the steps involved in arriving at an answer and try to see a pattern of steps that will take you all the way through the problem. Sometimes this may be a single equation that is presented in the text, but more often it is apt to involve a series of equations or operations. There are usually several different methods that can be used for solving problems and no single one of these is the right way. Any method that uses sound chemical and mathematical principles is correct.

The authors of the text and *Study Guide* favor the unit factor or dimensional analysis approach whenever possible, and it will be emphasized throughout the course.

| III Solving the problem | Once you have a sound plan or equation, the problem is already "solved." All you have to do is substitute the given data into your plan and calculate an answer. |

| IV The answer | Be sure to check to see if your answer seems reasonable. Take time to enjoy the sense of accomplishment when you arrive at this point. |

| V When the above steps do not work | If an honest effort does not bear fruit and the solution evades you, seek help. Outline the best approach you have taken to the problem and show it to someone. Explaining your material to someone else is often an effective learning technique. |

If this still does not help, go to your instructor. Do not go with general questions or complaints such as "I don't understand this chapter." Your instructor will not be able to guess what your problems are and will not have time to give special instructions for the whole chapter. Prepare specific questions and show your approach and methods. You can expect meaningful help if you are prepared.

| VI Electronic calculators | A pocket calculator is essentially a time-saving device. You can do the arithmetic without one, but the time spent can be invested more profitably doing other things. Science and engineering majors may want a programmable calculator for special uses, but for this course an inexpensive calculator will do all you need. It should have exponential or scientific display, a square root key, a log or ln key, and an inverse log or 10^x key. Most instructors allow calculators on exams and students with them spend less time working the arithmetic part of problems and thus have a definite advantage over students who use a slide rule or longhand technique. Calculators are well worth the small investment. |

Norman Eatough

STUDY GUIDE TO ACCOMPANY
RUSSELL · GENERAL CHEMISTRY

1 PRELIMINARIES AND PREMISES

CHAPTER OVERVIEW

In this introductory chapter we will be concerned with the basic methods and tools of chemistry. The first part of the chapter describes what chemistry is, why it is important, and how to study it. We will take a very brief look at historical aspects of the foundations of modern atomic theory to see how our ideas developed. There is a list of key terms at the end of the chapter. It is imperative that you become familiar with these terms as quickly as possible in each chapter you study. Being able to define and use scientific terms is basic to understanding the concepts and laws containing those terms. In many ways learning chemistry is much like learning a foreign language. You need to learn the vocabulary before you can learn to think in any language. So it is in chemistry. In this text each chapter builds on the previous work, and terms not learned will leave holes in your foundation chapters.

We will take an excursion into the world of mathematics as it is applied to problem solving in chemistry. There is no magic formula for working all chemistry problems, but you will see how a systematic approach to problems will solve the majority of challenges you will face.

**1-1
Chemistry: what, why, and how?**
Chemistry is the branch of science dealing with matter, its changes, and the laws describing those changes. If you have not yet read the To The Student section at the beginning of this *Study Guide*, do so now. Use the hints and suggestions there and in this section of the text and apply those that work for you personally.

**1-2
The way it all started**
As you read this section try to visualize the conditions under which these advances were made. Some of these important discoveries seem commonplace to us today, but they were made with very little data and much hard work and insight at the time.

Remember the discoveries that seem to be most important to today's ideas.

**1-3
Science and its methods**
Many important discoveries were made by accident or luck, but most come from an orderly and systematic approach to problems through the scientific method and the analysis of results of this method by a keen and well-trained mind. A major objective

of the entire course is to appreciate how the principles of chemistry are uncovered and then used to predict the changes and reactions that can occur in a system. This is the scientific method in action.

1-4
Words and definitions

Chemistry is an exact science. It can be exact only if we take care to define, understand, and use words and terms in a precise manner.

There are many new terms in this section. Learn them. If you have not yet found the glossary in the text, do so now and start using it.

1-5
Numbers: their use and misuse

Many concepts in chemistry involve numbers that are almost incomprehensibly small or large. Expressing this wide range of numbers in exponential notation has several advantages. It is more compact, shows the number of significant figures explicitly, gives a more accurate feeling for the magnitude of the number, makes mathematical operations involving these large and small numbers easier, and is the only way many numbers you will use can be displayed or entered in electronic calculators.

We will review the use of exponential notation in basic mathematical operations and the use and abuse of significant figures in this section. Although these concepts will not be mentioned again, they will be used continually throughout the course. Note how significant figures are handled slightly differently in addition and subtraction than in multiplication and division. Learn to round off answers to the correct number of significant figures and not just copy the digits that appear on your calculator. Appendix D in the text will help if you are rusty on algebraic concepts such as the quadratic formula and logarithms.

1-6
The metric system of units

The SI system and the metric system of units are not identical. The SI system is much more specialized than the general metric system. The seven base units from the metric system used to form the SI system are given in Table 1-1 in the text. They are often used in combination with the metric prefixes in Table 1-2. Most of the units in these tables should already be familiar to you.

There are some non-SI units in common use. They are millimeters of mercury (mmHg) and atmosphere (atm) for pressure, and liter and milliliter (ml) for volume. The text uses SI units in most cases, but other units are sometimes more convenient and so will be used occasionally.

1-7
Solving numerical problems

If you are not familiar with the dimensional analysis or unit factor method of problem solving, spend enough time on this section to see the advantages of this approach. Develop the habit of always including units on numbers you use in calculations. Observe how you can cancel units the same way you cancel numbers when multiplying or dividing. The strength in the unit factor method is its use of units as a guide in setting up problems. Proficiency in this only comes with practice. Work several problems by this method and you will soon see its power in setting up solutions to problems involving unit conversions.

The necessity of checking the units of your answer to be sure they are correct cannot be overemphasized. It is surprising how many errors can be detected and eliminated by making sure your answer always has the right units.

LEARNING OBJECTIVES

As a result of studying Chapter 1 you should be able to do the following:
Write the definition and give an example illustrating the use of each key term.

1-1
Chemistry: what,
why, and how?

1 Define chemistry.
2 Understand why you are studying it.
3 Understand how to study it.

1-2
The way it all
started

1 Understand how modern chemistry emerged from ancient beginnings. (Text Probs. 1-2, 1-3)
2 Understand the foundations of our modern concept of atoms. (Text Prob. 1-4)

1-3
Science and its
methods

1 Understand the use and limits of the scientific method. (Text Prob. 1-9)
2 Understand how scientific theories are formulated. (Text Probs. 1-1, 1-7, 1-8) (Self Test 8, 9)
3 List the steps in the scientific method. (Text Prob. 1-6)

1-4
Words and
definitions

1 Write the definitions and know the use of new terms as they are presented.
2 List the different states of matter. (Text Probs. 1-10, 1-11)
3 List some differences between physical and chemical properties of matter. (Text Probs. 1-13, 1-15, 1-16) (Self Test 18, 19)
4 List some distinctions among the various forms of matter: pure substance, compound, and mixture. (Text Probs. 1-12, 1-14) (Self Test 10, 11, 17)

1-5
Numbers: their use
and misuse

1 Express numbers in exponential notation. (Text Prob. 1-17) (New Skills Sec. 1-5:1; Self Test 12)
2 Use exponential notation in mathematical operations: addition, subtraction, multiplication, division, and taking roots. (Text Prob. 1-21) (New Skills Examples 1 to 10; Self Test 13, 14)
3 Give the number of significant figures in any number. (Text Prob. 1-18) (New Skills Examples 11, 12; Self Test 5)
4 Express answers to problems with the correct number of significant figures. (Text Probs. 1-19 to 1-22) (New Skills Examples 13 to 16; Self Test 20, 22)

1-6
The metric system
of units

1 List the seven base units of the SI system. (Text Prob. 1-23)
2 List the values of the prefixes kilo-, centi-, and milli- used in the metric system. (Text Probs. 1-24, 1-25, 1-26)
3 List the common non-SI units for pressure and volume.

1-7
Solving numerical
problems

1 Use the dimensional analysis or unit factor method in calculations. (Text Examples 1-1 to 1-5; Text Probs. 1-30 to 1-35) (New Skills Sec. 1-7, Examples 17, 18; Self Test 4, 22 to 25)

2 Express an equality as a unit factor. (Text Probs. 1-28, 1-29) (Self Test 3, 6, 15, 16, 21)

3 Use units to check the correctness of answers in your calculations.

NEW SKILLS

1-5
Numbers: their use
and misuse

1 Exponential notation

Often in solving chemical problems you will use numbers that are very large or very small. Most calculators will not accept these numbers unless they are entered in exponential notation. Some calculators automatically convert numbers to exponential notation after all the digits are used. Learning to convert large or small numbers to exponential notation will help you perform calculations easily and confidently on your calculator.

Multiplication and division are actually easier in exponential notation.

The general form of a number in exponential notation is

$$A \times 10^n$$

where A represents a number between 1 and 10 and n is the exponent. The number A (the coefficient) is multiplied by some power or multiple of 10. Thus

$$2 \times 10^6 \quad \text{is} \quad 2 \times 10 \times 10 \times 10 \times 10 \times 10 \times 10 \quad \text{or} \quad 2,000,000$$

If the exponent is negative we divide by 10 that number of times. Thus

$$3 \times 10^{-4} \quad \text{is} \quad 3 \times \frac{1}{10} \times \frac{1}{10} \times \frac{1}{10} \times \frac{1}{10} \quad \text{or} \quad 0.0003$$

To convert a number to exponential notation move the decimal point so the coefficient is between 1 and 10. Count the number of places the decimal point was moved. This is the value of the exponent, n. If the decimal point was moved to the left, the exponent is positive; if it was moved to the right, the exponent is negative. Thus

$$3,860,000 \quad \text{is} \quad 3.86 \times 10^6$$
$$0.000475 \quad \text{is} \quad 4.75 \times 10^{-4}$$

Negative numbers can be converted to exponential notation in the same manner

$$-10,400 \quad \text{is} \quad -1.04 \times 10^4$$
$$-0.000055 \quad \text{is} \quad -5.5 \times 10^{-5}$$

2 Mathematical calculations using exponential notation

(*a*) MULTIPLICATION USING EXPONENTIAL NOTATION. Multiplication of two numbers in exponential notation is performed by multiplying coefficients and adding exponents.

● **EXAMPLE 1**

Problem: Multiply 20,000 by 3,000,000 using exponential notation.

Solution: First express the numbers in exponential notation.

$$20,000 \quad \text{is} \quad 2 \times 10^4$$
$$3,000,000 \quad \text{is} \quad 3 \times 10^6$$

Now multiply coefficients and add exponents.

$$(2 \times 10^4)(3 \times 10^6) = 6 \times 10^{6+4} = 6 \times 10^{10} \bullet$$

● **EXAMPLE 2**　　**Problem:** Multiply 4,000 by 600,000 using exponential notation.

Solution:

$$(4 \times 10^3)(6 \times 10^5) = 24 \times 10^{3+5} = 24 \times 10^8$$

24×10^8 can be changed to normal exponential notation in which the coefficient is between 1 and 10 by moving the decimal one place to the left and adding 1 to the exponent

$$24 \times 10^8 \quad \text{is} \quad 2.4 \times 10^9$$

The answer should be given as 2.4×10^9. ●

● **EXAMPLE 3**　　**Problem:** Multiply 0.008 by 800,000 using exponential notation.

Solution: Negative exponents are added algebraically in multiplication.

$$(8 \times 10^{-3})(8 \times 10^5) = 64 \times 10^{-3+5} = 64 \times 10^2 = 6.4 \times 10^3$$

Note that in all mathematical operations the coefficient part of exponential notation is treated in a common, ordinary manner. ●

(*b*) DIVISION USING EXPONENTIAL NOTATION. Division is performed by dividing coefficients and subtracting exponents.

● **EXAMPLE 4**　　**Problem:** Divide 80,000 by 200 using exponential notation.

Solution:

$$\frac{8 \times 10^4}{2 \times 10^2} = 4 \times 10^{4-2} = 4 \times 10^2 \bullet$$

● **EXAMPLE 5**　　**Problem:** Divide 0.009 by 3,000,000 using exponential notation.

Solution:

$$\frac{9 \times 10^{-3}}{3 \times 10^6} = 3 \times 10^{-3-6} = 3 \times 10^{-9} \bullet$$

(*c*) ADDITION AND SUBTRACTION USING EXPONENTIAL NOTATION. Addition and subtraction can be performed only if all numbers involved have the same exponent. If the exponents are different they must be adjusted by moving the decimal point in the coefficient the same number of places to the left as the exponent is increased, or the same number of places to the right as the exponent is decreased. When the exponents are equal, the coefficients can be added and the exponent remains unchanged.

● **EXAMPLE 6**　　**Problem:** Add $(2 \times 10^3) + (4.0 \times 10^4) + (5.00 \times 10^5)$.

Solution:

$$2 \times 10^3 \quad \text{is} \quad 0.02 \times 10^5$$

$$4.0 \times 10^4 \quad \text{is} \quad 0.40 \times 10^5$$

$$5.00 \times 10^5 \quad \text{is} \quad \frac{5.00 \times 10^5}{5.42 \times 10^5}$$

Are the correct number of significant figures shown in the answer? •

Subtraction is done in the same manner. The coefficients are subtracted and the exponents must be kept constant. If this is still not clear, try converting the exponential notation to expanded form, carry out the mathematical operations, and compare the answer with your answer from the exponential notation method.

(*d*) POWERS OF NUMBERS USING EXPONENTIAL NOTATION. Raising a number in exponential notation to a power is performed by multiplying the exponent by the power and raising the coefficient to that power.

• **EXAMPLE 7**   **Problem:** Find the square of 400 using exponential notation.

Solution:

$$(4 \times 10^2)^2 = 16 \times 10^{2 \times 2} = 16 \times 10^4 = 1.6 \times 10^5 \bullet$$

• **EXAMPLE 8**   **Problem:** Find the cube of 0.003 using exponential notation.

Solution:

$$(3 \times 10^{-3})^3 = 27 \times 10^{-3 \times 3} = 27 \times 10^{-9} = 2.7 \times 10^{-8} \bullet$$

(*e*) ROOTS OF NUMBERS USING EXPONENTIAL NOTATION. Taking the root of a number in exponential notation is performed by taking the root of the coefficient and dividing the exponent by the root.

• **EXAMPLE 9**   **Problem:** Find the square root of 400 using exponential notation.

Solution:

$$\sqrt{4 \times 10^2} = (4 \times 10^2)^{1/2} = 2 \times 10^{2 \div 2} = 2 \times 10^1 = 20 \bullet$$

• **EXAMPLE 10**   **Problem:** Find the cube root of 27,000,000 using exponential notation.

Solution:

$$\sqrt[3]{2.7 \times 10^7} = (2.7 \times 10^7)^{1/3} = ?$$

The last example is easier to handle if the exponent is changed to a number evenly divisible by the root number.

$$(2.7 \times 10^7)^{1/3} = (27 \times 10^6)^{1/3} = 3 \times 10^{6 \div 3} = 3 \times 10^2 \bullet$$

Many pocket calculators have the capability of taking powers or roots of numbers. Check your owner's manual to see how this is done on your calculator.

3 Significant figures

Significant figures are an indication of the maximum reliability of an experimental measurement. Often the last significant figure in a measurement is estimated in the experiment and its accuracy may be in doubt.

For example, suppose you weighed yourself on a pair of scales and observe the pointer to be one-fifth of the way between the 55- and 56-kg marks. You would report your weight as 55.2 kg. This indicates you read the scales with a precision of ±0.1 kg. Even though there is some doubt in the precision of the last digit, the measured value is considered to be precise to three significant figures.

There are four simple rules to determine the number of significant figures in an experimentally determined number.

1 All digits other than zero are significant.
2 All zeros between nonzero digits are significant.
3 Zeros following a nonzero digit in a number with a decimal point are always significant.
4 Zeros that are not preceded by a nonzero digit simply locate the decimal point and are not significant figures.

NOTE: This does not mean to imply that locating the decimal point is an insignificant act; in fact, in some ways the choice of term *significant figures* is unfortunate. Significant figures tell us the significance of the error in measurement compared to the size of the number, not the location of the decimal point.

● **EXAMPLE 11**   **Problem**: How many significant figures are in each of the following: 4.073, 0.0072, 10, 0.0360?

Solution:

4.073	4 significant figures
0.0072	2 significant figures
10	1 significant figure
0.0360	3 significant figures ●

● **EXAMPLE 12**   **Problem**: Write the number four hundred to illustrate different measurements with one, two, three, and four significant figures.

Solution:

1 significant figure	400	or	4×10^2
2 significant figures	?		4.0×10^2
3 significant figures	400.	or	4.00×10^2
4 significant figures	400.0	or	4.000×10^2

The only way two significant figures can be indicated is by using exponential notation. ●

It is important that the precision of an answer reflect the precision of the data used in a problem. The answer cannot be more precise than the least precise data used. Care should be taken to preserve the correct number of significant figures in mathematical operations to show the right precision in your answers.

When numbers are added or subtracted, the measurement with the lowest precision determines the number of significant figures in the answer.

● **EXAMPLE 13**   **Problem**: The masses of four objects are found to be 473.1, 7.33, 0.14, and 0.0037 kg. What is the total mass of the four objects?

Solution: The least precise measurement has a precision of ±0.1 kg and the sum cannot be more precise than this. One might be tempted to add the masses as follows:

$$
\begin{array}{r}
473.1 \quad \text{kg} \\
7.33 \quad \text{kg} \\
0.14 \quad \text{kg} \\
\underline{0.0037 \text{ kg}} \\
481.5737 \text{ kg}
\end{array}
$$

Even though 473.1 has the most significant figures, in this case it is the least precise measurement. Since it is precise to only ±0.1 kg, the sum cannot be more precise than this and we must round off the answer to the nearest 0.1 kg.

The correct answer is 481.6 kg. Note that there are four significant figures in the answer even though some measurements have only two significant figures. ●

When numbers are multiplied or divided, the answer will have the same number of significant figures as the number in the data with the fewest significant figures. In multiplication and division it is the fewest number of significant figures in the data, not the location of the decimal point, that tells how to round off the answer to the correct number of significant figures. An example will show how exponential notation takes the guesswork out of determining significant figures.

● **EXAMPLE 14**   **Problem:** Multiply 400 by 27.1.

Solution: One might be tempted to write

$$400 \times 27.1 = 10,840$$

but that answer has too many significant figures and needs to be rounded off to correspond to the number with the least significant figures in the given data. The trouble is that there is no way of knowing how many significant figures the number 400 has. If the numbers had been given in exponential notation as 4.00×10^2 and 2.71×10, it would be obvious that there should be three significant figures in the answer and we would round off the answer to 1.08×10^4. ●

In exponential notation the coefficient always shows the correct number of significant figures and the exponent locates the decimal point.

● **EXAMPLE 15**   **Problem:** Find the product of 2.45×10^2 and 3.7×10^3.

Solution:

$$(2.45 \times 10^2)(3.7 \times 10^3) = 9.1 \times 10^5 \quad ●$$

● **EXAMPLE 16**   **Problem:** Divide 4.739×10^6 by 3.71×10^4.

Solution:

$$\frac{4.739 \times 10^6}{3.71 \times 10^4} = 1.28 \times 10^2 \quad ●$$

The concept of significant figures is easy to understand, but students often forget to apply it in calculations. Problems usually will not specifically ask for the correct number of significant figures, but you should always be aware of the precision your answer deserves in each problem in the text or *Study Guide.*

4 Rounding off numbers

A number is rounded off by dropping digits to the right of the last significant figure. The following rules can be used to round off answers to the correct number of significant figures.

a When the digit to the right of the last significant figure is less than 5, the last significant figure remains unchanged. For example, 9.7346 becomes 9.73 to three significant figures.

b When the digit to the right of the last significant figure is greater than 5, the last significant figure is increased by 1. For example, 83.478 becomes 83.5 to three significant figures.

c When the digit to the right of the last significant figure is 5, the last significant figure is increased by 1 if it is odd but remains unchanged if it is even. For example, 57.55 and 57.65 both give 57.6 when rounded off to three significant figures.

1-7
Solving numerical
problems

Most instructors will assume you have a basic understanding of algebra and handling algebraic equations. If you are rusty in this area, consult your bookstore for a paperback book on basic mathematics for chemistry. There are several good ones available.

We will proceed directly to the dimensional analysis or unit factor approach to problem solving. Many students who say they are having trouble with chemistry actually understand the chemistry but are stumbling over the mathematics. We have already seen how exponential notation simplifies the arithmetic. If you are still unconvinced, work Prob. 1-21 in the text. The general approach of the unit factor method will simplify calculations in a wide field of problems in chemistry. You will use the method extensively in later chapters, so now is the time to learn it well. It will take practice to get used to the method. It is simply a method of analyzing the units (dimensions) of numbers and using these units to set up factors to convert from the quantity given in a problem to the answer desired. Let the units guide you through the problem. It is important to recognize the information given in a problem and separate it from the question asked. This takes practice and persistence.

In dimensional analysis units are treated just like numbers in algebraic operations: they may be canceled or multiplied just like numbers.

Let us analyze Example 1-1 in the text.

● **EXAMPLE 17**

Problem: If you are 147 cm tall, what is your height in inches?

Solution: First: What is given and what is desired in the problem? 147 cm is given. The number of inches equal to 147 cm is the desired value. The problem could be rewritten to read "How many inches are equal to 147 cm?"

To solve the problem we need a unit factor that relates the given units to the desired units, in this case a conversion equation for centimeters and inches. Several conversion equations are given in Table 1-3 in the text. There are two that relate centimeters to inches. They are

$$1 \text{ cm} = 0.394 \text{ in}$$

$$1 \text{ in} = 2.54 \text{ cm}$$

Let us divide both sides of the first conversion equation by 0.394 in

$$\frac{1 \text{ cm}}{0.394 \text{ in}} = \frac{0.394 \text{ in}}{0.394 \text{ in}} = 1$$

We have formed a unit factor for changing inches to centimeters

$$\frac{1 \text{ cm}}{0.394 \text{ in}} = 1$$

Let us go back and divide both sides of the first conversion equation by 1 cm

$$\frac{1 \text{ cm}}{1 \text{ cm}} = 1 = \frac{0.394 \text{ in}}{1 \text{ cm}}$$

We have formed a second unit factor from the conversion equation

$$\frac{0.394 \text{ in}}{1 \text{ cm}} = 1$$

Similarly, we can form two unit factors from the second conversion equation: one by dividing both sides by 2.54 cm

$$\frac{1 \text{ in}}{2.54 \text{ cm}} = \frac{2.54 \text{ cm}}{2.54 \text{ cm}} = 1$$

and another by dividing by 1 in

$$\frac{1 \text{ in}}{1 \text{ in}} = 1 = \frac{2.54 \text{ cm}}{1 \text{ in}}$$

We have formed four unit factors from the two conversion equations. Indeed, each conversion equation in Table 1-3 in the text can be used to form two unit factors.

The four unit factors are

$$\frac{1 \text{ cm}}{0.394 \text{ in}} = 1 \qquad \frac{0.394 \text{ in}}{1 \text{ cm}} = 1$$

$$\frac{1 \text{ in}}{2.54 \text{ cm}} = 1 \qquad \frac{2.54 \text{ cm}}{1 \text{ in}} = 1$$

These are all fractions, or unit factors, equal to unity.

To solve the problem you must multiply the given quantity, 147 cm, by the unit factor that will make the answer appear in the correct units. To do this you must plan ahead from the given data to the answer. Given units are centimeters; desired units are inches.

$$\text{cm} \times \frac{\text{in}}{\text{cm}} = \text{in}$$

If centimeters are multiplied by in/cm, centimeters can be canceled to leave the desired inches.

The problem is essentially solved; all we need to do is add the correct numbers to the unit factors. We have a choice of two unit factors for in/cm. Either will work.

$$147 \text{ cm} \times \frac{0.394 \text{ in}}{1 \text{ cm}} = 57.9 \text{ in}$$

or
$$147 \ \cancel{cm} \times \frac{1 \ in}{2.54 \ \cancel{cm}} = 57.9 \ in$$

Choosing one of the other unit factors leads to an incorrect answer:

$$147 \ cm \times \frac{2.54 \ cm}{1 \ in} = 373 \ cm^2/in \quad \bullet$$

You may not recognize that the number 373 is incorrect, but the units cm^2/in tell you the answer is not correct. Always look at the numerical answer *and* the units to help tell if the answer is correct.

The same reasoning and principles can be applied to the unit factor method for problems in which more than one unit factor is needed to get the answer.

● **EXAMPLE 18**   **Problem:** An imported car has a fuel economy rating of 15.0 km/liter. How many miles per gallon is this?

Solution: The problem asks us to convert from units of km/liter to miles per gallon. The "per" in miles per gallon can be read as "divided by," or mi/gal.
    We need to convert

$$\frac{km}{liter} \quad to \quad \frac{mi}{gal}$$

Two conversions are required here: kilometers to miles and liters to gallons. Examine Table 1-3 in the text for equations that can be used to give the necessary unit factors.

$$1 \ km = 0.621 \ mi$$

from which

$$\frac{0.621 \ mi}{1 \ km} = 1$$

is a unit factor. The conversion of liters to gallons does not appear in Table 1-3, but we can accomplish the desired conversion by first converting liters to quarts and then use a familiar relation to convert quarts to gallons.

$$1 \ liter = 1.06 \ qt \quad or \quad \frac{1 \ liter}{1.06 \ qt} = 1$$

and
$$4 \ qt = 1 \ gal \quad or \quad \frac{4 \ qt}{1 \ gal} = 1$$

Now we can use these unit factors in a systematic fashion to obtain the desired units.

$$\frac{\cancel{km}}{\cancel{liter}} \times \frac{mi}{\cancel{km}} \times \frac{\cancel{liter}}{\cancel{qt}} \times \frac{\cancel{qt}}{gal} = \frac{mi}{gal}$$

The unit factors are assembled to cancel the given units and introduce the desired units. If the units are not right in the answer, go back and see if a unit factor has been inverted. Now we add the numbers to the unit factors to get the answer.

$$\frac{15.0 \ km}{liter} \times \frac{0.621 \ mi}{1 \ km} \times \frac{1 \ liter}{1.06 \ qt} \times \frac{4 \ qt}{1 \ gal} = 35.2 \ mi/gal$$

Check the significant figures also. Since 1 km, 1 liter, 4 qt, and 1 gal are all defined quantities, they have very high precision compared to the other numbers. They do not determine the number of significant figures in the answer. ●

Now work Examples 1-2 through 1-5 in the text.

SELF TEST

(Answers to Self Tests may be found at the back of this *Study Guide*.)

True or False

_F_ 1 Science vocabulary is relatively easy because each term has a precise meaning.

_T_ 2 An understanding of mathematics is necessary for an understanding of chemistry.

_T_ 3 All unit factors are equal to unity.

_F_ 4 If you can select the right unit factor you can convert a mass measurement to a density (mass per volume) measurement.

_F_ 5 The number 45.70 has three significant figures.

_T_ 6 If 1 ml = 0.001 liters, the unit factor to convert liters to milliliters is

$$\frac{10^3 \text{ ml}}{1 \text{ liter}}$$

_F_ 7 When you divide 3.976 by 2.062 your calculator displays 1.9282250. The correct answer is 1.9282250.

Completion

8 A tentative answer or explanation of scientific observations is called a _____.

9 A _____ describes a well tested law or model.

10 A _____ is composed of two or more pure substances.

11 A _____ is composed of two or more elements in a fixed ratio.

12 The number 0.000370 can be expressed as _____ in exponential notation.

13 The product of 3.00×10^7 and 5.0×10^5 is _____.

14 8.00×10^{-4} divided by 2.0×10^6 is _____.

15 The unit factor for converting milliliters to liters is _____.

16 The unit factor for converting kilograms to grams is _____.

Multiple choice

17 A pure substance composed of two or more elements is called a (an)
(a) element   (b) mixture   (c) compound   (d) atom

18 Which of the following does not involve a chemical change?
(a) Iron rusting
(b) Wood burning in air
(c) Milk turning sour
(d) Melting an iron nail

19 Which of the following represents a chemical change?
(a) Salt melts at 800°C.
(b) Diamond is the hardest known substance.
(c) Sulfur flows when heated.
(d) Burning a chemistry textbook.

20 The individual masses of four different objects are 5.0, 0.33, 50.0, and 3.05 g. The total mass of the four objects is

(a) 58.38 g   (b) 58.3 g   (c) 58.4 g   (d) 58 g

21 The correct unit factor to convert inches to centimeters is

(a) $\dfrac{2.54 \text{ cm}}{1 \text{ in}}$ (b) $\dfrac{0.394 \text{ in}}{1 \text{ cm}}$ (c) $\dfrac{1 \text{ in}}{2.54 \text{ cm}}$ (d) $\dfrac{0.1 \text{ in}}{1 \text{ cm}}$

22 Given 1 lb = 454 g, the mass of a person weighing 125 lb is

(a) 0.28 kg   (b) 56750 kg   (c) 56.8 kg   (d) 56.750 kg

23 How many miles are there in 1 kilometer? (1 in = 2.54 cm, 1 ft = 12 in, 1 mi = 5280 ft)

(a) 1.61   (b) 0.58   (c) 0.621   (d) 173

24 If there are 10 chunks in a glob and you have 30 globs, the number of chunks you have is

(a) 3   (b) 10   (c) 30   (d) 300

25 How many kilometers per hour is the 55 mph speed limit? See Prob. 23 for conversion equations.

(a) 34   (b) 55   (c) 88   (d) 225

2 MATTER AND ENERGY

CHAPTER OVERVIEW

If you have already had a course in science you have studied many of the concepts presented in this chapter. As you study, try to develop a better understanding of the kinds of matter, the types of energy, and how the nature of matter and energy are observed and measured. This chapter is about changes in the nature and types of matter and energy and how they relate to each other.

2-1
Matter: what is it?

The concept of mass becomes meaningful only when we measure and observe its effects manifest in inertia and weight. The difference between mass and weight should be clearly understood. Mass is a measure of the amount of matter. Weight is the effect of a gravitational field on mass. When an object is removed from the influence of a gravitational field it has no weight but its mass does not change. An astronaut has a certain mass and weight on earth but in space becomes weightless. He or she still has the same mass, but in the absence of a gravitational field has no weight.

The concept of density is useful to describe the compactness of matter. It is a measure of the mass of a given volume of matter. In SI units the mass is in kilograms (kg) and the volume is in cubic meters (m^3), so the density is in $kg\,m^{-3}$. More commonly, the mass will be expressed in grams (g) and the volume in cubic centimeters (cm^3) or milliliters (ml), so the density is in $g\,cm^{-3}$ or $g\,ml^{-1}$. Since a cubic centimeter is essentially equal to a milliliter, the last two units for density are equivalent. The concept of density is simple, but note in the example problems and homework how the manner in which data are presented can make the simplicity hard to find. You will experience the chance to transform word problems into solutions and apply the techniques of problem solving discussed in the introduction to this *Study Guide* as you work density problems.

2-2
Kinds of matter

Since chemistry is a study of matter and its changes, it is important to be aware of the structure of matter. Elements are the fundamental units of matter. There are 105 different elements, each represented by a unique chemical symbol. It would be worthwhile to learn the names and symbols of the first 30 elements. Elements interact to form aggregates called compounds. The combination of elements in a compound is denoted by combining the chemical symbols into a chemical formula such as NaCl, H_2O, or H_2SO_4. Elements and compounds can be mixed in any proportions to form various types of mixtures. The differences between compounds and mixtures of elements are described in the text.

Throughout the course we will study the physical and chemical changes of matter. These changes are governed by several laws, two of which are introduced here. The law of conservation of mass states that there is no gain or loss of mass during physical or chemical changes. The law of definite composition states that a given compound always has the same, definite, fixed ratio of elements.

2-3
The microstructure
of matter

It is easy to measure the properties of bulk matter such as temperature, pressure, volume, and mass, but much more challenging to make measurements on atoms, the fundamental building blocks of the elements. No one has ever seen an atom, yet we have a large amount of information about atomic behavior. We will have much more to say about atoms in Chaps. 3, 5, and 6.

2-4
Energy: what is it?

Work is the movement of a mass against an opposing force such as gravity. Energy is the ability or capacity to do work. There are many types of energy, and energy can be transformed from one type into another. Mechanical energy can be energy of motion (kinetic energy) or energy of position (potential energy). Heat energy and electrical energy are also commonly encountered in the study of chemistry. As the course progresses, we will also see how the concepts of energy and matter are interrelated and will become aware of the energy changes that accompany changes in matter.

2-5
Heat and
temperature

The differences between the terms *heat, energy,* and *temperature* should be clearly understood. Heat is energy in transit. Temperature is a measure of the average kinetic energy of the particles in an object. When heat is added to a substance its energy increases. This may result in an increase in temperature or a change in the phase of the substance which takes place at constant temperature. This concept of adding heat to a substance during a phase change while the temperature remains constant should be clearly understood.

The units used for energy and temperature measurements throughout the text are joules, degrees Celsius, and kelvins. Note that temperature on the Kelvin scale is measured in kelvins, not degrees Kelvin. The relationship between degrees Celsius and kelvins must be memorized.

LEARNING OBJECTIVES

As a result of studying Chap. 2 you should be able to do the following:

Write the definition and give an example illustrating the use of each key term.

2-1
Matter: what is it?

1 Explain how mass and matter are related. (Text Prob. 2-1)
2 Explain how inertia and weight are related to mass.
3 Explain the meaning and use of density. (Text Prob. 2-6) (Self Test 1)

4 Given the mass and volume of a substance, calculate its density. (Text Example 2-1; Text Probs. 2-4, 2-7) (New Skills Examples 1, 2; Self Test 21)

5 Calculate the volume of a given mass of substance if the density is known. (Text Example 2-2; Text Prob. 2-3) (New Skills Example 3; Self Test 22)

6 Calculate the mass of a given volume if the density is known. (Text Example 2-3; Text Prob. 2-9) (New Skills Example 4)

2-2
Kinds of matter

1 Understand the classification of matter in Fig. 2-1 of the text. (Self Test 2)

2 List the differences between pure substances, mixtures, elements, and compounds. (Text Probs. 2-19, 2-20) (Self Test 9, 17)

3 Understand the meaning and use of chemical symbols and formulas. (Self Test 3)

4 Show the differences between phases, homogeneous mixtures, heterogeneous mixtures, and solutions. (Text Probs. 2-13, 2-16) (Self Test 8)

5 List some differences between physical and chemical changes. (Self Test 5, 18, 19)

6 State and understand the law of conservation of mass and use it in chemical calculations. (Text Example 2-4; Text Prob. 2-23) (New Skills Example 5; Self Test 4)

7 State and understand the law of definite composition as applied to chemical compounds.

8 Calculate the percentage composition of a compound. (Text Example 2-5; Text Probs. 2-22, 2-25, 2-26) (New Skills Example 6; Self Test 23)

9 Calculate the grams of product formed from a given mass of reactant when the percentage composition of the product is known. (Text Example 2-6; Text Probs. 2-21, 2-24) (New Skills Example 7; Self Test 24)

2-3
The microstructure of matter

1 Understand the meaning and use of the terms *atom* and *molecule.* (Self Test 10)

2 Understand why some substances are not composed of molecules.

3 Explain the basic differences in the microstructure (molecular structure) of solids, liquids, and gases. (Text Prob. 2-14)

2-4
Energy: what is it?

1 Understand the meaning and use of the terms *energy* and *work* and the relationship between them. (Self Test 7, 11)

2 Understand the meaning of kinetic energy and potential energy and the relationship between them. (Text Probs. 2-30, 2-32, 2-33) (Self Test 15, 16, 20)

3 Tell how energy is transformed from one form into another. (Text Prob. 2-29)

2-5
Heat and temperature

1 Explain the difference between heat and temperature. (Text Prob. 2-27; Self Test 6, 12)

2 Relate temperature to kinetic energy.

3 Understand what happens when heat is added to a substance. (Text Prob. 2-28)

4 Use the SI basic unit of temperature, the kelvin.

5 Make conversions between degrees Fahrenheit, degrees Celsius, and kelvins. (Text Probs. 2-34 to 2-36) (Self Test 14, 25)

NEW SKILLS

2-1
Matter: what is it?

1 Calculation of density

Density is an important physical property of matter defined as the mass of substance per unit volume. Recalling that "per" means to divide:

$$\text{Density} = \frac{\text{mass}}{\text{volume}}$$

Mass is usually expressed in grams and volume in cubic centimeters

$$\text{Density} = \frac{g}{cm^3} = g\ cm^{-3}$$

The volume of a substance changes with temperature since most substances expand on heating. This means that density decreases as temperature increases. Density values are usually given at 25°C, and unless a different temperature is specified we will assume the densities in the text are for 25°C.

● **EXAMPLE 1**   **Problem:** A piece of copper metal has a volume of 50.0 cm^3 and weighs 447 g. What is the density of copper?

Solution: In the metric system mass and weight are the same so the mass of the copper is 447 g. Density is the mass of an object divided by its volume.

$$\text{Density} = \frac{447\ g}{50.0\ cm^3} = 8.94\ g\ cm^{-3}\ ●$$

● **EXAMPLE 2**   **Problem:** An empty container weighs 87.63 g. When 10.00 ml of a certain liquid is placed in the container, the total weight is 95.71 g. What is the density of the liquid?

Solution: The volume of the liquid is 10.00 ml or 10.00 cm^3 since 1 ml is the same as 1 cm^3. The mass of liquid is found by subtracting the mass of the empty container from the total mass

$$\text{Total mass} = \text{mass empty container} + \text{mass liquid}$$

$$\text{Mass liquid} = \text{total mass} - \text{mass empty container}$$

$$= 95.71\ g - 87.63\ g = 8.08\ g$$

$$\text{Density} = \frac{\text{mass}}{\text{volume}} = \frac{8.08\ g}{10.00\ cm^3} = 0.808\ g\ cm^{-3}\ ●$$

Now go through Example 2-1 in the text.

The units of density are g cm^{-3}. This means that density can be used as a unit factor between mass and volume. In fact, the importance of density in calculations is its use in converting mass to an equivalent volume or vice versa.

Let us examine this use. First we will find the volume equivalent to a given mass.

● **EXAMPLE 3**   **Problem:** Mercury (Hg) is sold commercially in flasks containing 70 lb of mercury. What is the volume (in liters) of 70.0 lb of mercury? The density of mercury is 13.54 g cm^{-3}.

Solution: The given quantity in the problem is 70.0 lb of mercury. The desired quantity is the volume in liters. We need a unit factor to convert pounds to liters. Since we do not have the density expressed in units of lb liter^{-1} (is this a consistent set of units for density?) we must convert pounds to grams with the unit factor

$$\frac{454 \text{ g}}{1 \text{ lb}} = 1$$

and cm^{-3} to $liter^{-1}$ with the unit factor

$$\frac{1 \times 10^3 \text{ cm}^3}{1 \text{ liter}} = 1$$

The density of Hg is given as 13.54 g cm^{-3}. This means 1 cm^3 of Hg has a mass of 13.54 g or, in equation form

$$1 \text{ cm}^3 \sim 13.54 \text{ g Hg}$$

where $\sim$ is read "is equivalent to"

The unit factors

$$\frac{1 \text{ cm}^3}{13.54 \text{ g}} = 1 \quad \text{and} \quad \frac{13.54 \text{ g}}{1 \text{ cm}^3} = 1$$

can be assembled from the given density.

To convert from a given mass to a volume we select the unit factor

$$\frac{1 \text{ cm}^3}{13.54 \text{ g}} = 1$$

Assemble the unit factors to give the desired units, liters of Hg, as follows

$$\text{lb Hg} \times \frac{\text{g Hg}}{\text{lb Hg}} \times \frac{\text{cm}^3 \text{ Hg}}{\text{g Hg}} \times \frac{\text{liter Hg}}{\text{cm}^3 \text{ Hg}} = \text{liters Hg}$$

If the wrong unit factor had been chosen $\left(\dfrac{13.54 \text{ g}}{1 \text{ cm}^3}\right)$, what would be the units in the answer?

The above equation shows how the unit factor method is used to solve density problems.

Now we insert the appropriate numbers into the unit factors and find the numerical answer.

$$70.0 \text{ lb Hg} \times \frac{454 \text{ g Hg}}{1 \text{ lb Hg}} \times \frac{1 \text{ cm}^3 \text{ Hg}}{13.54 \text{ g Hg}} \times \frac{1 \text{ liter Hg}}{10^3 \text{ cm}^3 \text{ Hg}} = 2.35 \text{ liters Hg} \ \bullet$$

Now try Example 2-2 in the text.

2 Use of density in calculations

Another use of density is to find the mass of a volume of substance.

● **EXAMPLE 4**   **Problem:** What is the mass of 1.00 ft^3 of air? The density of air at 25°C is 1.18 g $liter^{-1}$.

Solution: We will do this problem in parts. First we will find the mass of 1.00 liter of air and then convert this to the mass of 1.00 ft^3. The density tells us that 1 liter of air weighs 1.18 g.

$$\text{Density} = \frac{1.18 \text{ g}}{1 \text{ liter}}$$

We can convert the volume from liters to cubic feet with unit factors from Table 1.3 in the text.

$$\frac{1.18 \text{ g}}{1 \text{ liter}} \times \frac{1 \text{ liter}}{10^3 \text{ ml}} \times \frac{1 \text{ ml}}{6.10 \times 10^{-2} \text{ in}^3} \times \frac{12^3 \text{ in}^3}{1 \text{ ft}^3} = 33.4 \text{ g ft}^{-3}$$

Thus 1 ft^3 of air has a mass of 33.4 g. ●

Now try Example 2-3 in the text.

2-2
Kinds of matter

1 Conservation of mass
The law of conservation of mass assures us that in a chemical reaction the weight of the products of the reaction must be equal to the weight of the reactants (starting materials). No weight is gained or lost in a chemical reaction.

This concept allows us to make calculations involving the masses of products and starting materials in a reaction.

● **EXAMPLE 5**
Problem: Under certain conditions water can be decomposed into its elements, hydrogen and oxygen. When 18.0 g of water is decomposed, 16.0 g of oxygen is produced. How much hydrogen is produced?

Solution: The law of conservation of mass tells us

Mass reactants = mass products

In this decomposition water is the reactant and hydrogen and oxygen are the products, so the law of conservation of mass becomes:

Mass water = mass hydrogen + mass oxygen

Solving for mass of hydrogen

Mass hydrogen = mass water − mass oxygen

= 18.0 g − 16.0 g = 2.0 g ●

Now do example 2-4 in the text.

2 Law of definite composition: percentage composition of compounds
The law of definite composition tells us that a given compound contains the same percentages of each element no matter how the compound was made. We can determine the percentage composition of the elements in a compound and know that it will always be the same.

● **EXAMPLE 6**
Problem: Using the data in the previous example find the percentage composition of water.

Solution: The percentage composition means the percent of the total mass that is hydrogen and the percent that is oxygen.

$$\% \text{ oxygen} = \frac{\text{mass of oxygen}}{\text{total mass of compound}} \times 100$$

$$= \frac{16.0 \text{ g oxygen}}{18.0 \text{ g water}} \times 100 = 88.9\%$$

$$\% \text{ hydrogen} = \frac{\text{mass of hydrogen}}{\text{total mass of compound}} \times 100$$

$$= \frac{2.0 \text{ g hydrogen}}{18.0 \text{ g water}} \times 100 = 11.1\%$$

CHECK: % hydrogen + % oxygen = 100%

$$11.1\% + 88.9\% = 100\% \bullet$$

3 Law of definite composition: calculation of amounts of chemicals reacting
The law of definite composition can also be used to calculate the mass of reactants needed to produce a given mass of products if the percentage composition is known.

● **EXAMPLE 7**   **Problem:** Teflon is a compound containing the elements carbon and fluorine. Its percentage composition is 38.7 percent carbon and 61.3 percent fluorine. How many grams of fluorine would be needed to react with carbon to produce 50.0 g of Teflon? How many grams of carbon would be used?

Solution: We can use the definition of percent fluorine to find the mass of fluorine needed to produce 50.0 g of Teflon.

$$\% \text{ flourine} = \frac{\text{mass of fluorine}}{\text{mass of Teflon}} \times 100$$

Solving for the mass of fluorine gives

$$\text{Mass of fluorine} = \frac{\% \text{ flourine}}{100} \times \text{mass of Teflon}$$

$$= \frac{61.3}{100} \times 50.0 \text{ g} = 30.6 \text{ g}$$

The mass of carbon required can be found from the law of conservation of mass

Mass of Teflon = mass of carbon + mass of fluorine

Solving for mass of carbon

Mass of carbon = mass of Teflon − mass of fluorine

$$= 50.0 \text{ g} - 30.6 \text{ g} = 19.4 \text{ g} \bullet$$

Now work Example 2-5 in the text.

SELF TEST

True or False   ____ 1 A possible unit of density would be kg ft^{-3}.
____ 2 Pasteurized milk is a pure substance.
____ 3 NaCl is a chemical symbol.
____ 4 The mass of products produced in a chemical reaction is always equal to the mass of reactants consumed.
____ 5 Frying an egg is an example of a physical change.
____ 6 Heat is the same as temperature.
____ 7 Energy is the capacity to do work.

Completion   8 A _____ mixture consists of a single phase.

9 A _____ consists of two or more atoms bonded together.

10 All matter is composed of small particles called _____.

11 _____ is the movement of a mass against an opposing force.

12 _____ is energy moving from one object to another.

13 The SI unit of energy is the _____.

14 Absolute zero on the Kelvin scale is the same as _____ on the Celsius scale.

15 Energy of position is called _____.

16 Energy of motion is called _____.

Multiple choice   17 A pure substance that can be decomposed into two or more elements by ordinary chemical means is called

(a) an element   (b) an atom   (c) a compound   (d) a mixture

18 Which of the following represents a chemical change?

(a) Boiling water

(b) Forming of frost in a refrigerator

(c) Turning on an electric stove

(d) Turning on a gas stove

19 Which of the following represents a physical change?

(a) Rusting of a car door

(b) Cooking an egg

(c) Dissolving sugar in water

(d) Tarnishing of silverware

20 Which of the following is the best example of kinetic energy?

(a) A book on a table

(b) An automobile waiting at a street light

(c) Pulling against a spring

(d) A moving golf ball

21 A block of steel has a volume of 85.0 cm³ and weighs 655 g. What is its density?

(a) $7.71 \text{ cm}^3 \text{ g}^{-1}$ (b) 7.71 g cm^{-3} (c) 0.130 g cm^{-3} (d) 5.57 g cm^{-3}

22 The density of aluminum is 2.70 g cm^{-3}. What is the volume of a block of aluminum that weighs 35.0 g?

(a) 94.5 cm^3 (b) 37.7 cm^3 (c) 13.0 cm^3 (d) 0.077 cm^3

23 The elements potassium and chlorine combine to form the compound potassium chloride. If 39.3 g potassium combines with 35.7 g chlorine, what is the percentage of potassium in the compound potassium chloride?

(a) 52.4 percent   (b) 47.6 percent   (c) 1.10 percent   (d) 91.0 percent

24 The percentage composition of carbon dioxide is 27.3 percent carbon and 72.7 percent oxygen. How many grams of oxygen would be required to react with 50.0 g of carbon to form carbon dioxide?

(a) 266 g   (b) 50.0 g   (c) 18.8 g   (d) 133 g

25 Normal body temperature is 98.6°F. What temperature is this on the Kelvin scale?

(a) 310 K   (b) 131 K   (c) 120 K   (d) 37 K

3 FORMULAS, EQUATIONS, AND STOICHIOMETRY

CHAPTER OVERVIEW

We saw in Chap. 2 how chemical symbols are used as a shorthand notation to describe chemical changes. Chap. 3 expands on this concept by introducing several different kinds of chemical formulas and applying them quantitatively to chemical changes. You should become familiar with the uses and limitations of each type of chemical formula.

3-1
Combinations and collections of atoms

Chemical formulas are a shorthand method of conveying information about the composition of a compound. Sometimes we may want to convey different types of information about a compound and this can be done by using the appropriate kind of formula. There are three types: empirical, molecular, and structural. Notice how each type has definite limitations to its ability to present a complete picture of a compound and its structure.

3-2
Atomic weights and other masses

The atomic weight of an element is much more than just a number. It represents the relative masses of atoms of different elements on the microscale (world of atoms), but it has another meaning on the macroscale (observable scale on which we can make convenient measurements). It is the weight in grams of Avogadro's number of atoms. Molecular weight is simply the extension of the atomic weight concepts from atoms into molecules: the weight in grams of Avogadro's number of molecules. Formula weight is a more general term and applies to any chemical formula.

3-3
The mole

The word *mole* was coined as an abbreviation of the term "molecule" or "molecular weight." The molecular weight is the weight of one mole of any given compound. Avogadro's number of particles is called a mole. The term *mole* means two things: (1) Avogadro's number of particles of the substance; (2) the mass of substance contained in that number of particles. The numerical value of a mole, in grams, depends on the formula weight of the substance. You will see as you study this chapter that a mole of substance is the basic measuring quantity or unit used in chemical calculations. It is important that you feel confident about your understanding of the meaning and use of *mole*. Spend enough time on the concept until you do. It will be used throughout the course, so get a firm understanding of it now. Calculating molecular weights should become second nature to you before you finish this section.

3-4
Formula
stoichiometry

Stoichiometry is a large word that means the arithmetic of chemical formulas and equations. The dual meaning of atomic weight is seen again in the interpretation of chemical formulas. They represent the atomic composition of a compound on the microscale but also have another meaning relating to the macroscale. On a macroscopic scale the formula represents one mole of the compound. A molecular formula tells the number of atoms in a molecule and also the number of moles of atoms in a mole of molecules of a compound. It is essential that you understand each of these meanings and how they are different yet intimately related.

Calculating empirical formulas and molecular formulas from experimental data will help you develop an understanding of formula stoichiometry.

3-5
Chemical equations

The dual microscale and macroscale meaning of atomic weights and chemical formulas extends into chemical equations. Both meanings must be clearly understood. It may help you understand chemical equations if you treat them like algebraic equations. Reactants are written on the left-hand side of the equation and products on the right. The arrow separating reactants and products signifies "yields," "forms," or "reacts to form." The equation becomes a shorthand method of describing a chemical change in which reactants react to form products.

Chemical reactions obey the law of conservation of mass so the total mass of reactants always equals the total mass of products. Atoms are conserved so each element must have the same number of atoms on the reactant side of the equation as on the product side, and the total number of atoms must be the same in the reactants as in the products. The total number of moles is not necessarily conserved and may change. It is often troublesome to students to call an equation balanced that does not have the same total number of moles in reactants and products, but it is only the atoms that must be balanced, not the total number of moles.

3-6
Reaction
stoichiometry

In this section you will see the quantitative aspects of chemical formulas applied directly to chemical changes. You will work several problems showing the application of stoichiometry to chemical reactions. In these applications the adage "learn by doing" takes on a very significant meaning. It will take much effort and practice to become proficient at these calculations. There is no easy way out and no free lunch here. Get to work.

LEARNING OBJECTIVES

As a result of studying Chapter 3 you should be able to do the following:

Write the definition and give an example illustrating the use of each key term.

3-1
Combinations and
collections of atoms

1 Give an example showing how the composition of a compound is represented by its chemical formula.

2 List the differences in information conveyed by molecular and empirical formulas. (Self Test 1)

3-2
Atomic weights and
other masses

1 Relate the mass of an atom to its atomic weight. (Text Probs. 3-1, 3-4)
2 Give an example illustrating the dual meaning of atomic weight on the microscopic (or molecular) scale and the macroscopic (or observable) scale.
3 Explain how amu and atomic weight are related and how they differ. (Text Probs. 3-2, 3-13)
4 Determine the molecular weight of a compound if its molecular formula is known. (Text Example 3-1, 3-2) (New Skills Example 1; Self Test 15)
5 Calculate molecular weights from atomic weights given the molecular formula.
6 Give an example showing how molecular weight and formula weight are related.

3-3
The mole

1 Define a mole and give an example showing how it is related to formula weight. (Self Test 2)
2 Use atomic weights and molecular weights as unit factors in calculations.
3 Use Avogadro's number as a unit factor in calculations.
4 Perform calculations involving number of atoms, molecules, moles, or grams of a substance and the conversion of an amount of matter given in one of these quantities to any other, that is:
  a Calculate the number of moles in a given number of molecules or atoms of a substance and the number of molecules or atoms in a given number of moles. (Text Examples 3-3, 3-4) (New Skills Examples 3, 8 to 10; Self Test 12, 18)
  b Calculate the number of grams in a given number of moles or molecules of a substance and the number of moles or molecules in a given number of grams. (Text Examples 3-5 to 3-10; Text Probs. 3-5 to 3-8, 3-12) (New Skills Examples 4 to 7, 10; Self Test 8, 10 to 12)

3-4
Formula
stoichiometry

1 Show an understanding of quantitative relationship between atoms and molecules on both the micro- and macroscales by:
  a Calculating the number of each kind of atom in a given molecule or in a given number of moles of a substance. (Text Examples 3-11, 3-12; Text Prob. 3-17) (Self Test 7, 17)
  b Calculating the number of moles of each kind of atom in a given number of moles of a substance. (Text Examples 3-13 to 3-15; Text Probs. 3-10, 3-11) (Self Test 4, 6, 21)
2 Define empirical formula and give an example illustrating its relation to molecular formula. (Text Prob. 3-14) (Self Test 19)
3 Calculate the empirical formula of a substance from its composition. (Text Examples 3-17, 3-19; Text Probs. 3-15, 3-23, 3-24) (New Skills Example 12; Self Test 22, 25)
4 Determine the molecular formula from the empirical formula and molecular weight of a compound. (Text Examples 3-18, 3-19; Text Probs. 3-16, 3-28 to 3-31) (New Skills Example 13)
5 Calculate the percentage composition from the molecular formula of a compound. (Text Example 3-16; Text Probs. 3-25 to 3-27) (New Skills Example 11; Self Test 14, 20)
6 Calculate the amounts of chemicals reacting or produced in the formation or decomposition of simple compounds. (Text Probs. 3-19 to 3-22, 3-40) (Self Test 23)

3-5
Chemical equations

1 Write and balance simple chemical equations. (Text Examples 3-20, 3-21; Text Probs. 3-32 to 3-34) (New Skills Example 14; Self Test 3, 24)

3-6
Reaction stoichiometry

1 Calculate the amount of a substance reacting with or produced from a given amount of another substance using a balanced chemical equation. (Text Examples 3-22 to 3-28; Text Probs. 3-35 to 3-43) (New Skills Examples 15, 16, 17)

2 When reactants are not present in stoichiometric amounts, determine which reactant is the limiting reagent. (Text Example 3-27; Text Probs. 3-39, 3-40) (New Skills Example 17; Self Test 16)

NEW SKILLS

As you have no doubt observed, this chapter consists mostly of worked example problems. There are several areas of application of mathematics to chemistry (stoichiometry) that need to be mastered. Let us get started.

3-2
Atomic weights and other masses

Determination of molecular weight from atomic weights
For substances composed of molecules, the mass of 6.02×10^{23} molecules is the molecular weight in grams. The molecular weight in atomic mass units (amu's) is the sum of the atomic weights of all the atoms contained in the molecule.

● **EXAMPLE 1**

Problem: What is the molecular weight of carbon dioxide, CO_2?

Solution: A molecule of CO_2 is composed of one atom of carbon and two atoms of oxygen. The atomic weights of carbon and oxygen are found in the periodic table inside the front cover of the text.

The molecular weight of carbon dioxide is found as follows:

	Masses on Microscale (1 molecule of CO_2)	Masses on Macroscale (6.02×10^{23} molecules of CO_2)
1 atom of carbon/ molecule CO_2	12 amu C/molecule CO_2	12 g C/mol CO_2
2 atoms of oxygen/ molecule CO_2	2×16 amu O/molecule CO_2	32 g O/mol CO_2
Molecular weight	44 amu/molecule CO_2	44 g/mol CO_2

Thus the molecular weight has the same numerical value in the microscale and macroscale, but the units are different. ●

3-3
The mole

1 The concept of a mole
It is important to be able to convert a quantity of matter given in units of moles, number of atoms, or grams to one of the other quantities. To see how this works, let us investigate the concept of a mole further.

A mole is a quantity like a dozen. It is a fixed number of particles but not a fixed weight. You will not find a balance or scale in the laboratory with units of "mole."

The following illustration shows how a mole is like a dozen. There are 12 things in a dozen, so the unit factor is

$$\frac{12 \text{ things}}{\text{dozen}}$$

You can calculate the number of dozens in a given number of things:

$$\text{Number of dozens} = \frac{\text{number of things}}{12 \text{ things/dozen}}$$

● **EXAMPLE 2**   **Problem:** There are 4.0×10^9 people in the world. How many dozens of people are there?

Solution: The number of dozens $= \dfrac{4.0 \times 10^9 \text{ people}}{12 \text{ people/dozen}}$

$$= 3.3 \times 10^8 \text{ dozens}$$

The number of moles is calculated in the same way as the number of dozens. There are 6.02×10^{23} things in a mole, so the unit factor is

$$\frac{6.02 \times 10^{23} \text{ things}}{\text{mol}}$$

$$\text{Number of moles} = \frac{\text{number of things}}{60.2 \times 10^{23} \text{ things/mol}} \quad ●$$

● **EXAMPLE 3**   **Problem:** There are 4.0×10^9 people in the world. How many moles of people are there?

Solution: Number of moles $= \dfrac{4.0 \times 10^9 \text{ people}}{6.02 \times 10^{23} \text{ people/mol}}$

$$= 6.6 \times 10^{-15} \text{ mol} \quad ●$$

Things can have mass; therefore, moles and dozens may be related to mass.

● **EXAMPLE 4**   **Problem:** If an average person weighs 70 kg, how much would one dozen people weigh?

Solution: Use the unit factor approach:

$$\frac{70 \text{ kg}}{\text{person}} \left(\frac{12 \text{ people}}{\text{dozen}} \right) = 840 \text{ kg dozen}^{-1} \quad ●$$

● **EXAMPLE 5**   **Problem:** Using the data from Example 4, how much would 1 mol of people weigh?

Solution: The unit factor method used in Example 4 applies here also. One mole of people would weigh

$$\frac{70 \text{ kg}}{\text{person}} \left(\frac{6.02 \times 10^{23} \text{ people}}{\text{mol}} \right) = 4.2 \times 10^{25} \text{ kg mol}^{-1} \quad ●$$

When the things are atoms, the mass of 1 mol, or 6.02×10^{23} atoms, is the atomic weight. The weight of a carbon atom is 12.0 amu.

$$\frac{12 \text{ amu}}{\text{C atom}} \left(6.02 \times 10^{23} \frac{\text{C atoms}}{\text{mol C}} \right) = 7.2 \times 10^{24} \text{ amu/mol C}$$

To convert this large number to the unit of mass common to macroscale applications

$$\frac{7.2 \times 10^{24} \text{ amu}}{\text{mol C}} \left(\frac{1 \text{ g}}{6.02 \times 10^{23} \text{ amu}} \right) = 12 \text{ g/mol C}$$

Did you notice the versatility of Avogadro's number in that last step? When things are molecules, the mass of 1 mol or 6.02×10^{23} molecules is the molecular weight.

2 Calculations involving moles and grams of a substance

If you are given the number of grams of a compound you can calculate the number of moles provided you know the molecular or formula weight.

$$\text{Number of moles} = \frac{\text{grams}}{\text{grams mole}^{-1}} = \frac{\text{grams}}{\text{molecular weight}}$$

● **EXAMPLE 6**   **Problem:** The air in an average dormitory room contains about 20.0 kg of O_2. How many moles is this?

Solution: The molecular weight of O_2 is 32.0 g mol^{-1}.

$$\text{Number of moles of } O_2 = \frac{20{,}000 \text{ g } O_2}{32.0 \text{ g mol}^{-1}} = 625 \text{ mol } O_2 \quad ●$$

● **EXAMPLE 7**   **Problem:** If there are 250 g of H_2O in a glass, how many moles of H_2O are there?

Solution: The molecular weight of H_2O is

$$
\begin{array}{ll}
2 \text{ atoms of H} & 2.0 \\
1 \text{ atom of O} & \underline{16.0}
\end{array}
$$

$$\text{Molecular weight of } H_2O = 18.0 \text{ g mol}^{-1}$$

$$\text{Number of moles of } H_2O = \frac{250 \text{ g}}{18.0 \text{ g mol}^{-1}} = 13.9 \text{ mol } H_2O \quad ●$$

Text Examples 3-5, 3-6, 3-9, and 3-10 give additional examples of calculations involving moles and grams of a substance.

3 Calculations involving moles and number of particles of a substance

The number of particles can be calculated from the number of moles by using Avogadro's number as a unit factor.

$$\text{Number of particles} = \text{number of moles} \left(\frac{6.02 \times 10^{23} \text{ particles}}{1 \text{ mol}} \right)$$

● **EXAMPLE 8**   **Problem:** How many molecules of O_2 are there in the average dormitory room of Example 6?

Solution:

$$\text{Number of molecules} = 625 \text{ mol } O_2 \left(\frac{6.02 \times 10^{23} \text{ molecules } O_2}{\text{mol } O_2} \right)$$

$$= 3.76 \times 10^{26} \text{ molecules } O_2 \quad ●$$

● **EXAMPLE 9**   **Problem:** How many molecules of H_2O are there in the glass of water in Example 7?

Solution:

$$\text{Number of molecules} = 13.9 \text{ mol } H_2O \left(\frac{6.02 \times 10^{23} \text{ molecules } H_2O}{\text{mol } H_2O} \right)$$

$$= 8.37 \times 10^{24} \text{ molecules } H_2O \ ●$$

Examples 3-3, 3-4, 3-7, and 3-8 in the text give additional examples of calculations involving moles and number of particles in a substance.

4 Calculations relating mass to the number of particles in a substance
Now let us tie all these concepts together in one typical example in which you are asked to calculate the number of atoms of an element in a given mass of substance.

● **EXAMPLE 10**   **Problem:** How many atoms of sodium could be obtained from a salt shaker that contains 20.0 g of salt?

Solution: First calculate the number of moles of salt (NaCl) in the salt shaker. The formula weight of NaCl is

$$\begin{array}{ll} 1 \text{ atom of Na} & 23.0 \\ 1 \text{ atom of Cl} & \underline{35.5} \end{array}$$

$$\text{Formula weight of NaCl} = 58.5 \text{ g mol}^{-1}$$

$$\text{Number of moles of NaCl} = \frac{20.0 \text{ g}}{58.5 \text{ g mol}^{-1}} = 0.342 \text{ mol NaCl}$$

The number of molecules of NaCl is found as follows:

$$\text{Number of molecules of NaCl} = 0.342 \text{ mol NaCl} \left(\frac{6.02 \times 10^{23} \text{ molecules NaCl}}{1 \text{ mol NaCl}} \right)$$

$$= 2.06 \times 10^{23} \text{ molecules NaCl}$$

We could obtain one atom of Na from each molecule of NaCl, so

$$\text{Atoms of Na} = \text{molecules of NaCl} = 2.06 \times 10^{23} \text{ atoms Na}$$

This calculation can be performed in a single step if the appropriate unit factors are chosen and assembled correctly.

$$\text{Molecules of Na} = 20.0 \text{ g NaCl} \times \frac{1 \text{ mol NaCl}}{58.5 \text{ g NaCl}} \times \frac{6.02 \times 10^{23} \text{ molecules NaCl}}{1 \text{ mol NaCl}}$$

$$\times \frac{1 \text{ atom Na}}{1 \text{ molecule NaCl}}$$

$$= 2.06 \times 10^{23} \text{ atoms Na} \ ●$$

3-4
Formula
stoichiometry

1 Calculation of percentage composition (elemental composition) of a compound when the chemical formula is given

● **EXAMPLE 11**   **Problem:** Calculate the percentage composition of NaCl.

Solution: This problem asks us to find the percent by weight of Na and Cl in a sample of NaCl. We need a basis for calculation, so for convenience let us base our calculations on 1 mol of NaCl. One mole of NaCl contains 1 mol of Na atoms and 1 mol of Cl atoms.

$$
\begin{aligned}
1 \text{ mol Cl atoms} &= 35.5 \text{ g} \\
1 \text{ mol Na atoms} &= \underline{23.0 \text{ g}} \\
1 \text{ mol NaCl molecules} &= 58.5 \text{ g}
\end{aligned}
$$

The percent of an element is the weight of that element divided by the total weight (weight fraction) times 100.

$$
\% \text{ Na} = \frac{23.0 \text{ g Na}}{58.5 \text{ g NaCl}} \times 100 = 39.3\%
$$

$$
\% \text{ Cl} = \frac{35.5 \text{ g Cl}}{58.5 \text{ g NaCl}} \times 100 = 60.7\% \; \bullet
$$

Now go through Example 3-16 of the text.

2 Determination of empirical formula of a compound when the percentage composition (elemental composition) is given

When a new compound is synthesized or the identification of an unknown compound is sought, a standard procedure for determining the chemical formula of the compound is by experimentally determining its percentage or elemental composition.

● **EXAMPLE 12**   **Problem:** It was experimentally determined that a compound containing only phosphorus and oxygen contained 43.7 percent phosphorus. What is the empirical formula of the compound?

Solution: We need to establish a basis for calculation. A convenient basis is usually 100 g of the compound under consideration. Since 100 g of the compound is 43.7 percent P, the weights of P and O are found by

$$
\text{g P in 100 g compound} = 100(0.437) = 43.7 \text{ g P}
$$

$$
\text{g O} = 100 \text{ g} - 43.7 \text{ g} = 56.3 \text{ g O}
$$

Since the empirical formula is a ratio of moles of atoms in the compound rather than a weight ratio, we need to convert the weights to number of moles for each type of atom.

$$
\text{mol P} = 43.7 \text{ g P} \times \frac{1 \text{ mol P}}{31.0 \text{ g P}} = 1.41
$$

$$
\text{mol O} = 56.3 \text{ g O} \times \frac{1 \text{ mol O}}{16.0 \text{ g O}} = 3.52
$$

We have determined the ratio of phosphorus to oxygen is 1.41 mol of P to 3.52 mol of O. The formula of our compound could be written as $P_{1.41}O_{3.52}$, strictly speaking this is an accurate indication of the mole ratio, but it is not very easy to interpret on a microscale. It is difficult to visualize 1.41 atoms of P. Conventionally we express the subscripts in chemical formulas as small whole numbers. To do this we normalize the numbers by dividing both by the smaller number

$$\text{mol P} = \frac{1.41}{1.41} = 1.00$$

$$\text{mol O} = \frac{3.52}{1.41} = 2.50$$

The formula could now be written as $PO_{2.5}$, but the subscripts are still not both whole numbers. If we begin multiplying the normalized ratios by small integers, sooner or later we get integers that represent the moles of component and preserve the original ratio.

$$\text{mol P} = 1.00 \times 2 = 2.00$$

$$\text{mol O} = 2.50 \times 2 = 5.00$$

The formula is P_2O_5.
  Use your calculator to show all the ratios are equal.

$$\frac{1.41}{3.52} = \frac{1.00}{2.50} = \frac{2.00}{5.00} = 0.400$$

P_2O_5 is the simplest formula with whole numbers for subscripts and is called the empirical formula. ●
  Example 3-17 in the text illustrates the determination of the empirical formula of a compound containing four different kinds of atoms. The procedure is no different.

3 Determination of molecular formulas from empirical formulas
The molecular formula can be obtained from the empirical formula if the molecular weight is known.

● **EXAMPLE 13** **Problem:** The molecular weight of the compound of phosphorus and oxygen in the previous example was found to be 284 g mol^{-1}. What is the molecular formula of the compound?

Solution: First we determine the empirical weight for the empirical formula, P_2O_5.

$$
\begin{array}{lll}
\text{2 mol of P} & 2 \times 31 = & 62\text{ g} \\
\text{5 mol of O} & 5 \times 16 = & \underline{80\text{ g}} \\
\text{Empirical weight of } P_2O_5 & & 142\text{ g mol}^{-1}
\end{array}
$$

The molecular formula must be some integral multiple of the empirical formula. This means the molecular formula is composed of some number of empirical formulas. It might be written as $(P_2O_5)_x$, where x is a whole number. It follows that the molecular weight must be x times the empirical weight, or:

$$x = \frac{\text{molecular weight}}{\text{empirical weight}}$$

For our compound

$$x = \frac{284\text{ g mol}^{-1}}{142\text{ g mol}^{-1}} = 2$$

and the molecular formula consists of two empirical formulas. We could write it as $(P_2O_5)_2$ or better and more conventionally as P_4O_{10}. ●

Now work through Examples 3-17 and 3-18 in the text.

3-5   *1 Interpreting chemical equations*
Chemical equations   Let us analyze the chemical equation

$$2H_2(g) + O_2(g) \rightarrow 2H_2O$$

The equation can be read "two molecules of hydrogen react with one molecule of oxygen to produce two molecules of water." An equally valid interpretation is "2 mol of H_2 react with 1 mol of O_2 to produce 2 mol of H_2O." We need to analyze the microscopic and macroscopic interpretations further.

	$2H_2(g)$	+	$O_2(g)$	$\rightarrow$	$2H_2O$
Microscale interpretation	2 molecules of H_2	react with	1 molecule of O_2	to produce	2 molecules of water
Macroscale interpretation (mole basis)	2 mol of H_2	react with	1 mol of O_2	to produce	2 mol of water
Macroscale interpretation (gram basis)	4 g of hydrogen	react with	32 g of oxygen	to produce	36 g of water

The microscopic interpretation of a chemical reaction is relatively straightforward. It tells the number of molecules of each reacting substance and of the products. The equation is said to be balanced when the same number of atoms of each different element appears on each side of the equation. The macroscopic interpretation (gram basis) illustrates the weight information conveyed by a chemical equation. This information is not as readily apparent from the equation itself, but can you see how a combination of the equation and the molecular weights gives the weights of each compound? If not, come back to this concept after you have worked some of the example problems and it should become clear. The conservation of mass requirement for a chemical reaction should be quite apparent. The total mass of reactants (4 + 32 = 36 g) is the same as the total mass of products; thus mass is conserved (or, in other words, remains constant).

Now let us look at the macroscopic interpretation (mole basis). If you think of a mole as being an abbreviation of molecular weight, you see that the equation seems to say "2 molecular weights (mol) of H_2 react with 1 molecular weight (mol) of O_2 to produce two molecular weights (mol) of water." Notice that while mass is conserved, the total number of moles of substance is not. We start with 2 mol of hydrogen plus 1 mol of oxygen, or 3 mol total, and we end with 2 mol of water. There was a decrease in total number of moles as the reaction proceeded. If this is troublesome, go back to the microscopic interpretation and observe that the total number of molecules also changes from three molecules of reactants to two molecules of product. A balanced chemical equation does *not* require the same total number of moles on each side of the equation; only the individual atoms need be balanced.

2 Balancing chemical equations
Chemical equations are balanced when the law of conservation of mass is obeyed and the chemical formulas are correct. The same number of atoms of each element must

appear in the reactants and in the products. Care must be taken to represent the reacting substances by their correct chemical formulas when balancing an equation.

● **EXAMPLE 14**   **Problem:** Write a balanced chemical equation for the combustion of methane gas, CH_4, in oxygen to form carbon dioxide and water. Methane is the main component of natural gas.

Solution: A balanced chemical reaction shows the ratio of compounds involved in the reaction. We need to know the formulas of reactants and products of the reaction. You will be given these formulas at first, but you should gradually become able to predict the products of a reaction if you know the reactants. For the complete combustion (reaction with oxygen) of a compound containing carbon and hydrogen the products are CO_2 and H_2O. The unbalanced equation for the reaction is

$$CH_4 + O_2 \rightarrow CO_2 + H_2O$$

We need to balance the equation. You could balance it by selecting coefficients (the number in front of the formula) at random until you hit on a set giving the same number of atoms of C, H, and O on each side of the arrow, but usually it is best to start by balancing carbon first, then hydrogen, and finally oxygen. Since there is one atom of carbon on each side of the equation, carbon is already balanced. (When the coefficient of a compound is unity, it is not indicated in the equation.) There are four atoms of H in CH_4 and only two in H_2O. We certainly do not want to put four atoms of H on the right-hand side of the equation by changing the subscript from H_2O to H_4O because it would no longer represent water. We can, however, indicate more than one molecule (mole?) of water by putting a coefficient of 2 in front of the H_2O which gives four atoms of H on each side of the equation.

$$CH_4 + O_2 \rightarrow CO_2 + 2H_2O$$

Now we can balance the O atoms. The coefficients of CH_4, CO_2, and H_2O have been determined and we do not wish to change them because it will disrupt the balancing we have done so far. There are four atoms of O on the right-hand side of the equation. We can indicate four atoms of O on the left-hand side by placing a coefficient of 2 in front of the O_2 formula. The balanced equation is

$$CH_4 + 2O_2 \rightarrow CO_2 + 2H_2O \quad ●$$

3-6
**Reaction
stoichiometry**

1 Stoichiometric calculations using balanced chemical equations

If you have developed a sound understanding of the mole, chemical formulas, unit factors, and chemical equations, stoichiometric calculations will be straightforward. You will need to practice to become confident about your approach to the problems, but you should soon see that the same fundamental technique and approach is used for all problems of stoichiometry.

Let us work through a problem using a balanced chemical equation to calculate amounts of substances undergoing reaction.

● **EXAMPLE 15**   **Problem:** How many moles of oxygen are needed for complete combustion of 10 mol of methane?

Solution: We can use the balanced chemical equation from Example 14 to work this problem.

$$CH_4 + 2O_2 \rightarrow CO_2 + 2H_2O$$

The balanced equation tells us 2 mol of O_2 are required for each mole of CH_4. The number of moles of O_2 required for combustion of 10 mol of CH_4 is

$$mol\ O_2 = 10\ mol\ CH_4 \left(\frac{2\ mol\ O_2}{1\ mol\ CH_4}\right)$$

$$= 20\ mol\ O_2$$

Note how the unit factor needed to convert the given moles of CH_4 to the required moles of O_2 was constructed from the coefficients in the balanced equation. •

Now work carefully through Examples 3-20, 3-21, 3-22, and 3-23 in the text.

• **EXAMPLE 16**   **Problem:** How many grams of CO_2 are produced when 100 g of CH_4 undergo complete combustion?

Solution: From the previous example the balanced reaction is

$$CH_4 + 2O_2 \rightarrow CO_2 + 2H_2O$$

The reaction gives the ratio of compounds on a mole basis. The problem asks us to find the mass of substance produced. We need to change the quantity of CH_4 to number of moles before using the coefficients to give a ratio of substances reacting.

$$mol\ CH_4 = 100\ g\ CH_4 \times \frac{1\ mol\ CH_4}{16.0\ g\ CH_4} = 6.25\ mol\ CH_4$$

A unit factor can be constructed from the coefficients in the balanced reaction to give the moles of CO_2 produced from the given amount of CH_4.

$$mol\ CO_2 = 6.25\ mol\ CH_4 \times \frac{1\ mol\ CO_2}{1\ mol\ CH_4} = 6.25\ mol\ CO_2$$

Now we can determine the grams of CO_2

$$g\ CO_2 = 6.25\ mol\ CO_2 \times \frac{44\ g\ CO_2}{1\ mol\ CO_2} = 275\ g\ CO_2$$

We can combine these steps in one equation by compiling the unit factors in a systematic manner to proceed from the given quantity to the desired quantity.

$$g\ CO_2 = 100\ g\ CH_4 \times \frac{1\ mol\ CH_4}{16.0\ g\ CH_4} \times \frac{1\ mol\ CO_2}{1\ mol\ CH_4} \times \frac{44.0\ g\ CO_2}{1\ mol\ CO_2} = 275\ g\ CO_2$$

Notice how this chain of unit factors proceeds in a systematic manner. Grams of given substance are converted to moles by using the molecular weight as a unit factor; then the stoichiometric coefficients from the chemical equation are used to convert to moles of the desired substance; and finally the molecular weight of the desired substance is used as a unit factor to convert the moles to grams. •

Now work through Examples 3-24 and 3-25 in the text.

2 Concept of limiting reagent
Often the reactants in a process are not present in stoichiometric amounts (the mole ratio indicated by the ratio of coefficients in the balanced equation). When this is

true, one of the reactants will be consumed first and the excess of the other will remain unreacted. The reactant consumed first in a chemical reaction is the limiting reagent because it limits or determines the amount of product that can form.

● **EXAMPLE 17**   **Problem:** How many moles of water can be produced when 100 g of CH_4 is placed in a container with 100 g of O_2 and combustion is allowed to go to completion?

Solution: Again, the balanced chemical reaction is

$$CH_4 + 2O_2 \rightarrow CO_2 + 2H_2O$$

At this point we do not know whether the CH_4 or the O_2 will be consumed first as the reaction proceeds. It is not apparent from the masses of reacting substances. We need to change their masses to number of moles.

$$\text{mol of } CH_4 \text{ available} = 100 \text{ g } CH_4 \times \frac{1 \text{ mol } CH_4}{16.0 \text{ g } CH_4} = 6.25 \text{ mol } CH_4$$

$$\text{mol of } O_2 \text{ available} = 100 \text{ g } O_2 \times \frac{1 \text{ mol } O_2}{32.0 \text{ g } O_2} = 3.12 \text{ mol } O_2$$

Since 2 mol of O_2 are used for each mole of CH_4, the number of moles of CH_4 used for 3.12 mol of O_2 is

$$\text{mol } CH_4 \text{ used} = 3.12 \text{ mol } O_2 \times \frac{1 \text{ mol } CH_4}{2 \text{ mol } O_2} = 1.56 \text{ mol } CH_4 \text{ used}$$

So there are 6.25 – 1.56 = 4.69 mol of CH_4 in excess; O_2 is the limiting reagent and limits the amount of H_2O that can be produced.

$$\text{mol } H_2O = 3.12 \text{ mol } O_2 \times \frac{2 \text{ mol } H_2O}{2 \text{ mol } O_2} = 3.12 \text{ mol } H_2O \; ●$$

Now work through Example 3-27 in the text.

SELF TEST

True or False

____T____ 1 The formula $MgCl_2$ indicates 1 mol of magnesium chloride contains 1 mol of magnesium atoms and 2 mol of chlorine atoms.

____F____ 2 A mole signifies a certain number of particles rather than specific mass of substances.

____F____ 3 In balancing a chemical reaction you always make the total moles of product equal the total moles of reactant.

____T____ 4 There are 12 mol of oxygen atoms in 1 mol of $Al_2(SO_4)_3$.

____T/F____ 5 Structural formulas depict the spatial geometry of atoms in molecules.

Completion

6 There are ____12____ mol of oxygen atoms in 2 mol of $Ca(NO_3)_2$.

7 There are _____ atoms of oxygen in 32 g of O_2.

8 There are _____ mol of O_2 in 16 grams of O_2.

9 The formula weight of $Ba_3(PO_4)_2$ is _____.

10 3.01×10^{23} molecules of CH_4 weighs _____ g.

11 The number of grams in 5.00 mol of ZnO is _____ .

12 The number of grams in 1.20×10^{25} molecules of NH_3 is _____ .

13 The number of moles of borax, $Na_2B_4O_7$, that could be prepared from 2.16 g of boron is _____ .

14 The percent by weight of bromine in NaBr is _____ .

15 One mole of acetic acid, $HC_2H_3O_2$, weighs _____ g.

16 When reactants are not present in stoichiometric amounts, one of them must be the _____ .

Multiple choice

17 In a mole of NH_3 there are Avogadro's number of
(a) hydrogen atoms   (b) hydrogen molecules
(c) nitrogen atoms   (d) nitrogen molecules

18 Avogadro's number of hydrogen atoms weighs
(a) 6.02×10^{23} g   (b) $\dfrac{1}{6.02} \times 10^{23}$ g   (c) 1 g   (d) 2 g

19 The empirical formula of the compound $C_{12}H_8O_4$ is
(a) CHO   (b) $C_6H_4O_2$ (c) C_3H_2O (d) $C_4H_2O_2$

20 Sulfur dioxide, SO_2, is a troublesome pollutant generated from sulfur in coal during combustion in coal-fired power plants. The percent of oxygen in SO_2 is
(a) 50 percent   (b) 67 percent   (c) 25 percent   (d) 10 percent

21 The number of grams of Ca in 4.00 mol of $CaCO_3$ is
(a) 4   (b) 8   (c) 24   (d) 160

22 A compound is composed only of elements X and Y. An analysis shows the elemental composition is 50 percent X and 50 percent Y. Which of the following is true about the compound?
(a) The molecular formula is XY.
(b) The empirical formula is XY.
(c) The formula weight is 100 g.
(d) The empirical formula cannot be determined without more information.

23 How many grams of phosphorus are required to make 2 mol of calcium phosphate, $Ca_3(PO_4)_2$?
(a) 482 g   (b) 241 g   (c) 80 g   (d) 40 g

24 Gasoline is a complex mixture of compounds containing carbon and hydrogen. It is often represented by a single compound, octane, C_8H_{16}. When the chemical reaction for the combustion of octane

$$C_8H_{16} + O_2 \rightarrow CO_2 + H_2O$$

is balanced the coefficients are (from left to right)
(a) 1, 1, 1, 1   (b) 1, 12, 8, 16   (c) 1, 12, 8, 8   (d) 1, 6, 8, 16

25 A compound has an elemental analysis of 56.3 percent Mn and 43.7 percent S. What is the empirical formula of the compound?
(a) MnS   (b) Mn_2S_3 (c) MnS_2 (d) Mn_3S_4

4
IDEAL GASES

CHAPTER OVERVIEW

4-1
Observing gas
behavior

Matter exists in three states: solid, liquid, or gas. Depending on the temperature and pressure, most substances can exist in any one of these states. We are familiar with water in each state: solid (ice), liquid (water), and gas (steam or water vapor). Chapter 4 introduces us to the gaseous state. It is the best understood and probably the simplest state to study. We will learn the ABC's of gas behavior (Avogadro's principle, Boyle's law, Charles' law, Dalton's law) and see how they are used to predict gas behavior.

The gas laws use four variables to describe gas behavior.

1 Pressure, P, defined as force per unit area and usually measured in units of atmospheres or torrs
2 Volume, V, usually measured in liters
3 Absolute temperature, T, measured in kelvins
4 Number of moles, n

The gas laws allow us to calculate the effect of changes in these variables.

4-2
Pressure-volume
relationship:
Boyle's law

It is very important to keep track of which variables are changing and which remain constant as you use the gas laws. In Boyle's law the temperature and number of moles of gas remain constant and we determine the changes in pressure and volume. We know from experience that a large volume of air escapes from a tire when the pressure is released. That is, as the pressure decreases, the volume increases. This is an inverse proportion. If we decrease the volume by half, the pressure doubles. We can say, therefore, that at constant temperature the volume of a given number of moles of gas is inversely proportional to the pressure. Suppose we have a sample of gas at pressure P_1 and volume V_1. If the pressure is decreased to P_2 while the temperature is held constant, the volume will increase to V_2 and the change can be depicted as

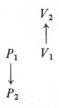

Since this is an inverse proportion, the volume increases as the pressure decreases. Mathematically this becomes

$$P_1 V_1 = P_2 V_2$$

This equation is Boyle's law. It allows calculation of changes in pressure and volume when the amount of gas and the temperature remain constant.

4-3
Temperature effects:
Charles' law

1 Charles' law

A gas expands as it is heated at constant pressure. That is, when the temperature increases, the volume increases. The temperature is directly proportional to the volume. If one increases, the other must increase also. This means that at constant pressure the volume of a given number of moles of gas is directly proportional to the absolute temperature. This is Charles' law. Mathematically, it is stated as

$$\frac{V_1}{T_1} = \frac{V_2}{T_2}$$

2 The combined law

We could develop a law between the pressure and temperature changes that would look very much like Charles' law if we desired, but instead let us examine the equation resulting from combining Boyle's and Charles' laws to give the combined law.

$$\frac{P_1 V_1}{T_1} = \frac{P_2 V_2}{T_2}$$

For a given quantity of gas this law allows calculations of pressure, volume, and temperature changes. Note that if the temperature is held constant ($T_1 = T_2$), the combined law reduces to Boyle's law. If the pressure is held constant so that $P_1 = P_2$, the combined law reduces to Charles' law. This is especially significant because if you recognize which variables are constant and which are changing, the combined law can be used to calculate all problems in the Boyle's law, Charles' law, and combined law sections of the text. Try this and see.

The text describes two methods to use the gas laws. Method 1 simply plugs the given values into the appropriate formula and calculates the answer. Method 2 tries to get you to visualize the effect of changing the pressure, volume, or temperature and set up ratios that change the desired variable in the right direction (increase or decrease). If you take a few minutes to think about what is happening in the problem and have an understanding of how these variables affect each other, the quantitative calculations should not be too difficult. If you rely on memorized formulas to solve the problem, you will probably become confused and discouraged.

4-4
Ideal-gas behavior

1 Avogadro's principle

Avogadro's principle, molar volume, and combining volumes of gases are closely related principles. Avogadro's principle states: At a given temperature and pressure, equal volumes of all gases contain equal numbers of molecules or moles. Consequently, 1 liter of all gases contains the same number of moles and 1 mol of all gases must occupy the same volume. At standard conditions of 0°C and 1 atm, 1 mol of any gas occupies 22.4 liters. This is the standard molar volume. Since chemical reactions involve fixed numbers of moles of chemicals, gaseous chemical reactions involve fixed volumes of the gases. This allows a new interpretation of chemical reactions for gases

$$2H_2\,(g) \quad + \quad O_2\,(g) \quad \longrightarrow \quad 2H_2O\,(g)$$

2 liters of	react	1 liter of	to	2 liters of
hydrogen	with	oxygen	produce	water

Thus, we see that volume relations are the same as mole relations. This is Gay-Lussac's law of combining volumes. It will be used in calculations of stoichiometry of gases.

2 The ideal-gas law

Boyle's law, Charles' law, and Avogadro's principle may be combined into one equation, the ideal gas law:

$$PV = nRT$$

R is called the ideal gas constant and has a value of 0.0821 liter atm mol^{-1} K^{-1}, when P is in atmospheres, V is in liters, n is in moles, and T is in kelvins.

Most gas problems, even those involving Boyle's, Charles', and the combined laws, can be solved with the ideal gas law. You must pay particularly close attention to the units on each variable when using this equation. Make sure your units are consistent. Problems involving molecular weight and density of gases are simply applications of the ideal gas law.

The equations we have discussed so far apply only to "ideal gases." Actually there is no such thing as an ideal gas. It is a simplified model or representation of gas behavior that allows fairly accurate calculations to be carried out in a simple manner. The imaginary ideal or perfect gas is one in which there are no interacting forces between molecules and the volume of the atoms is negligible compared to the total volume. If such a gas existed, it would obey the gas laws exactly. Its pressure would be exactly reduced by half when the volume is doubled. Atoms of real or actual gases attract or repel each other and occupy some space, so they do not follow the ideal gas equations exactly. Fortunately, most gases exhibit very close to ideal behavior at normal conditions of temperature and pressure, so the ideal gas equations are a very good approximation to real gas behavior under normal conditions.

3 Dalton's law

In a mixture of gases that do not react chemically, each gas acts independently, as if it were alone in the container, unaffected by the presence of other gases. Thus, each gas exerts its own, independent pressure called a partial pressure, and the sum of partial pressures of all gases in the container gives the total pressure. This is Dalton's law. Stated mathematically it becomes:

$$P_{\text{total}} = P_A + P_B + P_C$$

where P_{total} is the pressure that would be measured by a barometer or pressure gauge and P_A, P_B, and P_C are partial pressures of gases A, B, and C. Dalton's law can be used to find the total number of moles of gas in a mixture. The total number of moles of gas is the sum of the moles of each individual gas in a mixture:

$$n_{\text{total}} = n_A + n_B + n_C$$

where n_A, n_B, and n_C are the moles of gases A, B, and C present in the mixture. Notice that Dalton's law is simply saying: "The total (pressure) is the sum of the parts (partial pressures)," and the same reasoning applies to total moles. Dalton's law is frequently used to find the partial pressure of a gas collected over water in a laboratory experiment (Text Example 4-13).

4 Graham's law
Diffusion and *effusion* are terms used to describe the same gas behavior under different situations, the relative rate of movement or mixing of gases. Graham's law says the rate of movement of a gas (diffusion or effusion) is inversely proportional to its molecular weight. Mathematically this is stated

$$\frac{\text{Rate}_A}{\text{Rate}_B} = \frac{\sqrt{M_B}}{\sqrt{M_A}}$$

Usually the rates of movement are determined experimentally to find the molecular weight of an unknown gas in calculations involving Graham's law.

4-5
Kinetic-molecular
theory

The kinetic-molecular theory is a physical model of the behavior of gases based on a few very basic assumptions which correlate very well with experimental measurements. Developed in full, it provides convincing evidence that molecules exist and beautifully joins a simple but efficient theory or model to experimental observations. The assumptions of the kinetic-molecular theory are:

1 A gas is composed of a large number of tiny particles (molecules).
2 The molecules of a gas are in violent motion and collide frequently. The total energy remains constant on collision. Energy may be transferred from one molecule to another, but there is no loss of total energy.
3 There are no forces of attraction or repulsion between molecules.
4 The average kinetic energy of the gas molecules is proportional to the absolute temperature.

A successful theory should adequately describe experimental observations. Note that the observed behavior of gases described below can be correlated with the assumptions of the kinetic-molecular theory listed above:

1 Gases are compressible.
2 Gases expand to fill the container and diffuse rapidly. This accounts for the observed brownian motion in gases. Since gases do not lose energy, the gaseous state is permanent.
3 The gaseous state is permanent even at high pressures. Real gases may have signifi-

cant forces of attraction or repulsion which cause deviation from ideal behavior at high pressures.

4 Assumption 4 leads to Graham's law of diffusion.

KEY EQUATIONS

4-2
Pressure-volume
relationship:
Boyle's law

Boyle's law

$$PV = k \quad \text{or} \quad P_1 V_1 = P_2 V_2$$

4-3
Temperature effects:
Charles' law

Charles' law

$$V = aT \quad \text{or} \quad \frac{V_1}{T_1} = \frac{V_2}{T_2}$$

Combined law

$$\frac{PV}{T} = c \quad \text{or} \quad \frac{P_1 V_1}{T_1} = \frac{P_2 V_2}{T_2}$$

4-4
Ideal-gas behavior

Ideal gas law

$$PV = nRT$$

Dalton's law

$$P_{\text{total}} = P_A + P_B + P_C$$

Graham's law of diffusion

$$\frac{\text{Rate}_A}{\text{Rate}_B} = \frac{\sqrt{M_B}}{\sqrt{M_A}}$$

LEARNING OBJECTIVES

As a result of studying Chap. 4 you should be able to:
Write the definition and give an example illustrating the use of each key term.

4-1
Observing gas
behavior

1 Define pressure and make a sketch showing how barometers and manometers measure it. (Text Prob. 4-1)

2 Give the common units for pressure, volume, and temperature. (Self Test 7)

4-2
Pressure-volume
relationship:
Boyle's law

1 Write a mathematical statement of Boyle's law and use it to calculate pressure-volume relations in gases at constant temperature. (Text Examples 4-1 to 4-3; Text Probs. 4-3, 4-4) (Self Test 1, 2, 11, 16, 20)

2 Make a sketch showing the PV behavior of an ideal gas at constant temperature.

4-3
Temperature effects:
Charles' law

1 Describe a method of determining absolute zero and explain why the Kelvin temperature scale is used in Charles' law. (Self Test 3, 8, 9)

2 Write a mathematical statement of Charles' law and use it to calculate temperature-

volume changes at constant pressure for gases. (Text Examples 4-4, 4-5; Text Probs. 4-5 to 4-7) (New Skills Example 1; Self Test 10, 17)

3 Use pressure ratios, volume ratios, and temperature ratios in combined gas law calculations. (Text Examples 4-6, 4-7; Text Probs. 4-14 to 4-16) (New Skills Example 2; Self Test 12, 18, 19)

4-4
Ideal-gas behavior

1 Give an example illustrating Gay-Lussac's law of combining volumes.

2 State Avogadro's principle and give an example showing how it relates volume to moles of a gas.

3 Write the ideal-gas law and use it to calculate pressure-volume-temperature-weight relationships in gases. (Text Examples 4-8, 4-9; Text Probs. 4-17 to 4-20)

4 Memorize the numerical value and units of the ideal-gas constant. (Self Test 15)

5 Give the values of temperature and pressure at STP.

6 Memorize the value of the molar volume of a gas at STP, and calculate molar volumes at any value of temperature and pressure. (Text Probs. 4-12, 4-13)

7 Calculate the molecular weight of a gas from its measured density. (Text Examples 4-10, 4-12; Text Probs. 4-30 to 4-32, 4-37 to 4-39) (Self Test 23)

8 Use an example to show what is meant by the partial pressure of a gas. (Self Test 4, 13)

9 Write Dalton's law and use it to calculate the total pressure when partial pressures are known and to find the partial pressure of a gas collected over water. (Text Examples 4-11, 4-12; Text Probs. 4-22 to 4-25) (New Skills Example 4)

10 Calculate the density of a gas from its molecular weight. (Text Prob. 4-27) (Self Test 21)

11 Explain the difference between diffusion and effusion and use their measured values to calculate molecular weights of gases. (Text Prob. 4-8)

12 Use Graham's law to calculate (*a*) the molecular weight of a gas from measured effusion rates and (*b*) the relative rates of diffusion of gases. (Text Example 4-13; Text Probs. 4-10, 4-11) (Self Test 6, 14, 24)

4-5
Kinetic-molecular theory

1 List the assumptions of the kinetic-molecular theory.

2 Give examples to show how observed properties of gases are explained by the theory. (Text Probs. 4-9, 4-33)

3 Explain how Boyle's law, Charles' law, Graham's law, and Avogadro's principle relate to kinetic theory.

4 Explain why real gases do not behave exactly like an ideal gas.

4-6
Gas stoichiometry

1 Calculate the volume of gases used or produced in chemical reactions. (Text Examples 4-14 to 4-16; Text Probs. 4-40 to 4-42) (New Skills Examples 5 to 7; Self Test 5, 22, 25)

NEW SKILLS

4-2
Pressure-volume relationship: Boyle's law

Boyle's law states that the product of the pressure and volume of a gas at constant temperature is equal to a constant number.

$$PV = k$$

If the pressure or volume of a gas changes while the temperature remains the same, Boyle's law says the pressure × volume product does not change.

The mathematical equation for the constant PV relation is

$$P_1 V_1 = P_2 V_2$$

Subscript 1 refers to an initial state and subscript 2 refers to a final state after the change in pressure or volume.

Solving for V_2

$$V_2 = V_1 \frac{P_1}{P_2}$$

Note that the final volume is found by multiplying the initial volume by a ratio of pressures. We can use this reasoning to assemble a pressure ratio without referring to the equation. When pressure is reduced, the volume increases, so the pressure ratio must have a value greater than 1. On the other hand, if the pressure is increased, the volume will decrease. For V_2 to be less than V_1, the pressure ratio must be less than 1. This is the key to the reasoning approach used in Method 2 of Examples 4-1 through 4-7 in the text.

Knowing how pressure and volume are related, you can predict whether the volume will increase or decrease and set up the pressure ratio accordingly.

Work through Examples 4-1 to 4-3 of the text, paying close attention to the Method 2 solutions.

4-3
Temperature effects:
Charles' law

1 Charles' law problems

Charles' law problems can be worked by the same approach as Boyle's law problems. Reasoning out temperature, pressure, or volume ratios to calculate changes is possible in most problems. Using the formula (Method 1 in the text) is just as valid and you should use the method that suits you best. If you understand both methods, so much the better.

One very important fact must be remembered when using Charles' law, whether you use the formula method or the ratio method. The temperature must be in kelvins rather than degrees Celsius. If the temperature is given in degrees Celsius it must be converted to kelvins before the problem can be worked.

● **EXAMPLE 1**

Problem: A 5.00-liter sample of gas has its temperature raised from 10 to 40°C at constant pressure. What is the new volume?

Solution: Will the final volume be more or less than 5.00 liters? Since an increase in temperature causes an increase in volume, the volume must increase, so the final volume is more than the initial.

Would the ratio $\frac{10}{40}$ or $\frac{40}{10}$ be used to multiply the initial volume? Be careful. Neither of these temperature ratios is correct because the ratio must be in kelvins not degrees Celsius.

$$T_1 = 273 + 10 = 283 \text{ K}$$

$$T_2 = 273 + 40 = 313 \text{ K}$$

Now, is the ratio $\frac{283}{313}$ or $\frac{313}{283}$ correct? Since the volume must increase, we select the ratio greater than 1.

$$V_2 = V_1 \left(\tfrac{313}{283}\right)$$

$$V_2 = 5.00 \text{ liters} \left(\tfrac{313}{283}\right) = 5.53 \text{ liters} \bullet$$

Now work through Examples 4-4 and 4-5 in the text.

2 Combined law problems

Combined law problems are approached exactly as Boyle's law and Charles' law problems. The difference is that two variables change instead of one. A separate ratio can be set up for each changing variable and both ratios are used as multipliers to find the final conditions.

● **EXAMPLE 2**

Problem: A helium-filled weather balloon has a volume of 325 liters at 750 torr and 25°C. It is released and rises through the atmosphere to an altitude where the pressure is 200 torr and the temperature is -30°C. What is the volume of the balloon at that altitude?

Solution: First we convert the temperature to kelvins.

$$T_1 = 273 + 25 = 298 \text{ K}$$

$$T_2 = 273 - 30 = 243 \text{ K}$$

Now we reason through the problem to set up the required ratios. Since the pressure decreases, the volume will increase, so the pressure ratio must be greater than 1 or $\tfrac{750}{200}$. The temperature decreases and this will cause a decrease in volume, so the temperature ratio must be less than 1.

$$V_2 = 325 \text{ liters} \left(\tfrac{750}{200}\right)\left(\tfrac{243}{298}\right) = 994 \text{ liters} \bullet$$

Now work Examples 4-6 and 4-7 in the text.

4-4
Ideal-gas behavior

1 Using the ideal-gas law in calculations

Watch for problems that are tailor-made for using the ideal-gas law. There are four variables in the equation $PV = nRT$: pressure, volume, temperature, and number of moles. When a problem gives three of the four variables P, V, T, and n and asks for the value of the fourth, use the ideal-gas law. Problems that ask for a gas density or molecular weight can also be solved by the ideal-gas law. Be sure you use consistent units. The units of all variables must be consistent with the units of R.

$$R = 0.0821 \text{ liter atm mol}^{-1} \text{ K}^{-1}$$

so volume must be in liters, temperature in kelvins, and pressure in atmospheres. Work through Examples 4-9 and 4-10 in the text for experience with this type of problem.

2 Calculation of the density of a gas

Let us try a variation of the ideal-gas law problem.

● **EXAMPLE 3**

Problem: What is the density of hydrogen at 30°C and 1.00 atm?

Solution: Density = mass/volume. We can find the number of moles of hydrogen from the ideal-gas law, convert the moles to grams, and find the density. The volume is not given in the problem, but we are interested in the number of moles or grams per liter so we choose 1 liter of gas as the basis for calculations. Then n will be the number of moles in 1 liter. Solve the ideal-gas law for number of moles.

$$T = 273 + 30 = 303 \text{ K}$$

$$n = \frac{PV}{RT} = \frac{1.00 \text{ atm } (1.00 \text{ liter})}{0.0821 \text{ liter atm mol}^{-1} \text{ K}^{-1} (303 \text{ K})} = 0.0402$$

Now find the number of grams in the liter.

$$\text{No. of g} = n \times \text{mol. wt.}$$

$$= 0.0402 \text{ mol } (2.00 \text{ g mol}^{-1}) = 0.0804 \text{ g}$$

Since this is the grams per liter, it is also the density.

$$\text{Density} = \frac{\text{grams}}{V} = \frac{0.0804 \text{ g}}{1.00 \text{ liter}} = 0.0804 \text{ g liter}^{-1} \quad \bullet$$

3 Calculation of molecular weight from gas density

A common variation in applying the ideal-gas law is to find the molecular weight of a gas from an experimentally measured density. Example 4-11 in the text illustrates this calculation.

4 Dalton's law of partial pressures

Dalton's law of partial pressure states that the total pressure of a mixture of gases is the sum of the partial pressures of the individual gases.

$$P_{\text{total}} = P_A + P_B + P_C$$

If oxygen gas were collected by displacement of water from a container there would be two gases present in the container, oxygen and water vapor. The total pressure would be

$$P_{\text{total}} = P_{O_2} + P_{H_2O}$$

● **EXAMPLE 4**   **Problem:** Calculate the partial pressure of oxygen collected by displacement of water on a day when atmospheric pressure is 750.0 torr and the temperature is 25°C. The vapor pressure of water at 25°C is 23.76 torr.

Solution: We will assume that the total pressure of the gas is the same as atmospheric pressure. Dalton's law can be solved for the partial pressure of oxygen

$$P_{O_2} = P_{\text{total}} - P_{H_2O}$$

$$= 750.0 \text{ torr} - 23.76 \text{ torr} = 726.2 \text{ torr} \quad \bullet$$

Now try Examples 4-13 and then 4-12 in the text.

4-6
Gas stoichiometry

When gases are involved in chemical reactions, we sometimes want to know the volume of the gases involved. The principles of Chap. 4 enable us to make these calculations.

● **EXAMPLE 5**   **Problem:** Oxygen was discovered by the decomposition of mercury (II) oxide, HgO.

$$2HgO(s) \longrightarrow 2Hg(l) + O_2(g)$$

What volume of oxygen at STP could be obtained from the decomposition of 50.0 g of HgO?

Solution: We can determine the moles of O_2 from regular stoichiometry and use the molar volume at STP to find the volume.

$$\text{mol } O_2 = 50.0 \text{ g HgO} \times \frac{1 \text{ mol HgO}}{217 \text{ g HgO}} \times \frac{1 \text{ mol } O_2}{2 \text{ mol HgO}} = 0.115 \text{ mol } O_2$$

Since 1 mol of any gas at STP occupies 22.4 liters we can find the volume at STP in 0.115 mol O_2.

$$\text{liters } O_2 = 0.115 \text{ mol } O_2 \times \frac{22.4 \text{ liters}}{1 \text{ mol}} = 2.58 \text{ liters } \bullet$$

If more than one gas is involved in the reaction, unit factors for volume ratios of reacting chemicals can be set up directly from the stoichiometric coefficients.

● **EXAMPLE 6**   **Problem**: Nitric oxide, NO, is produced during the combustion of gasoline in an automobile engine. It rapidly reacts with oxygen to form nitrogen dioxide, NO_2, which is responsible for the brown haze common during air pollution episodes in many cities. If 10.0 liters of NO_2, measured at STP, are produced from NO, how many liters of O_2, also measured at STP, would be consumed?

$$2NO(g) + O_2(g) \longrightarrow 2NO_2(g)$$

Solution: Since all the gases are measured under the same conditions, the number of moles reacting is directly proportional to the volumes. The coefficients of the equation can be used to give the volume ratios.

$$\text{liters } O_2 = 10.0 \text{ liters } NO_2 \times \frac{1 \text{ liter } O_2}{2 \text{ liter } NO_2} = 5.0 \text{ liters } O_2 \bullet$$

We can extend our gas stoichiometry problems beyond the STP conditions to any temperature, pressure, and volume with the ideal-gas law.

● **EXAMPLE 7**   **Problem**: How many liters of hydrogen measured at 730 mmHg and 20°C are required to react with chlorine to produce 15.0 g HCl?

$$H_2(g) + Cl_2(g) \longrightarrow 2HCl(g)$$

Solution: First we will find the number of moles of HCl produced. Use the chemical equation to find how many moles of H_2 are required, and then use the ideal-gas law to determine the volume of the hydrogen.

$$\text{mol HCl} = 15.0 \text{ g HCl} \times \frac{1 \text{ mol HCl}}{36.5 \text{ g HCl}} = 0.411 \text{ mol HCl}$$

$$\text{mol } H_2 = 0.411 \text{ mol HCl} \times \frac{1 \text{ mol } H_2}{2 \text{ mol HCl}} = 0.206 \text{ mol } H_2$$

Now the volume of HCl is found from the ideal-gas law

$$V = \frac{nRT}{P}$$

$$= \frac{0.206 \ \text{mol}(0.0821) \ \text{liter atm mol}^{-1} \ \text{K}^{-1})(293 \ \text{K})}{(730 \ \text{mmHg}) \ \dfrac{1 \ \text{atm}}{760 \ \text{mmHg}}}$$

$$= 5.16 \ \text{liters}$$

Now try Examples 4-15 to 4-17 in the text.

SELF TEST

True or false

_____ 1 The product of the pressure and volume of a fixed amount of gas is constant.

_____ 2 When a gas is compressed the number of moles increases.

_____ 3 The absolute temperature of a gas is directly proportional to its volume at constant pressure.

_____ 4 In a mixture of two gases A and B, the total pressure is 680 mmHg. The partial pressure of A is 340 mmHg. We are sure that half the molecules in the mixture are gas A.

_____ 5 The volume ratio of gases in a chemical reaction is always a small whole number.

_____ 6 Nitrogen gas will diffuse faster than oxygen gas at a fixed temperature and pressure.

Completion

7 Pressure is equal to force per _____.

8 In the gas laws temperature is always used in _____ units.

9 Temperature in kelvins is equal to degrees Celsius plus _____.

10 If the temperature of a gas at constant pressure increases, the volume _____.

11 If the pressure of a gas at constant temperature increases, the volume _____.

12 The volume of a gas at STP is _____ than the volume at 700 mmHg and 300 K.

13 The pressure of a gas alone in a container is the _____.

14 According to Graham's law the relative rate of diffusion of two gases is inversely proportional to the square root of their _____.

15 The value of the ideal-gas constant is _____ liter atm mol^{-1} K^{-1}.

Multiple choice

16 If a gas occupies 5.0 liters at 380 mmHg, what volume will it occupy at 760 mmHg? The temperature remains constant.
(a) 2.5 liters   (b) 5.0 liters   (c) 10.0 liters   (d) 25.0 liters

17 If a gas occupies 5.0 liters at 0°C, what volume will it occupy at 273°C? The pressure remains constant.
(a) 2.5 liters   (b) 5.0 liters   (c) 10.0 liters   (d) 25.0 liters

18 The proper ratios of temperature and pressure to find the volume of a gas initially at 100°C and 760 mmHg when its temperature and pressure are changed to 200°C and 400 mmHg are
(a) $\frac{400}{760}, \frac{100}{200}$ (b) $\frac{400}{760}, \frac{373}{473}$ (c) $\frac{760}{400}, \frac{200}{100}$ (d) $\frac{760}{400}, \frac{473}{373}$

19 A sample of a gas has a volume of 10.0 liters. If the pressure is doubled and the absolute temperature is increased by a factor of 3, the final volume of the gas will
(a) increase by a factor of 6   (b) increase by a factor of 1.5
(c) decrease by a factor of $\frac{2}{3}$ (d) decrease by a factor of 1.5

20 The density of a gas at $0°C$ and 3 atm pressure is 1.5 g liter^{-1}. What will be the density at STP?
(a) 4.5 g liter^{-1} (b) 1.5 g liter^{-1}
(c) 0.5 g liter^{-1} (d) insufficient information to tell

21 The density of a gas at STP is
(a) The molar volume divided by the molecular weight
(b) The molecular weight multiplied by 0.0821 liter atm mol^{-3} K^{-1}
(c) The molecular weight divided by the molar volume
(d) The molecular weight divided by the number of moles

22 The reaction for formation of ammonia from nitrogen and hydrogen is the basis for a large fertilizer industry.

$$N_2(g) + 3H_2(g) \rightleftharpoons 2NH_3(g)$$

What volume of hydrogen, measured at STP, is required to produce a ton of ammonia for use as fertilizer?
(a) 895 liters   (b) 8.01×10^4 liters
(c) 1.36×10^6 liters   (d) 1.79×10^6 liters

23 It is found that 1.43 g of an unidentified gas fills a 1.00-liter container at STP. Which of the following is most likely to be the gas?
(a) H_2 (b) CH_4 (c) O_2 (d) SO_2

24 It is found that a sample of an unidentified gas effuses through a small opening half as fast as helium. Which of the following is most likely to be the gas?
(a) H_2 (b) CH_4 (c) O_2 (d) SO_2

25 What volume of O_2 is consumed by complete combustion of 12 liters of CH_4 at $500°C$ and 650 mmHg?
(a) 6 liters   (b) 12 liters   (c) 24 liters   (d) 36 liters

5 THE ATOM

CHAPTER OVERVIEW

5-1
The divisible atom

Our present concepts of the structure of atoms are so widely accepted and applied that it is difficult to imagine how matter was visualized before the discoveries described in this section. Dalton's theory of the atom showed amazing insight for his time. Compare his 1803 ideas with your present understanding of atoms. His theory successfully explained the chemical observations of his day and still account for the basic aspects of chemical behavior as we understand it today. His ideas were the beginning of modern atomic theory.

Several other important discoveries followed Dalton in the nineteenth century. Faraday found a basic relationship between matter and electricity, which meant that understanding the behavior of electrons became important to understanding matter. The experiments of Crookes, Thomson, and Millikan established two basic properties of electrons: their charge and mass. Further experiments with Crookes tubes revealed a relation between negative and positive electrical charges in matter.

Our present idea of atomic structure in which a nucleus is surrounded by electrons originated with Rutherford's experiment. Study Figs. 5-4 and 5-5 in the text until you understand how these observations showed the Thomson model for the structure of an atom could not be correct. Rutherford interpreted his observations as evidence of a small, dense, positively charged nucleus surrounded by space containing the electrons.

Further work showed the nucleus is composed of protons and neutrons. There are some important facts to be remembered from the last few paragraphs of Sec. 5-1.

1 The atomic number is the positive charge on the nucleus and is equal to the number of protons in the nucleus.
2 The number of protons in the nucleus equals the number of electrons in the extra-nuclear region.
3 The mass number is equal to the number of neutrons plus protons in the nucleus.
4 Isotopes are atoms with the same number of protons but different numbers of neutrons in the nucleus. They account for atomic weights being nonintegral numbers.

5-2
Atomic weights

Elements exist in nature as a mixture of isotopes. Since different isotopes of any given element have different weights, we use an average of these isotope weights for the atomic weight. The average is based on the isotope abundance found in nature for each element. The mass and abundance of the isotopes are determined by mass spectrometry as shown in Fig. 5-6 in the text. Text Example 5-1 shows how the mass and abundance values from mass spectrometry are used to calculate atomic weights. Note the difference between mass number and atomic weight pointed out in the last paragraph of the section.

5-3
Electrons in atoms

1 The noncollapsing atom

The first ideas about behavior of electrons in the space around the nucleus were unsatisfactory right from the start. They were (1) the electron was moving and (2) the electron was not moving. Strange as it may seem, neither of these alternatives was possible. If the electron were stationary, the electrostatic attraction of its negative charge to the positive charge of the nucleus would cause the atom to collapse. On the other hand, according to classical physics, an electron changing its direction, as in a circular orbit, must emit radiation. Electrons emitting radiation would lose energy and slow down and gradually spiral into the nucleus and the atom would collapse. Rutherford suggested that electrons in atoms travel in trajectories around the nucleus, much as planets travel around the sun, but could not explain why this structure would not collapse.

Either Rutherford's ideas of atomic structure were wrong, or classical physics did not apply to the atom. A new kind of physics was needed to explain atomic structure. This new physics was introduced by Niels Bohr. It is called quantum mechanics and is based on application of wave theory to electrons and radiant energy.

2 Radiant energy

Radiant energy is often called electromagnetic energy or light energy. The text discusses several characteristics of radiant energy:

1 Radiant energy travels by wave motion much like waves on a surface of water.
2 The frequency, ν, of a wave is the number of crests (or troughs) passing a point per second and is measured in hertz.
3 The wavelength, λ, is the distance between successive corresponding points (crests or troughs).
4 The velocity of a wave is the product of its frequency and wavelength: $c = \nu\lambda$, where c is the velocity of light in a vacuum, 3×10^8 m sec^{-1}.
5 Radiant energy in the form of light can be refracted, or separated by a prism into its different wavelengths. The pattern of wavelengths is called a spectrum. Figure 5-10 in the text illustrates a spectrum.

3 Atomic spectroscopy

When atoms are sufficiently excited by receiving radiant energy, they emit a line spectrum which consists of only certain, discrete wavelengths. The spectral pattern is distinctive for each element, much like a fingerprint. Figure 5-11 in the text shows a line spectrum of hydrogen. The wavelengths observed in the hydrogen spectrum can be calculated very accurately from the Rydberg equation. Note how atoms with more electrons than hydrogen give a more complex line spectrum as shown in Fig. 5-12 in the text.

4 Quantum mechanics

Bohr's application of wave theory to radiant energy led to the development of quantum mechanics and the concept of quantization. This simply means that energy comes in specific discrete amounts. When this idea is applied to electrons, it means the electron is restricted to only certain energy values. It turns out that the differences between these energy values are numerically the same as the radiant energies of the lines observed in atomic spectra. Thus, there is a basic connection between the energy of electrons and the wavelength of light emitted by an atom. Planck and Einstein showed how to relate the energy of a photon to its wavelength, and Bohr showed the connection between photon energy or wavelength and the energy levels of electrons in atoms. It appeared that electrons behave like waves.

5 The Bohr atom

The Bohr model of an atom consists of electrons moving around the nucleus in circular orbits much as planets revolve around the sun. Electrons can change orbits by absorbing or emitting photons which have exactly the same energy as the difference in energy between the two electron orbits. Since the emitted energy is quantized (has a fixed value), the wavelength of the energy is fixed and gives a single line in the line spectrum of the atom. In a given atom, many different transitions between different energy levels are possible for an electron, giving rise to the total line spectrum.

The values of energies of the observed line spectrum for hydrogen agree very well with energies calculated from the Bohr model, but agreement between calculated energies and experimental energies from observed spectra is poor for atoms other than hydrogen.

LEARNING OBJECTIVES

As a result of studying Chap. 5 you should be able to do the following:
Write the definition and give an example illustrating the use of each key term.

5-1
The divisible atom

1 List four ideas of modern atomic theory that came from John Dalton. (Text Prob. 5-3) (Self Test 1)
2 List the important discoveries made from observations of gas discharge tubes. (Text Probs. 5-4, 5-7, 5-10) (Self Test 2, 3, 7, 8, 16)
3 Explain how the mass and charge of the electron were determined. (Self Test 17)
4 Make a sketch illustrating how Rutherford showed that the atom consists of a small, heavy, positively charged nucleus surrounded by extranuclear electrons. (Text Prob. 5-2)
5 List three contributions of Rutherford's experiment to the theory of atomic structure. (Text Prob. 5-6) (Self Test 9)
6 List the relative characteristics (mass and charge) of the three subatomic particles: proton, neutron, and electron. (Text Prob. 5-8)
7 Explain the difference between mass number and atomic weight. (Self Test 10, 21)
8 List three items of information about the structure of an atom conveyed by the atomic number. (Text Prob. 5-12) (Self Test 5, 18)

9 Determine the number of protons, electrons, and neutrons in the nucleus of an element from its atomic number and mass number. (Text Probs. 5-12, 5-13) (New Skills Examples 1 to 3; Self Test 22, 23)

5-2
Atomic weights

1 Calculate atomic weights from isotope masses and isotope abundances. (Text Example 5-1; Text Probs. 5-16 to 5-19) (New Skills Example 4; Self Test 6, 24)
2 Understand the operation and significance of a mass spectrometer. (Self Test 11)

5-3
Electrons in atoms

1 Explain how application of classical physics to electrons in atoms leads to predictions of collapsing atoms. (Self Test 19)
2 Use the relationship between the speed of a wave, its frequency, and its wavelength in calculations. (Text Example 5-2; Text Probs. 5-24 to 5-26) (New Skills Example 5; Self Test 12, 20)
3 Understand the difference between continuous and line spectra. (Self Test 15)
4 Show how line spectra arise from transition of electrons between available energy levels in the atom. (Text Prob. 5-27)
5 Calculate the wavelengths of the line spectrum of hydrogen using the Rydberg equation.
6 Explain why new concepts in physics, replacing classical mechanics, were needed to explain the observations of Rutherford.
7 Know how the work of Bohr, Planck, and Einstein led to quantum mechanics to replace classical mechanics in explaining the behavior of small particles. (Text Prob. 5-23)
8 Calculate the energy of a photon from its frequency using $E = \hbar\nu$, or from its wavelength using $E = \hbar c/\lambda$. (Text Prob. 5-22)
9 Understand the concept of quantized energy. (Self Test 13)
10 Describe the Bohr model of an atom. (Text Prob. 5-20) (Self Test 14)
11 Make calculations that show how the energies calculated from the Bohr model (Rydberg equation) agree with the energies of the observed line spectrum for hydrogen. (Text Prob. 5-21)
12 Use the Rydberg equation to calculate wavelengths of lines in the hydrogen spectrum. (Text Prob. 5-28) (New Skills Example 6; Self Test 25)

NEW SKILLS

5-1
The divisible atom

1 Atomic numbers and mass numbers
The atomic number and mass number give valuable information about the structure of the atom. The atomic number indicates the number of protons in the nucleus and the number of electrons surrounding the nucleus in a neutral atom. The mass number is the number of protons plus neutrons in the nucleus and is designated by a superscript before the atomic symbol. For example, ^{23}Na signifies the isotope of sodium with mass number 23. The atomic number can be found from the periodic table on the inside front cover of the text and is included in the symbol as $^{23}_{11}$Na. However, since sodium can have only one atomic number, 11, this information is already specified by the atomic symbol, Na.

2 The use of atomic numbers and mass numbers to determine the number of protons, neutrons, and electrons in atoms

● **EXAMPLE 1**   **Problem:** How many protons and neutrons are present in the nucleus of ^{208}Pb? How many electrons are in the neutral atom?

Solution: The atomic number of Pb is found from the periodic table on the inside front cover of the text to be 82, so there are 82 protons in the nucleus. We find the number of neutrons as follows:

$$\text{Mass number} = \text{number of protons} + \text{number of neutrons}$$

$$\text{Number of neutrons} = \text{mass number} - \text{number of protons}$$

$$= \quad 208 \quad - \quad 82 \quad = 126$$

The number of electrons is always equal to the number of protons in a neutral atom, so there are 82 electrons in Pb. ●

● **EXAMPLE 2**   **Problem:** How many protons, neutrons, and electrons are present in $^{208}Pb^{2+}$?

Solution: The mass number and atomic number are the same for ^{208}Pb and $^{208}Pb^{2+}$, so the number of protons and neutrons is the same as in Example 1. The atom has acquired a +2 charge by losing two electrons. The two electrons took their negative charge with them, so the atom was left with two more protons than electrons, hence the +2 charge. The number of electrons left is 82 - 2 = 80. ●

● **EXAMPLE 3**   **Problem:** Complete the following table:

Symbol	Mass number	Atomic number	Protons	Neutrons	Electrons
^{27}Al					
$^{27}Al^{3+}$					
	200	80			
			17	20	
	84		36		

Solution:

Symbol	Mass number	Atomic number	Protons	Neutrons	Electrons
^{27}Al	27	13	13	14	13
$^{27}Al^{3+}$	27	13	13	14	10
^{200}Hg	200	80	80	120	80
^{37}Cl	37	17	17	20	17
^{84}Kr	84	36	36	48	36

●

5-2   **Atomic weights**   Most elements found in nature are composed of mixtures of isotopes. The atomic weight of an element is the average of the masses of the isotopes in the element. The average is weighted, or adjusted for the percent abundance of the isotopes. The percent abundance and masses of the isotopes are determined by mass spectrometry, and atomic weights are calculated from these data. You need to be able to perform these calculations, so the method is illustrated in the following example.

● **EXAMPLE 4**   **Problem:** A naturally occurring sample of lithium was analyzed in a mass spectrometer and found to consist of two isotopes: 92.75 percent of the sample was ^{7}Li (mass 7.01 amu) and 7.25 percent was ^{6}Li (mass 6.01 amu). What is the atomic weight of Li for this sample?

Solution: Each isotope contributes weight to the sample in proportion to its percent abundance. For the weight of 100 atoms:

$$^7\text{Li contributes} \quad 92.75\%(7.01 \text{ amu}) = 650 \quad \text{amu}$$
$$^6\text{Li contributes} \quad 7.25\%(6.01 \text{ amu}) = \underline{\ 43.6 \text{ amu}}$$
$$694 \quad \text{amu}$$

The weight of 100 atoms of Li is 694 amu, so the weight of one atom of Li (the atomic weight) is

$$\frac{694 \text{ amu}}{100} = 6.94 \text{ amu} \quad ●$$

Now do Example 5-1 in the text.

5-3   *1 The wavelength of radiant energy*
Electrons in atoms   The speed, frequency, and wavelength of a wave are related by the equation

$$\text{Speed} = \nu\lambda$$

In chemical applications we are interested in electromagnetic waves. These are the waves by which radiant energy travels. They behave in a manner analogous to water waves, but travel at the speed of light, designated by c and equal to 3.00×10^8 m s^{-1}. For radiant energy or light waves the product of the frequency ν and wavelength λ is equal to the speed of light

$$c = 3.00 \times 10^8 \text{ m s}^{-1} = \nu\lambda$$

This relation can be used to find the frequency of radiation if its wavelength is known, or to find the wavelength if the frequency is given.

● **EXAMPLE 5**   **Problem:** The wavelength of red light is 650 nm. What is its frequency?

Solution: 650 nm is 650 nanometers or 650×10^{-9} m. Solve the equation $c = \nu\lambda$ for ν and use $c = 3.00 \times 10^8$ m s^{-1}.

$$\nu = \frac{3.00 \times 10^8 \text{ m s}^{-1}}{\lambda}$$

$$= \frac{3.00 \times 10^8 \text{ m s}^{-1}}{650 \times 10^{-9} \text{ m}} = 4.6 \times 10^{14} \text{ s}^{-1} \quad ●$$

Example 5.2 and Probs. 5-24 to 5-26 in the text are very similar to this.

2 Calculation of wavelengths using the Rydberg equation
You may be asked to calculate the wavelength of a line in the hydrogen spectrum using the Rydberg equation. Let us see how this is done. Equation 5-1 in the text is the Rydberg equation

$$\frac{1}{\lambda} = R\left(\frac{1}{n_1^2} - \frac{1}{n_2^2}\right)$$

where λ is the wavelength of lines in the hydrogen spectrum, R is the Rydberg constant $(1.10 \times 10^{-2}\ \text{nm}^{-1})$ and n_1 and n_2 are integers. If $n_1 = 1$, the equation gives the Lyman series; if $n_1 = 2$, the Balmer series; and if $n_1 = 3$, the Paschen series of hydrogen lines. In all cases n_2 is an integer larger than n_1. We will investigate the significance of the values of n in Chap. 6.

We can generate several equations for each series by giving different values to n_2.

● **EXAMPLE 6**   **Problem**: Calculate the wavelength of the line in the Lyman series of the hydrogen spectrum for which $n_2 = 4$.

Solution: The Rydberg equation for the Lyman series is

$$\frac{1}{\lambda} = 1.10 \times 10^{-2}\ \text{nm}^{-1}\left(\frac{1}{1^2} - \frac{1}{n_2^2}\right)$$

For $n_2 = 4$ the equation becomes

$$\frac{1}{\lambda} = 1.10 \times 10^{-2}\ \text{nm}^{-1}\left(1 - \frac{1}{2^2}\right)$$

$$= 1.10 \times 10^{-2}\ \text{nm}^{-1}\ (1 - \tfrac{1}{4})$$

$$= 8.25 \times 10^{-3}\ \text{nm}^{-1}$$

$$\lambda = \frac{1}{8.25 \times 10^{-3}}\ \text{nm} = 121\ \text{nm}\ ●$$

Now try Prob. 5-28 in the text.

SELF TEST

True or false   ____ 1 John Dalton proposed that all matter is composed of identical atoms.
____ 2 Cathode rays are attracted to a positive charge.
_T_ ③ Electrons are present in all matter.
_T_ ④ Removal of an electron from an atom leaves the atom with a positive charge.
_F_ ⑤ The atomic number gives the number of protons in the nucleus and number of extranuclear electrons in an atom.
_F_ ⑥ All isotopes of a given element have the same mass.

Completion   7 The cathode ray in a discharge tube is made up of particles called _____.
8 Cathode rays are repelled from _____ charges.
⑨ Rutherford showed the atom has a dense massive _nucleus_ surrounded by _e-s_ .
⑩ The sum of protons and neutrons in an atom is its _mass #_ .
11 The mass of an isotope can be determined by a technique known as _____.
12 A hertz is the same as a _____.
13 Energy in certain permitted amounts is said to be _____.

14 The model of an atom consisting of electrons in circular orbits around a nucleus is called the _____ .

15 Many energy transitions are possible for the electrons in an atom and these transitions are observed as a _____ spectrum.

Multiple choice

16 Which of the following does not pertain to cathode rays?
  (a) They are emitted from the cathode of a gas-discharge tube.
  (b) They are attracted toward a positive charge.
  (c) They are radiant energy.
  (d) They carry a negative charge.

17 The charge on the electron was determined by
  (a) Thomson simultaneously applying an electric and a magnetic field to cathode rays
  (b) Goldstein's measurements on canal rays
  (c) Millikan's oil drop experiment
  (d) Rutherford's gold foil experiment

18 Which of the following is not given by the atomic number of an atom?
  (a) The number of neutrons in the nucleus
  (b) The number of protons in the nucleus
  (c) The number of extranuclear electrons
  (d) The mass number minus the number of neutrons

19 According to classical physics, an atom should
  (a) Consist of a nucleus and stationary electrons.
  (b) Collapse
  (c) Fly apart because of centrifugal force on the electron
  (d) Emit a line spectrum

20 Channel 19 on CB radios broadcasts at 27.185 megahertz (MHz). What is the wavelength of Channel 19?
  (a) 11.0 m   (b) 8.10×10^{16} m   (c) 0.0900 m   (d) 81.0 m

21 Which atom has the greatest mass?
  (a) ^{10}Be   (b) ^{10}Be   (c) ^{11}B   (d) ^{14}N

22 Which atoms have the same number of neutrons?
  (a) ^{10}Be and ^{10}B   (b) ^{10}Be and ^{11}B
  (c) ^{10}B and ^{11}B   (d) ^{10}Be and ^{14}N

23 Which atoms are isotopes?
  (a) ^{10}Be and ^{10}B   (b) ^{10}Be and ^{11}B
  (c) ^{10}B and ^{11}B   (d) ^{10}Be and ^{14}N

24 Bromine occurs naturally as a mixture of two isotopes: ^{79}Br (mass 79.0 amu) and ^{81}Br (mass 81.0 amu). The relative isotopic abundance of ^{79}Br is 55.0 percent. What is the atomic weight of Br?
  (a) 79.9   (b) 79.904   (c) 80.0   (d) 80.1

25 The Balmer series of the hydrogen spectrum falls in the visible region of electromagnetic waves. What is the wavelength for the transition of an electron from $n_2 = 5$ to $n_1 = 2$ in the Balmer series?
  (a) 2.30×10^{-3} nm   (b) 3.30×10^{-3} nm
  (c) 303 nm   (d) 433 nm

6 ELECTRONS: ENERGIES, WAVES, AND PROBABILITIES

CHAPTER OVERVIEW

A particle consisting of electrons flying around a nucleus in well-defined paths is the popular presentation of an atom. This picture is easy to visualize and agrees with our experience and observations of matter in the macroscopic world, but it is incorrect. The microscopic world of atoms is governed by an entirely different set of rules. To gain true insight into the behavior of atoms we must set aside our experience with matter on the macroscale and learn a whole new set of rules based on probability, quantized energy, and particles that behave like waves. Chapter 6 presents these new rules and applies them to atoms. Let the notion that electrons behave like little particles take a back seat for a while. Instead, think of electrons as waves of energy and the quantum-mechanical picture of an atom will begin to make sense.

6-1
The quantum-mechanical model

First of all, let us point out that quantum mechanics successfully predicts behavior of atoms but familiar classical physics is entirely inadequate to explain microscale behavior of particles. When Niels Bohr realized this, he opened the door to modern atomic theory.

In the microscopic world, particles can behave like waves and waves exhibit properties of particles. The fact that electrons can be diffracted provides the most convincing evidence that electrons are waves, or at least behave like waves. De Broglie's equation relates the wavelength of microscopic particles to their mass and velocity.

The application of quantum mechanics to behavior of electrons involves very difficult mathematics so only the results are presented in the text. This quantum-mechanical approach gives a systematic method of classifying electronic energy levels and helps us understand how electrons are distributed in an atom.

Figures 6-2 and 6-3 in the text summarize the electronic orbital classification scheme. The pattern of distribution of electrons in the orbitals of an atom is described in Figs. 6-3 and 6-5 in the text. There are two methods of showing this distribution pattern: electronic configurations and orbital diagrams. The electronic configuration of each element is shown in Table 6-2 in the text. Orbital diagrams are shown in Table 6-1.

The last half of the section emphasizes the Aufbau procedure for adding electrons to orbitals of lowest energy to determine ground-state electronic configurations of the atoms. The Aufbau filling sequence is shown in Figs. 6-3 and 6-5 in the text. You should become familiar enough with this filling sequence to write the electronic configurations for the elements given only the atomic number. The electronic configurations resulting from the Aufbau process are shown in Table 6-2 of the text.

The configuration consisting of full *s* and *p* subshells in the highest energy shell is very stable. We will see how this configuration, sometimes called the noble-gas configuration, is important in predicting general chemical behavior of the elements.

6-2
One-dimensional
standing waves

Sections 6-2, 6-3 and 6-4 describe the behavior of standing waves. The text introduces wave behavior in one dimension and shows how the nodes and antinodes become more complex in two and three dimensions, and how quantum numbers are used to describe the mode of vibration.

6-3
Two-dimensional
standing waves

Nodes in two-dimensional standing waves are along lines. While the mode of vibration in one dimension could be described by a single quantum number, description of the wave motion in two dimensions requires two quantum numbers, one to describe the frequency of vibration and one to specify its orientation.

6-4
Electrons: three-
dimensional waves

Extending the one- and two-dimensional concepts of the previous sections into three dimensions gets us into the wave description of electrons. Nodes in three dimensions become surfaces and describe the boundary limits for electrons in atoms.

The Heisenberg uncertainty principle introduces the concept of probability into describing the location of an electron. It tells us it is impossible to give a precise description of the location of electrons in atoms. Instead, we define a region of space which has a high probability of containing the electron, and call this region an electronic orbital. Figures 6-16, 6-23, and 6-26 in the text show the geometry of the *s*, *p*, and *d* orbitals defined in this fashion.

A quantitative description of electronic orbitals is obtained through the Schrödinger equation. Quantum numbers arise from solutions to this equation.

6-5
Quantum numbers

Quantum numbers are identification tags for electrons in atoms. Each electron can be assigned specific values of the four quantum numbers and no two electrons in an atom have the same values for all four quantum numbers. Table 6-3 in the text summarizes the basic information concerning quantum numbers.

LEARNING OBJECTIVES

As a result of studying Chap. 6 you should be able to do the following:
Write the definition and give an example illustrating the use of each key term.

6-1
The quantum-
mechanical model

1 Show why the notion of an atom consisting of electrons flying around the nucleus in well-defined paths is not correct. (Self Test 1)
2 Show why quantum mechanics replaced classical mechanics to explain the behavior of subatomic particles.
3 Calculate the de Broglie wavelength of a particle. (Text Example 6-1; Text Probs. 6-2, 6-3, 6-5) (Self Test 25)

4 Understand why diffraction of electrons is experimental evidence that electrons behave like waves. (Text Prob. 6-1)

5 Reproduce the organization of electron energy levels in an atom into shells, sub-shells, and orbitals. (Text Figs. 6-2, 6-3; Text Probs. 6-8, 6-9) (New Skills Example 1; Self Test 2, 6, 7, 17)

6 Determine the number of paired or unpaired electrons in an atom. (New Skills Example 5; Self Test 3, 12, 18)

7 Determine whether or not an atom is paramagnetic. (Text Probs. 6-10, 6-13) (New Skills Example 6, Self Test 8)

8 Write Hund's rule and the Pauli exclusion principle. (Text Prob. 6-31) (Self Test 14)

9 Write the filling order of electrons for the Aufbau procedure. (Text Fig. 6-5; Text Prob. 6-11) (New Skills 6-1 : 3; Self Test 4, 22)

10 Write the electronic configuration and orbital diagram of elements with atomic numbers 1 through 36. (Text Probs. 6-6, 6-7, 6-12) (New Skills Examples 2 to 4; Self Test 9, 10, 19, 21, 24)

6-2
One-dimensional standing waves

1 Represent a standing wave by a vibrating string and identify the nodes and anti-nodes. (Text Probs. 6-18, 6-26) (Self Test 5)

2 Understand why certain modes of vibration are allowed while others are forbidden.

3 Understand how standing wave vibrations are quantized and how quantum numbers apply to the allowed vibrational modes.

6-3
Two-dimensional standing waves

1 Understand that when the concepts of the vibrating string in text Sec. 6-2 is expanded to two dimensions, the nodes become more complex and a second quantum number is required to describe the orientation of the wave.

6-4
Electrons: three-dimensional waves

1 Explain why it is impossible to know the velocity and position of an electron simultaneously. (Text Prob. 6-4)

2 Understand how a three-dimensional wave represents an electron in an atom.

3 Relate the nodes and antinodes of three-dimensional waves to boundary surfaces for electron contours. (Text Probs. 6-19, 6-26)

4 Relate the lobes of three-dimension waves to orbitals of the electrons.

5 Understand how wave motion is described by the Schrödinger equation and relate the solutions of this equation to the wave function (Ψ).

6 Relate the square of the wave function (Ψ^2) to the probability of finding an electron in a particular region of space, and to the shape of the orbital lobes.

7 Draw sketches of the s, p, and d orbitals. (Text Figs. 6-18, 6-21, 6-26; Text Probs. 6-14 to 6-16, 6-20, 6-21, 6-27)

6-5
Quantum numbers

1 List the names, symbols, information provided, and possible values of the four quantum numbers. (Text Table 6-3; Text Probs. 6-29, 6-30, 6-32) (New Skills 6-5 : 1; Self Test 11, 16, 20, 23)

2 Write quantum numbers for electrons in atoms. (Text Table 6-4; Text Prob. 6-17) (New Skills Examples 7, 8; Self Test 13, 15)

3 Describe the overall shape of an atom in terms of the sum of the electron charge clouds. (Text Prob. 6-25)

4 Relate the principal quantum number to the total nodes in the charge cloud and the azimuthal quantum number to the angular nodes. (Text Prob. 6-28)

NEW SKILLS

6-1
The quantum-mechanical model

1 The wavelength of particles

The de Broglie relationship between wavelength, mass, and velocity describes what is sometimes called the dual nature of matter, its ability to behave like both a particle and a wave.

The wavelength associated with a particle can be calculated by the de Broglie relationship and is called the de Broglie wavelength. Even though it can be calculated, the wavelength of macroscopic particles is so small it has no practical meaning. Example 6-1 and Probs. 6-2 and 6-3 in the text involve calculations of de Broglie wavelengths of particles.

2 Classification of electron energy levels or shells

The electronic energy levels in an atom are organized into shells, subshells, and orbitals according to the following scheme:

1 The principal division of energy levels is into shells designated by the letters K, L, M, N, O . . . or specified by the number n of the shell where n is some integer, roughly equivalent to the Bohr atom integers. A shell represents a general region in space around the nucleus where the electron is found. Shells get progressively larger and have higher energy going through the sequence K, L, M, N, O.
2 Each shell consists of one or more subshells representing characteristic regions in space and designated s, p, d, f . . . .
3 Subshells are divided into orbitals which indicate the orientation of the subshell in space. Each orbital can hold two electrons.
4 Two electrons in an orbital always spin in opposite directions around their own axis.

● **EXAMPLE 1**

Problem: List the possible subshells in the fourth main energy level. How many orbitals are in each subshell? What is the maximum electron population possible for this level?

Solution: The fourth main energy level is the N shell. The number of subshells in a shell is equal to the shell number. Therefore, there are four subshells. They are the $s, p, d,$ and f subshells. There is one orbital in the s subshell, three in the p subshell, five in the d subshell, and seven in the f subshell, a total of 16 orbitals. Each orbital holds a maximum of two electrons so the total possible electrons in the fourth energy level is 32. Note that if n is the number of a main level, there are n^2 orbitals and $2n^2$ possible electrons in the energy level. ●

3 The Aufbau filling process

The Aufbau procedure for building up the electronic configuration of elements consists of assigning electrons to orbitals according to a systematic filling order. The diagram below will make it easy to remember the Aufbau filling order. Just follow the arrows beginning at the bottom (lowest energy).

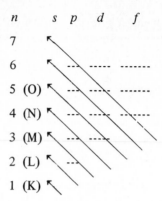

4 Electronic configurations

An electronic configuration shows the number of electrons in each occupied orbital of an atom. The only information needed to write an electronic configuration is the atomic number of the element and the Aufbau filling order.

● **EXAMPLE 2**   **Problem:** Write the electronic configuration for the element with atomic number 32.

Solution: The atomic number 32 signifies 32 electrons that need to be placed in orbitals. We place electrons in orbitals in order of increasing energy remembering that there is a maximum of two electrons per orbital. Each s orbital holds two electrons. There are three p orbitals and five d orbitals, so the p subshell holds six electrons and the d subshell holds ten. Starting with the lowest energy level (K) we have:

$$1s^2 2s^2 2p^6 3s^2 3p^6 3d^{10} 4s^2 4p^2$$

The electrons up to and including the $3p$ sublevel can be denoted by the symbol [Ar], which represents the configuration for argon. This shortens the configuration to

$$[Ar] 4s^2 3d^{10} 4p^2 \quad ●$$

Electronic configurations of other elements are written in the same fashion. The only exceptions to the Aufbau filling diagram occur when it is possible to half fill d or f subshells. Table 6-2 in the text shows that an electron is taken from a higher-energy-level s orbital in these cases.

● **EXAMPLE 3**   **Problem:** Write electronic configurations for the following particles: Ba, Ba^{2+}, I^-, and Xe.

Solution: The atomic number of Ba is 56, so it has 56 electrons. Ba^{2+} has lost two electrons so it has 54. I^- has one additional electron besides the 53 indicated by its atomic number for 54 total electrons. Xe has 54 electrons.

The electronic configurations are

Ba	($Z = 56$) (56 electrons)	[Xe] $6s^2$
Ba^{2+}	($Z = 56$) (54 electrons)	[Xe]
I^-	($Z = 53$) (54 electrons)	[Xe]
Xe	($Z = 54$) (54 electrons)	[Xe]

Ba^{2+}, I^-, and Xe all have the same electronic configuration and are called isoelectronic particles. ●

5 Orbital diagrams

An alternative method of depicting electron distribution in atoms is by orbital diagrams. These diagrams show the distribution of electrons among the orbitals of the higher energy subshells.

● **EXAMPLE 4**   **Problem:** Write the orbital diagram for the element in Example 2 above.

Solution: The orbital diagram is

$$[Ar] \quad \underset{}{\underline{\text{⥮}}} \ \underset{}{\underline{\text{⥮}}} \ \underset{3d}{\underline{\text{⥮}} \ \underline{\text{⥮}} \ \underline{\text{⥮}}} \qquad \underset{4s}{\underline{\text{⥮}}} \qquad \underset{}{\underline{\text{↑}}} \ \underset{4p}{\underline{\text{↑}}} \ \underline{\phantom{\text{↑}}}$$

The two electrons in the $4p$ subshell are placed in separate orbitals with parallel spins (both arrows point in the same direction) in accordance with Hund's rule. ●

6 Unpaired electrons

Lone electrons in an orbital are called unpaired electrons. Atoms containing unpaired electrons are attracted to a magnetic field and are said to be paramagnetic.

● **EXAMPLE**   **Problem:** How many unpaired electrons does the element in Example 4 contain?

Solution: The two $4p$ electrons occupy separate orbitals so they are unpaired. There are two unpaired electrons. ●

● **EXAMPLE 6**   **Problem:** Is titanium paramagnetic?

Solution: An atom is paramagnetic if it has unpaired electrons. An orbital diagram will show if they are present; the orbital diagram is

$$Ti \ (Z = 22) \quad [Ar] \quad \underset{}{\underline{\text{↑}}} \ \underset{3d}{\underline{\text{↑}}} \ \underline{} \ \underline{} \ \underline{} \qquad \underset{4s}{\underline{\text{⥮}}}$$

The two $3d$ electrons are unpaired according to Hund's rule, so titanium is paramagnetic. ●

6-5   ### 1 Information indicated by quantum numbers

Quantum numbers   Quantum numbers are identification tags for electrons in atoms. There are four quantum numbers.

1 The first quantum number is called the principal quantum number and given the symbol n. It tells the shell or main energy level of an electron and is a measure of its average distance from the nucleus. The allowed values for n are $1, 2, 3, 4, 5, \ldots$.

2 The second quantum number is called the azimuthal quantum number and has the symbol l. It specifies the subshell $s, p, d,$ or f containing the electron. The allowed values of l are integers from 0 to $(n - 1)$.

3 The third quantum number is the magnetic quantum number and is represented by the symbol m_l; it specifies the directional orientation of the subshell in space. m_l has integral values from $-l$ to $+l$.

4 The fourth quantum number is the spin quantum number represented by m_s. It specifies the direction of spin of the electron about its own axis and has values of $+\frac{1}{2}$ or $-\frac{1}{2}$.

The names, possible values, and information signified by the four quantum numbers are summarized in Table 6-3 in the text.

2 Assigning quantum numbers to electrons in atoms
The following rules can be used to determine the quantum numbers of electrons in specific orbitals.

1   n is the number of the main energy level
2   $l = 0$ for s electrons, $l = 1$ for p electrons, $l = 2$ for d electrons, and $l = 3$ for f electrons
3   m_l has any integral value from $-l$ to $+l$, including 0.
4   m_s is either $+\frac{1}{2}$ or $-\frac{1}{2}$.

● **EXAMPLE 7**   **Problem:** What are the possible quantum numbers for the last two Aufbau electrons in Si?

Solution: The last two Aufbau electrons in Si are the $3p^2$ electrons. Applying the rules for assigning quantum numbers gives

$$n = 3 \qquad l = 1 \qquad m_l = -1, 0, \text{ or } +1 \qquad m_s = +\tfrac{1}{2} \text{ or } -\tfrac{1}{2}$$

The three $3p$ orbitals corresponding to $m_l = -1$, 0, and $+1$ are all equivalent and the $3p^2$ electrons could be in any of them. The electrons must have parallel spin, so m_s must be $+\frac{1}{2}$ or $-\frac{1}{2}$ for both. The six possible quantum numbers are

$$3, 1, -1, +\tfrac{1}{2} \qquad 3, 1, 0, +\tfrac{1}{2} \qquad 3, 1, 1, +\tfrac{1}{2}$$
$$3, 1, -1, -\tfrac{1}{2} \qquad 3, 1, 0, -\tfrac{1}{2} \qquad 3, 1, 1, -\tfrac{1}{2}$$

Any two of these in which both electrons have the same sign for m_s represent the allowable quantum numbers. ●

● **EXAMPLE 8**   **Problem:** Which of the following sets of quantum numbers are possible in an atom?
(a) $1, 1, 0, +\frac{1}{2}$ (b) $2, 1, 1, -\frac{1}{2}$ (c) $3, 1, -2, -\frac{1}{2}$ (d) $4, 0, 1, +\frac{1}{2}$
(e) $5, 4, 3, +\frac{1}{2}$

Solution: The quantum numbers are always given in the order n, l, m_l, and m_s. (a) Not possible: l can only have values up to $n - 1$ (b) Possible. (c) Not possible: m_l can only have values up to $\pm l$.   (d) Not possible: m_l must be 0 if $l = 0$.   (e) Possible. ●

SELF TEST

True or false   ___F___ (1) Electrons move around the nucleus in well-defined paths called orbits.
___T___ (2) No matter what energy level it is in, each orbital can hold two electrons.
___F___ (3) Paired electrons have parallel spins.
___F___ (4) The filling sequence of orbitals by the Aufbau procedure follows a fixed order.
_____ 5 A stretched string may vibrate in many different modes.
___T___ (6) The third main energy level holds a maximum of 18 electrons.

Completion

7 The N shell has _____ (number) subshells and _____ orbitals.

8 Unpaired electrons cause an interaction with a _____ field.

9 An atom of nitrogen has _____ (number) electron(s) in a $1s$ orbital, _____ electron(s) in a $2s$ orbital, and _____ electron(s) in each of _____ different $2p$ orbitals.

10 The electronic configuration of the element with atomic number 24 is _____.

11 The smallest principal quantum number of an electron for which the magnetic quantum number is +3 is _____ .

12 The number of unpaired electrons in scandium (atomic number 21) are (is) _____ .

13 The atomic number of the element for which the last electron added in the Aufbau procedure has $n = 3$, $l = 1$, $m_l = -1$, and $m_s = -\frac{1}{2}$ is _____.

14 Two electrons in the same orbital must have different _____.

15 All electrons in a p subshell have quantum number l equal to _____.

16 There are _____ (number) different possible orientations in space for orbitals having $l = 3$.

Multiple choice

17 The maximum number of electrons in the energy level with $n = 5$ is
(a) 5   (b) 25   (c) 32   (d) 50

18 Which of the following has the most unpaired electrons?
(a) $_7N$ (b) $_{13}Al$ (c) $_{17}Cl$ (d) $_{24}Cr$

19 Which of the following is the electronic configuration for Fe?
(a) $[Ar]\,3d^8$ (b) $[Ar]\,3d^6\,4s^2$ (c) $[Ar]\,3d^7\,4s^1$ (d) $[Ar]\,3p^6\,4s^2$

20 Which quantum number designates the orientation in space of electron orbitals?
(a) principal   (b) azimuthal   (c) magnetic   (d) spin

21 Which element has its $3p$ orbitals half full of electrons?
(a) $_{13}Al$ (b) $_{14}Si$ (c) $_{15}P$ (d) $_{16}S$

22 In which of the following subshells would an electron have the lowest energy?
(a) $4d$ (b) $4f$ (c) $5s$ (d) $5p$

23 How many different values of the magnetic quantum number are possible for azimuthal quantum number $l = 2$?
(a) one   (b) three   (c) five   (d) ten

24 Which of the following does not represent a possible electronic configuration for an atom in its ground state?
(a) $1s^2\,2s^2\,2p^6$ (b) $1s^2\,2s^2\,2p^6\,3s^1$ (c) $[Ar]\,4s^1\,3d^3$ (d) $[Ar]\,4s^1\,3d^5$

25 What is the wavelength in meters of a proton (mass = 1 amu) traveling at $\frac{1}{100}$ of the speed of light? ($c = 3.00 \times 10^8$ m s^{-1})
(a) 1.33×10^{-13} (b) 1.33×10^{-16} (c) 2.21×10^{-40} (d) 3.67×10^{-64}

7 CHEMICAL PERIODICITY

CHAPTER OVERVIEW

There are 105 elements which interact to form millions of compounds. Each of these compounds has characteristic physical and chemical properties. If we were to approach chemistry in a haphazard manner and start learning about these compounds one by one, we would not get very far in a lifetime.

The concepts presented in this chapter make possible a systematic study of chemical trends and behavior of groups of elements. The periodic table organizes an immense amount of information to make the study of chemistry and chemicals meaningful and possible.

7-1
The discovery of the periodic law

Several attempts to correlate the behavior of elements before 1870 went largely unnoticed, but when Meyer and Mendeleev published their periodic table, they predicted the existence of unknown elements and accurately estimated their properties. These predictions were soon verified and the periodic table became a standard tool of chemists.

7-2
The periodic law

When elements are arranged in order of increasing atomic number, certain properties are seen to repeat at definite intervals. This repetition is the periodic law and forms the basis for the modern periodic table shown as Fig. 7-2 in the text. Using the periodic table to understand and predict chemical behavior is what Chap. 7 is all about. Elements in groups or columns have similar chemical properties, so we can learn the chemistry of the group rather than studying each element individually. The noble gases, alkali metals, and halogens are groups that show striking similarities in their properties.

The correlation of electronic configuration with position in the periodic table is at least as important as the correlation of observable properties. Study Fig. 7-3 to see the relationship between the Aufbau orbital-filling process and the periodic table. You should be able to correlate the electronic configuration of the last Aufbau filling orbital with the position of elements in the periodic table.

The divisions of the periodic table shown in Fig. 7-3 are very important and should be learned.

7-3
Trends in atomic
properties

One of the main uses of the periodic table is the correlation of trends in several physical and chemical properties of the elements. The text shows periodic correlations for atomic radius, ionization energy, electron affinity, density, and melting point by presenting data in six figures and six tables. You do not need to memorize these data, but you should see the trends, recognize the exceptions to the trends, and learn the reasons for the trends and the exceptions.

The trends in size are easy to remember if you correlate what we have already learned about electronic configurations with the periodic chart. Each new period in the chart adds a new shell so, logically, each period is larger than the one(s) before it. Electrons added to the same shell across a period are approximately the same distance from the nucleus. The increasing nuclear charge pulls the entire shell closer, so size trends correlate beautifully with what we have learned about electronic structure. Notice how even the irregularities in trends are predicted by the stability of half-filled shells.

Trends in ionization energy show strong periodic behavior (Fig. 7-5 in the text) that can be closely correlated to electronic configuration and nuclear charge. Again, the irregularities in the trends are expected from the stability of filled or half-filled subshells.

Electron affinity shows general trends also but the irregularities here are not so easily explained in terms of simple electronic configuration.

7-4
Trends in physical
properties

All of the physical properties mentioned in the text show strong periodic trends, and plots like Figs. 7-8 and 7-9 could be made for any of them.

7-5
Trends in chemical
properties

In Chap. 8 we will see how the position of elements in the periodic table can be used to determine the formulas of simple ionic compounds. An understanding of the relationship between electronic configuration and the periodic table is essential for effective use of the table in predicting chemical formulas.

A diagonal line from boron to astatine divides the periodic table into two important divisions. Metals lie to the left and nonmetals to the right of this diagonal line. Elements close to the diagonal line are called metalloids.

LEARNING OBJECTIVES

As a result of studying Chap. 7 you should be able to do the following:
Write the definition and give an example illustrating the use of each key term.

7-1
The discovery of
the periodic law

1 Explain how the concept of periodic behavior was discovered and why it was so successful. (Text Prob. 7-4)

7-2
The periodic law

1 Write the periodic law and give three examples of periodic behavior.
2 Identify periods and groups on the periodic table. (Text Prob. 7-5) (Self Test 6)

3 Identify the alkali metals, halogens, noble gases, and transition metals in the periodic table (Text Probs. 7-7, 7-8) (Self Test 8)

4 Predict electronic configurations from the position of an element in the periodic table. (Text Probs. 7-9 to 7-11)

5 Determine the number of valence shell electrons from the position of an atom in the periodic table. (Text Probs. 7-10, 7-12) (Self Test 1, 11, 14, 24)

7-3
Trends in atomic properties

1 Using a halogen atom as an example, clearly distinguish between ionization energy and electron affinity. (Text Prob. 7-18)

2 Predict the trends in atomic radius, ionic radius, ionization energy, and electron affinity among atoms in the same group or period. (Text Probs. 7-15, 7-17, 7-20 to 7-22, 7-26 to 7-28) (Self Test 2, 3, 7, 10, 16 to 20, 25)

3 Explain the trends in atomic radius and ionization energy in terms of electronic configurations and nuclear charge.

4 List irregularities of trends in atomic radius and ionization energy for second-period elements and justify these irregularities on the basis of electronic configurations and nuclear charge.

5 Explain why second-period elements often behave differently from other members of their group.

6 Explain why the chemical behavior and physical properties of the transition elements, lanthanoids, and actinoids show strong similarities.

7-4
Trends in physical properties

1 Predict trends in density and melting point among adjacent atoms in the periodic table. (Text Prob. 7-29) (Self Test 4, 23)

7-5
Trends in chemical properties

1 List some advantages of studying chemical behavior by groups of elements rather than individually.

2 Identify elements as metals, nonmetals, or metalloids from their position in the periodic table. (Text Probs. 7-30, 7-31) (Self Test 5, 13)

NEW SKILLS

7-3
Trends in atomic properties

If we represent the periodic chart by a rectangle, it becomes easy to represent the general trends in atomic properties by remembering values of the properties for two corners of the periodic table.

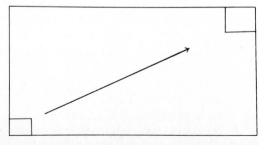

Smallest atomic radius, highest ionization energy, highest electron affinity

Largest atomic radius, lowest ionization energy, lowest electron affinity

The diagonal points in the direction of decreasing atomic size and increasing ionization energy and electron affinity.

The correlations of atomic properties among groups and periods may be summarized as follows:

1 The atomic radius of elements decreases from left to right in a period and increases from top to bottom in a group.
2 The ionization energy of elements increases from left to right in a period and decreases from top to bottom in a group.
3 Electron affinity shows the same trend as ionization energy.

SELF TEST

True or false

_T_ 1 The concept that a completed valence shell is a very stable electronic configuration is called the octet rule.

_T_ 2 The atomic radii decrease from left to right in a period.

_F_ 3 The atomic radii decrease from top to bottom in the representative groups.

_F_ 4 Chemical properties generally obey the periodic law but physical properties do not.

_T_ 5 Metals are on the left of the periodic table and nonmetals are on the right.

Completion

6 In the periodic table elements having similar chemical and physical properties appear together in _columns_.

7 Ionization energy and _____ show similar trends in the periodic table.

8 Elements whose differentiating electrons are in the d subshell of an energy level below the valence shells are called _____.

9 The first ionization energy of an element is always _____ (less, greater) than the second ionization energy.

10 Sodium is _____ (smaller, larger) than the atom just under it in the periodic table.

11 The number of valence electrons is the same as the _____ for A group elements.

12 The element that follows lanthanum in the periodic table is _____.

13 The elements that show both metallic and nonmetallic behavior are called _____ _____.

Multiple choice

14 The electrons in the highest energy level comprise which shell?
   (a) transition   (b) valence   (c) periodic   (d) main

15 The size change associated with filling the $4f$ subshell is called the
   (a) atomic radius trend   (b) electron screening
   (c) lanthanoid contraction   (d) actinoid contraction

16 The element with the largest atomic radius is located in which part of the periodic table?
   (a) upper left   (b) upper right   (c) lower left   (d) lower right

17 The element with the highest ionization potential is located in which part of the periodic table?
   (a) upper left   (b) upper right   (c) lower left   (d) lower right

18 The element with the highest electron affinity is located in which part of the periodic table?

(a) upper left   (b) upper right   (c) lower left   (d) lower right

19 Which of the following has an atomic radius less than that of chlorine?

(a) Na   (b) S   (c) Ar   (d) K

20 Which of the following are arranged in order of increasing ionization energy?

(a) Na, K, Rb   (b) Cl, Ar, K   (c) O, F, Ne   (d) Ne, Cl, Se

21 Which of the following are arranged in order of increasing atomic radius?

(a) B, C, N   (b) F, Ne, Na   (c) Kr, Ar, Ne   (d) Li, Na, K

22 Which of the following would be expected to have chemical properties similar to Cl?

(a) S   (b) Br   (c) Ne   (d) Se

23 Which of the following has a melting point and boiling point similar to Sr?

(a) Rb   (b) Y   (c) Ca   (d) Xe

24 Which of the following has the same number of valence electrons as As?

(a) N   (b) V   (c) Ge   (d) Kr

25 Which element has the highest electron affinity?

(a) Li   (b) He   (c) F   (d) At

8 CHEMICAL BONDING

CHAPTER OVERVIEW

In Chaps. 5, 6, and 7 we studied the electronic structure and properties of atoms. In Chap. 8 we investigate the forces that bond atoms together into molecules. The two general types of bonds are ionic and covalent. Each type is formed by a specific process and gives unique properties to a molecule. The opening paragraph of the text emphasizes that actual bonds are usually intermediate between these two idealized bond types.

Polyatomic ions are held together by covalent bonds, and their structures are determined by the manner of distribution of valence electrons among the atoms. We will investigate this electron distribution in considerable detail. Chemical properties of a molecule are related to the charge distribution and we will see how this distribution is described by oxidation numbers of the atoms.

8-1
Ionic bonding

An ionic bond is the electrostatic force of attraction between particles with opposite electrical charges. It is formed by the transfer of one or more electrons from a metal to a nonmetal. Metals tend to lose electrons and nonmetals gain electrons to attain a noble-gas electronic configuration called a stable octet. The ionic charge for representative elements can be found by inspection from their position in the periodic table. Since molecules are always electrically neutral, positive and negative ions combine in ratios determined by their charges. The total positive and negative charge always balance in a molecule. When one atom has a low ionization energy (metal) and another has a high electron affinity (nonmetal), an electron transfer takes place to form an ionic bond. The overall process releases energy, so the ionic product is energetically more stable than the original atoms. This process is illustrated for NaCl in Fig. 8-3 in the text.

8-2
Covalent bonding

When two atoms with similar tendencies to gain or lose electrons interact, electrons are shared between the atoms to form a covalent bond. Sharing of two or three pairs of electrons between two atoms gives double or triple covalent bonds. The distribution of valence electrons in covalent compounds is conveniently shown by Lewis structures.

Although electrons are shown on specific atoms in Lewis structures, in reality all electrons in a molecule are indistinguishable. Lewis structures are only a bookkeeping technique and they fail to show a true picture of bonding when resonance is possible. Then, the actual molecule is a resonance hybrid of the different Lewis structures. However, drawing Lewis structures helps to predict how atoms combine to form molecules and what geometry these molecules will have. We will use Lewis structures as an aid to understanding molecular geometry throughout the text, so you should learn the rules for drawing them. Examples 8-5 through 8-9 in the text illustrate Lewis structures.

8-3
Electronegativity

Electronegativity is the tendency of a bonded atom to attract additional electrons. The electron pair in a covalent bond responds to differences in electronegativities between the bonded atoms. When atoms of equal electronegativity are bonded, the electrons are shared equally and the bond is nonpolar.

When atoms of different electronegativity are bonded, the atom with higher electronegativity attracts the electron pair more strongly, resulting in unequal sharing of the electrons.

The atom with higher electronegativity becomes the negative end of the bond, leaving the other end positive and making a polar covalent bond.

Most bonds exhibit a mixture of ionic and covalent characteristics and so are polar to some extent.

Bonds with a high degree of ionic character are called ionic; those with a high degree of covalent character are called covalent or polar covalent.

The amount of ionic character of a bond can be estimated from the difference in electronegativities of the bonding atoms.

Atoms in the upper left of the periodic chart have highest electronegativities; atoms in the lower left corner have the lowest electronegativities.

8-4
Electronic bookkeeping

This section deals with the distribution of electrical charge in molecules. There are two methods of assigning charges to atoms in molecules: formal charges and oxidation numbers. Formal charges give a more accurate description of the actual charge distribution in molecules, but oxidation numbers are more convenient and are the usual method used. The rules applying to both methods are given in the text.

Oxidation numbers are used to organize and relate descriptive chemistry to the charge distribution of compounds, and to balance and interpret reactions involving electron transfer [called oxidation-reduction reactions (Chaps. 13 and 19)].

LEARNING OBJECTIVES

As a result of studying Chap. 8 you should be able to do the following:
Write the definition and give an example illustrating the use of each key term.

8-1
Ionic bonding

1 Explain how an ionic bond results from the electrostatic attraction between ions formed by transfer of electrons from an atom with low ionization energy to one with a high electron affinity. (Text Prob. 8-3) (Self Test 6, 15)

2 Draw Lewis structures for simple molecules and ions. (Text Examples 8-1, 8-2; Text Probs. 8-19, 8-20) (New Skills Example 2; Self Test 8)

3 Identify lone-pair and shared-pair electrons in Lewis structures. (Self Test 1)

4 Write empirical formulas for ionic compounds given the charges on the cation and anion. (Text Examples 8-3, 8-4) (New Skills Example 1; Self Test 7)

5 Predict the number of electrons an atom will lose or gain (hence its ionic charge) from the number of valence electrons as determined by its position in the periodic table. (Self Test 7)

8-2
Covalent bonds

1 Explain how covalent bonds are formed between atoms by sharing electrons. (Text Prob. 8-4)

2 Explain the change in potential energy and electron probability density that occurs as separated atoms are brought together to form a covalent bond.

3 Draw Lewis structures for molecules or polyatomic ions with covalent bonds. (Text Examples 8-5 to 8-9; Text Probs. 8-5, 8-6, 8-22) (New Skills Examples 2 to 4; Self Test 9, 10, 16 to 18, 25)

4 Give examples showing the limitations of the octet rule and Lewis structures for large atoms, resonance hybrids, and odd-electron compounds. (Text Probs. 8-23, 8-25) (Self Test 2, 16)

5 Draw the contributing Lewis structures for resonance hybrid molecules. (Text Prob. 8-11)

8-3
Electronegativity

1 Define electronegativity and know the general trend of electronegativity with respect to the position of atoms in the periodic table. (Text Prob. 8-12) (Self Test 3, 11, 19)

2 Predict whether a bond will be normal covalent, polar covalent, or ionic based on the difference in electronegativity between the bonded atoms. (Text Probs. 8-13, 8-14, 8-16, 8-18) (Self Test 4, 12, 20)

3 Relate the electronegativity value of an atom to metallic or nonmetallic behavior.

8-4
Electronic
bookkeeping

1 Understand how formal charge and oxidation numbers are used to keep track of the distribution of valence electrons among atoms in a molecule. (Self Test 5)

2 Understand why formal charge and oxidation number are not generally the same as an electrical charge on an ion.

3 Determine the formal charge and oxidation number on each atom in a molecule or polyatomic ion with the aid of a Lewis structure. (Text Examples 8-10 to 8-13; Text Probs. 8-24, 8-26, 8-27, 8-30) (New Skills Examples 5; Self Test 13, 14, 21 to 24)

NEW SKILLS

8-1
Ionic bonding

1 Writing Lewis structures

Lewis structures are an important aid to understanding the kind of bonding in a molecule. We will use them in writing structures for resonance hybrids, determining bond polarity, and, later, predicting geometry of molecules and types of hybrid bonds.

The following procedure can be used to write Lewis structures:

1 Write the symbol for each atom in a position showing the geometry of the molecule. In most cases the arrangement of atoms will be obvious; if it is not, you may need to try several arrangements to find one that works.

2 Determine the total number of valence electrons in the molecule. Add an electron for each negative charge or subtract an electron for each positive charge if the particle is an ion.

3 Assign a pair of electrons to each bond between adjacent atoms.

4 Assign the remaining electrons to complete the octet for each atom except hydrogen. This may require sharing of two or three pairs of electrons between atoms.

You will usually be given the geometrical (spatial) position of atoms relative to each other in the molecule. If you are not given this information, and there are three or more atoms in the molecule, remember that oxygen and hydrogen atoms are usually bonded to a central atom. The central atom is the one closest to the lower left-hand corner of the periodic table. Remember that carbon has four covalent bonds, and almost never has a lone pair of electrons.

The completed Lewis structure should show:

1 Which atoms in the molecule are bonded together
2 How the valence electrons are assigned in the molecule
3 Which pairs of electrons are bonding and which are lone pairs
4 Any double or triple bonds in the molecule

Although electrons are shown as belonging to, or coming from specific atoms in Lewis structures, in reality all electrons are indistinguishable, and Lewis structures are only a bookkeeping technique.

Example 8-1 in the text shows how to write the Lewis structure for the ionic compound calcium chloride. Since all ionic compounds must be electrically neutral (you do not get an electrical shock when you touch a chemical), they combine in the ratio of one calcium ion to two chloride ions. Notice that in Lewis structures brackets and ionic charges are added to the chemical symbol and all the electrons in the original valence shell are shown. The number of chloride ions is indicated by a coefficient in the Lewis structure and by a subscript in the chemical formula.

2 Writing chemical formulas from ionic charges

Chemical formulas of binary ionic compounds can be written easily if the charges on the ions are known. Charges of the representative elements in binary ionic compounds are determined from their position in the periodic table. Group IA, IIA, and IIIA metals have one, two, and three valence electrons, respectively. They lose these electrons to form their respective ions and so have ionic charges of +1, +2, and +3, respectively. Therefore, the group number is the charge for elements in the first three groups. When elements in groups VA, VIA, and VIIA form binary ionic compounds they gain three, two, and one electrons, respectively, to complete their valence octets. Their resulting charges are -3, -2, and -1, respectively. Thus we have

Group	IA	IIA	IIIA	VA	VIA	VIIA
Ionic charge	+1	+2	+3	-3	-2	-1

Thus we can determine ionic charges from the group number of the representative elements.   Transition elements sometimes have ionic charges as indicated by their group number, but the technique is not as reliable as for the representative elements.

● **EXAMPLE 1**   **Problem**: What is the chemical formula for the ionic compound between strontium and nitrogen?

Solution: Strontium is in group IIA and nitrogen in in group VA, so they have charges of +2 and −3, respectively. A neutral compound can be formed by combining three strontium ions with two nitride ions to give a total +6 charge and −6 charge. The formula is Sr_3N_2. ●

Now try Examples 8-3 and 8-4 in the text.

8-2   *Lewis structures*
Covalent bonding   Lewis structures are much more meaningful and informative for covalent compounds than for ionic, but first the geometry must be known or determined. Usually you will be given the spatial arrangement of the atoms, but if you are not, remember that oxygen and hydrogen are almost always bonded to a larger central atom or carbon. Carbon atoms are often bonded to each other.

● **EXAMPLE 2**   **Problem**: Write the Lewis structure of chloroform, $CHCl_3$.

Solution: No information or hints were given about the geometry of the molecule so we resort to the general observation that carbon usually serves as the central atom and other atoms are bonded to it. The carbon atom must have four bonds. The geometry is

$$Cl$$
$$H \ C \ Cl$$
$$Cl$$

The position of H and Cl around the carbon is arbitrary; the H can be exchanged with any Cl and the geometry is still the same, as we shall see in Chap. 9. Next we need to determine the total number of valence electrons. From their positions in the periodic table we see that H has one valence electron, C has four, and each Cl has seven for a total of $1 + 4 + 3(7) = 26$ valence electrons. Eight of these are required for the four bonds on the carbon.

$$\overset{\cdot\cdot}{Cl}$$
$$H:C:Cl$$
$$\underset{Cl}{\cdot\cdot}$$

Note how the shared pairs needed for bonding satisfy the need for two electrons to fill hydrogen's valence shell and eight to fill carbon's shell. There are $26 − 8 = 18$ additional electrons to be distributed among the chlorine atoms. This gives six more electrons to each Cl, just the right amount to complete the octet on each Cl and finish the Lewis structure for $CHCl_3$. ●

$$:\overset{\cdot\cdot}{Cl}:$$
$$H:\overset{}{C}:\overset{\cdot\cdot}{Cl}:$$
$$:\underset{\cdot\cdot}{Cl}:$$

● **EXAMPLE 3**   **Problem:** Write the Lewis structure for formaldehyde, CH_2O.

Solution: In this molecule the two hydrogens and the oxygen will be bonded to the carbon. By looking at the position of the atoms in the periodic table, we can predict considerable information about the bonding even before we complete the Lewis structure. Hydrogen with one valence electron normally forms one bond. Carbon, as we have seen, with four electrons forms four bonds. Oxygen has six electrons (two less than an octet) so it normally forms two bonds. Since there are only three atoms to form four bonds with carbon, one of the atoms must form a double bond; this has to be the oxygen. Thus, we know the molecule will appear as

$$H—C=O$$
$$\underset{\textstyle H}{|}$$

even before we write the Lewis structure. Nevertheless, let us proceed with the Lewis structure.

There are $1 + 1 + 4 + 6 = 12$ valence electrons. (Be sure you understand how we arrive at the number 12.) Eight of these have been committed to bonds on carbon

$$\underset{\textstyle \overset{\displaystyle ..}{H}}{H:C::O}$$

leaving four electrons to provide the two lone pairs necessary to complete the octet on oxygen

$$\underset{\textstyle H}{H:C::\overset{..}{\underset{..}{O}}:}$$

thus giving a completed valence shell to each atom and finishing the Lewis structure. ●
Now let us try a Lewis structure for a charged particle (ion).

● **EXAMPLE 4**   **Problem:** Write the Lewis structure for the phosphate ion, $PO_4{}^{3-}$.

Solution: In this ion the four oxygens are bonded to the central phosphorus atom.

$$\left[\begin{array}{c} O \\ | \\ O—P—O \\ | \\ O \end{array} \right]^{3-}$$

The total valence electrons are five from phosphorus, six from each of the four oxygens, and three for the 3- charge on the ion.

$$5 + 4(6) + 3 = 32$$

There is only one way the 32 electrons can be distributed so each atom obeys the octet rule

$$\left[\begin{array}{c} :\overset{..}{O}: \\ :\overset{..}{O}:P:\overset{..}{O}: \\ :\overset{..}{O}: \end{array} \right]^{3-}$$

Now try Examples 8-5 through 8-9 in the text.

8-4
Electronic
bookkeeping

1 Formal charges

When more than one Lewis structure is possible for a molecule, formal charges can be used to decide which Lewis structure is correct. The true Lewis structure will have formal charges consistent with known electronegativities for the atoms in the molecule.

Rules for assigning formal charges to atoms in a Lewis structure are given in the text and their application is shown in Examples 8-10 and 8-11.

2 Oxidation numbers

The assignment of oxidation numbers to atoms in molecules is straightforward if the rules given in the text are followed. These rules may be summarized as follows:

1   Fluorine always has −1 oxidation number in compounds.
2   Oxygen has −2 oxidation number in compounds except for peroxides, super-oxides, and with fluorine.
3   Hydrogen has +1 oxidation number when combined with nonmetals and −1 when combined with metals.
4   Groups IA, IIA, and IIIA metals have oxidation numbers equal to the charge on the ion.
5a The oxidation number of atoms unbonded, or in their elemental state, is zero.
5b For simple, monatomic (one-atom) ions, the oxidation number is equal to the charge on the ion.
5c The sum of oxidation numbers of atoms in a molecule is 0.
5d The sum of oxidation numbers of all atoms in an ion is equal to the charge on the ion.

● **EXAMPLE 5**

Problem: Assign oxidation numbers to each atom in the following: Cl_2, Cl^-, NaCl, $CaSO_4$, CN^-, NH_4^+, $K_2Cr_2O_7$, and CH_2O.

Solution: We will apply the appropriate rules to each particle and write the oxidation number over each atom.

$\overset{(0)}{Cl_2}$ Rule 5a: The oxidation number is zero in an uncombined element.

$\overset{(-1)}{Cl^-}$ Rule 5b: The oxidation number is equal to the ionic charge for monatomic ions.

$\overset{(+1)}{Na} \overset{(-1)}{Cl}$ Rule 5b: The oxidation number is equal to the charge on the ions for binary ionic compounds.

$\overset{(+2)}{Ca} \overset{(+6)}{S} \overset{(-2)}{O_4}$ Rule 4:   Gives oxidation number of Ca as +1.
          Rule 2:   Gives oxidation number of O as −2.
          Rule 5c: Gives oxidation number of sulfur as +6 from the sum of oxidation numbers of the atoms.

$$Ca + S + 4(O) = 0$$
$$(+2) + x + 4(-2) = 0$$
$$x = 6$$

$\overset{(+2)(-3)}{\text{C N}^-}$

Rule 4: (extension) Gives N an oxidation number of -3 from its position in group VA in the periodic table.

Rule 5d: Gives C an oxidation number of $+2$ from the simple equation

$$x - 3 = -1$$
$$x = 2$$

$\overset{(-3)(+1)}{\text{N H}_4^+}$

Rule 3: Gives H an oxidation number of $+1$.

Rule 5d: Gives N an oxidation number of -3 from the equation

$$x + 4 (+1) = +1$$
$$x = -3$$

Note that in a binary ion N takes the oxidation number predicted from its position in group VA (-3).

$\overset{(+1)\,(+6)\,(-2)}{\text{K}_2 \text{ Cr}_2 \text{ O}_7}$

Rule 2: Gives oxygen -2.

Rule 4: Gives potassium $+1$.

Rule 5c: Gives Cr $+6$ from the equation

$$2x + 2(1) + 7(-2) = 0$$
$$x = 6$$

The coefficient of 2 for x is required because there are two Cr atoms in the molecule.

$\overset{(0)(+1)(-2)}{\text{C H}_2 \text{ O}}$

Rule 2: Gives oxygen -2.

Rule 3: Gives hydrogen $+1$.

Rule 5c: Gives carbon an oxidation number of 0 from the equation

$$x + 2(1) - 2 = 0$$
$$x = 0 \quad \bullet$$

Now you should be able to work Problems 8-27, 8-28 and 8-30 in the text.

SELF TEST

True or false

F ____ 1 Lone pairs of electrons are not attached to an atom.

____ 2 Large atoms such as iodine can use vacant *d* orbitals to expand their valence shell.

F ____ 3 Electronegativity is the same as electron affinity.

____ 4 A polar covalent bond is formed by two atoms of similar but different electro-negativities.

____ 5 Oxidation numbers attempt to indicate the distribution of electrical charge on atoms in a molecule or ion.

Completion

6 The ionization of aluminum may be represented by the equation _____.

7 Element X is in group IIA and element Y is in group VA. The chemical formula formula for an ionic compound between X and Y is _____.

8 The Lewis structure for NaCl is _____.

9 The Lewis structure for CH_2Cl_2 is _____.

10 The Lewis structure for $SO_2{}^{2-}$ is _____.

11 The tendency of a bonded atom to attract electrons is indicated by its _____
_____.

12 A covalent bond in which the electrons are not shared equally is a _____
_____.

13 The oxidation number of S in $KHSO_4$ is _____.

14 The oxidation number of I in $ICl_4{}^-$ is _____.

Multiple choice

15 Ionic bonds are formed when
(a) A metal atom gains electrons and a nonmetal atom loses electrons.
(b) A metal atom loses electrons and a nonmetal atom gains electrons.
(c) A metal atom shares electrons with a nonmetal atom.
(d) Two nonmetal atoms share electrons.

16 Lewis structures
(a) Have eight electrons around all atoms
(b) Do not show lone-pair electrons
(c) Show the distribution of electrons on atoms
(d) Accurately describe the structure of a resonance hybrid

17 The total number of valence electrons in $SO_3{}^{2-}$ is
(a) 12   (b) 14   (c) 24   (d) 26

18 The total number of shared pairs of electrons in CO_2 is
(a) one   (b) two   (c) three   (d) four

19 Which element has the greatest electronegativity?
(a) F   (b) I   (c) Li   (d) Cs

20 Which of the following bonds is most polar?
(a) H—C   (b) F—F   (c) Cs—F   (d) Na—Cl

21 The formal charge on S in the ion $SO_4{}^{2-}$ is
(a) 0   (b) +2   (c) -2   (d) +4

22 The oxidation number of Cl in the compound $KClO_4$ is
(a) -1   (b) +3   (c) +5   (d) +7

23 The oxidation number of carbon in the compound CH_4 is
(a) 0   (b) +2   (c) +4   (d) -4

24 The oxidation number of lead in the compound Pb_3O_4 is
(a) $+\frac{4}{3}$ (b) +2   (c) $+2\frac{2}{3}$ (d) +4

25 The correct Lewis structure(s) for the compound C_2H_6O is (are)

$$\begin{array}{ccc}
\begin{array}{c} H\ \ H \\ \ddots\ \ \ddots \\ H{:}\overset{\ \ \ }{C}{:}\overset{\ \ \ }{C}{:}\overset{\ddots}{\underset{\ddots}{O}}{:}H \\ \ddot{H}\ \ \ddot{H} \end{array} &
\begin{array}{c} H\ \ \ \ H \\ \ddots\ \ \ \ \ddots \\ H{:}\overset{\ \ \ }{C}{:}\overset{\ddots}{\underset{\ddots}{O}}{:}\overset{\ \ \ }{C}{:}H \\ \ddot{H}\ \ \ \ \ddot{H} \end{array} &
\begin{array}{c} H \\ \ddots \\ H{:}\overset{\ \ \ }{C}{:}\overset{\ddots}{\underset{\ddots}{O}}{:}\overset{\ \ \ }{C}{:}H \\ \ddot{H}\ \ \ \ \ddot{H} \end{array} \\
\textbf{(a)} & \textbf{(b)} & \textbf{(c)}
\end{array}$$

(a) A, B, and C   (b) A   (c) A and B   (d) B and C

9

THE COVALENT BOND

CHAPTER OVERVIEW

9-1
Electron-pair repulsion and molecular geometry

In this chapter we will take a close look at the properties of the covalent bond. One important aspect of a covalent molecule is its geometry, or the physical arrangement of its atoms in space.

A lot of terms from basic geometry will be used to describe the shape of molecules. Refer to a dictionary or geometry text if you need help understanding these terms. Atoms tend to arrange themselves to minimize the repulsion between electron pairs and maximize the electron-nucleus attractions. The VSEPR (pronounced "vesper") method is a way to predict the orientation of atoms most favorable for strong covalent bonding.

The steps in using the VSEPR method are outlined in Sec. 9-1. First draw the Lewis structure, determine the steric number, and use Table 9-1 to find the general geometry of the molecule. Tables 9-1 and 9-2 apply the VSEPR method for you if you know the steric number and number of lone pairs on the central atom. These are quickly seen from the Lewis structure. Remember that the geometrical shape of a molecule is found by connecting the nuclei of the outside atoms by straight lines. Lone pairs on the central atom are not included in the overall geometry of the molecule.

Another important aspect of covalent molecules is their polarity. Often molecules contain polar bonds, but the shape of the molecule causes the bond dipoles to cancel each other so the overall molecule is nonpolar. If an imaginary plane can be passed through the center of mass and separate a center of positive charge from a center of negative charge, the molecule is polar.

9-2
Valence-bond theory and orbital overlap

Two separate and distinct theories describe covalent bonds and electronic structure of molecules. Each theory has its own advantages and limitations and each explains certain observations well.

1 Valence-bond (VB) theory considers a bonding pair to occupy atomic orbitals on the bonded atoms. Bonding is the result of overlap of the atomic orbitals.
2 Molecular-orbital (MO) theory considers the atomic orbitals to be replaced by new molecular orbitals. Bonding is determined by the number of electrons in certain molecular orbitals.

The VB theory explains molecular geometry best while MO theory explains molecular spectra, bond strength, and magnetic properties best.

The concepts of σ (sigma) and π (pi) bonds are very important. Make sure you understand how each arises from atomic orbitals, which orbitals give σ and which give π bonds, and how the atomic orbitals overlap to make σ and π molecular orbitals. Remember that one bond of a double or triple bond is always a σ bond; the other(s) π bond(s).

9-3
Hybrid orbitals

The geometry and bonding of many molecules cannot be explained from simple atomic orbitals. Apparently, atomic orbitals merge (hybridize) to form new orbitals as molecular bonding takes place. There are several types of possible hybrid orbitals and they are summarized in Table 9-4 of the text. The type of hybridization is determined by the geometry of the molecule, so try to relate these two concepts as you study.

Remember: The number of hybrid orbitals obtained during hybridization must equal the number of atomic orbitals used. Hybrid orbitals are a powerful aid in explaining the geometry of and bonding in molecules.

9-4
The molecular
orbital model

A molecular orbital (MO) is formed by mixing atomic orbitals of two bonding atoms. The resulting MO can either increase or decrease the density of electrons between the bonding nuclei. If the electron density is increased, the MO is bonding and the nuclei are drawn closer together. If it is decreased, the MO is antibonding and the nuclei are allowed to repel each other. An asterisk (*) is used to designate antibonding orbitals and is read as "star," so $\pi*$ is read "pi star."

The relationship between energies of the molecular orbitals and the atomic orbitals from which they were derived is shown in Figs. 9-31 to 9-33 in the text. Note that the bonding MO is always lower in energy (more stable) than the atomic orbitals that generated it, while the antibonding MO is always higher in energy than the atomic orbitals.

Molecular orbitals are filled with electrons by an Aufbau-type procedure to give molecular electronic configurations for homonuclear molecules of second-period elements. Figures 9-34 to 9-39 and Table 9-5 in the text show the filling order.

If the bond order is greater than 0, the molecule should exist; otherwise it will not. The strength and utility of the MO theory is best seen in the successful predictions of stable molecules, bond energies, and magnetic properties which correlate well with experimental observations.

LEARNING OBJECTIVES

As a result of studying Chap. 9 you should be able to do the following:
Write the definition and give an example illustrating the use of each key term.

9-1
Electron-pair
repulsion and
molecular geometry

1 Understand the VSEPR method of predicting molecular geometry by minimizing electron-pair repulsion. (Self Test 15)
2 Determine the steric number of a central atom in a molecule or ion and relate this to the general geometry of the atoms. (Text Table 9-1; Text Example 9-1) (New Skills Example 1; Self Test 1, 18 to 20)

3 Make sketches of the arrangements of atoms for each of the geometries listed in Table 9-1.

4 Further specify the molecular geometry by determining the number of lone-pair electrons and finding the geometry corresponding to the steric number and number of lone pairs in Table 9-2. (Text Probs. 9-15, 9-16) (New Skills Examples 1, 2; Self Test 2, 18, 19, 21)

5 Predict whether or not a molecule is polar by passing an imaginary plane through the center of mass and determining if there is a separation of positive and negative charges. (Text Fig. 9-12; Text Probs. 9-17, 9-18, 9-21, 9-22) (Self Test 16)

**9-2
Valence-bond
theory and orbital
overlap**

1 Explain the basic difference in VB and MO theories with respect to atomic orbital overlap and formation of molecular orbitals.

2 Explain how σ bonds and π bonds result from overlap of atomic orbitals. (Text Probs. 9-2, 9-4, 9-5) (Self Test 6, 7, 11)

3 Explain the arrangement of σ and π bonds in single, double, and triple bonds. (Text Prob. 9-3) (Self Test 23)

**9-3
Hybrid orbitals**

1 Understand that overlap of atomic orbitals does not predict correct geometry or bonding for molecules. Hybrid orbitals are generated from atomic orbitals to describe covalent bonding in molecules.

2 Know the types of hybrid orbitals in Table 9-4, and how they arise from atomic orbitals. (Text Prob. 9-9) (Self Test 8)

3 Predict the hybrid orbitals used in bonding by period 2 elements. (Text Prob. 9-13) (New Skills Example 3; Self Test 17)

4 Understand the geometry terms in text Table 9-4 and sketch the arrangement of atoms in each of these geometries. (Self Test 9)

5 Know which hybrid orbitals correspond to a given type of geometry. (Text Table 9-4; Text Probs. 9-9, 9-14)

**9-4
The molecular
orbital model**

1 Understand that molecular orbitals (MOs) in molecules are analogous to atomic orbitals (AOs) in atoms.

2 Know which MOs are generated from mixing given s and p atomic orbitals. (Text Prob. 9-30)

3 Know the filling order of MOs for period 2 elements. (Text Figs. 9-31 to 9-33; Text Prob. 9-33)

4 Understand the difference between bonding and antibonding MOs. (Text Prob. 9-23) (Self Test 10)

5 Use the Aufbau type of procedure to write the configuration of valence electrons in MOs for homonuclear molecules of period 2. (Text Figs. 9-35 to 9-39; Text Probs. 9-24, 9-25, 9-36) (New Skills Example 4; Self Test 14, 22)

6 Explain why the sequence of filling MOs changes between N_2 and O_2 as you proceed across period 2. (Self Test 4)

7 Extend the filling sequence of MOs to heteronuclear molecules or diatomic ions of period 2 elements. (Text Probs. 9-26, 9-27) (Self Test 12, 22, 24)

8 Determine bond order and relate it to the stability of a molecule. (Text Table 9-5; Text Example 9-2; Text Probs. 9-24, 9-28, 9-29, 9-34, 9-35) (New Skills Examples 5, 6; Self Test 5, 12, 13, 24, 25)

NEW SKILLS

9-1
Electron-pair
repulsion and
molecular geometry

Predicting the shape of molecules from Lewis structures by the VSEPR method
The valence-shell electron-pair repulsion theory (designated **VSEPR** and pronounced "vesper") is a way of determining the geometry or shape of a molecule from the Lewis structure. The VSEPR method is based on the idea that electron pairs repel each other so that the most stable shape for a molecule is one that allows the electron pairs to get as far apart as possible.

Tables 9-1 and 9-2 in the text make the VSEPR method very simple. First, use the Lewis structure to determine the steric number (total electron pairs) and the number of lone pairs on the central atom. Tables 9-1 and 9-2 give the geometry, bond angles, and type of hybridization on the central atom for several combinations of steric numbers and lone pairs. Double or triple bonds count as only one electron pair when determining the steric number.

● **EXAMPLE 1**   **Problem:** Predict the geometry (shape) of the XeF_4 molecule.

Solution: We will apply the steps in the VSEPR method as given in Sec. 9-1 of the text. First we write a Lewis structure. The molecule is symmetrical with the four fluorines arranged around Xe. There are $8 + 4(7) = 36$ valence electrons. The octet rule only allows distribution of 32 valence electrons.

$$:\ddot{F}:$$
$$:\ddot{F}:\ddot{Xe}:\ddot{F}:$$
$$:\ddot{F}:$$

Since there is a total of 36 valence electrons, the valence shell of Xe must be expanded to contain 12 electrons. There are four bonding pairs and two nonbonding pairs on Xe so the steric number is $4 + 2 = 6$. Table 9-1 gives octahedral orientation around atoms with a steric number of 6 and shows the hybridization on Xe to be sp^3d^2. All bonds are 90° to each other. Note that the two lone pairs occupy points on the octahedron, but that these sites are not part of the overall geometry of the molecule.

Using Table 9-2, we find that a molecule with a steric number of 6 and two lone pairs on the central atom has square planar geometry. All five atoms are in the same plane with the four fluorine atoms at the corners of a square surrounding Xe. The lone pairs on Xe are oriented at 90° above and below the plane.

Note how the lone pairs help determine the bond directions even though they are not considered part of the overall shape of the molecule. Without the lone pairs, the geometrical shape would be tetrahedral. ●

Now try Example 9-1 in the text.

● **EXAMPLE 2**   **Problem:** Predict the geometry of the following using the VSEPR method: **(a)** CO_2 **(b)** SO_2 **(c)** NF_3 **(d)** ClF_3

Solution: Lewis structures are:

$$:\ddot{O}::C::\ddot{O}: \qquad :\ddot{O}:S::\ddot{O}: \qquad :\ddot{F}:N:\ddot{F}: \qquad :\ddot{F}:\ddot{C}l:\ddot{F}:$$
$$:\ddot{F}: \qquad\quad :\ddot{F}:$$

| | (a) | (b) | (c) | (d) |

Compound	Number of atoms bonded to central atom	Lone pairs	Steric number	Molecular geometry
(a) CO_2	2	0	2	Linear
(b) SO_2	2	1	3	Angular
(c) NF_3	3	1	4	Trigonal pyramidal
(d) ClF_3	3	2	5	T-shaped

The Lewis structure is used to determine the steric number and then Table 9-2 in the text gives the geometry having least electron-pair repulsion. ●

9-3
Hybrid orbitals

Hybrid orbitals for second-period elements

In Sec. 9-1 we learned how to use Lewis structures and the VSEPR method to determine the geometry of molecules. The atomic orbital overlap described in Sec. 9-2 successfully describes the bonding in diatomic molecules but is inadequate for polyatomic molecules. The text describes why tetrahedral geometry of CH_4 with four equivalent C—H bonds cannot be explained with simple atomic orbitals.

According to Table 9-4 in the text, BF_3 is a trigonal planar molecule. There are three B—F bonds, all in the same plane, and $120°$ apart. However, the boron atomic orbitals are not in the same plane and not $120°$ apart. For instance, the three $2p$ orbitals are $90°$ apart. The trigonal planar geometry is quite different from the simple atomic orbital geometry. The correct geometry for BF_3 is described by mixing atomic orbitals to form new orbitals oriented toward the bonded atoms. The new orbitals are called hybrid orbitals, and the process of mixing is called hybridization. The text illustrates the hybridization process for several second-period elements. No additional orbitals are created during hybridization because the number of hybrid orbitals generated is always equal to the number of atomic orbitals used, and all hybrid orbitals on an atom are equivalent. Second-period elements do not have d-orbital electrons, so they only form hybrid orbitals from s and p atomic orbitals. The type of hybridization is determined by the steric number (number of bonded atoms plus number of lone pairs) as shown in Table 9-1 in the text. Hybridization is not intended to predict molecular geometry, but is used to describe the bonding of a given geometry once it has been determined by experiment or the VSEPR method.

● **EXAMPLE 3**   **Problem:** Determine the hybridization on the central atom of each molecule in Examples 1 and 2.

Solution: The hybrid orbital geometry determined by the VSEPR method is used in conjunction with text Tables 9-1, 9-2, and 9-4 to find the hybridization.

Compound	Steric number	Molecular geometry	Hybrid orbital geometry	Hybridization
XeF_4	6	Square planar	Octahedral	d^2sp^3
CO_2	2	Linear	Linear	sp
SO_2	3	Angular	Trigonal planar	sp^2
NF_3	4	Trigonal pyramidal	Tetrahedral	sp^3
ClF_3	5	T-shaped	Trigonal bipyramidal	dsp^3

The molecular geometry is different from the hybrid orbital geometry when lone pairs of electrons are present, so be sure to include lone pairs when you determine the hybrid orbital geometry. ●

9-4
The molecular orbital model

Writing molecular orbital configurations for diatomic molecules and ions
The filling order of MOs for homonuclear molecules H_2 through N_2 is:

$$\sigma_{1s}, \sigma^*_{1s}, \sigma_{2s}, \sigma^*_{2s}, \pi_{2p_y}, \pi_{2p_z}, \sigma_{2p_x}, \pi^*_{2p_y}$$

From O_2 to Ne_2 the σ_{2p_x} MO has lower energy than the π_{2p_y} and π_{2p_z} MOs so the filling order becomes

$$\sigma_{1s}, \sigma^*_{1s}, \sigma_{2s}, \sigma^*_{2s}, \sigma_{2p_x}, \pi_{2p_y}, \pi_{2p_z}, \pi^*_{2p_y}, \pi^*_{2p_z}, \sigma^*_{2p_x}$$

The molecular electronic configurations for these homonuclear diatomic atoms is given in Table 9-5 of the text.

The same general rules apply for filling molecular orbitals as for the Aufbau procedure with atomic orbitals. Each of the orbitals holds two electrons and electrons enter the available orbital with lowest energy first. The π_{2p_y} and π_{2p_z} orbitals have equal energy so they are each occupied by single electrons before electron pairing takes place. The same is true for $\pi^*_{2p_y}$ and $\pi^*_{2p_z}$.

The filling order for homonuclear molecules can be used for heteronuclear molecules or ions as long as the atoms are close together in the periodic table and the total number of valence electrons is consistent with the filling order for homonuclear molecules.

● **EXAMPLE 4**   **Problem:** Write the molecular electronic configuration for N_2, N_2^-, and N_2^+.

Solution: The filling order for molecules from H_2 to N_2 can be used for each of these. KK designates the inner core $1s$ electrons.

N_2^+ 9 valence electrons $KK(\sigma_{2s})^2(\sigma^*_{2s})^2(\pi_{2p_y})^2(\pi_{2p_z})^2(\sigma_{2p_x})^1$
N_2 10 valence electrons $KK(\sigma_{2s})^2(\sigma^*_{2s})^2(\pi_{2p_y})^2(\pi_{2p_z})^2(\sigma_{2p_x})^2$
N^- 11 valence electrons $KK(\sigma_{2s})^2(\sigma^*_{2s})^2(\pi_{2p_y})^2(\pi_{2p_z})^2(\sigma_{2p_x})^2(\pi^*_{2p_y})^1$ ●

● **EXAMPLE 5**   **Problem:** Find the bond order for each of the particles in the previous example.

Solution: Antibonding electrons are those in the "star" orbitals.

$$\text{Bond order} = \frac{\text{bonding electrons} - \text{antibonding electrons}}{2}$$

Particle	Bonding electrons	Antibonding electrons	Bond order
N_2^+	7	2	$2\frac{1}{2}$
N_2	8	2	3
N_2^-	8	3	$2\frac{1}{2}$ •

● **EXAMPLE 6**   **Problem:** Compare the bond energies and bond lengths in the particles of the previous example.

Solution: Bond order is a measure of the strength of the bond. For bonding atoms of similar atomic number, the bond length is inversely proportional to bond order. A strong bond pulls the nuclei closer together and gives a shorter bond. In the above example, N_2 has the strongest bond. Its bond energy will be highest and its bond length shortest. N_2^+ and N_2^- should have similar bond energies and bond lengths. ●

SELF TEST

True or false   ___ 1 The steric number is the total number of valence electron pairs in a molecule.
___ 2 Lone pairs are not included in the designation of the overall geometry of a molecule.
___ 3 Molecules with sp^3 hybridization on the central atom always show tetrahedral geometry.
___ 4 σ_{2p} MOs are always lower energy than π_{2p} MOs.
___ 5 Bond strength is directly proportional to amount of atomic orbital overlap.

Completion   6 The overlap of two atomic s orbitals gives a _____ bond.
7 Sideways overlap of two atomic p orbitals gives a _____ bond.
8 Combination of an s atomic orbital with two p orbitals gives _____ hybridization.
9 sp^3 hybrid orbitals point toward the corners of a _____.
10 Molecular orbitals that increase the density of electrons between bonding atoms are called _____ orbitals.
11 End-to-end overlap of two p orbitals leads to a _____ bond.
12 The bond order of CO is _____.
13 MO theory predicts the molecule Be_2 is _____.
14 MO theory predicts O_2 has two unpaired electrons in _____ (bonding, antibonding) MOs.

Multiple choice   15 Which of the following is not essential to the VSEPR method?
(a) Drawing a Lewis structure
(b) Determining the steric number
(c) Minimizing the repulsion between lone pairs
(d) Minimizing the repulsion between bonding pairs

16 Which of the following is polar?
(a) CO_2 (b) $BeCl_2$ (c) NH_4^+ (d) NH_3

17 sp^3 hybridization is present in
(a) H_2O (b) BeF_2 (c) BH_3 (d) SF_6

18 The molecular geometry of the compound PCl_3 should be
(a) T-shaped   (b) pyramidal   (c) tetrahedral   (d) trigonal planar

19 Which of the following has a tetrahedral shape?
(a) H_2O (b) NH_3 (c) C_2H_2 (d) SiH_4

20 The steric number of XeF_2 is
(a) 2   (b) 3   (c) 4   (d) 5

21 How many lone pairs of electrons are present in H_2Se?
(a) zero   (b) one   (c) two   (d) four

22 How many antibonding electrons are in NO^+?
(a) one   (b) two   (c) four   (d) eight

23 How many sigma bonds are in the molecule $H-C\equiv C-H$?
(a) two   (b) three   (c) four   (d) five

24 Which of the following has the lowest bond order?
(a) NF   (b) BN   (c) BeC   (d) He_2^+

25 Which of the following has the shortest bond length?
(a) O_2 (b) O_2^+ (c) O_2^- (d) O_2^{2-}

10

IDEAL SOLIDS
AND LIQUIDS

CHAPTER OVERVIEW

10-1
Solids: some preliminary observations

In a true solid, the atoms or particles are arranged in an orderly array. The geometry and type of particles determine the properties of the solid and we will see how they fall into definite groups or types. Sometimes the external appearance of a large crystal gives clues to the internal structure of the crystal, but there are also powerful techniques that reveal the microstructure of crystals.

10-2
X-ray diffraction

Crystals diffract x rays into a pattern of spots or rings which can be analyzed to determine the internal microstructure and bonding in the crystal. The mathematics of analyzing x-ray diffraction patterns is based on the Bragg relation. It relates the angle of diffraction and wavelength of x rays to the spacing of atoms in parallel planes in the crystal

$$n\lambda = 2d \sin \theta$$

The variables in this equation are defined in the text and in the New Skills section. The term $\sin \theta$ is a trigonometric function. It can be determined from θ by looking in a table of trigonometric functions in any mathematics or chemical handbook or by using most pocket calculators. Laue patterns or Debye-Scherrer patterns are often recorded on film. Values of θ can be measured directly from the film and d values can be calculated with the Bragg relation. You should be able to make this calculation. (See Example 10-1 in the text.)

10-3
The crystal lattice

The unit cell is the key to understanding the geometry of any crystal lattice since the entire crystal is generated by repeating the unit cell. Of the six different crystal types shown in Fig. 10-14, you should become familiar with the cubic and hexagonal structures. Learn the differences and similarities of the three types of cubic structures: primitive, face-centered, and body-centered. Most of the problems and calculations you will do are based on these three types.

10-4
Close packing

There are two types of close-packed crystal structures: cubic close-packed and hexagonal close-packed. They differ only in the way layers of atoms are stacked upon each other. These stacking sequences are illustrated in Figs. 10-19 through 10-23 in the text. It should be apparent that face-centered cubic and cubic close-packed are different names for the same structure. Close-packed structures are important because all the noble gases and about 40 metals crystallize in these structures.

The concept of tetrahedral holes and octahedral holes in close-packed structures will not be difficult to understand if you examine Fig. 10-24 in the text closely. These void spaces are often occupied by atoms or ions that are the right size to fit into the space. Size relations of atoms play an important part in determining the type of crystal structure of a compound. Many ionic compounds crystallize with one ion in a close-packed structure pattern and the other in tetrahedral or octahedral holes in the structure.

10-5
Bonding and
properties of solids

The four types of solids have different physical properties as a result of the different crystal structures and types of particles. You should become very familiar with the physical properties of each type of solid (summarized in Table 10-1 in the text).

Van der Waals forces are much weaker than the ionic and covalent bonds we have studied previously, but they are important in determining the structure of solids. There are two types of van der Waals or intermolecular forces: (1) dipole-dipole forces between polar molecules, illustrated in Fig. 10-28 in the text, and (2) London forces (also called dispersion forces) illustrated in Fig. 10-29.

The concept of delocalized electrons, or electron gas, is important in explaining the high thermal and electrical conductivity of metallic solids.

Lattice energy is an indication of the strength of bonds in a crystal. It is usually quite difficult to measure experimentally and so is calculated from other experimental measurements by a Born-Haber calculation. You will become familiar with this type of calculation in several problems in the text.

10-6
Liquids

Liquids contain particles that are close together but have neither the orderly arrangement characteristic of solids nor the randomness of gases. Liquids have physical properties quite different from gases or solids. Study the concepts of viscosity, diffusion, surface tension, and vapor pressure as applied to liquids. Note how evaporation rates and vapor pressure are related to temperature. Note the difference between boiling point and normal boiling point. The appearance of gas bubbles as a liquid is heated does not always signify boiling since dissolved gases often appear as vapor bubbles as they come out of solution.

The Clausius-Clapeyron equation relates vapor pressure of a liquid to temperature and the molar heat of vaporization. There are three kinds of calculations normally carried out with this equation and they are covered later in the New Skills section.

Note that freezing point and melting point are identical temperatures for pure substances.

LEARNING OBJECTIVES

As a result of studying Chap. 10 you should be able to do the following:
Write the definition and give an example illustrating the use of each key term.

10-1
Solids: some
preliminary
observations

1 Define a solid in terms of the internal arrangement of its particles in a crystal structure. (Text Prob. 10-5)
2 Understand the difference between a true solid and an amorphous substance. (Text Prob. 10-1) (Self Test 7)
3 Relate the properties of a solid to its crystal structure. (Text Probs. 10-2, 10-3)

10-2
X-ray diffraction

1 Describe the diffraction of x rays from layers in a crystal lattice. (Text Prob. 10-7)
2 Use the Bragg equation to calculate spacing between layers when the angle of diffraction and wavelength of an x ray is given. (Text Example 10-1; Text Probs. 10-8 to 10-11) (Self Test 17)
3 Understand how the geometry and dimension of a unit cell are obtained from x-ray diffraction patterns. (Self Test 8)

10-3
The crystal lattice

1 Understand the geometry of simple crystal structures. (Text Probs. 10-12, 10-16) (Self Test 2, 15, 16)
2 Understand that all crystals belong to one of six different crystal systems.
3 Understand how the unit cell describes the entire geometry of a crystal. (Text Probs. 10-13 to 10-15) (Self Test 9)
4 Understand how the properties and kind of particles determine the type of crystal lattice of a solid.
5 Calculate the length of a unit cell for body-centered or face-centered cubic structures from the atomic radius or density of the substance. (Text Probs. 10-17, 10-18, 10-22) (New Skills Examples 1, 3; Self Test 19, 20)
6 Determine the number of atoms per unit cell and the type of cell for cubic structures given the density and unit cell dimensions. (Text Probs. 10-19, 10-20) (New Skills Example 2; Self Test 18)

10-4
Close packing

1 Define packing efficiency. (Self Test 10)
2 Calculate packing efficiency given the type of crystal lattice for simple crystals. (Text Example 10-2)
3 Know the types of crystals that have high packing efficiencies. (Text Prob. 10-24)
4 Understand the difference in layering sequence between cubic close-packed and hexagonal close-packed structures. (Self Test 1)
5 Understand how tetrahedral and octahedral holes arise in close-packed structures and how these holes are occupied by particles in some substances. (Text Probs. 10-25 to 10-28) (Self Test 3, 4)

10-5
Bonding and
properties of solids

1 Understand how properties of solids depend on the geometry of the crystal structure, the type of particles, and the kind of bonding. (Text Probs. 10-31, 10-32, 10-36, 10-37, 10-44) (Self Test 13, 14, 21)
2 Know the properties and kind of bonding of the four types of solids. (Text Probs. 10-29, 10-30, 10-34, 10-35) (Self Test 11)
3 Describe the van der Waals forces, including dipole-dipole forces and London or dispersion forces. (Self Test 5, 12)
4 Calculate the lattice energy of a crystal by a Born-Haber type of calculation. (Text Probs. 10-38 to 10-40) (New Skills Example 4; Self Test 22)

10-6
Liquids

1 Compare the structure of liquids to those of solids and gases. (Text Probs. 10-45, 10-46, 10-59)
2 Explain why liquids have higher viscosity than gases.
3 Compare the rates of diffusion of liquids and gases.
4 Explain the cause and effects of surface tension. (Text Prob. 10-47)
5 Explain the process of evaporation. (Text Prob. 10-49)
6 Understand the effect of intermolecular forces and types of molecules on vapor pressure of a liquid. (Text Probs. 10-48, 10-50, 10-51)
7 Understand the effect of temperature on vapor pressure. (Text Prob. 10-52) (Self Test 23)
8 Use the Clausius-Clapeyron equation to calculate vapor pressure at different temperatures, to determine the normal boiling point of a liquid, and to determine the molar heat of vaporization given sufficient information. (Text Examples 10-3 to 10-5; Text Probs. 10-53 to 10-58) (New Skills Example 5; Self Test 24, 25)
9 Define boiling point and freezing point. (Self Test 6)

NEW SKILLS

10-2
X-ray diffraction

Determining the spacing between layers in a crystal using the Bragg equation
Data taken by x-ray diffraction techniques can be used in the Bragg equation to reveal the microstructure of crystals. The Bragg equation relates the measured angle of diffraction to the spacing between layers in a crystal.

$$n\lambda = 2d \sin \theta$$

where $\sin \theta$ = sine of the angle between the incoming x ray and the plane of the atoms in the crystal layer
d = distance between two parallel planes
λ = wavelength of the x ray
n = a positive integer

In actual practice the x-ray wavelength and the angle of diffraction can be measured very accurately. Values of d are calculated for several values of n for each measured angle of diffraction and the unit cell is deduced by analyzing the d values through geometric relations. Each substance has a unique set of diffraction angles called a diffraction pattern that can be used to easily identify complex compounds and minerals.

We will carry this process only as far as determining the distance between parallel planes of atoms in the crystal as shown in Example 10-1 in the text. The Bragg relation can be used to solve for any of the variables d, n, λ, or θ if values for the others are known.

10-3
The crystal lattice

A knowledge of the geometry of the unit cell reveals much about the substance. You need to be able to analyze several different aspects of the unit cell.

1 Calculation of dimensions of a unit cell when the type of cell and atomic radius of the substance are given
If the type of cell and the atomic radius of the substance are known, the dimensions of the unit cell can be determined.

● **EXAMPLE 1**   **Problem:** The atomic radius of gold is 0.144 nm and it crystallizes in the face-centered cubic structure. What is the length of a side of a unit cell for a gold crystal?

Solution: In a face-centered cubic structure, atoms along a diagonal of the face of the cell just touch each other. See Fig. 10-15a in the text. The length of the face diagonal is four times the radius of the atom, $d = 4r$, where d is the diagonal length and r is the atomic radius. Since the diagonal forms the base of an isosceles triangle with two cell edges, the pythagorean theorem of geometry gives $d^2 = 2l^2$ where d is the hypotenuse of the isosceles triangle and l is the length of the cell edge. Equating these two relations for d gives

$$4r = \sqrt{2}\, l \qquad l = \frac{4}{\sqrt{2}} r$$

For the gold crystal

$$l = \frac{4}{\sqrt{2}} (0.144 \text{ nm}) = 0.407 \text{ nm} \quad ●$$

2 Calculation of the number of atoms in a unit cell when the type of cell and density of the substance are given

Since the unit cell contains a fixed number of atoms, its weight is fixed. It also has a fixed volume, so the mass of a unit cell is actually a mass per unit volume, or density. If we know the type of cell and the density of the substance, we can find the number of atoms or molecules in the unit cell.

● **EXAMPLE 2**   **Problem:** The density of silver metal is 10.5 g cm^{-3}. It crystallizes in a cubic structure with a side length of 0.41 nm. How many atoms are there in the unit cell?

Solution: The volume of the unit cell is

$$V = l^3 = (0.41)^3 = 0.069 \text{ nm}^3$$

From the density we can determine the mass of the unit cell

$$\text{Mass of unit cell} = 10.5 \text{ g cm}^{-3}\ (0.069 \text{ nm}^3) \left(\frac{1 \text{ cm}}{10^7 \text{ nm}}\right)^3 = 7.2 \times 10^{-22} \text{ g}$$

The atomic weight of silver is 108 g mol^{-1}, so there are

$$7.2 \times 10^{-22} \text{ g} \left(\frac{1 \text{ mol}}{108 \text{ g}}\right) = 6.7 \times 10^{-24} \text{ mol}$$

in the unit cell. We can use Avogadro's number to find the number of atoms in the unit cell.

$$\left(6.7 \times 10^{-24}\ \frac{\text{mol}}{\text{unit cell}}\right)\left(6.02 \times 10^{23}\ \frac{\text{atoms}}{\text{mol}}\right) = 4.0\ \frac{\text{atoms}}{\text{unit cell}}$$

Note that the face-centered cubic structure must have four atoms per unit cell, corresponding to the number we calculated. (See Fig. 10-15a in the text.) ●

3 Calculation of unit cell dimensions when the type of cell and density of the substance are given

The reverse of the previous procedure can be used to find the dimensions of the unit cell if the type of crystal structure is known.

● **EXAMPLE 3**   **Problem:** The density of platinum is 21.4 g cm^{-3} and it crystallizes in a body-centered cubic structure. What is the length of the unit cell?

Solution: The body-centered cubic structure has two atoms per unit cell. Let us consider the placement of atoms in the unit cell to show how this is so. There is one atom at each corner, but each of these belongs to eight different unit cells (see Fig. 10-12 in the text), so $\frac{1}{8}(8) = 1$ atom contributed to a unit cell from the corner positions. The atom in the center of the unit cell belongs entirely to the cell, so each unit cell has, effectively, two atoms. These two atoms comprise the mass of the unit cell.

$$\text{Mass of unit cell} = 195 \text{ g mol}^{-1} \left(\frac{1 \text{ mol}}{6.02 \times 10^{23} \text{ atoms}} \right) \left(\frac{2 \text{ atoms}}{\text{unit cell}} \right)$$

$$= 6.48 \times 10^{-22} \text{ g (unit cell)}^{-1}$$

The volume of the cell can be found from the mass of the cell and the bulk density

$$\text{Volume of unit cell} = 6.48 \times 10^{-22} \text{ g (unit cell)}^{-1} \left(\frac{1 \text{ cm}^3}{21.4 \text{ g}} \right)$$

$$= 3.03 \times 10^{-23} \text{ cm}^3 \text{ (unit cell)}^{-1}$$

The length of a cube is the cube root of the volume

$$l = V^{1/3} = (3.03 \times 10^{-23} \text{ cm}^3)^{1/3} = 3.12 \times 10^{-8} \text{ cm}$$

or

$$3.12 \times 10^{-8} \text{ cm} \left(\frac{10^7 \text{ nm}}{1 \text{ cm}} \right) = 0.312 \text{ nm} \bullet$$

10-5
Bonding and
properties of solids

Born-Haber calculations

The Born-Haber calculation is a method of determining the energy released when a crystal lattice is formed from gaseous ions. This quantity is difficult to measure experimentally, but the enthalpy change between reactants and products in a reaction is always the same regardless of the path or sequence of steps by which the reaction proceeds. Figure 10-31 of the text shows two possible paths for forming an NaCl crystal. Since both paths start with the same reactants and end with the same products, the overall enthalpy change must be the same for the two paths. The enthalpy change for the path on the right is the sum of the enthalpy change for each step

$$\Delta H_{\text{overall}} = \Delta H_{\text{step 1}} + \Delta H_{\text{step 2}} + \Delta H_{\text{step 3}} + \Delta H_{\text{step 4}} + \Delta H_{\text{step 5}}$$

Since all of the enthalpy changes except the lattice energy ($\Delta H_{\text{step 5}}$) can be measured experimentally, the lattice energy can be calculated.

● **EXAMPLE 4**   **Problem:** Calculate the lattice energy of sodium bromide from the following experimental data. ΔH of formation of NaBr from the elements is -360 kJ mol^{-1}, ΔH_{subl} of Na is 108 kJ mol^{-1}, ΔH_{diss} of Br$_2$ is 112 kJ mol^{-1}, ΔH_{ion} of Na is 496 kJ mol^{-1}, and $\Delta H_{\text{e.a.}}$ of Br is -330 kJ mol^{-1}.

Solution: The lattice energy is the enthalpy of the reaction

$$Na^+(g) + Cl^-(g) \longrightarrow NaCl(s)$$

The energy of this reaction cannot be determined directly from the reaction given. Instead, we will design a different path for the reaction which incorporates the lattice energy as part of the overall path (similar to Fig. 10-31 of the text).

Step 1	$Na(s) \longrightarrow Na(g)$	$\Delta H_1 = \Delta H_{subl}$	$=$ 108 kJ
Step 2	$Na(g) \longrightarrow Na^+(g) + e^-$	$\Delta H_2 = \Delta H_{ion}$	$=$ 496 kJ
Step 3	$\frac{1}{2} Br_2(g) \longrightarrow Br(g)$	$\Delta H_3 = \frac{1}{2}\Delta H_{diss}$	$=$ 56 kJ
Step 4	$e^- + Br(g) \longrightarrow Br^-(g)$	$\Delta H_4 = \Delta H_{e.a.}$	$= -330$ kJ
Step 5	$Na^+(g) + Br^-(g) \longrightarrow NaBr(s)$	$\Delta H_5 = \Delta H_{lat}$	

Overall	$Na(s) + \frac{1}{2}Br_2(g) \longrightarrow NaBr(s)$	$\Delta H_{overall} = \Delta H_{form} = -360$ kJ	

The overall chemical reaction is the algebraic sum of the reactions for steps 1 through 5. To find the enthalpy change for an overall reaction, we sum the enthalpy changes for the individual steps in the same manner as the chemical reactions for the steps were combined to give the overall reaction

$$\Delta H_{overall} = \Delta H_1 + \Delta H_2 + \Delta H_3 + \Delta H_4 + \Delta H_5$$

Solving for ΔH_{lat}

$$\Delta H_5 = \Delta H_{lat} = \Delta H_{overall} - (\Delta H_1 + \Delta H_2 + \Delta H_3 + \Delta H_4)$$

Now we can substitute numerical values and solve for ΔH_{lat}.

$$\Delta H_{lat} = -360 \text{ kJ} - (108 \text{ kJ} + 496 \text{ kJ} + 56 \text{ kJ} - 330 \text{ kJ}) = -690 \text{ kJ mol}^{-1} \bullet$$

10-6
Liquids

One of the most important relations in physical chemistry is the Clausius-Clapeyron equation. It relates equilibrium vapor pressure to temperature and the enthalpy of vaporization. You will find its most useful form to be

$$\log \frac{P_1}{P_2} = \frac{-\Delta H_{vap}}{2.303R} \left(\frac{1}{T_1} - \frac{1}{T_2} \right)$$

The Clausius-Clapeyron equation makes three kinds of calculations possible.

1 Calculation of ΔH_{vap} when the vapor pressure is given at two different temperatures
Example 10-3 in the text illustrates this calculation. ΔH_{vap} changes somewhat with temperature and 42.2 kJ mol^{-1} is an average value for temperatures between 20 and 60°C.

2 Use the Clausius-Clapeyron equation to find the vapor pressure at one temperature when ΔH_{vap} and the vapor pressure at a second temperature are known
This calculation is illustrated in text Example 10-4.

*3 Use of the Clausius-Clapeyron equation to find the temperature at which a liquid
has a certain vapor pressure if ΔH_{vap} and the vapor pressure at some other
temperature are known.*

● **EXAMPLE 5**   **Problem:** Calculate the temperature at which the vapor pressure of water is 1000
mmHg given that ΔH_{vap} is 40,700 J mol^{-1} at 100°C.

Solution: We will use the normal boiling point for our reference vapor pressure

$$T_1 = 100°C + 273 = 373 \text{ K}$$

$$T_2 = ?$$

$$P_1 = 760 \text{ mmHg}$$

$$P_2 = 1000 \text{ mmHg}$$

$$R = 8.31 \text{ J mol}^{-1} \text{ K}^{-1}$$

$$\Delta H_{vap} = 40,700 \text{ J mol}^{-1}$$

Substituting these values into the Clausius-Clapeyron equation gives

$$\log \frac{760 \text{ mmHg}}{1000 \text{ mmHg}} = \frac{-40,700 \text{ J mol}^{-1}}{2.303(8.31 \text{ J mol}^{-1} \text{ K}^{-1})}\left(\frac{1}{373 \text{ K}} - \frac{1}{T_2}\right)$$

$$\log 0.760 = -2.13 \times 10^3 \left(2.681 \times 10^{-3} - \frac{1}{T_2}\right)$$

$$-0.1192 = -2.13 \times 10^3 \left(2.681 \times 10^{-3} - \frac{1}{T_2}\right)$$

$$2.681 \times 10^{-3} - \frac{1}{T_2} = \frac{-0.1192}{-2.13 \times 10^3} = 5.60 \times 10^{-5}$$

$$\frac{1}{T_2} = 2.681 \times 10^{-3} - 5.60 \times 10^{-5} = 2.625 \times 10^{-3}$$

$$T_2 = 381 \text{ K} \quad \text{or} \quad 381 \text{ K} - 273 = 108°C$$

Notice how the logarithmic relation between vapor pressure and temperature gives a
very large increase in vapor pressure for a small temperature increase. ●
     The normal boiling point of a liquid can be calculated in the same manner. It is
simply the temperature at which the vapor pressure is 760 mmHg. Text Example
10-5 shows this calculation.

SELF TEST

True or false ____ 1 Cubic close-packed and hexagonal close-packed structures differ only in layer-
                          ing sequence.
                 ____ 2 Face-centered cubic structures have four particles per unit cell.
                 ____ 3 All close-packed structures have both tetrahedral and octahedral holes.

____ 4 Atoms often occupy tetrahedral or octahedral holes and expand the original close-packed structure.

____ 5 Van der Waals forces are electrostatic and form a strong ionic bond.

____ 6 The melting point of a pure substance is a little higher than the freezing point.

Completion
7 Rubber and glass are examples of _____.

8 The Bragg relation allows calculation of _____ from the x-ray wavelength and diffraction angle.

9 The small portion of a crystal structure that can be used to generate the entire structure is called a _____.

10 _____ is a measure of ratio of volume of spheres to the volume of a unit cell.

11 There are four types of solids. They are _____, _____, _____ and _____.

12 The two types of van der Waals forces are _____ and _____.

13 Ionic solids are _____ (good, poor) conductors of electricity.

14 Molecular solids have _____ (high, low) melting points.

Multiple choice
15 How many particles are in the unit cell of a body-centered cubic structure?
(a) 1   (b) 2   (c) 3   (d) 4

16 How many other atoms surround each atom in a hexagonal close-packed structure?
(a) 4   (b) 6   (c) 8   (d) 12

17 X-rays of wavelength 1.54 nm are diffracted from a crystal at an angle of $25°\ 30'$. If this is a first-order diffraction, what is the spacing of the planes of atoms responsible for the diffraction?
(a) 3.58 nm   (b) 1.79 nm   (c) 0.895 nm   (d) 0.559 nm

18 An ionic compound crystallizes with the positive ions (M) in a close-packed cubic pattern and the negative ions (X) occupying all the tetrahedral holes of the positive ion lattice. What is the formula for the compound?
(a) M_2X (b) MX   (c) MX_2 (d) MX_4

19 The density of tungsten (W) is 19.3 g cm^{-3}. It crystallizes in a body-centered cubic structure. What is the volume of a unit cell for tungsten?
(a) 0.0158 nm   (b) 0.0316 nm^3 (c) 0.331 nm^3 (d) 11.8 nm^3

20 Referring to the unit cell for tungsten from Prob. 19, what is the radius of the tungsten atom in nanometers?
(a) 0.112   (b) 0.137   (c) 0.274   (d) 0.316

21 Which of the following types of solids ordinarily have low melting points?
(a) ionic   (b) molecular   (c) covalent   (d) metallic

22 Given that the enthalpy of formation of LiF is -612 kJ mol^{-1}, the enthalpy of sublimation of Li is 155 kJ mol^{-1}, the enthalpy of dissociation of F_2 is 79 kJ mol^{-1}, the enthalpy of ionization of Li is 520 kJ mol^{-1}, and the electron affinity of F is -333 kJ mol^{-1}, what is the lattice energy of LiF in kilojoules per mole?
(a) -994   (b) -1034   (c) -1660   (d) -1700

23 Data for the equilibrium vapor pressure of any liquid as a function of temperature can be represented on a straight line by plotting
(a) P against T (b) $\log P$ against T
(c) P against $1/T$ (d) $\log P$ against $1/T$

24 The molar heat of vaporization of propane is 11.2 kJ mol^{-1} and its normal boiling

point is $-42.1°C$. What is the pressure in a closed container of propane at room temperature $(25°C)$?

(a) 0.27 atm   (b) 1.00 atm   (c) 3.71 atm   (d) 92.0 atm

25 The molar heat of vaporization of butane is 21.0 kJ mol^{-1}. At room temperature $(25°C)$ it has a vapor pressure of 1820 mmHg. What is the normal boiling point of butane?

(a) $-3°$ (b) $0°C$ (c) $59.1°C$ (d) $270°C$

11 REAL MATTER AND CHANGES OF STATE

CHAPTER OVERVIEW

**11-1
Real gas**
In Chap. 4 we discussed the behavior of ideal gases and made several calculations using the ideal-gas law. Although real gases do not follow the ideal-gas law exactly, it gives quite accurate results unless the pressure becomes very large or the temperature is very low. Figures 11-1 and 11-2 in the text show how the actual pressure-volume behavior of N_2 and CO_2 deviates from PV behavior predicted by the ideal-gas law. Over what range of temperature and pressure would you say the ideal-gas law holds for these gases?

The van der Waals equation attempts to account for the two main reasons for non-ideal behavior in gases: (1) molecules occupy space and (2) they attract or repel each other. It is easy to calculate pressure with the van der Waals equation but difficult to solve for volume. The values of a and b are different for different gases, so each real gas has its own van der Waals constants. The van der Waals equation predicts real gas behavior better than the ideal-gas law but is still not exact. More complicated equations and calculations are used to get more accurate results. Industrial firms often buy and sell gases at very high pressures and low temperatures where there is considerable deviation from ideal-gas or van der Waals behavior; thus, more complex equations are required to determine the amounts of gas bought or sold.

Recall from Chap. 4 that the ideal-gas law predicts no temperature change as an ideal gas expands into a vacuum. Most real gases cool during expansion. Carbon dioxide from a CO_2 fire extinguisher cools enough to form dry ice as it expands because forces of attraction between CO_2 molecules must be overcome as the gas expands. The energy to overcome these forces comes from the CO_2 molecules and they cool as they give up their kinetic energy.

Hydrogen and helium have repelling forces at room temperature and pressure so they become warmer during expansion. This makes hydrogen a hazardous gas to handle under pressure because enough heat can be generated as H_2 expands to cause combustion or explosion.

11-2
Real liquids

There is no model of an ideal liquid comparable to an ideal gas, so we cannot analyze the behavior of liquids in the same way we analyzed gases. However, nonideal behavior of liquids is observed in superheating during boiling and supercooling during freezing. The text discusses some problems in making experimental measurements of boiling and melting points that arise from these effects.

Liquid crystals are not true crystals. They are actually highly supercooled liquids which have some ordering, but much less than described in Chap. 10 for crystalline solids. Nematic liquid crystals are used in the readout displays (LCD) on many pocket calculators and other electronic devices. They use very little current so the batteries in LCD devices last much longer than those in other types of displays.

11-3
Real solids

Nonideal behavior in solids is caused by imperfections (called defects) in the ideal crystal. The two main types of defects are line defects and point defects. Line defects are edge or screw dislocations of the normal crystal pattern and tend to weaken the crystal structure. Point defects give rise to changes in color and conductivity in crystals and are used to make semiconductors and transistors. Figure 11-8 in the text shows that point defects or impurities are intentionally introduced into certain crystals to make semiconductors. Impurity defects can change the physical properties of alloys and metals dramatically. For instance, carbon in the interstices of iron crystals makes steel hard, but sulfur or hydrogen in the same positions greatly weakens the iron structure.

11-4
Changes of state

Figure 11-12 in the text shows what happens when heat is added to a substance. You are familiar with an increase in temperature of a substance as it is heated. This is an increase in the kinetic energy or speed of movement of the molecules. An increase in the kinetic energy of molecules is just another way of saying the temperature increases.

There are instances, however, when adding heat to a substance does not change its temperature or kinetic energy. This occurs at the melting point and the boiling point. It is important to note that changes of state (solid to liquid or liquid to vapor) occur at constant temperature. Even though heat is added to a substance during a change of state, the temperature does not change. When heat is removed during a change of state (condensation or freezing), the temperature does not change. Heat added during a change of state breaks the forces between molecules and increases their potential energy rather than their kinetic energy. The kinetic energy and temperature remain constant.

The text presents solid-liquid, solid-vapor, and liquid-vapor equilibrium data for water in Figs. 11-14 and 11-16. These data are combined in Fig. 11-19 to give a phase diagram which can be used to determine what phases are present at a given pressure and temperature.

Pay close attention to the text discussion of Le Châtelier's principle. We will encounter this effect several times in chemistry as we study shifts in equilibrium.

11-5
Phase diagrams

You should learn several important aspects about phase diagrams. A line represents the pressure-temperature conditions where two phases are in equilibrium. The intersection of lines represents the only point (triple point) at which all three phases coexist in equilibrium. The area between the lines represents single-phase conditions.

Phase diagrams can become quite complicated when several polymorphs exist in the solid state or when more than a single compound is present.

LEARNING OBJECTIVES

As a result of studying Chap. 11 you should be able to do the following:
Write the definition and give an example illustrating the use of each key term.

11-1
Real gases

1 Explain how the volume of molecules and intermolecular forces cause departure from ideal-gas behavior for real gases. (Text Probs. 11-1, 11-11, 11-12) (Self Test 17)

2 Explain why departure from ideal behavior is most pronounced at high pressures and low temperatures. (Self Test 1)

3 Calculate the pressure or temperature of a gas using the van der Waals equation. (Text Example 11-1; Text Probs. 11-7 to 11-9) (New Skills Example 1; Self Test 25)

4 Explain the physical significance of the constants a and b in the van der Waals equation. (Text Probs. 11-4 to 11-6)

5 Compare the free expansion of an ideal gas and a real gas and explain the difference in temperature changes for the two gases. (Text Prob. 11-2) (Self Test 2, 8)

11-2
Real liquids

1 Explain the cause, results, and cure of superheating in liquids. (Text Probs. 11-14 to 11-16) (Self Test 9)

2 Explain why the structure of glass is more like a liquid than a solid. (Text Prob. 11-17) (Self Test 10)

3 Explain how certain molecules form liquid crystals and list some of the special properties of these substances. (Text Prob. 11-18)

11-3
Real solids

1 Distinguished between edge dislocations and screw dislocations and explain how they affect the properties of crystals. (Text Probs. 11-19 to 11-21) (Self Test 3, 11, 18)

2 Understand how atoms or ions occupying lattice vacancies or lattice interstitial positions can affect the electrical properties of the crystal. (Text Prob. 11-22) (Self Test 4, 5, 12, 19)

3 Understand how metalloids are doped to make n-type and p-type semiconductors and explain the difference between the two types. (Text Probs. 11-22, 11-23, 11-26) (Self Test 5, 13)

4 Understand how nonstoichiometric compounds result from ions occupying interstices.

11-4
Changes of state

1 Explain what changes of state take place as a substance is heated and why the temperature is constant during a change of state. (Text Prob. 11-28) (Self Test 20)

2 Understand why potential energy changes while kinetic energy remains constant during changes of state. (Text Prob. 11-32) (Self Test 6, 21)

3 Use the Clausius-Clapeyron equation to calculate molar heat of vaporization, molar heat of sublimation, and equilibrium vapor pressure of a phase change. (Text Probs. 11-36, 11-37)

4 Compare the behavior of substances above and below their critical temperature. (Text Probs. 11-38, 11-39)

5 Understand the application of the Le Châtelier principle to shifts in equilibrium and use the principle to predict what will happen when the equilibrium of a system is shifted. (Text Probs. 11-41 to 11-45) (Self Test 14)

11-5
Phase diagrams

1 Use a phase diagram to predict what phases will exist at equilibrium in a system at a given temperature and pressure. (Text Probs. 11-35, 11-49) (Self Test 23)

2 Understand how areas, lines, and points on a phase diagram relate to the number of phases present. (Self Test 7, 22)

3 Use a phase diagram to predict what phases will be encountered as a substance is heated or cooled at constant pressure. (Text Probs. 11-48, 11-49) (Self Test 24)

4 Use a phase diagram to predict the changes of phase encountered as the pressure on a substance is changed at constant temperature. (Text Probs. 11-47, 11-52) (Self Test 15)

5 Draw a simple phase diagram from information obtained from cooling curves. (Text Probs. 11-49, 11-51, 11-53)

NEW SKILLS

11-1
Real gases

1 The van der Waals equation

There are many equations of state for gases besides the ideal-gas law. You will be expected to solve for pressure and temperature of a gas using one of these equations, the van der Waals equation.

$$\left(P + \frac{n^2 a}{V^2}\right)(V - nb) = nRT$$

In this equation P, V, n, R, and T have the same meanings and units as in the ideal-gas law. The constants a and b have different values for each gas. Some of these values are included in Table 11-1 in the text. Be sure your units are consistent as you use the equation.

2 Calculation of pressure or temperature of a gas using the van der Waals equation

The van der Waals equation can be solved for pressure to give

$$P = \frac{nRT}{V - nb} - \frac{n^2 a}{V^2}$$

or for temperature to give

$$T = \frac{1}{nR}\left(P + \frac{n^2 a}{V^2}\right)(V - nb)$$

● **EXAMPLE 1**

Problem: Oxygen is often sold in high-pressure cylinders containing 28.5 lb of O_2 at 2200 lb in^{-2}. The cylinder has a volume of 60 liters. Calculate the temperature of the oxygen using (a) the ideal-gas law and (b) the van der Waals equation.

Solution:

$$P = 2200 \text{ lb in}^{-2} \left(\frac{1 \text{ atm}}{14.7 \text{ lb in}^{-2}}\right) = 150 \text{ atm}$$

$$V = 60 \text{ liters}$$

$$n = 28.5 \text{ lb } (454 \text{ g lb}^{-1})\left(\frac{1 \text{ mol } O_2}{32 \text{ g}}\right) = 404 \text{ mol } O_2$$

(a) Solving the ideal-gas law for T and substituting the given values

$$T = \frac{PV}{nR} = \frac{150 \text{ atm (60 liters)}}{404 \text{ mol (0.082 liter atm mol}^{-1} \text{ K}^{-1})} = 272 \text{ K} \quad \text{or} \quad -1°C$$

(b) Now solve the van der Waals equation for T and substitute the given values. The constants a and b are found in Table 11-1 in the text.

$$a = 1.36 \text{ liter}^2 \text{ atm mol}^{-2} \qquad b = 0.0318 \text{ liter mol}^{-1}$$

$$T = \frac{1}{nR} \left(P + \frac{n^2 a}{V^2} \right) (V - nb)$$

$$T = \frac{1}{404 \text{ liters (0.082 liter atm mol}^{-1} \text{ K}^{-1})}$$

$$\cdot \ 150 \text{ atm} + \frac{(404 \text{ mol})^2 \ (1.36 \text{ liter}^2 \text{ atm mol}^{-2})}{(60 \text{ liters})^2}$$

$$\cdot \ [60 \text{ liters} - (404 \text{ mol}) (0.0318 \text{ liter mol}^{-1})]$$

$$T = 301 \text{ K} \quad \text{or} \quad 28°C \ \bullet$$

Example 11-1 in the text illustrates the calculation of pressure using the van der Waals equation.

SELF TEST

True or false   ___ 1 Departure from ideal-gas behavior is most pronounced at high pressures and low temperatures.

___ 2 Most gases cool during a free adiabatic expansion because the molecules expend energy to overcome intermolecular forces of attraction.

___ 3 Edge dislocations and screw dislocations increase the chemical reactivity and reduce the mechanical strength of crystals.

___ 4 Lattice vacancies, interstitial atoms, and impurity defects are all examples of point defects.

___ 5 Semiconductors are crystals which have impurity defects introduced on purpose.

___ 6 Heat of fusion is a measure of the increase in potential energy of the molecules during melting.

___ 7 Only the solid phase exists at temperatures below the triple point.

Completion   8 A gas becomes hotter during expansion if it is above its _____ temperature.

9 Superheating and bumping may be controlled or eliminated by adding _____ to the liquid.

10 Glass is an example of a highly _____ liquid.

11 Two types of line defects in crystals are _____ and _____.

12 Atoms occupying small holes in a crystal structure which are not lattice sites are _____ atoms.

13 The electrical conductivity of semiconductors _____ (increases, decreases) as temperature is increased.

14 Increasing the pressure on a gas-liquid equilibrium mixture causes the system to shift towards the _____ phase.

15 The melting point of water _____ (increases, decreases) as the pressure increases, contrary to most substances.

16 Substances having more than one possible solid phase are called _____.

Multiple choice   **17** Real gases do not follow the ideal gas law exactly because
- **(a)** All collisions are perfectly elastic.
- **(b)** They are below their critical temperature.
- **(c)** Real gases are mixtures.
- **(d)** Intermolecular forces are present.

18 Edge dislocations and screw dislocations in crystals are examples of
- **(a)** Point defects
- **(b)** Line defects
- **(c)** Schottky and Frenkel defects
- **(d)** Impurity defects

19 Impurity defects consist of
- **(a)** Interstitial atoms
- **(b)** Foreign atoms present at lattice sites
- **(c)** Vacant lattice sites
- **(d)** A pair of lattice vacancies of opposite charge

20 The change of a substance from the gaseous state to the liquid state is known as
- **(a)** fusion   **(b)** evaporation   **(c)** condensation   **(d)** supercooling

21 The heat of vaporization is a measure of
- **(a)** The increase in kinetic energy when a substance changes from the liquid to the gaseous state
- **(b)** The increase in potential energy when a substance changes from the liquid to the gaseous state
- **(c)** The average potential energy during the vaporization process
- **(d)** The heat of fusion plus the heat of sublimation.

22 The triple point is
- **(a)** The temperature at which the vapor pressure of the solid and liquid states are equal
- **(b)** The temperature and pressure at which solid, liquid, and gas are at equilibrium
- **(c)** The temperature at which the gas-liquid equilibrium curve starts
- **(d)** All of the above

23 The sketch shows a simple phase diagram for a pure substance. Which of the following is correct?

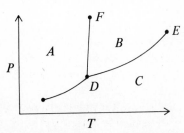

    (a) A represents solid, B represents liquid, C represents gas, D is the triple point, and E is the critical point.

    (b) A represents solid, B represents gas, C represents liquid, D is the triple point, and E is the critical point.

    (c) A represents liquid, B represents gas, C represents solid, D is the triple point, and F is the critical point.

    (d) A represents gas, B represents liquid, C represents solid, D is the triple point, and F is the critical point.

24 In the phase diagram sketched in Prob. 43, if the temperature and pressure are changed from region A to region B, what would be observed?

    (a) freezing   (b) melting   (c) condensation   (d) evaporation

25 What is the pressure of 2.00 mol of ammonia gas in a 1.00-liter container at 25°C as predicted by the van der Waals equation? (For ammonia, $a = 4.17$ liters^2 atm mol^{-2} and $b = 0.0371$ liter mol^{-1}.)

    (a) 21.1 atm   (b) 36.1 atm   (c) 44.5 atm   (d) 48.9 atm

12 SOLUTIONS

CHAPTER OVERVIEW

Chapter 12 is a fairly long chapter and it is full of new and important concepts fundamental to understanding the behavior of solutions. It will require intensive study.

12-1
Mixtures

There are many different kinds of mixtures and the classification into heterogeneous or homogeneous is not sharp. Nevertheless, if we cannot distinguish different phases in a mixture on a molecular scale we say we have a homogeneous mixture or a solution.

Colloids are borderline cases in between solutions and heterogeneous mixtures. Their particles are just the right size to scatter visible light passed through them. This scattering is called the Tyndall effect and is characteristic of colloids. See Fig. 12-2 in the text.

12-2
Types of solutions

Of the several types of solutions mentioned in the text, most of your attention and study will be centered on solids, gases, and liquids dissolved in water. In fact, the remainder of the chapter deals almost exclusively with aqueous (water) solutions of a solute.

12-3
Concentration and solubility

You will quickly discover there are many different ways of expressing the concentration of the solute. The amount of solute dissolved in the solvent may be expressed qualitatively as dilute, concentrated, weak, or strong; or semiquantitatively as unsaturated, saturated, or supersaturated. These terms only give a relative idea of concentration. Of more importance to you will be an understanding of the quantitative expressions of concentration: mole fraction, mole percent, molarity, molality, and percent by weight. Most of the calculations in this chapter deal with these quantitative terms. Molarity is the most common concentration unit used to describe solutions but, as you will see, each of the other quantitative expressions is also used in calculations. We will work several examples showing the use of each. Study these examples and Examples 12-1 through 12-6 in the text and you should become proficient at handling concentration in any units.

The solvation process is explained and understood best in terms of interactions between solute and solvent molecules. If the solute-solvent attraction is strong enough to overcome solvent-solvent and solute-solute attractions, the substance will be soluble. In certain substances hydrogen bonding takes place and greatly increases the solute-solvent attraction to make these substances more soluble. The adage "like dissolves like" is worth remembering to help predict solubilities. In general, the solubility of solids in water increases as temperature increases, while the solubility of gases decreases, but there are several exceptions. Figure 12-8 in the text shows some solubilities.

Le Châtelier's principle helps predict the effect of temperature on solubility if the sign of ΔH_{soln} is known. Many solids have positive ΔH_{soln} (that is, are endothermic), so their solubility tends to increase as the temperature increases. Figure 12-8 in the text shows how the solubility of some solutes increases with increasing temperature while that of others decreases. The sign of ΔH_{soln} depends on the relative values of ΔH_{lat} and ΔH_{hyd}. A high lattice energy tends to make the solute less soluble while a high hydration energy makes it more soluble.

Gases have negative ΔH_{soln} so the rule that the solubility of gases decreases as temperature increases generally holds.

Pressure has little effect on the solubility of solids but a pronounced effect on the solubility of gases. Use Henry's law to determine the solubility of a gas at a given pressure.

12-4 Colligative properties

Pure liquids have characteristic values of vapor pressure, osmotic pressure, boiling point, and freezing point. When a solute is added, these properties are affected.

Vapor-pressure lowering by a solute is given by Raoult's law. If a solution follows Raoult's law it is said to be an ideal solution; thus, departure from Raoult's law is a measure of nonideal behavior in solutions. Figure 12-13 in the text illustrates this behavior. The direction of deviation from Raoult's law depends on the relative attractions of solute-solvent molecules. The distillation diagram shown in Fig. 12-15 in the text follows from Raoult's law. Study it to see how liquid mixtures can be separated by fractional distillation.

Boiling-point elevation and freezing-point depression are related colligative properties. Remember that if compounds dissociate you get two or more moles of ions from one mole of solute. One mole of ions dissolved in one kilogram of solvent lowers the freezing point by K_f degrees or raises the boiling point by K_b degrees. Values for K_f and K_b are given in Table 12-4 in the text.

Note the similarity between the van't Hoff equation for osmotic pressure and the ideal-gas law. The similarity is coincidental, but it makes the van't Hoff equation easy to remember. Study Figs. 12-19 to 12-21. They explain osmosis, osmotic pressure, and reverse osmosis.

An important use of colligative properties is to determine the molecular weight of nonelectrolyte solutes.

12-5 Electrolytes

Electrolytes are solutes that dissociate to give ions when they dissolve. The ions are electrical conductors. Compounds whose solutions do not conduct electricity are called nonelectrolytes. Strong electrolytes are completely dissociated into ions while weak electrolytes are only partially dissociated. Nearly all salts are strong electrolytes. Le Châtelier's principle predicts that dissociation of weak electrolytes will be greater at low concentrations than at high concentrations. The hydrated proton, H_3O^+, is called a hydronium or oxonium ion. It is a very important ion in acid-base chemistry.

12-6 Ions in aqueous solution

Hydronium ions and hydroxide ions are important to aqueous solutions and we will use them extensively in the next few chapters. The Arrhenius definition of acids and bases applies to aqueous solutions and is based on the H^+ and OH^- ions. We will learn other definitions of acids and bases in Chap. 13, so be sure you have a firm understanding of the Arrhenius definition now.

All ions in aqueous solution are hydrated and this often affects their properties. Smaller ions with high charge densities are hydrated to the greatest extent, so the Na^+ hydrated ion is actually larger than the K^+ hydrated ion, exactly the opposite of the size ratio of the corresponding unhydrated ions.

Dilute solutions of electrolytes behave ideally and obey the Debye-Hückel theory, but significant nonideal behavior may be observed for concentrations greater than $0.01\ M$.

KEY EQUATIONS

12-3 Concentration and solubility

1 Mole fraction
$$X_A = \frac{n_A}{n_A + n_B + n_C + \cdots} = \frac{\text{mol A}}{\text{total mol}}$$

2 Mole percent
$$\text{mol \% A} = X_A(100) = \frac{\text{mol A}}{\text{total mol}} \times 100$$

3 Molarity
$$M_A = \frac{\text{mol solute}}{\text{liters solution}} = \frac{\text{mol}}{\text{liter}} = \frac{n_A}{V}$$

Note that the number of moles of solute is fixed by the molarity and volume of solution.

$$n_A = M_A V$$

4 Molality
$$M_A = \frac{\text{mol solute}}{\text{kg solvent}} = \frac{\text{mol}}{\text{kg}} = \frac{n_A}{\text{kg solvent}}$$

5 Percent by mass
$$\text{Mass \% A} = \frac{\text{mass A}}{\text{total mass}} \times 100$$

6 Solubility of a gas (Henry's law)
$$X = KP$$

where X = mole fraction of the dissolved gas
P = partial pressure of the gas above the liquid
K = Henry's law constant (see Table 12-2 in the text)

12-4 Colligative properties

1 Vapor pressure of a solution
$$P_1 = X_1 P_1^\circ$$
(Raoult's law)

where P_1 = vapor pressure of the solution
P_1° = vapor pressure of pure solvent
X_1 = mole fraction of the solvent

2 Boiling-point elevation $\Delta T_b = K_b m$

where ΔT_b = boiling-point elevation
K_b = boiling-point elevation constant (see Table 12-4 in the text)
m = molality of the solute

3 Freezing-point depression $\Delta T_f = -K_f m$

where ΔT_f = freezing-point depression
K_f = freezing-point depression constant (see Table 12-4 in the text)
m = molality of the solute

4 Osmotic pressure $\pi V = n_2 RT$

where π = osmotic pressure
n_2 = moles of solute
V = volume of solution containing n_2 mol of solute
R = ideal-gas constant
T = temperature in kelvins

LEARNING OBJECTIVES

As a result of studying Chap. 12 you should be able to do the following:
Write the definition and give an example illustrating the use of each key term

12-1
Mixtures
1 Tell whether a mixture is heterogeneous or homogeneous.
2 List the different kinds of colloids.
3 List some properties peculiar to colloids. (Text Probs. 12-1, 12-3, 12-4)
4 Explain the Tyndall effect.

12-2
Types of solutions
1 Describe how different phases combine to make solutions. (Text Prob. 12-9)
2 Understand how the properties of a solution relate to its pure components. (Text Prob. 12-8)

12-3
Concentration and solubility
1 Write definitions for the terms used to describe concentration. (Text Prob. 12-10) (Self Test 2, 8, 10)
2 Use the quantitative terms for concentration in calculations, that is, calculate the following:
   a Mole fraction and mole percent, given the weights of solute and solvent. (Text Examples 12-1, 12-2; Text Probs. 12-18 to 12-20) (New Skills Examples 1, 2; Self Test 1, 17, 18)
   b Molarity, given the weight of solute and volume of solution. (Text Example 12-3; Text Probs. 12-16, 12-54) (New Skills Example 3)
   c Molarity, given the weights of the solute and solvent and density of the solution. (Text Example 12-4; Text Probs. 12-19, 12-20, 12-22, 12-65) (New Skills Example 5; Self Test 20)
   d Molality, given the weights of solute and solvent. (Text Example 12-5; Text Prob. 12-17) (New Skills Example 6; Self Test 19)
   e Molality, given the weight of solute and volume and density of solution. (Text Probs. 12-19, 12-20) (New Skills Example 7; Self Test 21)

    f Percent by weight, given the weight of solute and solvent. (Text Example 12-6; Text Probs. 12-19, 12-20) (New Skills Example 8; Self Test 13)

3 Calculate the number of moles in a given volume of solution if the molarity is known. (Text Prob. 12-41) (New Skills Example 4)

4 Determine the concentration of ions given the concentration of solute. (Text Probs. 12-25, 12-26) (New Skills Examples 11, 12)

5 Calculate the molarity of a solution made by diluting a solution of known molarity with a given quantity of water. (Text Probs. 12-27, 12-28) (New Skills Examples 9, 10; Self Test 7, 22)

6 Calculate the solubility (mole fraction) of a gas using Henry's law. (Text Probs. 12-30, 12-38 to 12-40) (New Skills Example 13; Self Test 23)

7 Explain why solute-solvent molecular attractions determine the solubility and dissociation of substances. (Text Probs. 12-37, 12-59)

8 Understand the concept "like dissolves like." (Text Probs. 12-11, 12-32, 12-62) (Self Test 9)

9 Explain why hydrogen bonding affects the solubility of some compounds and predict what compounds are likely to form hydrogen bonds.

10 Combine lattice energy and hydration energy to determine heat of solution. (Text Probs. 12-15, 12-34) (Self Test 3)

11 Predict the effect of temperature on the solubility of a solute if the sign of ΔH_{soln} is known. (Text Probs. 12-29, 12-36) (Self Test 4)

12 Understand the relationship between size of a ion and its charge density to its hydration energy and solubility. (Text Prob. 12-33)

**12-4
Colligative
properties**

1 Explain why colligative properties are affected by the number of particles in solution but not by the type of particles.

2 Calculate the vapor pressure of a solution using Raoult's law. (Text Example 12-7; Text Prob. 12-43) (New Skills Example 14; Self Test 24)

3 Understand how deviation from Raoult's law is a measure of nonideal behavior in real solutions. (Text Fig. 12-13; Text Probs. 12-12, 12-57) (Self Test 6)

4 Calculate the partial pressure and mole fraction of each component of an ideal solution. (Text Example 12-9; Text Probs. 12-49, 12-50, 12-60) (New Skills Example 15)

5 Determine the composition of a vapor phase in equilibrium with a known liquid phase from a distillation diagram (Text Fig. 12-15) and explain how solutions of volatile liquids can be separated into pure components by fractional distillation. (Self Test 11)

6 Calculate the boiling-point elevation and the freezing-point depression of solutions. (Text Example 12-10; Text Probs. 12-42, 12-47, 12-61) (New Skills Example 16; Self Test 14, 25, 26)

7 Explain the processes of osmosis and reverse osmosis. (Text Figs. 12-19 to 12-21; Text Prob. 12-58)

8 Calculate the osmotic pressure of a solution. (Text Prob. 12-43) (New Skills Example 17; Self Test 27)

9 Calculate the molecular weight of a nonelectrolyte solute by its effect on a colligative property. (Text Examples 12-8, 12-11 to 12-13; Text Probs. 12-6, 12-44 to 12-46, 12-48, 12-63) (Self Test 28, 29)

12-5
Electrolytes

1 Explain the differences between strong and weak electrolytes and nonelectrolytes. (Text Prob. 12-52; Text Table 12-5) (Self Test 15)
2 Use Le Châtelier's principle to predict the extent of dissociation of weak electrolytes as a function of concentration. (Text Prob. 12-51)
3 Write a reaction showing how hydronium ions are formed.
4 Make calculations relating the extent of dissociation of a weak electrolyte to the change of a colligative property. (Text Example 12-14; Text Probs. 12-55, 12-56) (New Skills Examples 18, 19; Self Test 30)

12-6
Ions in aqueous solution

1 Write the Arrhenius definitions of acid, base, and salt and write a chemical equation to show how a salt is formed in a neutralization reaction. (Text Prob. 12-64)
2 List some differences between the properties of hydrated and nonhydrated ions.
3 Understand the mechanism of hydration. (Text Prob. 12-14)
4 Give examples showing how nonideal behavior of solutes can be determined from colligative property measurements.
5 Understand that the Debye-Hückel theory predicts the extent of nonideal behavior of electrolytes in dilute solutions.

NEW SKILLS

There are a lot of important computational skills to be mastered in conjunction with Chap. 12. Many of these will be used extensively in the following chapters, so now is the time to learn them.

12-3
Concentration and solubility

It may seem that the quantitative expressions for concentration are just a lot of different ways of saying the same thing, and in a sense that is true. However, each expression has its own applications and so all must be understood.

1 Mole fraction: (X_A) and mole percent
Mole fraction is used in Henry's law, Raoult's law, and distillation diagrams. It is simply the moles of a component divided by the total moles in the mixture.

● **EXAMPLE 1**

Problem: Determine the mole fraction of each gas if 2 mol of SO_2, 4 mol of N_2, and 6 mol of H_2 are mixed together.

Solution:

$$X_{SO_2} = \frac{\text{mol } SO_2}{\text{total mol}} = \frac{\text{mol } SO_2}{\text{mol } SO_2 + \text{mol } N_2 + \text{mol } H_2}$$

$$= \frac{2 \text{ mol}}{2 \text{ mol} + 4 \text{ mol} + 6 \text{ mol}} = 0.17$$

Notice that mole units cancel so mole fraction is a unitless number.

$$X_{N_2} = \frac{\text{mol } N_2}{\text{total mol}} = \frac{4 \text{ mol}}{12 \text{ mol}} = 0.33$$

The total of mole fractions of all components must equal unity

$$X_{SO_2} + X_{N_2} + X_{H_2} = 1$$

so we can find X_{H_2} by

$$X_{H_2} = 1 - (X_{SO_2} + X_{N_2})$$
$$= 1 - (0.17 + 0.33) = 0.50 \ \bullet$$

● **EXAMPLE 2** **Problem:** What is the mole percent of each compound in Example 1?

Solution:

$$\text{Mol} \ \% = \text{mole fraction}(100)$$

$$\text{Mol} \ \% \ SO_2 = X_{SO_2}(100) = 0.17(100) = 17\%$$

$$\text{Mol} \ \% \ N_2 = X_{N_2}(100) = 0.33(100) = 33\%$$

The sum of the mole percents of all components must equal 100%.

$$\text{Mol} \ \% \ SO_2 + \text{mol} \ \% \ N_2 + \text{mol} \ \% \ H_2 = 100$$

$$\text{Mol} \ \% \ H_2 = 100 - (\text{mol} \ \% \ SO_2 + \text{mol} \ \% \ N_2)$$

$$= 100 - (17 + 33) = 50\% \ \bullet$$

Now work Examples 12-1 and 12-2 in the text.

2 Molarity

Molarity is the most common concentration unit used for stoichiometric calculations. We will make extensive use of molarity in calculations throughout the rest of the course. Molarity is simply the moles of solute per liter of solution

$$M = \frac{\text{mol solute}}{\text{liters of solution}} = \frac{\text{mol}}{\text{liter}}$$

● **EXAMPLE 3** **Problem:** What is the molarity of the solution when 2.5 mol of substance are dissolved in enough water to make 6 liters of solution?

Solution:

$$M = \frac{\text{mol}}{\text{liter}} = \frac{2.5 \ \text{mol}}{6.0 \ \text{liters}} = 0.42 \ M$$

The solution is 0.42 M. ●

● **EXAMPLE 4** **Problem:** How many moles of solute are needed to make 5.00 liters of 0.15 M solution?

Solution: Note that the problem does not specify the amount or type of solvent in the solution. It is slightly less than 5.00 liters because the solute occupies some volume. We do not need to know the specific amount of solvent to solve the problem. Solve the equation defining molarity for number of moles.

$$\text{Moles} = \text{molarity volume} = MV$$

$$\text{moles solute} = (0.15 \ \text{mol liter}^{-1}) \ (5.00 \ \text{liters}) = 0.75 \ \text{mol}$$

Notice that the number of moles in solution is not dependent on the formulas of the

compounds. No matter what substances were used for solute and solvent, 0.75 mol of solute would be needed. ●
  Now work Example 12-3 in the text.
  Molarity can also be calculated from the mass of the solute and solvent if the density of the solution is known.

● **EXAMPLE 5** **Problem:** Dilute hydrochloric acid used in the laboratory can be prepared by dissolving 25.0 g HCl in 100 g H_2O. The resulting solution has a density of 1.10 g cm^{-3}. What is the molarity of the HCl?

Solution: The number of moles of HCl is

$$\text{Mol HCl} = 25.0 \text{ g HCl} \, \frac{1 \text{ mol HCl}}{36.5 \text{ g HCl}} = 0.685 \text{ mol}$$

Total weight of solution = g HCl + g H_2O = 25.0 + 100 = 125 g

$$\text{Volume of solution} = \frac{g}{\text{density}} = \frac{125 \text{ g}}{1.10 \text{ g cm}^{-3}} = 114 \text{ cm}^3 \quad \text{or} \quad 0.114 \text{ liter}$$

$$M = \frac{\text{mol}}{\text{volume}} = \frac{0.685 \text{ mol}}{0.114 \text{ liter}} = 6.01 \text{ } M \text{ ●}$$

Now work Example 12-4 in the text.

3 Molality
Molality (*m*) is used as a measure of concentration in boiling-point elevation and freezing-point depression equations and is defined as the moles of solute per kilogram of solvent

$$m = \frac{\text{mol solute}}{\text{kg solvent}} = \frac{\text{mol}}{\text{kg}}$$

● **EXAMPLE 6** **Problem:** What is the molality of the solution when 1.2 mol of solute are dissolved in 600 g of solvent to make a solution.

Solution: In the case of molality, it is necessary to know the mass of solvent. (Remember: The volume of solution was used to determine molarity.)

$$m = \frac{1.2 \text{ mol solute}}{0.600 \text{ kg solvent}} = 2.00 \text{ } m$$

The solution is 2.00 *m*. As with molarity, the molality is independent of the kind of molecules used as solute or solvent. ●

● **EXAMPLE 7** **Problem:** An aqueous solution of NaCl contains 20 g of NaCl in 600 ml. What is the molality of the solution if its density is 1.04 g cm^{-3}?

Solution: We need to find the mass of water in the solution.

Total mass of solution = mass of solute + mass of solvent
Total mass of solution = (volume) (density)

$$= (600 \text{ ml}) (1.04 \text{ g cm}^{-3}) = 624 \text{ g}$$

The mass of NaCl is 20 g.

$$\text{Mass of water} = \text{mass of solution} - \text{mass of NaCl}$$

$$= 624 - 20 = 604 \text{ g}$$

$$m = \frac{\text{mol NaCl}}{\text{kg H}_2\text{O}} = \frac{0.342 \text{ mol}}{0.604 \text{ kg}} = 0.566 \; m \; \bullet$$

Now work Example 12-5 in the text.

4 Percent by mass

Percent by mass or weight percent is commonly used in laboratories because it is easy to relate to the way a solution is prepared. It is not very convenient to use in making stoichiometric calculations, however.

$$\text{Mass \%} = \frac{\text{mass of solute}}{\text{mass of solution}} \times 100$$

• **EXAMPLE 8**   **Problem:** If 30 g of solution is evaporated to dryness and leaves 6.5 g of salt, what was the percent by mass of salt in the solution?

Solution:

$$\text{Mass \% salt} = \frac{\text{g salt}}{\text{g solution}} \times 100$$

$$= \frac{6.5 \text{ g}}{30 \text{ g}} \times 100 = 22\% \; \bullet$$

Work Example 12-6 in the text.

5 Change of molarity on dilution of a solution

Solutions used in chemical laboratories are normally prepared from a fairly concentrated stock solution by adding solvent to obtain the desired concentration. It is easy to calculate the molarity of a dilute solution prepared from a concentrated solution.

• **EXAMPLE 9**   **Problem:** What is the molarity of a solution prepared by adding 1.00 liter of solvent to 100 ml of an 8.0 M concentrated solution?

Solution: We can develop a general formula for dilution problems as follows: The number of moles of solute does not change when the solvent is added.

$$(n_A)_{\text{conc}} = (n_A)_{\text{dil}}$$

If we solve the equation defining molarity for the moles of solute we have

$$n_A = MV$$

Substituting this into the equation for n_A gives

$$(MV)_{\text{conc}} = (MV)_{\text{dil}}$$

or

$$M_{\text{dil}} = M_{\text{conc}} \frac{V_{\text{conc}}}{V_{\text{dil}}}$$

Thus, the change in concentration on dilution is proportional to the ratio of the volumes of the concentrated and diluted solutions.

In the case of our solution

$$M_{dil} = 8.0\ M\ \frac{0.1\ \text{liter}}{1 + 0.1\ \text{liter}} = 0.73\ M\ \bullet$$

• **EXAMPLE 10**   **Problem:** How may milliliters of 15.0 M (concentrated) nitric acid (HNO_3) would you dilute to prepare 500 ml of 6.0 M (dilute) nitric acid?

Solution: The dilution equation of Example 9 can be solved for V_{conc}

$$V_{conc} = V_{dil}\ \frac{M_{dil}}{M_{conc}}$$

$$= 500\ \text{ml}\ \frac{6.0\ M}{15.0\ M} = 200\ \text{ml}$$

The dilute solution is prepared by carefully adding 200 ml of concentrated nitric acid to 300 ml of water. •

6 Relating molarity of ions to molarity of solute

Before we leave concentration units we should investigate the relationship between the molarity of ions and the molarity of their parent salt.

• **EXAMPLE 11**   **Problem:** What is the molarity of NO_3^- ions in a solution 2.0 M in aluminum nitrate, $Al(NO_3)_3$?

Solution: The dissociation of $Al(NO_3)_3$ gives

$$Al(NO_3)_3 \longrightarrow Al^{3+} + 3NO_3^-$$

Three moles of NO_3^- ions are produced from each mole of $Al(NO_3)_3$

$$M_{NO_3^-} = \frac{2.0\ \text{mol}\ Al(NO_3)_3}{1\ \text{liter}} \times \frac{3\ \text{mol}\ NO_3^-}{1\ \text{mol}\ Al(NO_3)_3} = \frac{6\ \text{mol}\ NO_3^-}{1\ \text{liter}} = 6\ M\ \bullet$$

• **EXAMPLE 12**   **Problem:** What is the molarity of Cl^- ions in a solution containing 0.5 mol NaCl, 1.5 mol $FeCl_3$, and 0.3 mol $CaCl_2$ in 1500 ml of solution?

Solution: We need to find the total number of moles of Cl^- ions.

$$\text{Mol}\ Cl^-\ \text{from NaCl} = 0.5\ \text{mol NaCl} \times \frac{1\ \text{mol}\ Cl^-}{1\ \text{mol NaCl}} = 0.5\ \text{mol}\ Cl^-$$

$$\text{Mol}\ Cl^-\ \text{from}\ FeCl_3 = 1.5\ \text{mol}\ FeCl_3 \times \frac{3\ \text{mol}\ Cl^-}{1\ \text{mol}\ FeCl_3} = 4.5\ \text{mol}\ Cl^-$$

$$\text{Mol}\ Cl^-\ \text{from}\ CaCl_2 = 0.3\ \text{mol}\ CaCl_2 \times \frac{2\ \text{mol}\ Cl^-}{1\ \text{mol}\ CaCl_2} = 0.6\ \text{mol}\ Cl^-$$

$$\text{Total mol}\ Cl^- = 0.5 + 4.5 + 0.6 = 5.6\ \text{mol}$$

$$M_{\text{Cl}^-} = \frac{\text{mol Cl}^-}{\text{liters solution}} = \frac{5.6 \text{ mol}}{1.5 \text{ liters}} = 3.7 \, M \bullet$$

7 Solubility of gases using Henry's law
Henry's law states that the mole fraction of a dissolved gas is proportional to the partial pressure of the gas above the solution.

$$X = KP$$

where X = mole fraction of gas in solution
          K = Henry's law constant (Table 12-2 in the text)
          P = partial pressure of the gas above the solution

• **EXAMPLE 13**   **Problem:** Compare the composition of "air" dissolved in water at $20°C$ to that of the air above the water.

Solution: Air consists essentially of 21 percent oxygen and 79 percent nitrogen so the partial pressures in air at 1 atm are

$$P_{\text{O}_2} = 0.21 \text{ atm} \qquad P_{\text{N}_2} = 0.79 \text{ atm}$$

and the mole fractions are

$$X_{\text{O}_2 \text{(air)}} = 0.21 \qquad X_{\text{N}_2 \text{(air)}} = 0.79$$

The ratio of O_2 to N_2 in air is $0.21 : 0.79 = 0.27$. The mole fractions in solution are found from Henry's law. The constants at $20°C$ from Table 12-2 in the text have been multiplied by 10^5 so

$$K_{\text{O}_2} = 2.58 \times 10^{-5} \text{ atm}^{-1} \qquad K_{\text{N}_2} = 1.32 \times 10^{-5} \text{ atm}^{-1}$$

$$X_{\text{O}_2 \text{(soln)}} = K_{\text{O}_2} P_{\text{O}_2} = 2.58 \times 10^{-5} \text{ atm}^{-1} \, (0.21 \text{ atm}) = 5.4 \times 10^{-6}$$

$$X_{\text{N}_2 \text{(soln)}} = K_{\text{N}_2} P_{\text{N}_2} = 1.32 \times 10^{-5} \text{ atm}^{-1} \, (0.79 \text{ atm}) = 1.04 \times 10^{-5}$$

The ratio of O_2 to N_2 dissolved in water is

$$\frac{5.4 \times 10^{-6}}{1.04 \times 10^{-5}} = 0.52$$

Note that the ratio of O_2 to N_2 is nearly twice as high in solution as in the air. This shows that each gas behaves independently when dissolved and, strictly speaking, we should not refer to "air" dissolved in water. •

12-4   Quantitative relationships between changes in colligative properties and concentration
Colligative of solute can be calculated by the methods discussed in this section. We will consider
properties   each colligative property separately.

1 Vapor-pressure lowering (Raoult's law)
The relationship between the lowering of vapor pressure of a solvent by a solute to the solute concentration is given by Raoult's law (for ideal solutions).

$$P_1 = X_1 P_1^\circ$$

where P_1 = vapor pressure of the solution
P_1° = vapor pressure of pure solvent
X_1 = mole fraction of solvent

• **EXAMPLE 14**   **Problem:** The vapor pressure of water at $25°C$ is 23.79 mmHg. What is the vapor pressure of a 20.0 percent by weight solution of sucrose (table sugar; MW = 342) in water if Raoult's law is followed?

Solution: If we take 100 g of solution as a basis to determine mole fraction we have

$$g \text{ sucrose} = 20 \text{ g} \qquad g \text{ } H_2O = 80 \text{ g}$$

$$\text{Mol sucrose} = \frac{20.0 \text{ g}}{342 \text{ g mol}^{-1}} = 0.0585 \text{ mol}$$

$$\text{Mol } H_2O = \frac{80.0 \text{ g}}{18 \text{ g mol}^{-1}} = 4.44 \text{ mol}$$

$$X_{H_2O} = \frac{\text{mol } H_2O}{\text{total mol}} = \frac{4.44 \text{ mol}}{4.44 \text{ mol} + 0.0585 \text{ mol}} = 0.987$$

$$P_{soln} = X_{H_2O} P_{H_2O}^\circ = 0.987 \, (23.79 \text{ mmHg}) = 23.48 \text{ mmHg}$$

It takes a lot of sugar to lower the vapor pressure of water significantly! •

Now work Example 12-7 in the text.
Raoult's law applies to both components in a solution of volatile compounds, so the vapor pressure of each component can be determined and their sum will be the total vapor pressure of the solution.

• **EXAMPLE 15**   **Problem:** The vapor pressure of gasoline (average MW = 114) produced for summer consumption is 517 mmHg measured at $100°F$. Gasohol is a mixture of alcohol and gasoline and its use has been proposed as a method of reducing our imports of petroleum products. What is the vapor pressure of a gasohol mixture made of 90 percent by weight gasoline and 10 percent methyl alcohol (CH_3OH)? The vapor pressure of pure methyl alcohol at $100°F$ is 230 mmHg.

Solution: We will apply Raoult's law to each component separately to determine their partial pressures and then find their sum to determine the total pressure. First find the mole fractions using 100 g of solution as the basis of calculation.

$$\text{Mol gasoline} = \frac{90 \text{ g}}{114 \text{ g mol}^{-1}} = 0.79 \text{ mol}$$

$$\text{Mol } CH_3OH = \frac{10 \text{ g}}{32 \text{ g mol}^{-1}} = 0.31 \text{ mol}$$

$$X_{gasoline} = \frac{0.79 \text{ mol}}{1.1 \text{ mol}} = 0.72$$

$$X_{CH_3OH} = 1 - 0.72 = 0.28$$

Now use Raoult's law to find the partial pressures.

$$P_{\text{gasoline}} = X_{\text{gasoline}} \, P^{\circ}_{\text{gasoline}} = 0.72 \, (517 \text{ mmHg}) = 372 \text{ mmHg}$$

$$P_{\text{CH}_3\text{OH}} = X_{\text{CH}_3\text{OH}} P_{\text{CH}_3\text{OH}} = 0.28 \, (230 \text{ mmHg}) = 64.4 \text{ mmHg}$$

The vapor pressure of the gasohol is

$$P_{\text{gasoline}} + P_{\text{CH}_3\text{OH}} = 372 \text{ mmHg} + 64.4 \text{ mmHg} = 436 \text{ mmHg} \quad \bullet$$

One of the criticisms of gasohol use is that it has a higher vapor pressure than gasoline and will cause vapor-lock problems. That is, the formation of gas bubbles will interfere with the flow of the fluid. How do you feel about this criticism of gasohol? Ethyl alcohol has also been used in gasohol. Its vapor pressure at 100° F is 116 mmHg.

Try Example 12-9 in the text.

2 Boiling-point elevation

The elevation of the boiling point of a solvent by a nonvolatile solute is proportional to the molality of the solute. The boiling-point elevation is the difference between the boiling points of the solution and the pure solvent.

$$\Delta T_b = T_{b(\text{soln})} - T_{b(\text{solv})}$$

The boiling-point elevation equation which holds for dilute solutions is

$$\Delta T_b = K_b m$$

where m is the molality of the solute and K_b is the molal boiling-point elevation constant. Each solvent has its own value of K_b. Values for some liquids are given in Table 12-4 in the text. Example 12-10 in the text illustrates the calculation of boiling-point elevation of a solution.

3 Freezing-point lowering

The freezing point of a solvent is lowered by the addition of a solute. The amount of lowering is again proportional to the molality of the solute

$$\Delta T_f = -K_f m$$

where ΔT_f = freezing-point lowering = $T_{f(\text{soln})} - T_{f(\text{solv})}$
       K_f = molal freezing-point lowering constant
       m = molality

Since $T_{f(\text{solv})}$ is greater than $T_{f(\text{soln})}$, ΔT_f is a negative quantity. Both K_f and m are positive, so the minus sign in front of K_f is necessary to preserve the sign conventions.

● **EXAMPLE 16**   **Problem:** Ethylene glycol, $C_2H_6O_2$, is used as a permanent antifreeze in autombile coolant systems. Calculate the number of grams of ethylene glycol per kilogram of water that will prevent freezing of the coolant down to 15.0°F.

Solution:

$$^{\circ}C = (15.0^{\circ}F - 32)\tfrac{5}{9} = -9.4^{\circ}C$$

$$\Delta T_f = T_{f(\text{soln})} - T_{f(\text{H}_2\text{O})} = -9.4 - 0 = -9.4^{\circ}C$$

The molality required is obtained from the freezing-point depression equation; $K_f = 1.855°C\ m^{-1}$ is found from Table 12-4 in the text.

$$m = \frac{-\Delta T_f}{K_f} = \frac{-(-9.4°C)}{1.855°C\ m^{-1}} = 5.07\ m$$

We can convert molality into grams of ethylene glycol per kilogram of water as follows:

$$\frac{5.07\ \text{mol}\ C_2H_6O_2}{1\ \text{kg}\ H_2O} \cdot \frac{62.0\ \text{g}\ C_2H_6O_2}{1\ \text{mol}} = 314\ \text{g}\ C_2H_6O_2\ (\text{kg}\ H_2O)^{-1}\quad \bullet$$

4 Osmotic pressure

Osmotic pressure is another colligative property that is directly proportional to the concentration of solute. Its value is calculated from the van't Hoff equation

$$\Pi V = n_2 RT$$

where Π = osmotic pressure
n_2 = moles of solute in V liters of solution
R = ideal-gas constant
T = temperature in kelvins

● **EXAMPLE 17**   **Problem**: Calculate the osmotic pressure of a solution of 30.0 g of sucrose (table sugar) in 1.00 liter of solution at 25°C. The molecular weight of sucrose is 342.

Solution: Solve the van't Hoff equation for Π and substitute the given values.

$$n_2 = \frac{30.0\ \text{g}}{342\ \text{g mol}^{-1}} = 0.0877\ \text{mol}$$

$V = 1$ liter

$R = 0.082$ liter atm mol^{-1} K^{-1}

$T = 25°C + 273 = 298$ K

$$\Pi = \frac{n_2 RT}{V} = \frac{0.0877\ \text{mol}\ (0.082\ \text{liter atm mol}^{-1}\ \text{K}^{-1})\ (298\ \text{K})}{1.00\ \text{liter}} = 2.14\ \text{atm}\quad \bullet$$

5 Calculation of molecular weight from measured colligative properties

An important use of colligative properties is to calculate the molecular weight of a solute. Any of the colligative properties discussed in Chap. 12 can be used for this. The text gives an example of each type of calculation. Text Example 12-8 shows the use of Raoult's law to calculate the molecular weight of a solute from measurements of vapor pressure. Text Examples 12-11, 12-12, and 12-13 show how to calculate molecular weight from measurements of boiling-point elevation, freezing-point depression, and osmotic pressure, respectively.

12-5
Electrolytes

Determination of the number of particles produced by the dissociation of a strong electrolyte

Colligative properties measure the total number of particles in solution without regard to what kind of particles are present. Therefore, when a known number of molecules of a strong electrolyte is introduced into a solvent, the freezing-point lowering will tell how many particles have been produced by dissociation.

● EXAMPLE 18   **Problem:** A solution containing 1.25 g of a strong electrolyte (MW = 162.5) in 100 g of water freezes at $-0.573°C$. How many particles are formed from each molecule of solute?

Solution: The molality of the solute is calculated first:

$$m_{\text{solute}} = \frac{1.25 \text{ g}}{0.100 \text{ kg H}_2\text{O}} \cdot \frac{1 \text{ mol solute}}{162.5 \text{ g solute}} = 0.0769 \ m$$

If no dissociation had occurred the freezing-point depression would have been the amount caused by a 0.0769 m solution. We can calculate the freezing-point depression for the undissociated solute

$$\Delta T_{f(\text{undissociated solute})} = -K_f m = -(1.855°C \ m^{-1})(0.0769 \ m) = -0.143°C$$

The ratio of molality of dissociated particles to molality of undissociated solute is equal to the ratio of freezing-point depressions. If we divide the two freezing-point depression equations we get

$$\frac{\Delta T_{f(\text{dissociated particles})}}{\Delta T_{f(\text{undissociated solute})}} = \frac{-K_f m_{\text{diss}}}{-K_f m_{\text{undiss}}} = \frac{\text{mol dissociated/kg solvent}}{\text{mol undissociated/kg solvent}} = \frac{\text{mol dissociated}}{\text{mol undissociated}}$$

The observed freezing-point depression for the dissociated state was $-0.573°C$. Therefore, the ratio of moles of dissociated particles to moles of undissociated solute is

$$\frac{\text{mol dissociated}}{\text{mol undissociated}} = \frac{-0.573°C}{-0.143°C} = 4.01$$

Apparently, four particles are produced from each solute molecule that dissociates. ●
   This same approach can be used to determine the percent dissociation of weak electrolytes as shown in the next example. Note that text Example 12-14 uses a very different approach to work this same problem.

● EXAMPLE 19   **Problem:** Hydrogen fluoride, HF, produces a solution of hydrofluoric acid when dissolved in water. HF is only partly dissociated in aqueous solutions. A $5.00 \times 10^{-2} \ m$ solution of HF in water has a freezing-point depression of $-0.103°C$. What is the percent dissociation of HF in the solution?

Solution: If no dissociation had taken place, the freezing-point depression would have been

$$\Delta T_{f(\text{undiss})} = -K_f m = -(1.86°C \ m^{-1})(5.00 \times 10^{-2} \ m) = -0.0930°C$$

The ratio of observed moles to undissociated moles (see previous example) is

$$\frac{\text{mol dissociated}}{\text{mol undissociated}} = \frac{\Delta T_{f(\text{diss})}}{\Delta T_{f(\text{undiss})}} = \frac{-0.103}{-0.0930} = 1.11$$

   After dissociation, there is an increase of 0.11 mol of ions for each mole of HF. For the case of HF, the numbers of moles of positive ions and negative ions produced are equal, so the number of moles of HF dissociated is equal to the *increase* in moles of ions produced. The percent dissociation is

$$\% \text{ dissociation} = \frac{\text{mol dissociated}}{\text{total mol}} = \frac{0.11}{1} \times 100 = 11\% \bullet$$

SELF TEST

True or false

___ 1 If a solution is made of 50 g of methyl alcohol (MW = 32) and 50 g of water, the mole fraction of each is 0.50.

___ 2 In dilute aqueous solutions molarity is essentially equal to molality.

___ 3 Energy is released when a substance dissolves in water if the hydration energy is greater than the lattice energy.

___ 4 The solubility of a substance will increase with increasing temperature if the heat of solution is negative.

___ 5 Water saturated with oxygen at 25°C becomes supersaturated when cooled to 10°C.

___ 6 A solution of two volatile components in which the attractions between solute and solvent molecules are stronger than solute-solute or solvent-solvent attractions will show negative deviation from Raoult's law.

___ 7 When a solution of a strong electrolyte is diluted the number of moles of solute remains constant.

Completion

8 _____ is the moles of solute divided by the total moles of solution.

9 If _____ to _____ interactions are stronger than _____ to _____ interactions or _____ to _____ interactions, the solute will be soluble.

10 Molality is defined as _____ of solute per _____ of solvent.

11 Solutions of volatile components can be separated by the process of _____.

12 Four examples of colligative properties are _____, _____, _____, and _____.

13 A 30 percent by weight solution of NaCl in water contains 30 g of NaCl and _____ g of H_2O.

14 The normal boiling point of an aqueous solution containing 1 m nonelectrolyte solute will be _____°C if the solution is ideal.

15 Nearly all _____ are completely dissociated in aqueous solutions.

16 The formula of the oxonium ion is _____.

Multiple choice

17 What is the mole fraction of $CaCl_2$ in a solution of 16.0 g of $CaCl_2$ dissolved in 500 g of water?
  (a) 0.00515   (b) 0.00757   (c) 0.0310   (d) 0.288

18 What is the mole percent of $CaCl_2$ in the solution in Prob. 17?
  (a) 0.515%   (b) 0.757%   (c) 3.10%   (d) 28.8%

19 What is the molality of the solution in Prob. 17?
  (a) 0.00515 m (b) 0.00757 m (c) 0.0320 m (d) 0.288 m

20 The density of the solution in Prob. 17 is 1.010 g cm^{-3}. What is the molarity of the $CaCl_2$?
  (a) 0.032 M (b) 0.142 M (c) 0.282 M (d) 0.288 M

21 A solution is prepared by dissolving 18.0 g of NaCl in enough water to make 100 ml of a solution whose density is 1.10 g cm^{-3}. What is the molality of the solution?
(a) $3.08 \, m$ (b) $3.34 \, m$ (c) $5.28 \, m$ (d) $15.3 \, m$

22 You are asked to prepare 1.00 liter of 0.350 M NaCl from a stock solution which is 6.00 M. How many milliliters of stock solution should you use?
(a) 35.9   (b) 58.3   (c) 171   (d) 210

23 How many grams of oxygen can be dissolved in 1 liter of water at $20°C$ if the oxygen pressure is 2.00 atm? Henry's law constant for O_2 in water at $20°C$ is $2.58 \times 10^{-5} \text{ atm}^{-1}$.
(a) $9.18 \times 10^{-2} \text{ g}$ (b) $2.87 \times 10^{-3} \text{ g}$
(c) $2.58 \times 10^{-5} \text{ g}$ (d) $5.16 \times 10^{-5} \text{ g}$

24 The vapor pressure of pure water at $35°C$ is 42.18 mmHg. What is the vapor pressure of an aqueous solution which is 3.000 m in a nonvolatile nonelectrolyte?
(a) 12.65 mmHg   (b) 21.60 mmHg
(c) 40.02 mmHg   (d) cannot be determined from the information given

25 The normal boiling point of a 0.1 m solution of NaCl in water would be
(a) $100.05°C$ (b) $100.10°C$ (c) $100.19°C$ (d) $100.37°C$

26 What is the freezing point of a solution made of 8.90 g of toluene (C_7H_8) in 200 g of benzene (C_6H_6). The freezing point of pure benzene is $5.50°C$ and its molal freezing-point depression constant is $5.12°C \text{ m}^{-1}$.
(a) $-5.08°C$ (b) $2.58°C$ (c) $3.02°C$ (d) $5.31°C$

27 The redwoods in California often grow to heights of 100 m. Assuming that osmotic pressure is responsible for carrying water from the roots to the upper leaves, what molarity of salts in the tree sap would be required to raise water 100 m at $25°C$? ($13.55 \text{ mmH}_2\text{O} = 1$ mmHg)
(a) 0.211 M (b) 0.244 M (c) 2.52 M (d) 0.397 M

28 An aqueous solution containing 2.50 g of a nonelectrolyte in 200 g of H_2O freezes at $-0.415°C$. What is the molecular weight of the nonelectrolyte?
(a) 11.2   (b) 15.4   (c) 27.9   (d) 55.8

29 What is the molecular weight of a substance if an aqueous solution containing 5.00 g liter^{-1} has an osmotic pressure of 2.30 mmHg at $25°C$?
(a) 53.1   (b) 3.390   (c) 40,400   (d) 80,600

30 Acetic acid, $HC_2H_3O_2$, is a weak electrolyte which partially dissociates in water to form H^+ and $C_2H_3O_2^-$ (acetate) ions. In a 0.150 m solution of acetic acid in water, the freezing point is $-0.308°C$. What is the percent dissociation of acetic acid in this solution?
(a) 5.5%   (b) 6.7%   (c) 11.0%   (d) 13.3%

13 AQUEOUS-SOLUTION REACTIONS

CHAPTER OVERVIEW

13-1
Acid-base reactions

Water is the most common solvent on earth yet it has unique properties that give it special significance in chemistry. In Chap. 12 we studied the effect of molecular solutes on the properties of water. In this chapter we will investigate water as a solvent for reactions of electrolytes.

Water is in equilibrium with H^+ and OH^- ions and these ions are responsible for much of the chemical activity of water. Acid-base reactions are very important in the chemistry of aqueous solutions. You should become familiar with the different ways of defining acids and bases.

The Arrhenius definition is probably most familiar, but it is also the most limited and applies only to aqueous solutions. The Brønsted-Lowry definition is more general and includes NH_3 as a base, an important advantage over the Arrhenius definition. The Lewis definition is very general; it is based on electron-pair transfer and includes many compounds omitted by the other two definitions.

13-2
Precipitation and complexation reactions

There are two keys to writing equations for precipitation reactions: (1) knowing how the reactants dissociate and then recombine into products and (2) knowing which products precipitate (come out of solution as an insoluble compound) or form weak electrolytes. Being successful in the first key step requires knowledge of formulas and charges of common ions. We studied this in Chap. 8 for simple ions. You should remember how to determine the charge on an ion from its position in the periodic table. You need to memorize the formulas and charges of common polyatomic ions such as NH_4^+, OH^-, NO_3^-, $C_2H_3O_2^-$, CO_3^{2-}, PO_4^{3-}, and any others your instructor may suggest. Some reactions involve two salts as reactants. To write an equation for these reactions you first write the ions which result from the dissociation of the salts and then pair each cation with a different anion, remembering to preserve electrical neutrality in the product compounds. If these products fall into the classification scheme for reactions in Sec. 13-3 of the text a chemical reaction will occur; otherwise, there will be no actual reaction for the equation.

Being successful at the second key requirement is straightforward. Simply learn to recognize which products are weak electrolytes and know the guidelines for soluble and insoluble compounds in Sec. 13-3. of the text. There are no short cuts to learning this material. It takes hard work and memorization and must be done before you can be proficient at writing precipitation reactions. Learn the guidelines and then practice writing reactions.

Writing a reaction for the formation of a complex ion generally involves the combination of reactants into a single product or complex. Table 13-2 in the text shows the ligands and metal ions that commonly react to form complex ions. This concept will be discussed in detail in Chap. 22.

13-3
Net equations for
aqueous-solution
reactions

This section is really the application of the concepts presented in Sec. 13-2. Follow the examples closely and work as many problems as you can. In this chapter the adage "learn by doing" is of paramount importance.

The net reaction eliminates all spectator ions and shows only the components that react.

13-4
Electron-transfer
reactions

Electron-transfer reactions are commonly called redox reactions, short for reduction-oxidation. This section is an intensive application of the oxidation number concept we studied in Sec. 8-4. You will probably need to review the rules presented there for determining oxidation numbers before you can understand this section

There are many new terms concerning oxidation and reduction. It is best to learn them immediately so the semantics do not become a stumbling block to understanding redox concepts.

Ordinarily you will not have to balance redox equations by both the oxidation-number and half-reaction methods, but your instructor will set the requirements. The half-reaction method will help you in understanding the concepts of Chap. 19. Becoming proficient at balancing redox equations is largely a matter of practice.

13-5
Solution
stoichiometry

This section combines the concepts of concentration units from Chap. 12 and the stoichiometry of Chap. 3. As you can see, the possible types of problems are growing rapidly, but if you have learned the concepts presented so far, you should be able to work these problems. The concepts of equivalent weight and normality are widely used in stoichiometric calculations, so become familiar with them. Normality and equivalents are related in exactly the same way as molarity and moles.

$$M = \frac{moles}{liter} \qquad N = \frac{equivalents}{liter}$$

KEY EQUATIONS

13-5
Solution
stoichiometry

1 Equivalents: acid-base

$$\text{Equivalent weight} = \frac{\text{formula weight}}{\text{No. of ionizable } H^+ \text{ or } OH^-}$$

$$\text{Number of equivalents} = \frac{\text{grams}}{\text{equivalent weight}}$$

$$\text{Normality} = N = \frac{\text{No. of equivalents of solute}}{\text{liters solution}}$$

$$= \text{molarity (No. of ionizable } H^+ \text{ or } OH^-)$$

For monoprotic acids or bases with one OH^-: $N = M$

For diprotic acids or bases with two OH^-: $N = 2M$

For triprotic acids or bases with three OH^-: $N = 3M$

For neutralization: $(NV)_{\text{acid}} = (NV)_{\text{base}}$

2 Equivalents: redox

$$\text{Equivalent weight} = \frac{\text{formula weight}}{\text{change in oxidation number}}$$

$$\text{Number of equivalents} = \frac{\text{grams}}{\text{equivalent weight}}$$

$$\text{Normality} = N = \frac{\text{number of equivalents of solute}}{\text{liters solution}}$$

$$= \text{molarity (change in oxidation number)}$$

For redox

$$(NV)_{\text{oxidant}} = (NV)_{\text{reductant}}$$

LEARNING OBJECTIVES

As a result of studying Chap. 13 you should be able to do the following:
Write the definition and give an example illustrating the use of each key term.

13-1
Acid-base reactions

1 Explain why water is the most important solvent for many chemical reactions and why the reactions occur much faster in aqueous solution.
2 Explain why the autodissociation of water plays an important part in acid-base chemistry. (Text Prob. 13-3)
3 Give the Arrhenius definition of acids, bases, and salts and explain its limitations. (Text Probs. 13-1, 13-11) (Self Test 1, 6)
4 Understand why neutralization is the combination of H^+ and OH^- ions no matter what the source of the H^+ and OH^- ions. (Self Test 4, 7)
5 Understand how the solvent-system definition of acids and bases extends the Arrhenius concept to solvents other than water. (Text Probs. 13-7, 13-8)
6 Give the Brønsted-Lowry definition of acids and bases. (Text Probs. 13-4, 13-11)
7 Explain and give examples of conjugate acid-base pairs. (Text Prob. 13-2)
8 Explain what is meant by the strength of an acid and how the leveling effect of water affects the strengths of certain acids. (Text Probs. 13-5, 13-9) (Self Test 3)

9 Give the Lewis definition of acids and bases and explain why this definition is more general than the others. (Text Prob. 13-6) (Self Test 2)

13-2
Precipitation and
complexation
reactions

1 List all of the ions present in a given solution of electrolytes. (Text Probs. 13-17, 13-18)
2 Understand what is meant by precipitation and what causes a compound to precipitate.
3 Write molecular, ionic, and net ionic equations given the reactants when an insoluble product or weak electrolyte is formed. (Text Example 13-1; Text Probs. 13-19, 13-20) (New Skills Examples 1 to 3)
4 Understand what complex ions are and how they are formed. (Text Probs. 13-14 to 13-16)

13-3
Net equations
for aqueous-solution
reactions

1 Know the scheme given in the text for classifying aqueous-solution reactions.
2 Know the guidelines given in the text for classifying compounds as soluble or insoluble. (Text Probs. 13-12, 13-13) (Self Test 16)
3 Know the guidelines given in the text for classifying electrolytes as strong or weak. (Self Test 14)
4 Use the guidelines to predict when a chemical reaction will occur in aqueous solutions and write an equation for the reaction. (Text Examples 13-2 to 13-5; unworked examples 1 through 10; Text Probs. 13-21 to 13-23) (New Skills Examples 4, 5; Self Test 10, 15)

13-4
Electron-transfer
reactions

1 Identify the components oxidized and reduced in redox reactions. (Text Probs. 13-26, 13-27, 13-32) (New Skills Examples 6 to 11; Self Test 8, 9, 17)
2 Use the oxidation-number method to balance redox reactions taking place in the absence of a solvent. (Text Examples 13-6, 13-7; Text Prob. 13-25) (New Skills Examples 6, 7; Self Test 18)
3 Use the oxidation-number method to balance redox reactions in acidic or basic solutions. (Text Examples 13-8, 13-9; Text Probs. 13-28, 13-30) (New Skills Examples 8, 9; Self Test 19)
4 Use the half-reaction or ion-electron method to balance redox equations in aqueous solutions. (Text Examples 13-10, 13-11; Text Probs. 13-29, 13-31) (New Skills Examples 10, 11; Self Test 19, 20)

13-5
Solution
stoichiometry

1 Solve stoichiometric problems based on neutralization of acids and bases. (Text Examples 13-12 to 13-14, 13-18; Text Probs. 13-37 to 13-43, 13-51) (New Skills Examples 15, 16; Self Test 21)
2 Perform calculations relating equivalent weight to molecular weight, equivalents to moles, and normality to molarity. (Text Examples 13-15 to 13-17; Text Probs. 13-33 to 13-35, 13-39, 13-44, 13-45) (New Skills Examples 12 to 14; Self Test 5, 11 to 13, 22 to 24)
3 Solve stoichiometric problems involving redox reactions. (Text Examples 13-19 to 13-21; Text Probs. 13-46 to 13-50, 13-53, 13-54) (New Skills Examples 17, 18; Self Test 25)
4 Solve stoichiometric problems involving precipitation reactions. (Text Example 13-22)

NEW SKILLS

13-2
Precipitation and complexation reactions

You cannot write chemical equations until you can write chemical formulas and predict the ions that result when electrolytes are dissolved. If you have not yet learned the charges and formulas of common ions, you will find this chapter bewildering; if you have learned them, it should be understandable but will still require time to practice the skills.

Precipitation reactions

When two soluble electrolytes are mixed in solution a chemical reaction occurs if any combination of the mixed ions results in an insoluble compound. The insoluble compound will precipitate (come out of solution as a solid).

● **EXAMPLE 1**   **Problem**: A solution of sodium chloride is mixed with a solution of silver nitrate and an insoluble compound is formed. Write a molecular equation for the reaction.

Solution: The first step in writing a reaction is to find what ions are present when the solutions are mixed. Sodium chloride dissociates according to the reaction

$$NaCl \longrightarrow Na^+ + Cl^-$$

and silver nitrate dissociates according to

$$AgNO_3 \longrightarrow Ag^+ + NO_3^-$$

The ions present from dissociation of the reactants are Na^+, Ag^+, Cl^-, and NO_3^-. Only ions of opposite charge combine into products because the resulting molecules must be electrically neutral; therefore the *only* possible products, besides the reactant molecules, are $NaNO_3$ and $AgCl$. One of these must be insoluble. The molecular reaction is

$$NaCl + AgNO_3 \longrightarrow NaNO_3 + AgCl$$

The positive and negative ions have simply traded partners. ●

● **EXAMPLE 2**   **Problem**: Write an ionic equation for the reaction in the previous example.

Solution: To write an ionic equation we need to know which product is the insoluble compound. The solubility guidelines in the text tell us that $NaNO_3$ is soluble but $AgCl$ is insoluble. The ionic equation is

$$Na^+ + Cl^- + Ag^+ + NO_3^- \longrightarrow Na^+ + NO_3^- + AgCl(s)$$

$AgCl$ is not written in ionic form because it is insoluble and so does not form an appreciable concentration of ions. ●

● **EXAMPLE 3**   **Problem**: Write a net ionic equation for the reaction in Example 2.

Solution: To convert an ionic equation to a net ionic equation we simply eliminate the spectator ions. Spectator ions are those that stay in solution while the other ions participate in the reaction. They always occur on both sides of the equation in the same form. In this case, Na^+ and NO_3^- are spectator ions. Elimination of these from both sides of the equation gives the net ionic equation.

$$Cl^- + Ag^+ \longrightarrow AgCl(s) \quad \bullet$$

Now work Example 13-1 in the text.

13-3
Net equations for
aqueous-solution
reactions

A real challenge in writing chemical equations is figuring out the products for a given set of reactants. You must know the classification schemes and guidelines in Sec. 13-3 of the text to figure out reactions. The rest is a matter of "learning by doing."

● **EXAMPLE 4**

Problem: Will a reaction occur if solutions of sodium hydroxide and lead(II) chloride are mixed?

Solution: The ions produced by dissociation of the reactants are Na^+, OH^-, Pb^{2+}, and Cl^-. They can combine to form only two new compounds: $NaCl$ and $Pb(OH)_2$. According to solubility guideline 8, $Pb(OH)_2$ is insoluble and a precipitation reaction will occur. ●

● **EXAMPLE 5**

Problem: Hydrochloric acid is added to a sample of solid sodium carbonate. Give equations for the reactions that occur.

Solution: Sodium carbonate is soluble, but we should look for a chemical change which could result in different products. The hydrochloric acid furnishes H^+ and Cl^- ions. H^+ ions react with CO_3^{2-} ions to form HCO_3^-, a weak acid; therefore, acids dissolve carbonate salts to give hydrogen carbonate products. The molecular reaction is

$$Na_2CO_3(s) + HCl \longrightarrow NaCl + NaHCO_3$$

The ionic reaction is

$$Na_2CO_3(s) + H^+ + Cl^- \longrightarrow 2Na^+ + Cl^- + HCO_3^-$$

and the net ionic reaction is

$$Na_2CO_3(s) + H^+ \longrightarrow 2Na^+ + HCO_3^-$$

Check the last reaction to convince yourself that it is balanced atomically and with respect to charge.

If additional HCl is present the reaction can go further because HCO_3^- and H^+ can combine to give the weak acid H_2CO_3. The net ionic equation for this reaction is

$$HCO_3^- + H^+ \longrightarrow H_2CO_3$$

The Na^+ ions are in solution and become spectator ions. ●

Now work Examples 13-3 to 13-5 in the text and try to explain why reactions 1 through 10 following Example 13-5 take place.

13-4
Electron-transfer
reactions

Redox reactions are the basis of several important chemical changes. We will study their applications later in Chap. 19. Right now we are concerned with understanding the concepts involved and becoming familiar with them by learning two techniques used to balance redox equations. Each technique has its own advantages and the choice of one over the other is largely a matter of personal preference.

1 Oxidation-number method
There are often several possible products from a given set of reactants in redox reactions, so information about the product composition must be given before an equation can be written. Balancing the equation is a matter of following the steps as outlined in the text. We can illustrate this by example, starting with a simple one.

● **EXAMPLE 6**   **Problem**: Balance the following equation by the oxidation-number method.

$$Fe + O_2 \longrightarrow Fe_2O_3$$

Solution: We will apply the steps outlined in the text.
Step 1: Assign oxidation numbers

$$\textcircled{0} \quad \textcircled{0}\textcircled{+3}\textcircled{-2}$$
$$Fe + O_2 \ Fe_2O_3$$

Step 2: Determine the number of electrons (oxidation numbers) gained and lost. The oxidation number of Fe increases from 0 to +3 so Fe is oxidized (hence it is the reducing agent because it reduces the oxygen). The oxidation number of O_2 decreases from 0 to -2 so O_2 is reduced (hence it is the oxidizing agent since it oxidizes Fe to Fe^{3+}).
Step 3: If a molecule has more than one atom that gains or loses electrons (changes in oxidation number), find the net gain or loss for that molecule. Step 3 does not apply in this equation.
Step 4: Balance the electron transfer by inserting coefficients into the equation to make the number of electrons lost equal to the number of electrons gained. It is generally easiest to balance the left-hand side of the equation first, and our first consideration is to balance the changes in oxidation number (electrons transferred). Often arrows are used as a bookkeeping aid in this step.

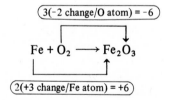

The lowest common denominator for -2 and +3 is 6. Two Fe atoms have +6 change and three O atoms have -6 change; the gain in oxidation number (six electrons lost) equals the decrease in oxidation number (six electrons gained). The Fe and O_2 on the left-hand side can be balanced by taking two Fe atoms and three O atoms (or $\frac{3}{2}O_2$ molecules) and the partially balanced equation becomes

$$2Fe + \tfrac{3}{2}O_2 \longrightarrow Fe_2O_3$$

Step 5: Complete the balancing. Now that we have balanced the electron transfer, we do not want to change the coefficients on the elements already balanced. Balance the rest of the equation using these coefficients as a guide. In this case, one molecule of Fe_2O_3 gives us the correct atomic balance. This equation could have been balanced by inspection quite easily, but it illustrates the steps involved in the oxidation-number method. The same approach will balance more difficult equations. ●

● **EXAMPLE 7**   **Problem:** Balance the following equation by the oxidation-number method.

$$As_2S_5 + HNO_3 \longrightarrow As_2O_5 + H_2SO_4 + NO + H_2O$$

Solution: We apply the steps as outlined in the text.

Step 1:

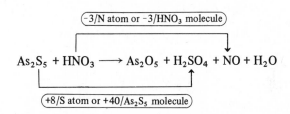

Step 2: The oxidation number of sulfur changes from -2 to +6, a gain of 8. The oxidation number of nitrogen changes from +5 to +2, a loss of 3.

Step 3: Does not apply to this equation.

Step 4: Using the arrow system to keep track of bookkeeping

Since there are five sulfur atoms per As_2S_5 molecule and the oxidation number of each sulfur atom changes by +8, the total change for an As_2S_5 molecule is $5(+8) = +40$. The lowest common denominator for balancing the electron transfer is $3 \times 40 = 120$. Three molecules of As_2S_5 have a total gain of 120 in oxidation number and 40 molecules of HNO_3 have a balancing loss of 120 in oxidation number; therefore, we balance the electron transfer by

$$3As_2S_5 + 40HNO_3 \longrightarrow As_2O_5 + H_2SO_4 + NO + H_2O$$

Step 5: The coefficients on the left-hand side balance the electron transfer so they must not be changed. We balance the rest of the equation using them as a guide. There are six atoms of As and 15 atoms of S on the left-hand side, so the same number must appear on the right-hand side. This requires the coefficient of As_2O_5 to be 3 and the coefficient of H_2SO_4 to be 15. The same reasoning requires 40 atoms of nitrogen on each side, so the coefficient of NO must be 40. The equation now becomes

$$3As_2S_5 + 40HNO_3 \longrightarrow 3As_2O_5 + 15H_2SO_4 + 40NO + H_2O$$

Next we balance the oxygen atoms. There are 120 atoms of O on the left-hand side and this number is fixed. So far we have assigned 15 atoms of O to As_2O_5, 60 atoms to H_2SO_4, and 40 atoms to NO, for a total of $15 + 60 + 40 = 115$ atoms of O already assigned. The remaining five atoms ($120 - 115 = 5$ atoms left) require the coefficient of H_2O to be 5, and the balanced equation is

$$3As_2S_5 + 40HNO_3 \longrightarrow 3As_2O_5 + 15H_2SO_4 + 40NO + 5H_2O$$

The hydrogen atoms are automatically balanced and can be used to check the coefficients.   There are $(2 \times 15) + (5 \times 2) = 40$ H atoms on the right-hand side which balances the 40 atoms on the left-hand side. Although this equation was more complex than Example 6, the balancing technique was the same. •

Now work Examples 13-6 and 13-7 in the text.

2 Balancing redox equations in aqueous solutions by the oxidation-number method
When a redox reaction occurs in acidic or basic solution, H^+, OH^-, and H_2O are often not included in the skeletal equation you are asked to balance. However, the amounts of these species are fixed by the reaction and are determined by applying the steps outlined in the text.

• **EXAMPLE 8**   **Problem**: The following reaction takes place in acidic solution. Complete and balance the equation by the oxidation-number method.

$$H_3AsO_3 + MnO_4^- \longrightarrow H_3AsO_4 + Mn^{2+}$$

Solution: We will apply the steps outlined in the text for balancing redox equations in aqueous solution by the oxidation-number method.

Step 1: $\overset{(+1)(+3)(-2)}{H_3 \ As \ O_3} + \overset{(+7)(-2)}{Mn \ O_4^-} \longrightarrow \overset{(+1)(+5)(-2)}{H_3 \ As \ O_4} + \overset{(+2)}{Mn^{2+}}$

Step 2: $H_3AsO_3 + MnO_4^- \longrightarrow H_3AsO_4 + Mn^{2+}$

with $\boxed{-5/Mn}$ from MnO_4^- to Mn^{2+} and $\boxed{+2/As}$ from H_3AsO_3 to H_3AsO_4

Step 4: $5H_3AsO_3 + 2MnO_4^- \longrightarrow H_3AsO_4 + Mn^{2+}$

Step 5: $5H_3AsO_3 + 2MnO_4^- \longrightarrow 5H_3AsO_4 + 2Mn^{2+}$

Step 7a: The net charge on the left-hand side is -2. The net charge on the right is $+4$. The left side is deficient $+6$ compared to the right. Since this is an acidic solution, we add $6H^+$ to the left to balance the charges

$$6H^+ + 5H_3AsO_3 + 2MnO_4^- \longrightarrow 5H_3AsO_4 + 2Mn^{2+}$$

Step 8: There are $15 + 8 = 23$ O atoms on the left and 20 O atoms on the right. We need to add three H_2O molecules to the right-hand side to balnce the oxygen

$$6H^+ + 5H_3AsO_3 + 2MnO_4^- \longrightarrow 5H_3AsO_4 + 2Mn^{2+} + 3H_2O$$

The hydrogen balance can be used as a check:

$6 + (5 \times 3) = 21$ H on the left $(5 \times 3) + (2 \times 3) = 21$ H on the right •

• **EXAMPLE 9**   **Problem**: Complete and balance the equation in Example 8 if it takes place in a basic solution.

Solution: Steps 1 through 6 are identical to those in Example 8 so we have

$$5H_3AsO_3 + 2MnO_4^- \longrightarrow 5H_3AsO_4 + 2Mn^{2+}$$

Step 7b: The net charge on the left is -2 and on the right $+4$. The right-hand side is deficient by six negative charges. Since this a basic solution we add $6OH^-$ to the right to balance the charges.

$$5H_3AsO_3 + 2MnO_4^- \longrightarrow 5H_3AsO_4 + 2Mn^{2+} + 6OH^-$$

Step 8: There are $(3 \times 5) + (2 \times 4) = 23$ O atoms on the left and $(5 \times 4) + 6 = 26$ O atoms on the right. We add three molecules of H_2O to the left-hand side to balance oxygen.

$$5H_3AsO_3 + 2MnO_4^- + 3H_2O \longrightarrow 5H_3AsO_4 + 2Mn^{2+} + 6OH^-$$

The hydrogen balance is used as a check

$$(5 \times 3) + (3 \times 2) = 21 \text{ H on the left} \qquad (5 \times 3) + 6 = 21 \text{ H on the right} \quad \bullet$$

Now work through Examples 13-8 and 13-9 in the text.

3 Balancing redox equations in aqueous solution by the half-reaction or ion-electron method

The second method of balancing redox equations does not use oxidation numbers; rather, the overall reaction is divided into an oxidation half-reaction and a reduction half-reaction. These half-reactions are balanced separately and then added to get the overall equation, making sure the number of electrons lost in the oxidation half-reaction equals the number of electrons gained in the reduction half-reaction. The step-by-step procedure for this method is given in the text.

● **EXAMPLE 10**   **Problem:** The following reaction takes place in acidic solution. Complete and balance it by the half-reaction method.

$$Cr_2O_7^{2-} + 3H_2S \longrightarrow Cr^{3+} + S$$

Solution: We will apply the steps for balancing redox reactions in aqueous solution by the half-reaction method.

Step 1: Step 1 requires that we recognize which species is oxidized and which is reduced. The easiest way to do this is to see which elements change in oxidation number. An increase in oxidation number is oxidation and a decrease is reduction. In our example, Cr is reduced from an oxidation number of $+6$ in $Cr_2O_7^{2-}$ to one of $+3$ in Cr^{3+}, while S is oxidized from oxidation number -2 in H_2S to 0 in S. $Cr_2O_7^{2-}$ is the oxidizing agent or oxidant and H_2S is the reducing agent or reductant.

The oxidation half-reaction includes the compounds containing sulfur in its different oxidation states

$$H_2S \longrightarrow S$$

and the reduction half-reaction shows Cr in its different oxidation states

$$Cr_2O_7^{2-} \longrightarrow Cr^{3+}$$

Step 2: Now we balance each half-reaction according to the sequence of steps given in the text. First the reduction half-reaction. Balance the Cr atoms first. There are two Cr atoms on the left, so we need two on the right

$$Cr_2O_7{}^{2-} \longrightarrow 2Cr^{3+}$$

Now balance the oxygen by adding seven H_2O molecules to the right side to balance the seven oxygen atoms in $Cr_2O_7{}^{2-}$ on the left

$$Cr_2O_7{}^{2-} \longrightarrow 2Cr^{3+} + 7H_2O$$

The reaction occurs in acidic solution so we balance H by adding H^+ as needed to the left side. It takes 14 H^+ ions to balance the H_2O

$$14H^+ + Cr_2O_7{}^{2-} \longrightarrow 2Cr^{3+} + 7H_2O$$

Complete the balancing by adding e^- as needed to balance the charges. There is $+14 - 2 = +12$ net charge on the left and $2(+3) = +6$ net charge on the right. We are adding negative charges (electrons), so it takes $6e^-$ on the left to make the charges balance at $+6$ on the left and right.

$$14H^+ + Cr_2O_7{}^{2-} + 6e^- \longrightarrow 2Cr^{3+} + 7H_2O$$

Now we can balance the oxidation half-reaction. The sulfur atoms are already balanced and there are no oxygen atoms to balance so we proceed directly to Step 2c and add 2 H^+ ions to the right to balance H:

$$H_2S \longrightarrow S + 2H^+$$

Now balance charges by adding $2e^-$ to the right

$$H_2S \longrightarrow S + 2H^+ + 2e^-$$

Step 3: Now we can combine the half-reactions. We must be sure the electron transfer is balanced; that is, the electrons lost in the oxidation half-reaction and the electrons gained in the reduction half-reaction must be equal. If we multiply the entire oxidation half-reaction by 3, there will be $6e^-$ lost and $6e^-$ gained. The two half-reactions can be added to give the overall reaction.

$$14H^+ + Cr_2O_7{}^{2-} + 6e^- \longrightarrow 2Cr^{3+} + 7H_2O$$
$$3H_2S \longrightarrow 3S + 6H^+ + 6e^-$$
$$\overline{14H^+ + 3H_2S + Cr_2O_7{}^{2-} + 6e^- \longrightarrow 3S + 6H^+ + 2Cr^{3+} + 7H_2O + 6e^-}$$

Common species on both sides of the equation can be canceled just as in algebraic equation, so cancel $6H^+$ and $6e^-$ from each side to leave the final equation.

$$8H^+ + 3H_2S + Cr_2O_7{}^{2-} \longrightarrow 3S + 2Cr^{3+} + 7H_2O \quad \bullet$$

● **EXAMPLE 11**   **Problem:** Complete and balance the following reaction taking place in basic solution by the half-reaction method.

$$MnO_4{}^- + AsO_3{}^{3-} \longrightarrow MnO_2 + AsO_4{}^{3-}$$

Solution: Apply the steps for the half-reaction method as given in the text.
Step 1: Mn is reduced from a $+7$ oxidation state to $+4$ and As is oxidized from $+3$ to $+5$. The reduction half-reaction is

$$MnO_4{}^- \longrightarrow MnO_2$$

and the oxidation half-reaction is

$$AsO_3^{3-} \longrightarrow AsO_4^{3-}$$

Step 2: Balance O, H, and charge for the reduction half-reaction first. **To balance O add $2H_2O$ to the right**

$$MnO_4^- \longrightarrow MnO_2 + 2H_2O$$

The left side has four fewer H atoms. Since this is a basic solution we **balance H by adding $4H_2O$ to the left and $4OH^-$ to the right**

$$MnO_4^- + 4H_2O \longrightarrow MnO_2 + 2H_2O + 4OH^-$$

The duplicate H_2O molecules can be canceled. Now balance charges by adding $3e^-$ to the left

$$MnO_4^- + 2H_2O + 3e^- \longrightarrow MnO_2 + 4OH^-$$

Now balance the oxidation half-reaction by the same steps. Balance O by adding $1H_2O$ to the left

$$AsO_3^{3-} + H_2O \longrightarrow AsO_4^{3-}$$

Balance H by adding $2H_2O$ to the right (it is deficient two H atoms) and $2OH^-$ to the left.

$$AsO_3^{3-} + H_2O + 2OH^- \longrightarrow AsO_4^{3-} + 2H_2O$$

Now cancel the duplicate H_2O and balance charges by adding $2e^-$ to the right

$$AsO_3^{3-} + 2OH^- \longrightarrow AsO_4^{3-} + H_2O + 2e^-$$

Step 3: Balance the electron transfer by multiplying the entire reduction half-reaction by 2 and the oxidation half-reaction by 3 to get six electrons transferred. Add the half-reactions to get the overall equation.

Reduction: $\quad 2MnO_4^- + 4H_2O + 6e^- \longrightarrow 2MnO_2 + 8OH^-$

Oxidation: $\quad\quad\quad 3AsO_3^{3-} + 6OH^- \longrightarrow 3AsO_4^{3-} + 3H_2O + 6e^-$

$\overline{\quad\quad 2MnO_4^- + 3AsO_3^{3-} + H_2O \longrightarrow 2MnO_2 + 3AsO_4^{3-} + 2OH^-}$

In the overall equation $6e^-$, $6OH^-$, and $3H_2O$ have been canceled from both sides. ●

Now work Examples 13-10 and 13-11 in the text and try to balance some of the following equations. Answers are included after the self-test answers for this chapter.

Balance redox reactions 1 to 10 by any method.

1 $As + HNO_3 \longrightarrow As_2O_5 + NO + H_2O$

2 $H_2S + KMnO_4 + HCl \longrightarrow S + KCl + MnCl_2 + H_2O$

3 $Fe_2(SO_4)_3 + KI \longrightarrow FeSO_4 + K_2SO_4 + I_2$

4 $Sb_2S_3 + HNO_3 \longrightarrow Sb_2O_5 + S + NO_2 + H_2O$

5 $C_2H_3OCl + Cr_2O_7^{2-} + H^+ \longrightarrow Cr^{3+} + Cl_2 + CO_2 + H_2O$

6 $C_2O_4^{2-} + MnO_4^- + H^+ \longrightarrow CO_2 + Mn^{2+} + H_2O$

7 $FeSO_4 + H_2SO_4 + KMnO_4 \longrightarrow Fe_2(SO_4)_3 + K_2SO_4 + MnSO_4 + H_2O$

8 $Br_2 + NH_3 \longrightarrow NH_4Br + N_2$

9 $F_2 + H_2O \longrightarrow HF + O_3$

10 $Cu_2S + SO_4{}^{2-} + H^+ \longrightarrow Cu^{2+} + H_2SO_3 + H_2O$

Reactions 11 to 17 occur in acidic solution. Complete and balance the equations by any method.

11 $Fe^{2+} + MnO_4{}^- \longrightarrow Fe^{3+} + Mn^{2+}$

12 $MnO_2 + Cl^- \longrightarrow Mn^{2+} + Cl_2$

13 $Zn + NO_3{}^- \longrightarrow Zn^{2+} + NH_4{}^+$

14 $Ag^+ + AsH_3 \longrightarrow H_3AsO_3 + Ag$

15 $C_2H_2 + MnO_4{}^- \longrightarrow Mn^{2+} + CO_2$

16 $ClO_3{}^- + Br^- \longrightarrow Cl^- + Br_2$

17 $MnO_4{}^- + H_2O_2 \longrightarrow Mn^{2+} + O_2$

Reactions 18 to 22 occur in basic solution. Complete and balance the equations by any method.

18 $Br_2 \longrightarrow Br^- + BrO_3{}^-$

19 $Cr(OH)_3 + Cl_2 \longrightarrow Cl^- + CrO_4{}^{2-}$

20 $P_4 \longrightarrow H_2PO_2{}^- + PH_3$

21 $CH_2O + Ag_2O \longrightarrow Ag + HCO_2{}^-$

22 $Bi(OH)_3 + SnO_2{}^{2-} \longrightarrow Bi + SnO_3{}^{2-}$

**13-5
Solution
stoichiometry**

It is often necessary to know the relationship between the amounts of reactants and products in aqueous-solution reactions. An important example of the calculations involved in solution stoichiometry is the determination of the amounts of acid and base reacting in a neutralization reaction. These calculations are quite easy once you understand some basic relationships.

1 Acid-base stoichiometry by molarity
When the acid donates a single H^+ and the base donates a single OH^-, the stoichiometry is completely represented by the simple neutralization reaction:

$$H^+ + OH^- \longrightarrow H_2O$$

An example of this type of reaction is

$$NaOH + HCl \longrightarrow NaCl + H_2O$$

When a solution of either acid or base is completely neutralized, equal moles of acid and base are used in the reaction.

$$\text{Moles acid = moles base}$$

Examples 13-12 and 13-13 in the text show how these relationships can be used in stoichiometric calculations of acid-base reactions.

Triprotic acids have three ionizable hydrogens. An example of the complete neutralization of a triprotic acid is given in Example 13-14 in the text. This time the number of moles of base required is three times the number of moles of acid present.

$$\text{Moles base} = 3(\text{moles acid})$$

The stoichiometry in terms of molarity is illustrated in the text example.

2 Determination of equivalent weight, equivalents, and normality

We could develop relationships for each different combination of acids and bases depending on how many hydrogens are donated by the acid and the number of hydroxides in the base, but we would have a different relationship for each type of problem using this approach. To get around this inconvenience the concepts of equivalents and normality were developed. Let us investigate the concepts of equivalents, equivalent weight, and normality and then apply them to neutralization reaction calculations.

An acid-base equivalent is defined as the weight in grams that supplies or reacts with one mole of H^+. An equivalent of base is one mole of available OH^-. Equivalents are related to moles as follows:

Equivalents of acid or base = moles of acid or base

$$\times \text{ number of ionizable } H^+ \text{ or } OH^- \text{ per molecule}$$

If there is one ionizable H^+ (monoprotic acid), equivalents and moles are equal. If there are two ionizable H^+ per acid molecule (diprotic acid), there are two equivalents per mole; there are three equivalents per mole of triprotic acid. Similar relations hold for bases.

Equivalent weight is the mass in grams of one equivalent. It is related to molecular weight for acids and bases as follows:

$$\text{Equivalent weight} = \frac{\text{molecular weight}}{\text{number of ionizable } H^+ \text{ or } OH^-}$$

Normality is a concentration unit based on equivalents in the same way that molarity is based on moles.

$$M = \text{molarity} = \frac{\text{moles}}{\text{liter}} \quad N = \text{normality} = \frac{\text{equivalents}}{\text{liter}}$$

$$N = M(\text{equiv mol}^{-1})$$

In acid-base relationships the normality is the number of moles of available H^+ or OH^- per liter. Some examples will illustrate the use of these new terms.

● **EXAMPLE 12**   **Problem**: How many equivalents are there in (a) 1.00 mol of HCl? (b) 1.00 mol of H_2CO_3? (c) 1.00 mol of $La(OH)_3$?

Solution: We will work each part by a slightly different approach to illustrate the different relationships between moles and equivalents.

(a) HCl is a monoprotic acid, so there is one ionizable hydrogen per molecule or 1 equiv per mole.

$$\text{Equivalents} = \text{mol of } H^+ = \text{mol HCl} \times \text{equiv mol}^{-1}$$

$$= 1.00 \text{ mol HCl} \times \frac{1 \text{ equiv}}{1 \text{ mol HCl}} = 1.00 \text{ equiv}$$

(b) H_2CO_3 is a diprotic acid, so there are two ionizable hydrogens per mole.

$$\text{Equivalents} = \text{mol } H_2CO_3 \times \frac{\text{mol } H^+}{\text{mol } H_2CO_3}$$

$$= 1.00 \text{ mol } H_2CO_3 \times \frac{2 \text{ mol } H^+}{1 \text{ mol } H_2CO_3} = 2.00 \text{ equiv}$$

(c) $La(OH)_3$ has three ionizable hydroxide ions per mole, so there are 3 equiv per mole.

$$\text{Equivalents} = \text{mol(No. of ionizable } OH^-) = 1.00 \text{ mol}(3) = 3.00 \text{ equiv} \; \bullet$$

• **EXAMPLE 13**   **Problem**: What is the equivalent weight of $Mg(OH)_2$?

Solution: There are two ionizable OH^- per mole of $Mg(OH)_2$, so the equivalent weight is

$$\text{Equivalent weight} = \frac{\text{mol. wt.}}{\text{No. of ionizable } OH^-} = \frac{58.3 \text{ g mol}^{-1}}{2 \text{ equiv mol}^{-1}} = 29.2 \text{ g equiv}^{-1} \; \bullet$$

• **EXAMPLE 14**   **Problem**: What is the normality of (a) $1.0 \, M$ HCl? (b) $2.0 \, M$ $Ca(OH)_2$?

Solution: (a) There is 1 equiv per mole for HCl so

$$N = M(\text{equiv mol}^{-1}) = 1.0 \, M(1 \text{ equiv mol}^{-1}) = 1.0$$

Normality equals molarity for monoprotic acids or bases with one hydroxide.

(b) $Ca(OH)_2$ has 2 equiv of OH^- per mole.

$$N = 2.0 \, M(2 \text{ equiv mol}^{-1}) = 4.0 \, N \; \bullet$$

Now work Examples 13-15 to 13-17 in the text.

3 Use of normality in acid-base stoichiometry

In all acid-base neutralization reactions the number of moles of H^+ equals the number of moles of OH^- at neutralization. Equivalents are the number of moles of available H^+ or OH^-, so the equivalents of acid always equal the equivalents of base at complete neutralization.

$$\text{Equiv acid} = \text{equiv base}$$

Since $N = \text{equiv liter}^{-1}$, the number of equivalents is

$$\text{Equiv} = N \times \text{liters} = NV$$

where N is the normality of the solution and V is the volume in liters. Substituting NV for equivalents in the neutralization equation gives

$$(NV)_{\text{acid}} = (NV)_{\text{base}}$$

Since the equivalents of acid always equal the equivalents of base at complete neutralization, this equation is a general relationship and the single equation works for all acids and bases. Any one of the variables can be determined if the other three are known.

● **EXAMPLE 15**   **Problem:** How many milliliters of 0.200 N Ca(OH)$_2$ are needed to completely neutralize 40.0 ml of 0.150 N H$_3$PO$_4$?

Solution: The neutralization reaction in terms of normality works in all cases, so simply substitute the known values and solve for milliliters of Ca(OH)$_2$.

$$(NV)_{\text{Ca(OH)}_2} = (NV)_{\text{H}_3\text{PO}_4}$$

$$V_{\text{Ca(OH)}_2} = V_{\text{H}_3\text{PO}_4} \frac{N_{\text{H}_3\text{PO}_4}}{N_{\text{Ca(OH)}_2}} = 40.0 \text{ ml} \frac{0.150 \, N}{0.200 \, N} = 30.0 \text{ ml} \; ●$$

● **EXAMPLE 16**   **Problem:** How many milliliters of 0.200 M Ca(OH)$_2$ are needed to completely neutralize 40.0 ml of 0.150 M H$_3$PO$_4$?

Solution: We first convert the molarity values to normality.

$$0.200 \, M \text{ Ca(OH)}_2 \frac{2 \text{ equiv Ca(OH)}_2}{1 \text{ mol}} = 0.400 \, N$$

$$0.150 \, M \text{ H}_3\text{PO}_4 \frac{3 \text{ equiv H}_3\text{PO}_4}{1 \text{ mol}} = 0.450 \, N$$

Now substitute these values into the neutralization equation as in the previous example

$$V_{\text{Ca(OH)}_2} = V_{\text{H}_3\text{PO}_4} \frac{N_{\text{H}_3\text{PO}_4}}{N_{\text{Ca(OH)}_2}} = 40.0 \text{ ml} \frac{0.450 \, N}{0.400 \, N} = 45.0 \text{ ml} \; ●$$

Now work Example 13-18 in the text.

4 Use of equivalents and normality in stoichiometric calculations of redox equations
In the case of redox equations an equivalent is defined as the weight in grams of a substance that accepts or donates one mole of electrons. It is related to moles by the equation

Equivalents = moles(change in oxidation number of the compound)

= moles(electrons transferred)

Equivalent weight = $\dfrac{\text{molecular weight}}{\text{change in oxidation number}}$

It should be apparent that since the change in oxidation number of an element is often different in different reactions, we need to specify the reaction to determine the equivalents of a compound in redox reactions.

The definition of normality is the same as for acid-base reactions and the equation

$$(NV)_{\text{oxidant}} = (NV)_{\text{reductant}}$$

holds for all redox reactions.

● **EXAMPLE 17**   **Problem:** If 2.00 mol of ClO_3^- undergoes reaction to form Cl^-, how many equivalents of ClO_3^- reacted?

Solution: Cl changes from oxidation state +5 in ClO_3^- to −1 in Cl^-. The net change in oxidation number is −6. In calculating equivalents we use the numerical value of the change without regard to algebraic sign.

$$\text{Equiv } ClO_3^- = 2 \text{ mol } ClO_3^- \frac{6e^- \text{ transferred}}{1 \text{ mol}} = 12 \text{ equiv } ●$$

● **EXAMPLE 18**   **Problem:** How many milliliters of 0.153 M $Cr_2O_7^{2-}$ are needed to react with 25.0 ml of 0.437 M H_2S if the $Cr_2O_7^{2-}$ is reduced to Cr^{3+} and the H_2S is oxidized to elemental sulfur?

Solution: If we change the molarity values to normality we can work the problem without having a balanced equation since one equivalent of oxidant reacts with one equivalent of reductant for all redox equations. The change in oxidation number of Cr is from +6 in $Cr_2O_7^{2-}$ to +3 in Cr^{3+} or −3 per Cr atom. Since there are two Cr atoms per $Cr_2O_7^{2-}$ the net change for $Cr_2O_7^{2-}$ is −6.

$$N_{Cr_2O_7^{2-}} = 0.153 \, M \frac{6 \text{ equiv}}{1 \text{ mol } Cr_2O_7^{2-}} = 0.918 \, N$$

The change in oxidation state for S in H_2S is from −2 in H_2S to 0 in S, or +2 total change.

$$N_{H_2S} = 0.437 \, M \frac{2 \text{ equiv}}{1 \text{ mol } H_2S} = 0.874 \, N$$

Now substitute into the equation

$$(NV)_{Cr_2O_7^{2-}} = (NV)_{H_2S}$$

and solve for $V_{Cr_2O_7^{2-}}$

$$V_{Cr_2O_7^{2-}} = V_{H_2S} \frac{N_{H_2S}}{N_{Cr_2O_7^{2-}}} = 25.0 \text{ ml } \frac{0.874 \, N}{0.918 \, N} = 23.8 \text{ ml } ●$$

Now work Examples 13-19 to 13-21 in the text.

SELF TEST

True or false   ___ 1 All Arrhenius acids are also Brønsted acids.

___ 2 According to the Lewis theory, an acid is an electron-pair donor.

___ 3 In an aqueous solution of HCl, H_3O^+ is the strongest acid possible.

___ 4 The reaction of an acid with an equivalent amount of base always gives a solution that is neutral.

___ 5 There are always 2 equiv per mole of $Ca(OH)_2$.

Completion   6 The Arrhenius concept of acids and bases is limited to _____ solutions.

7 The reaction $2H_2O \longrightarrow H_3O^+ + OH^-$ is an example of _____ .

8 Oxidation occurs when a substance _____ (loses, gains) electrons or _____ _____ (increases, decreases) in oxidation number.

9 $Cl_2 + 2e^- \longrightarrow 2Cl^-$ is a (an) _____ (oxidation, reduction) reaction.

10 Mixing solutions of $Sr(NO_3)_2$ and Na_2CO_3 _____ (will, will not) result in a chemical reaction.

11 There are _____ equiv per mole of $La(OH)_3$.

12 A 0.300 M solution of H_2SO_4 would be _____ N.

13 A 0.600 M solution of $FeCl_3$ reacts to form Fe. The normality of the $FeCl_3$ solution was _____ .

Multiple choice

14 Which of the following is a weak electrolyte?
(a) $Ca(OH)_2$ (b) H_2SO_4 (c) Na_2CO_3 (d) H_2CO_3

15 When solutions of $Pb(NO_3)_2$ and Rb_2SO_4 are mixed, the precipitate that forms is?
(a) $RbNO_3$ (b) $PbSO_4$
(c) both $RbNO_3$ and $PbSO_4$ (d) no precipitate forms

16 Which of the following ions form an insoluble compound with Ca^{2+}?
(a) $NO_3^-, C_2H_3O_2^-$ (b) F^-, SO_4^{2-}, CO_3^-
(c) Cl^-, PO_4^{3-}, OH^- (d) Br^-, SO_3^{2-}

17 In the redox reaction $Ca + 2H_2O \longrightarrow Ca(OH)_2 + H_2$, the oxidant is
(a) Ca   (b) H_2O (c) $Ca(OH)_2$ (d) H_2

18 What is the sum of the coefficients when the following redox equation is balanced?

$$AuCl_4^- + AsH_3 + H_2O \longrightarrow H_3AsO_3 + H^+ + Au + Cl^-$$

(a) 10   (b) 14   (c) 19   (d) 23

19 How many molecules of water are required to balance the following redox equation in acidic solution?

$$HBr + MnO_4^- \longrightarrow Br_2 + Mn^{2+}$$

(a) 2   (b) 3   (c) 5   (d) 8

20 Which set of coefficients will balance the following half-reaction?

$$H^+ + XeO_3 + e^- \longrightarrow Xe + H_2O$$

(a) 4, 1, 4, 1, 2   (b) 12, 2, 2, 2, 6   (c) 6, 1, 6, 1, 3   (d) 2, 1, 2, 1, 1

21 How many milliliters of 0.100 M $Ca(OH)_2$ are required to neutralize 30.0 ml of 0.250 M HNO_3?
(a) 12.0   (b) 24.0   (c) 37.5   (d) 75.0

22 How many equivalents are in 4.0 mol of H_2SO_4?
(a) 1.0   (b) 2.0   (c) 4.0   (d) 8.0

23 HNO_3 is reduced to NO in a chemical reaction. If the HNO_3 was 3.00 M, what was its normality?
(a) 1.50 N (b) 3.00 N (c) 6.00 N (d) 9.00 N

24 What is the equivalent weight of Na_2CO_3 in the reaction

$$Na_2CO_3 + HCl \longrightarrow NaHCO_3 + NaCl?$$

(a) 26.5   (b) 53.0   (c) 106.0   (d) 212.0

25 How many milliliters of 0.150 N $KMnO_4$ would be required to oxidize 20.0 ml of 0.250 N AsH_3?
(a) 4.0   (b) 12.0   (c) 33.3   (d) cannot tell without knowing the products

14

CHEMICAL KINETICS

CHAPTER OVERVIEW

14-1
Important terms and concepts

Chemical kinetics is the study of the rate or speed of chemical reactions and the step-by-step mechanism by which they proceed. Reaction rate is the speed of production of products or disappearance of reactants and is measured in units of concentration per time, usually moles per liter per second (mol liter^{-1} s^{-1}). As reactant molecules are consumed in the reaction, their concentration decreases; therefore, fewer collisions occur and the reaction gradually slows. The reaction rate depends mainly on the chemical properties and reactivity of the reactants, their concentration, and the temperature. Knowledge of the reaction rate allows calculation of the concentration of reactants at any time and of the length of time needed to reach a given concentration. It also helps us understand the mechanism of a reaction.

A knowledge of calculus will help in understanding the symbolism used in this section but is not essential to the concepts presented. If you have not yet had calculus just read

$$\frac{\Delta[A]}{\Delta t} \quad \text{or} \quad \frac{d[A]}{dt}$$

as the rate of change of concentration of A with time.

$$\text{Rate} = -\frac{d[A]}{dt}$$

simply says "the reaction rate is equal to the decrease in concentration of A per unit time." Note that the rate can be expressed as a function of the concentration of any reactant or product.

14-2
The rate law

A rate law is a mathematical equation that relates rate to the concentrations of reacting species, for example

$$\text{Rate} = -\frac{d[A]}{dt} = k[A][B]$$

The minus sign shows that [A] is decreasing as time increases. The term k is an important constant called the specific rate constant. Its magnitude reveals how fast the reaction tends to proceed at any given temperature. Its variation with temperature reveals much about the energy changes of a reaction, as we shall see later.

The concept of order of a reaction is simple, but make sure you understand it thoroughly. We will spend considerable time determining order of reactions. Knowledge of the order gives us basic clues about the reaction mechanism.

There are several techniques for finding values for reaction order and the specific rate constant depending on the type of data available. If you have rate data as a function of concentration (such as in Example 14-1) the method of initial rates works well. If you have concentration data as a function of time, a graphical method is best. Reaction order can have any value from 0 to 3, but first-order reactions are most common.

14-3 **Collision theory**	Collision theory assumes that gas molecules must collide in order to react and that only some of the collisions actually result in chemical reactions. According to this theory, the rate of reaction depends on the concentrations of the reactants; the frequency of collisions Z; the fraction of molecules that have enough energy to react when they collide $e^{-E_a/RT}$; and the probability that the molecules have the correct orientation, represented by the steric factor p. Altogether this gives

$$\text{Rate} = pe^{-E_a/RT}Z_0\,[A]\,[B]$$

from which $k = pe^{-E_a/RT}Z_0$ and can be calculated from theory. The collision theory works fairly well for very simple molecules, but there is no way to calculate p if the reacting molecules are very complex and so use of the collision theory is limited.

The Arrhenius equation is very important because it allows determination of the energy of activation from measurements of the specific rate constant at different temperatures (Text Examples 14-3 and 14-4). The activation energy E_a is the energy the reactants must have in order for the reaction to occur. It is usually in the range of 40 to 200 kJ mol^{-1}.

14-4 **The activated complex**	The activated complex is the intermediate state between reactants and products. It occurs at the top of the energy hill in Figs. 14-10 and 14-11. They show the energy relationships during a chemical reaction in a graphical manner and help us visualize the energy changes during reactions.

14-5 **Reaction mechanisms**	There is a saying "The only simple chemical reaction is one that hasn't been studied." Nearly all reactions take place through a series of steps or elementary reactions. Almost always, one of these steps is much slower than the others and limits the reaction rate. This rate-determining step is closely correlated with kinetic measurements. In fact, if the kinetics predicted by the mechanism through the rate-determining step do not agree with the kinetic rate law determined experimentally, the mechanism should be discarded. In this way kinetics is a guide to determining the correct mechanism and to better understanding (and hence controlling) chemical reactions.

Chain reactions are often explosively fast. Many are observed in nature, especially in the formation of photochemical smog.

14-6 **Catalysis**	A catalyst is a substance that speeds a chemical reaction but can be recovered intact when the reaction is over. Catalysts act by lowering the E_a thus allowing more molecules to react at lower temperatures. In the pharmaceutical industry drugs are pro-

duced that are very sensitive to heat. They would be destroyed by the temperatures needed to speed the reactions to the point at which the products could be manufactured at a commercially reasonable rate. Catalysts allow the production to proceed at a reasonable rate at temperatures low enough to preserve the product. Enzymes are very effective catalysts for biochemical reactions involving very large molecules that would have difficulty orienting themselves correctly (for reactions to occur) without the enzyme.

Catalysts are generally highly specific to a particular reaction, so each new need for a catalyst is a new challenge to research. A homogeneous catalyst is present in the same phase as the reactant molecules and functions by forming a reactive intermediate with one reactant which, in turn, reacts with the other reactant to form products. A heterogeneous catalyst is in a different phase than the reactants and usually provides a surface on which the reactants can make contact. Inhibitors are substances that slow down a reaction. Promoters are substances that make a catalyst more effective.

KEY EQUATIONS

14-2
The rate law

Order	Rate law	Concentration vs. time relationship	$t_{1/2}$	linear plot to test order
0	Rate $= \dfrac{-d[A]}{dt} = k_0$	$[A]_0 - [A] = k_0 t$	$\dfrac{[A]_0}{2k_0}$	$[A]$ vs. t
1	Rate $= \dfrac{-d[A]}{dt} = k_1[A]$	$\log[A] = \dfrac{-k_1 t}{2.303} + \log[A]_0$	$\dfrac{0.693}{k_1}$	$\log[A]$ vs. t
2	Rate $= \dfrac{-d[A]}{dt} = k_2[A]^2$	$\dfrac{1}{[A]} = k_2 t + \dfrac{1}{[A]_0}$	$\dfrac{1}{k_2[A]_0}$	$\dfrac{1}{[A]}$ vs. t

14-3
Collision theory

The rate of a bimolecular reaction according to collision theory is

$$\text{Rate} = pe^{-E_a/RT}Z_0[A][B]$$

from which it follows

$$k = pe^{-E_a/RT}Z_0$$

The Arrhenius equation is

$$k = Ae^{-E_a/RT}$$

It is also expressed in a somewhat more useful form for calculating E_a from specific rate constant values at two different temperatures as

$$\log\frac{k_2}{k_1} = \frac{E_a}{2.303R}\left(\frac{1}{T_1} - \frac{1}{T_2}\right)$$

Note how closely this form of the equation resembles the Clausius-Clapeyron equation of Chap. 10.

LEARNING OBJECTIVES

As a result of studying Chap. 14 you should be able to do the following:
Write the definition and give an example illustrating the use of each key term.

14-1
Important terms and concepts

1 List the factors that determine the rate of a chemical reaction. (Text Prob. 14-2)
2 Determine the average rate over a given time interval from a plot of concentration as a function of time. (Text Probs. 14-1, 14-8) (Self Test 7)
3 Determine the instantaneous rate from the slope of a tangent to a concentration versus time plot. (Text Probs. 14-1, 14-9)
4 Express the rate of reaction in terms of the change of concentration of any reactant or product with time. (Text Probs. 14-3, 14-5, 14-6) (New Skills Examples 1, 2; Self Test 1, 8, 14)
5 Understand what is meant by a reaction mechanism.

14-2
The rate law

1 Write rate laws to show the relationship between concentration and reaction rate. (Text Probs. 14-12, 14-13) (Self Test 15)
2 Identify the order of a reaction from the rate law. (Text Prob. 14-14) (Self Test 2)
3 Write a rate law given the order of reaction of each reacting species. (Self Test 15)
4 Determine the initial rate of a reaction from a concentration versus time plot such as Fig. 14-2 in the text.
5 Determine the order of reaction and specific rate constant using the method of initial rates. (Text Example 14-1; Text Probs. 14-15 to 14-19) (New Skills Examples 3, 4; Self Test 16)
6 Test reaction rate data for first or second-order kinetics by a graphical method using concentration versus time data and determine the specific rate constant. (Text Example 14-2; Text Probs. 14-20 to 14-24) (New Skills 14-2: 2; Self Test 3, 17, 18)
7 Calculate the half-life of first- and second-order reactions. (Text Probs. 14-25, 14-26) (New Skills Example 5; Self Test 20)
8 Calculate the concentration of reactants remaining after a given time, and the time required for concentrations to change by a given amount for first- and second-order reactions. (Text Probs. 14-27 to 14-30) (New Skills Example 6; Self Test 19, 21, 22)

14-3
Collision theory

1 Compare the relationship between molecularity and reaction order for general reactions and elementary processes. (Text Prob. 14-31)
2 List three factors that affect the efficiency with which collisions result in chemical reactions. (Text Probs. 14-33 to 14-36)
3 Understand how the factors in Learning Objective 14-3:2 are included in the rate equation according to collision theory.
4 Understand how collision theory is used to predict the correct form of rate laws for bimolecular gas reactions.
5 Understand the concept of activation energy. (Text Probs. 14-37, 14-41 to 14-44) (Self Test 11, 23)
6 Use the Arrhenius equation to calculate activation energy. (Text Examples 14-3, 14-4; Text Probs. 14-38, 14-45, 14-46) (Self Test 9, 23, 25)
7 Use the Arrhenius equation to calculate the specific rate constant when the activa-

tion energy and specific rate constant at a second temperature are known. (Text Probs. 14-39, 14-40) (New Skills Example 7; Self Test 6, 24)

14-4
The activated
complex

1 Give an example showing that the activated complex is an intermediate state between reactants and products. (Text Prob. 14-47) (Self Test 10)

2 Use a plot of change in potential energy during a reaction (such as Fig. 14-10 in the text) to show the relationships among energy of activation, energy of reaction, and energy of the reactants and products. (Text Probs. 14-48 to 14-51, 14-64) (Self Test 11)

14-5
Reaction
mechanisms

1 Show how a reaction mechanism is made of several elementary reactions. (Text Prob. 14-53)

2 Write rate laws for elementary processes. (Text Prob. 14-52)

3 Relate the kinetics of an overall reaction to the kinetics of the rate-determining step. (Text Prob. 14-54) (Self Test 4, 5)

4 Show how experimental kinetic data can be used to test the validity of a proposed reaction mechanism.

5 Give an example of a chain reaction. (Text Probs. 14-55, 14-56)

14-6
Catalysis

1 Explain the function of a catalyst and give an example showing how one functions. (Text Prob. 14-57) (Self Test 13)

2 Explain the difference between a homogeneous and a heterogeneous catalyst. (Text Prob. 14-60) (Self Test 12)

3 Explain how enzymes function as catalysts for biochemical reactions.

NEW SKILLS

14-1
Important terms
and concepts

1 Determining rates from concentration-time data
You will be expected to understand the concepts of average rate and instantaneous rate and be able to determine both of them from data showing how concentration changes as a reaction proceeds (concentration versus time data). (Learning Objectives 14-1:2, 3) Figure 14-1 in the text shows how this is done graphically. Text Probs. 14-8 and 14-9 will give you practice in applying these techniques.

2 Expressing rates in terms of concentration changes
You may be expected to express the rate of reaction in terms of change of concentration of any reactant or product with time. (Learning Objective 14-1:4) Basically, this makes use of the general reaction

$$aA + bB \longrightarrow cC + dD$$

where the rates in terms of each species are related as follows

$$\text{Rate} = -\frac{1}{a}\frac{d[A]}{dt} = -\frac{1}{b}\frac{d[B]}{dt} = \frac{1}{c}\frac{d[C]}{dt} = \frac{1}{d}\frac{d[D]}{dt}$$

● **EXAMPLE 1**   **Problem:** Write an expression which symbolizes the rate of the following reaction in terms of each species in the reaction:

$$C_3H_8 + 5\,O_2 \longrightarrow 3CO_2 + 4H_2O$$

Solution: Using the relationship for rates of the general equation as a guide, we can write the required relations. The values of a, b, c, and d are the stoichiometric coefficients from the chemical equation

$$\text{Rate} = -\frac{d\,[C_3H_8]}{dt} = -\frac{1}{5}\frac{d\,[O_2]}{dt} = \frac{1}{3}\frac{d\,[CO_2]}{dt} = \frac{1}{5}\frac{d\,[H_2O]}{dt} \;\bullet$$

● **EXAMPLE 2**   **Problem**: The rate in terms of O_2 in the previous example is

$$-\frac{d\,[O_2]}{dt} = 1.2 \times 10^{-4}\ M\,s^{-1}$$

What is the rate in terms of CO_2?

Solution: Using the rate relationships from the previous example we can see

$$-\frac{1}{5}\frac{d\,[O_2]}{dt} = \frac{1}{3}\frac{d\,[CO_2]}{dt}$$

Solving for $d\,[CO_2]/dt$ and substituting the value given for O_2, we find

$$\frac{d\,[CO_2]}{dt} = -\frac{3}{5}(-1.2 \times 10^{-4}\ M\,s^{-1}) = 7.2 \times 10^{-5}\ M\,s^{-1} \;\bullet$$

Problems 14-3, 14-5, and 14-6 in the text are similar.

14-2
The rate law

1 Determining the order of a reaction by the method of initial rates
Experimentally, we measure how concentration changes with time. In Sec. 14-1 we used these experimental measurements to determine rates. In this section we will go one step further by using rates to find the order of a reaction. One technique for doing this is the method of initial rates. The initial rates of several experiments are determined as shown in Fig. 14-2 in the text. If the experiments are arranged so the initial concentrations increase in a regular manner, the order can often be determined by inspection of the data.

● **EXAMPLE 3**   **Problem**: A set of experiments was run for the reaction $A + B \rightarrow C$. Initial rates were determined for each experiment as follows:

Experiment	Initial [A], M	Initial [B], M	Initial rate, $M\,s^{-1}$
1	1.0	1.0	2.0×10^{-3}
2	2.0	1.0	4.0×10^{-3}
3	2.0	2.0	16.0×10^{-3}

Determine the order of reaction for each reactant and the overall order.

Solution: The rate law for the reaction must take the general form

$$\text{Rate} = k\,[A]^x[B]^y$$

The experiments were designed so each reactant could be studied separately. In experiments 1 and 2, [B] is held constant so the change in rate is due only to [A]. As [A] doubles, the rate doubles. They are directly proportional so $x = 1$ and the reaction is first order with respect to A. In experiments 2 and 3, [A] is held constant so the change in rate is due only to [B]. As [B] doubles, the rate increases fourfold; thus $y = 2$, since $4 = 2^2$, and the reaction is second order with repsect to B and third order overall. When the experimental data are not arranged so conveniently, a more quantitative approach may be necessary. ●

● **EXAMPLE 4**   **Problem**: Write the rate law for the reaction $A + B \rightarrow C$ from the following initial rate data:

Experiment	Initial [A], M	Initial [B], M	Initial rate, $M\,s^{-1}$
1	0.734	0.0171	1.23×10^{-3}
2	0.734	0.0233	1.44×10^{-3}
3	0.304	0.0233	3.84×10^{-4}

Solution: Simple proportionalities cannot be readily seen in these data so we will use a quantitative approach. The rate law is of the general form

$$\text{Rate} = k\,[A]^x\,[B]^y$$

We need to determine numerical values of k, x, and y to write the rate law. There are three unknowns and we can write three equations from the experimental data to find values of k, x, and y. Substituting the experimental data into the general form of the rate law gives

Experiment 1: $\text{Rate}_1 = 1.23 \times 10^{-3} = k(0.734)^x(0.0170)^y$

Experiment 2: $\text{Rate}_2 = 1.44 \times 10^{-3} = k(0.734)^x(0.0233)^y$

Experiment 3: $\text{Rate}_3 = 3.84 \times 10^{-4} = k(0.304)^x(0.0233)^y$

Dividing the equation for experiment 1 by the equation for experiment 2 gives

$$\frac{1.23 \times 10^{-3}}{1.44 \times 10^{-3}} = \frac{k(0.0734)^x(0.0170)^y}{k(0.0734)^x(0.0233)^y}$$

This simplifies to

$$0.854 = (0.730)^y$$

Now take logarithms of both sides:

$$\log 0.854 = y \log 0.730$$

$$y = \frac{\log 0.854}{\log 0.730} = \frac{-0.0685}{-0.137} = 0.500$$

So the reaction is 0.5 order in B. We can use experiments 2 and 3 in the same manner to find x. Divide the equation for experiment 2 by the equation for experiment 3.

$$\frac{1.44 \times 10^{-3}}{3.84 \times 10^{-4}} = \frac{k(0.734)^x(0.0233)^y}{k(0.304)^x(0.0233)^y}$$

This simplifies to

$$3.75 = (2.41)^x$$

Take logarithms of both sides:

$$\log 3.75 = x \log 2.41$$

$$x = \frac{\log 3.75}{\log 2.41} = \frac{0.574}{0.383} = 1.50$$

The reaction is 1.5 order in A.

We can use the values of x and y in any of the rate equations to find k. Using the rate equation for experiment 3

$$3.84 \times 10^{-4} \, M \, s^{-1} = k(0.304 \, M)^{1.5}(0.0233 \, M)^{0.5}$$

Solving for k

$$k = \frac{3.84 \times 10^{-4} \, M \, s^{-1}}{(0.304 \, M)^{1.5}(0.0233 \, M)^{0.5}} = \frac{3.84 \times 10^{-4} \, M \, s^{-1}}{0.168 \, M^{1.5}(0.153 \, M^{0.5})} = 0.0149 \, M^{-1} \, s^{-1}$$

The complete rate law is

$$\text{Rate} = 0.0149 \, M^{-1} \, s^{-1} \, [A]^{1.5}[B]^{0.5} \quad \bullet$$

Now work through Example 14-1 in the text. For additional practice try Probs. 14-15 to 14-19 in the text.

2 Determination of order of a reaction by graphical methods

When it is suspected that a reaction is zero, first, or second order, we can test the experimental data directly, without determining rates, by a graphical technique. A linear plot of concentration versus time shows the reaction is zero order. When the logarithm of concentration is plotted against time and a straight line is obtained, the reaction is first order. If a straight line is obtained by plotting $1/[A]$ versus time, the reaction must be second order. For any given reaction only one of these plots can result in a straight line; the others must be curved. Figure 14-3 in the text shows a straight-line plot of a first-order reaction, while Fig. 14-4 is a linear plot of a second-order reaction. In each case the specific rate constant is found from the slope of the graph. Example 14-2 in the text illustrates this technique. Problem 14-20 in the text is designed to give further practice in using this method of determining order of reaction.

3 Half-life

The half-life of a reaction is the time it takes the concentration to decrease to half its initial values:

$$t_{1/2} = \frac{0.693}{k_1} \qquad \text{for a first-order reaction}$$

$$t_{1/2} = \frac{1}{k_2 [A]_0} \qquad \text{for a second-order reaction}$$

$$t_{1/2} = \frac{[A]_0}{2k_0} \qquad \text{for a zero-order reaction}$$

● **EXAMPLE 5**   **Problem:** The specific rate constant for the first-order reaction A → B + C is 0.0375 s^{-1} at 25°C. (a) What is the half-life of the reaction? (b) How long would it take the concentration of A to decrease from an initial value of 0.800 M to 0.100 M?

Solution: (a) The half-life of a first-order reaction is

$$t_{1/2} = \frac{0.693}{k_1}$$

Substituting the value for k gives

$$t_{1/2} = \frac{0.693}{0.0375 \ s^{-1}} = 18.5 \ s$$

(b) In going from 0.800 to 0.100 M the concentration is reduced by half three times, so the total time is three half-lives

$$t = 3t_{1/2} = 3(18.5 \ s) = 55.5 \ s \ ●$$

Problems 14-25 to 14-27 in the text will give you practice using half lives.

4 Calculation of concentration of a reactant at any time during a reaction
Mathematical relationships permitting calculations of concentration of reactants at any time during a reaction are developed in the text. (See the Key Equations section of this chapter in the *Study Guide*.) These equations can be used to find the concentration of reactants remaining after a given time has passed if the concentration at time zero, $[A]_0$, and the specific rate constant are known for zero-, first-, or second-order reactions. As usual, any of the variables in these equations can be determined if the rest are given.

● **EXAMPLE 6**   **Problem:** The reaction A → B + C is first order with $k = 3.75 \times 10^{-4} \ s^{-1}$ at 25°C. (a) If the initial concentration of A is 0.500 M, what will be the concentration after 1 h? (b) How long will it take for the concentration of A to decrease from 0.500 to 0.00226 M?

Solution: The equation relating concentration and time for a first-order reaction is

$$\log [A] = \frac{-k_1 t}{2.303} + \log [A]_0$$

We can substitute the given values into this equation and solve for $[A]$

$$\log [A] = \frac{-3.75 \times 10^{-4} \ s^{-1} \ (3600 \ s)}{2.303} + \log 0.500$$

$$= -0.586 + (-0.301) = -0.887$$

$$[A] = 10^{-0.887} = 0.130 \ M$$

(b) Solve the concentration-time equation for first-order reactions for t:

$$t = \frac{2.303}{k_1} \log \frac{[A]_0}{[A]}$$

Substitute the values given and solve for t:

$$t = \frac{2.303}{3.75 \times 10^{-4} \text{ s}^{-1}} \log \frac{0.500}{0.00226}$$

$$= \frac{2.303 \ (2.345)}{3.75 \times 10^{-4} \text{ s}^{-1}} = 1.44 \times 10^4 \text{ s} \quad \text{or} \quad 4.00 \text{ h} \ \bullet$$

Problems 14-28 to 14-30 in the text are similar to this.

14-3 *Determination of E_a and k using the Arrhenius equation*
Collision theory Probably the most useful form of the Arrhenius equation in calculations is

$$\log \frac{k_2}{k_1} = \frac{E_a}{2.303R} \left(\frac{1}{T_1} - \frac{1}{T_2} \right)$$

It can be used to find k_1, k_2, T_1, T_2, or E_a given values for the other four variables. The two most common uses are (1) calculating E_a when the specific rate constant is known at two temperatures and (2) calculating the specific rate constant at some desired temperature when it is given at a different temperature and E_a is known. Example 14-4 in the text uses two values of k in the Arrhenius equation to find E_a. Example 14-3 shows a graphical method for making this kind of calculation. Problems 14-45 and 14-46 in the text can be worked by either method.

• **EXAMPLE 7** **Problem:** A certain reaction has $E_a = 90.0 \text{ kJ mol}^{-1}$. The specific rate constant for this reaction is $4.17 \times 10^{-3} \text{ s}^{-1}$ at 35°C. What is the value of the specific rate constant at 75°C?

Solution: Using the Arrhenius equation we can substitute the given values and solve for k_2:

$$k_1 = 4.17 \times 10^{-3} \text{ s}^{-1}$$

$$T_1 = 35°C + 273 = 308 \text{ K}$$

$$T_2 = 75°C + 273 = 348 \text{ K}$$

$$E_a = 90,000 \text{ J mol}^{-1}$$

$$R = 8.31 \text{ J mol}^{-1} \text{ K}^{-1}$$

$$\log \frac{k_2}{4.17 \times 10^{-3}} = \frac{90,000 \text{ J mol}^{-1}}{2.303 \ (8.31 \text{ J mol}^{-1} \text{ K}^{-1})} \left(\frac{1}{308 \text{ K}} - \frac{1}{348 \text{ K}} \right) = 1.755$$

$$\frac{k_2}{4.17 \times 10^{-3}} = 10^{1.755} = 56.9$$

$$k_2 = 56.9 \ (4.17 \times 10^{-3}) = 0.237 \text{ s}^{-1} \ \bullet$$

Problems 14-39 and 14-40 in the text involve similar calculations.

SELF TEST

True or false   —— 1 Reaction rates can be expressed in terms of reactants but not products.
—— 2 A reaction mechanism for which the rate law is rate = k [A] [B]^2 is always first order in A.
—— 3 If a plot of concentration versus time is linear, the reaction is first order.
—— 4 The order of reaction is the same as the molecularity in a reaction mechanism.
—— 5 In a chemical reaction the steps in a mechanism all proceed simultaneously even though one of them is the slow, rate-determining step.
—— 6 According to the Arrhenius equation, a plot of log k versus T should be linear.

Completion   7 The slope of a tangent to a concentration versus time plot gives the ———————.
8 The units of rate are ———————.
9 The energy of activation can be determined from the slope of a (an) ———————— plot.
10 The unstable, short-lived particle at the top of the energy hill is called the ———— ————————.
11 The energy difference between reactants and the top of the energy hill is called the ————————.
12 A catalyst in the same phase as the reactants is called a (an) ————————.
13 A catalyst ———————— (alters, does not affect) the mechanism of a reaction.

Multiple choice   14 For the homogeneous gas phase reaction $2H_2 + O_2 \rightarrow 2H_2O$, the rate of reaction can be expressed in which of the following ways?

(a) Rate $= -\dfrac{1}{2}\dfrac{d\,[H_2]}{dt} = -\dfrac{1}{2}\dfrac{d\,[H_2O]}{dt}$

(b) Rate $= 2\dfrac{d\,[H_2]}{dt} = \dfrac{d\,[Q_2]}{dt}$

(c) Rate $= -\dfrac{1}{2}\dfrac{d\,[H_2]}{dt} = \dfrac{-d\,[O_2]}{dt}$

(d) Rate $= \dfrac{d\,[O_2]}{dt} = -\dfrac{1}{2}\dfrac{d\,[H_2O]}{dt}$

15 For the reaction $A + B \rightarrow 2C$, when [A] is doubled the rate doubles and when [B] is doubled the rate increases fourfold. The rate law is
(a) Rate = k [A]^2 [B]^4
(b) Rate = k [A] [B]^2
(c) Rate = k [A]
(d) Rate = k [B]^2

16 The following rate data for the reaction $A + B \rightarrow 2C$ were obtained experimentally.

Initial [A], M	Initial [B], M	Initial rate, $M\ s^{-1}$
0.001	0.002	1.5×10^{-4}
0.001	0.004	3.0×10^{-4}
0.002	0.002	6.0×10^{-4}

The rate law for this reaction is
(a) Rate = k [A] [B]^2

(b) Rate = $k[A]^2[B]$

(c) Rate = $k[A][B]$

(d) Rate = $k[A]^2[B]^2$

17 A reaction is known to be first order in A. A straight line will be obtained by plotting

(a) log [A] versus time   (b) log [A] versus reciprocal time

(c) [A] versus time   (d) 1/[A] versus time

18 If the reaction $2A \rightarrow B + C$ is second order, which of the following plots will give a straight line?

(a) $[A]^2$ versus time   (b) log [A] versus time

(c) 1/[A] versus time   (d) [A] versus time

19 A certain reaction is second order in A. When [A] is $0.030\,M$, the rate is 3×10^{-3} $M\,s^{-1}$. The rate when [A] is $0.015\,M$ is:

(a) $7.5 \times 10^{-4}\,M\,s^{-1}$ (b) $1.5 \times 10^{-3}\,M\,s^{-1}$

(c) $0.21\,M\,s^{-1}$ (d) $3.33\,M\,s^{-1}$

20 A certain reaction is first order in A. The specific rate constant is $3.0 \times 10^{-3}\,s^{-1}$. The half-life is

(a) $2.1 \times 10^{-3}\,s$ (b) 100 s   (c) 231 s   (d) 768 s

21 A certain reaction is first order in [A]. In 30 min [A] decreases from 0.55 to $0.15\,M$. How many minutes will it take for [A] to decrease from 0.35 to $0.15\,M$?

(a) 10.4   (b) 19.1   (c) 19.6   (d) 45.1

22 For the reaction in Prob. 21, if the initial concentration of A is $0.75\,M$, what will its concentration be after 1 h?

(a) $4.1 \times 10^{-2}\,M$ (b) $5.6 \times 10^{-2}\,M$ (c) $0.10\,M$ (d) $0.35\,M$

23 The activation energy of a reaction can be obtained from the slope of a plot of

(a) log k versus $1/T$ (b) log k versus T

(c) k versus log T (d) k versus log $1/T$

24 A certain reaction has $E_a = 125$ kJ mol^{-1}. The specific rate constant is $0.033\,s^{-1}$ at 55°C. What is the value of the specific rate constant at 100°C?

(a) $1.3 \times 10^{-4}\,s^{-1}$ (b) $0.037\,s^{-1}$ (c) $0.088\,s^{-1}$ (d) $8.3\,s^{-1}$

25 A certain reaction has specific rate constant of $4.27 \times 10^{-3}\,s^{-1}$ at 25°C and $7.35 \times 10^{-2}\,s^{-1}$ at 80°C. What is the energy of activation in kilojoules per mole?

(a) 5.44   (b) 45.2   (c) 104   (d) 860

15

CHEMICAL EQUILIBRIUM

CHAPTER OVERVIEW

**15-1
Homogeneous
chemical
equilibrium**

The use of an arrow ($\longrightarrow$) in chemical equations discussed so far in the text may have given you the impression that chemical reactions proceed until all the reactants have been converted to products. This is not true. Actually, all chemical reactions proceed in the forward direction (reactants forming products) and also in the reverse direction (products decomposing into reactants). They are called reversible reactions and should be denoted by a double arrow ($\rightleftharpoons$) or an equal sign. When the rate of the forward reaction equals the rate of the reverse reaction there is no net change in concentration and the reaction is said to be at equilibrium. Figure 15-1 in the text illustrates how the concentrations of reactants and products approach equilibrium in a general case.

Figure 15-2 shows how equilibrium can be approached from either direction.

If only a few molecules of reactants remain at equilibrium the reaction is said to "go to completion." Reactions which essentially go to completion include those in which an insoluble substance or a weak electrolyte is formed. Figure 15-3 in the text shows how a chemical reaction can be taken to completion by removing products as they are formed. Note how Le Châtelier's principle predicts what will happen as the equilibrium is stressed by changing the concentration of reactants or products in Fig. 15-3. Pay close attention to the concepts "shift to the right" and "shift to the left;" these are common terms used to describe changes in systems at equilibrium. "Stresses" on a system at equilibrium are changes in temperature, pressure, volume, or concentration of products or reactants. Changes in pressure or volume affect only gas-phase reactions in which the stoichiometric number of moles of reactants is different from the number of moles of products as indicated by the balanced chemical equation. An increase in pressure shifts the reaction toward the side of the equation having fewer moles of gaseous molecules because the increase in pressure is relieved by reducing the number of moles in a given volume. A decrease in volume has the same effect as an increase in pressure.

**15-2
The law of
chemical
equilibrium**

At any given temperature the mass-action expression can be equal to any numerical value depending on how closely the reaction has approached equilibrium. However, since there is only one equilibrium state possible under a given set of conditions, the equilibrium constant has only one value at a given temperature. It is *only* at equilibrium that $Q = K$. In the next few chapters we apply equilibrium concepts to several types of reactions. Different names will be given to the equilibrium constant depending on the type of reaction considered, but the basic concepts involved are presented in this chapter. Getting a good understanding of equilibrium now will form a strong foundation for work ahead. K_c is the main equilibrium constant you will use, but be familiar with its close relative K_P. Notice that when the number of moles of gaseous products and reactants are equal, $\Delta n = 0$ and $K_c = K_P$.

The equilibrium constant of a reaction is closely related to the specific rate constants of the forward and reverse reactions, as the equation $K = k_f/k_r$ signifies.

A very useful relation is the expression giving the equilibrium constant in terms of the concentration of reactants and products, often called the law of equilibrium. For the reaction $a\mathrm{A} + b\mathrm{B} \rightleftharpoons c\mathrm{C} + d\mathrm{D}$, the equilibrium constant expression is

$$K = \frac{[\mathrm{C}]^c [\mathrm{D}]^d}{[\mathrm{A}]^a [\mathrm{B}]^b}$$

Get used to the idea of products in the numerator of the equation and reactants in the denominator, usually called "products over reactants." We will see it often.

The same expression for K can be obtained by equating the forward and reverse rate equations, but no matter how you arrive at K, it has only one value at any given temperature. As the text explains, units on K are usually omitted. Notice how the magnitude of K tells how far the reaction has proceeded at equilibrium. If K is much greater than unity, the amount of products will be greater than the amount of reactants in the equilibrium mixture. If K is much less than unity, the amounts of reactants will be greater, so the magnitude of K gives us an idea of how far the reaction proceeds to "completion."

The mass-action quotient Q takes the same form as the expression for K but describes a reaction that is not at equilibrium, so Q is not constant. If Q is less than K, the reaction proceeds towards products to get to equilibrium. If Q is greater than K, more reactants are formed from products (reverse reaction) to get to equilibrium. Again we emphasize that only at equilibrium does $Q = K$.

It is important to remember that K depends on temperature so you should always give the temperature for any numerical value of K to avoid confusion. The van't Hoff equation is used to calculate K at any given temperature when the standard heat of reaction and K at a different temperature are known.

15-3
Equilibrium calculations

There are several types of calculations that can be made in conjunction with equilibrium constants. We will consider them in detail in the New Skills section.

KEY EQUATIONS

15-2
The law of chemical equilibrium

For the general equation $a\mathrm{A} + b\mathrm{B} \rightleftharpoons c\mathrm{C} + d\mathrm{D}$, the equilibrium constant expression is

$$K_c = \frac{[\mathrm{C}]^c [\mathrm{D}]^d}{[\mathrm{A}]^a [\mathrm{B}]^b}$$

In terms of pressure units

$$K_P = \frac{(P_C)^c (P_D)^d}{(P_A)^a (P_B)^b}$$

The two constants are related by

$$K_P = K_c(RT)^{\Delta n}$$

The effect of temperature on K_P is given by the van't Hoff equation

$$\log \frac{(K_P)_1}{(K_P)_2} = \frac{-\Delta H°}{2.303R} \left(\frac{1}{T_1} - \frac{1}{T_2} \right)$$

where $\Delta H°$ is the standard heat of reaction.

LEARNING OBJECTIVES

As a result of studying Chap. 15 you should be able to do the following:
Write the definition and give an example illustrating the use of each key term.

15-1
Homogeneous
chemic
equilibrium

1 Understand that all chemical reactions are reversible.
2 Explain why the rate of the forward reaction decreases and the rate of the reverse reaction increases when reactants are converted to products as a reaction approaches equilibrium. (Text Figs. 15-1, 15-2; Text Prob. 15-3)
3 Apply Le Châtelier's principle to predict the response of a system at equilibrium to a change in temperature, pressure, or concentration. (Text Probs. 15-4, 15-6 to 15-12) (New Skills Example 1; Self Test 6 to 9, 16 to 18)
4 List the factors that affect the value of K_c. (Self Test 5)

15-2
The law of chemical
equilibrium

1 Write expressions for the equilibrium constant and mass-action quotient for a reaction from the balanced chemical equation. (Text Probs. 15-14 to 15-16) (New Skills Examples 2, 3; Self Test 13)
2 Predict the direction a reaction will move to achieve equilibrium from the relative magnitudes of Q and K. (Text Example 15-2; Text Probs. 15-17 to 15-20) (New Skills Example 4; Self Test 1, 2, 15)
3 Calculate K_c from K_P or K_P from K_c. (Text Example 15-1; Text Probs. 15-21 to 15-24, 15-45) (Self Test 10, 14)
4 Understand how K_c is related to the specific rate constants of the forward and reverse reactions.
5 Calculate K_P at any temperature using the van't Hoff equation when K_P at one temperature and the standard heat of reaction are given. (Text Probs. 15-25 to 15-27) (New Skills Example 5; Self Test 19)
6 Calculate $\Delta H°$ using the van't Hoff equation given K_P at two temperatures. (Text Example 15-3; Text Probs. 15-28, 15-29)

15-3
Equilibrium
calculations

1 Calculate the value of K_c or K_P given equilibrium concentrations of all substances in a reaction. (Text Example 15-4) (New Skills Example 6; Self Test 11, 20)
2 Calculate the equilibrium concentration of a substance given the value of K_c and the concentration of other substances in the reaction at equilibrium. (Text Example 15-5; Text Probs. 15-30, 15-37) (New Skills Example 7; Self Test 12, 21)

3 Calculate the equilibrium concentration of all substances in a chemical reaction given the value of K_c and the initial concentration of reacting substances. (Text Examples 15-6 to 15-8; Text Probs. 15-31, 15-33 to 15-44, 15-46, 15-47) (New Skills Example 8; Self Test 22 to 25)

NEW SKILLS

15-1
Homogeneous chemical equilibrium

Using Le Châtelier's principle to predict the effect of a change on a system at equilibrium

According to Le Châtelier's principle, when a system at equilibrium is subjected to a stress or change in temperature, volume, pressure, or concentration of one of the substances, the system will shift to relieve that stress. The text considers concentration stresses on the $N_2 + 3H_2 \rightleftharpoons 2NH_3$ system in detail. Let us consider another example.

● **EXAMPLE 1**

Problem: The system

$$4NH_3(g) + 7\,O_2(g) \rightleftharpoons 4NO_2(g) + 6H_2O(l)$$

is initially at equilibrium. Predict the effect, if any, of each of the following changes on the equilibrium, using Le Châtelier's principle. $\Delta H°$ for the reaction is negative. (a) Increasing the pressure. (b) Increasing the volume. (c) Adding 1 mol of NH_3. (d) Adding 1 mol of NO_2. (e) Increasing the temperature.

Solution: According to Le Châtelier's principle the system will shift to reduce the stress which is applied.

(a) Increasing the pressure puts a stress on the side of the reactants with the most gaseous molecules. In this case there are 11 mol of gaseous reactants and only 4 mol of gaseous products. The reaction moves to the side with fewer gaseous molecules to relieve the pressure increase. This is a shift to the right.

(b) Increasing the volume is the opposite of increasing the pressure, so following the reasoning of part (a) there would be a shift to the left.

(c) Adding reactants puts a stress on the reactant side. The system reacts to relieve this stress by converting some of the reactants to products, resulting in a shift to the right.

(d) Adding products puts a stress on the product side, resulting in a shift to the left.

(e) Since $\Delta H°$ is negative the reaction is exothermic and we can think of heat as a product. Increasing the temperature puts a stress on the product side which is generating heat. This is relieved by a shift to the left. ●

15-2
The law of chemical equilibrium

1 Writing equilibrium expressions

You must be able to write and interpret correct chemical equilibrium expressions from a balanced chemical equation. It will be helpful if you understand the following guidelines:

1 The equilibrium expression is always the products over the reactants, with each term raised to the power indicated by its coefficient in the balanced overall equation.
2 If all the coefficients of a chemical equation are multiplied by 2, the equilibrium constant must be squared.
3 If a chemical equation is reversed, the new equilibrium constant and expression are the reciprocal of the original.

4 If two chemical equations are added, the equilibrium constant is the product of the
   K's of the added reactions.
5 Concentrations of pure liquids or solids such as $H_2O(l)$, $Hg(l)$, $Br_2(l)$, and $CaCO_3(s)$
   are not included in equilibrium expressions.

● **EXAMPLE 2**   **Problem:** Write the equilibrium condition or equilibrium expression for the Ostwald
reaction given in Example 1.

Solution: Always be certain the equation is balanced before you write the equilibrium
expression. The expression is always products over reactants, each to the power indicated by its coefficient in the chemical equation.

$$K_c = \frac{[NO_2]^4}{[NH_3]^4[O_2]^7}$$

H_2O does not appear in the expression because it is present as a pure liquid. ●

● **EXAMPLE 3**   **Problem:** Write the equilibrium expression for the pressure equilibrium constant for
the reaction

$$CaCO_3(s) \rightleftharpoons CaO(s) + CO_2(g)$$

Solution:

$$K_P = P_{CO_2}$$

$CaCO_3$ and CaO are both solids so are not included in the equilibrium expression. For
this reaction the equilibrium expression is just the partial pressure of CO_2 above the
solids. What would be the equilibrium expression for the concentration equilibrium
constant? ●

2 Using the mass-action expression to predict changes in systems not at equilibrium
The magnitude of the mass-action quotient can be compared to the value of K to determine which way a system will move to attain equilibrium.

1 If $Q < K$, more products will be formed until $Q = K$.
2 If $Q > K$, more reactants will be formed from products until $Q = K$.
3 If $Q = K$, the system is at equilibrium.

We can illustrate the use of Q to see how a system will react to attain equilibrium with
an example.

● **EXAMPLE 4**   **Problem:** For a certain reaction at 25°C the mass-action quotient is 0.05. The equilibrium constant at this temperature is 125. Predict which direction the reaction will
move to attain equilibrium.

Solution: For the reaction not at equilibrium

$$Q = \frac{[products]}{[reactants]} = 0.05$$

For the reaction at equilibrium

$$K = \frac{[\text{products}]}{[\text{reactants}]} = 125$$

Since Q is less than K, the reaction will move to increase Q by increasing products and reducing reactants. This is called a shift to the right or a shift to the products. This shift will continue until Q has increased enough to be equal to K. When $Q = K$ there will be no further reaction. ●

Example 15-2 in the text illustrates how to calculate Q from given concentrations.

3 The relationship between K_c and K_P

Equilibrium conditions can be expressed in terms of molarity or, in the case of gases, of partial pressures of the gases. The text shows these equilibrium constants are related by the equation.

$$K_P = K_c (RT)^{\Delta n}$$

where K_P = pressure equilibrium constant
$\quad K_c$ = concentration equilibrium constant
$\quad R$ = ideal-gas constant = 0.082 liter atm mol^{-1} K^{-1}
$\quad T$ = temperature in kelvins
$\quad \Delta n$ = moles of gaseous products – moles of gaseous reactants and is determined
$\qquad$ from the balanced chemical equation

Example 15-1 in the text illustrates the calculation of K_P from K_c.

4 The effect of temperature on K, the van't Hoff equation

The effect of temperature on the equilibrium constant of gas-phase reactions is given by the van't Hoff equation

$$\log \frac{(K_P)_1}{(K_P)_2} = \frac{-\Delta H°}{2.303R} \left(\frac{1}{T_1} - \frac{1}{T_2} \right)$$

This form of equation should be familiar by now (recall the Clausius-Clapeyron equation and the equation for E_a). As usual, any variable in the equation can be calculated if the others are known. Generally we want to determine K_P at some temperature different than the given values.

● **EXAMPLE 5**   **Problem:** The pressure equilibrium constant for a certain reaction at 25°C is 1.7×10^{-4} and its standard heat of reaction is 70 kJ mol^{-1}. What is the value of K_P at 100°C?

Solution: Substitute the given values into the van't Hoff equation and solve for $(K_P)_2$

$$(K_P)_1 = 1.7 \times 10^{-4}$$

$$T_1 = 25°C + 273 = 298 \text{ K}$$

$$T_2 = 100°C + 273 = 373 \text{ K}$$

$$\Delta H° = 70,000 \text{ J mol}^{-1}$$

$$R = 0.082 \text{ J mol}^{-1} \text{ K}^{-1}$$

$$\log \frac{1.7 \times 10^{-4}}{(K_P)_2} = \frac{-70,000 \text{ J mol}^{-1}}{2.303 \ (8.31 \text{ J mol}^{-1} \text{ K}^{-1})} \left(\frac{1}{298 \text{ K}} - \frac{1}{373 \text{ K}}\right)$$

$$\log \frac{1.7 \times 10^{-4}}{(K_P)_2} = -2.47$$

Taking antilogarithms and solving for $(K_P)_2$

$$\frac{1.7 \times 10^{-4}}{(K_P)_2} = 10^{-2.47} = 3.39 \times 10^{-3}$$

$$(K_P)_2 = \frac{1.7 \times 10^{-4}}{3.39 \times 10^{-3}} = 0.050 \quad \bullet$$

15-3

Equilibrium
calculations

1 General approach

Most equilibrium calculations can be approached in a general manner. The following guidelines will help you organize the data given to find the desired answer.

1 Write a balanced chemical equation for the reaction.
2 Write the equilibrium condition or expression for the reaction.
3 Prepare a table showing the given data and any changes from the initial conditions.
4 Calculate equilibrium concentrations in terms of the changes as far as possible.
5 Substitute equilibrium concentrations into the equilibrium expression and solve for the unknown quantity.
6 Be sure the unknown quantity is in the same units as requested by the problem.

We will illustrate the application of these guidelines to several types of equilibrium calculations.

2 Calculating K from equilibrium concentrations

● **EXAMPLE 6**   **Problem:** For the reaction

$$A(g) + 2B(g) \rightleftharpoons 4C(g) + 3D(g)$$

it was found that an equilibrium mixture in a 2-liter vessel contained 0.50 mol of A, 1.70 mol of B, 1.90 mol of C, and 2.30 mol of D at 25°C. Calculate the value of the equilibrium constant at 25°C.

Solution: We will apply the calculation guidelines. The chemical equation is already balanced so the equilibrium expression is

$$K_c = \frac{[C]^4 \, [D]^3}{[A] \, [B]^2}$$

Since we are given equilibrium amounts we can omit guidelines (3) and (4) and proceed to (5). The equilibrium concentrations are

$$[A] = 0.5 \text{ mol/2 liters} = 0.25 \text{ mol liter}^{-1} = 0.25 \ M$$

$$[B] = 1.70 \text{ mol/2 liters} = 0.85 \text{ mol liter}^{-1} = 0.85 \ M$$

$$[C] = 1.90 \text{ mol/2 liters} = 0.95 \text{ mol liter}^{-1} = 0.95 \ M$$

$$[D] = 2.30 \text{ mol/2 liters} = 1.15 \text{ mol liter}^{-1} = 1.15 \ M$$

Substitute these values into the equilibrium expression and solve for K_c

$$K_c = \frac{(0.95)^4 (1.15)^3}{(0.25)(0.85)^2} = \frac{(0.81)(1.52)}{(0.25)(0.72)} = 6.8 \bullet$$

Now work Example 15-4 in the text.

3 Calculating the equilibrium concentration of one substance when given the value of K and equilibrium concentrations of other substances in the reaction

• **EXAMPLE 7**   **Problem:** For the reaction $A + 2B \rightleftharpoons 3C$ an equilibrium mixture in a 2.00-liter vessel at 25°C contained 0.750 mol of A and 0.350 mol of B. How many moles of C were in the vessel? K_c for the reaction is 9.00 at 25°C.

Solution: We will apply the guidelines for equilibrium calculations. The equilibrium expression for the reaction is

$$K_c = \frac{[C]^3}{[A][B]^2}$$

We can omit steps (3) and (4) because equilibrium concentrations are already given, so we proceed directly to step (5).

$$K_c = 9.0$$

$$[A] = 0.750 \text{ mol}/2.00 \text{ liters} = 0.375 \text{ mol liter}^{-1}$$

$$[B] = 0.350 \text{ mol}/2.00 \text{ liters} = 0.175 \text{ mol liter}^{-1}$$

Solve the equilibrium expression for [C] and substitute the required values

$$[C]^3 = K_c [A][B]^2 = 9.00(0.375)(0.175)^2 = 0.103 \text{ mol}^3/\text{liter}^{-3}$$

$$[C] = (0.103)^{1/3} = 0.469 \text{ mol liter}^{-1}$$

Step (6) reminds us to check the problem to be sure we have answered the question asked. We calculated the concentration of C to be 0.469 mol liter^{-1}. The total number of moles of C in the reaction vessel is

$$\text{Mol C} = [C] \text{ (volume of vessel)} = (0.469)(2.00 \text{ liters}) = 0.939 \text{ mol} \bullet$$

Example 15-5 in the text is a similar problem.

4 Calculating the equilibrium concentration of any substance given the value of K and the initial concentrations or amounts of substances reacting

In calculations of this type we need to use stoichiometric methods to determine equilibrium concentrations from initial concentrations. This can be done conveniently using a tabular method for calculations as illustrated in the following example.

• **EXAMPLE 8**   **Problem:** For the reaction $A + B \rightleftharpoons 2C$ the value of K_c at 35°C is 16.0. Calculate the equilibrium concentrations of A, B, and C at 35°C if 2 mol of A and 2 mol of B are mixed in a 1-liter container and allowed to reach equilibrium.

Solution: The equilibrium expression for the balanced chemical equation is

$$K = \frac{[C]^2}{[A][B]}$$

We will use the stoichiometry of the chemical equation to determine the changes in concentration that take place as the system reaches equilibrium. Let x equal the number of moles of C formed during the reaction. According to stoichiometry, the number of moles of A reacted is

$$x \text{ mol C}\left(\frac{1 \text{ mol A}}{2 \text{ mol C}}\right) = \tfrac{1}{2}x$$

and the number of moles of B reacted is

$$x \text{ mol C}\left(\frac{1 \text{ mol B}}{1 \text{ mol C}}\right) = \tfrac{1}{2}x$$

These facts can readily be shown in tabular form and can be used to calculate equilibrium concentrations using the law of conservation of mass.

Amount present at equilibrium = amount present initially + change due to reaction

Substance	Initial amount, mol liter^{-1}	Change, mol liter^{-1}	Equilibrium amount, mol liter^{-1}
A	2	$-\tfrac{1}{2}x$	$2 - \tfrac{1}{2}x$
B	2	$-\tfrac{1}{2}x$	$2 - \tfrac{1}{2}x$
C	0	$+x$	x

The negative changes for A and B show that their concentrations were reduced during the reaction. Since [C] increases during reaction, its change is positive. Now we can apply guideline (5) by substituting the equilibrium concentrations in terms of the variable x into the equilibrium expression.

$$K_c = 16.0 = \frac{x^2}{(2 - \tfrac{1}{2}x)(2 - \tfrac{1}{2}x)}$$

We can take the square root of each side of the equation and solve for x

$$4.0 = \frac{x}{(2 - \tfrac{1}{2}x)}$$

$$x = 2.67 \text{ mol}$$

Therefore, the equilibrium concentrations are

$$[A] = 2 - \tfrac{1}{2}x = 2 - \tfrac{1}{2}(2.67) = 0.665 \text{ mol liter}^{-1}$$

$$[B] = 2 - \tfrac{1}{2}x = 2 - \tfrac{1}{2}(2.67) = 0.665 \text{ mol liter}^{-1}$$

$$[C] = x = 2.67 \text{ mol liter}^{-1} \quad \bullet$$

Example 15-6 in the text is a similar problem. If you have trouble following the reasoning involved in determining the concentration changes, try the tabular approach to calculations. Examples 15-7 and 15-8 in the text are very similar to Example 15-6 except that it is more difficult to solve the equations for x. Usually the simplifying assumptions used in Example 15-8 can be used to make the calculations easier.

SELF TEST

True or false
___ 1 At any given temperature the value for the mass-action expression for a given reaction at equilibrium is a constant.
___ 2 If the mass-action quotient is smaller than the equilibrium constant, the reaction will shift to the left.
___ 3 Equilibrium expressions do not apply to heterogeneous equilibria.
___ 4 If the equilibrium constant is greater than unity we are sure that there are more products present at equilibrium than reactants.
___ 5 If a reaction is exothermic K_c must increase as temperature is increased.

Completion The reaction $N_2(g) + 3H_2(g) \rightleftharpoons 2NH_3(g)$ applies to questions 6 to 9.

6 Adding N_2 will shift an equilibrium mixture to the _____ (right, left).
7 Removing H_2 will shift an equilibrium mixture to the _____ (right, left).
8 Increasing the pressure will shift an equilibrium mixture to the _____ (right, left).
9 The reaction is exothermic so increasing the temperature will shift an equilibrium mixture to the _____ (right, left).
10 K_P is equal to K_c if Δn is equal to _____.
11 If the equilibrium concentrations for the reaction $A + 2B \rightleftharpoons 3C$ are $[A] = 2.0\,M$, $[B] = 2.0\,M$, and $[C] = 3.0\,M$, the value of the equilibrium constant is _____.
12 If the equilibrium constant for the reaction $A + B \rightleftharpoons 2C$ is 8.0, the equilibrium concentration of A in equilibrium with $[B] = 2.5\,M$ and $[C] = 5.0\,M$ is _____.

Multiple choice
13 The correct equilibrium expression for the reaction $CaCO_3(s) \rightleftharpoons CaO(s) + CO_2(g)$ is

(a) $K_c = \dfrac{[CaO][CO_2]}{[CaCO_3]}$ (b) $K_c = \dfrac{[CaCO_3]}{[CaO][CO_2]}$

(c) $K_c = [CO_2]$ (d) $K_c = \dfrac{[CaO]}{[CaCO_3]}$

14 K_c for the reaction $A(g) + B(g) \rightleftharpoons 2C(g)$ is 16.0 at 25°C. What is K_P at this temperature?
(a) 2.56×10^{-3} (b) 6.25×10^{-2} (c) 16.0   (d) 391

15 A certain reaction $A(g) + B(g) \rightleftharpoons 2C(g)$ has $K = 9.0$ at 35°C. If $[A] = 2\,M$, $[B] = 4\,M$, and $[C] = 1.5\,M$, which of the following is true for the mixture?
(a) It will shift to the left.   (b) It will shift to the right.
(c) More A is needed to achieve equilibrium.   (d) The reaction is at equilibrium.

Questions 16 to 18 refer to the equilibrium reaction

$$N_2(g) + 3H_2(g) \rightleftharpoons 2NH_3(g) \qquad \Delta H° = -92.2 \text{ kJ}$$

16 The concentration of NH_3 at equilibrium will increase if
(a) the temperature is increased   (b) N_2 is added
(c) N_2 is removed   (d) an inert gas is added

17 The concentration of H_2 at equilibrium will increase if
(a) the pressure is increased   (b) N_2 is added
(c) NH_3 is removed   (d) the temperature is increased

18 The reaction will go to completion if
(a) the temperature is increased   (b) N_2 is removed
(c) NH_3 is removed   (d) N_2 is added

19 A certain reaction $A(g) + B(g) \rightleftharpoons C(g)$ has $K_P = 2.0$ at $25°C$ and $\Delta H° = -100$ kJ. What is the value of K_P at $100°C$?
(a) 5.96×10^{-4} (b) 0.596 (c) 0.888 (d) 1.39

20 For the gas-phase reaction $2A + B \rightleftharpoons 2C$, equilibrium measurements show $[A] = 0.250\ M$, $[B] = 0.300\ M$, and $[C] = 0.210\ M$. What is the value of K_c under these conditions?
(a) 0.425 (b) 2.35 (c) 2.80 (d) 4.72

21 For the reaction $CaCO_3(g) \rightleftharpoons CaO(s) + CO_2(g)$ at $700°C$, $K_P = 0.061$. What is the partial pressure of CO_2 in equilibrium with CaO and $CaCO_3$?
(a) 0.061 mmHg   (b) 16.4 mmHg   (c) 0.061 atm   (d) 16.4 atm

22 For the reaction $2C \rightleftharpoons A + B$, $K_c = 2.50$ at $25°C$. What is the concentration of A in equilibrium with $3.00\ M$ C if $[A] = [B]$?
(a) $0.211\ M$ (b) $2.74\ M$ (c) $4.74\ M$ (d) $22.5\ M$

23 For the reaction $A(g) + B(g) \rightleftharpoons C(s)$, $K_P = 4.00$ at $100°C$. What is the partial pressure of A in equilibrium with a system in which the partial pressure of B is 0.50 atm?
(a) 0.50 atm   (b) 1.00 atm   (c) 2.00 atm   (d) 4.00 atm

24 For the reaction $A(g) + B(g) \rightleftharpoons 2C(g)$, $K_c = 49$. What is the equilibrium concentration of C if 2.00 mol of it are placed in a 1-liter vessel and allow to reach equilibrium?
(a) $0.22\ M$ (b) $0.44\ M$ (c) $1.56\ M$ (d) $1.78\ M$

25 For the reaction $A(g) + B(g) \rightleftharpoons C(g)$, what is the equilibrium concentration of C if we start with $[A] = 1.00\ M$, $[B] = 2.00\ M$, $[C] = 0$, and $K_c = 1.00 \times 10^{-5}$?
(a) $1.00 \times 10^{-5}\ M$ (b) $2.00 \times 10^{-5}\ M$ (c) $4.47 \times 10^{-3}\ M$ (d) $2.00\ M$

16

AQUEOUS-SOLUTIONS: ACID-BASE EQUILIBRIA

CHAPTER OVERVIEW

16-1
The dissociation of weak acids

A large part of this chapter is the application of equilibrium concepts from Chap. 15 to acids and bases. In Chap. 12 we calculated the degree of dissociation of weak acids. This section investigates the concept of dissociation of weak acids from an equilibrium viewpoint. The concepts are all familiar but some new terms are introduced. The equilibrium constant for the dissociation reaction of a weak acid in aqueous solution is called an acid dissociation constant, K_a, but it is no different than the equilibrium constants of Chap. 15. Since it applies to a special process it is given a special name.

The magnitude of K_a reveals the strength of the acid. Strong acids dissociate completely so the equilibrium is shifted far to the right in the chemical equation, making K_a very large. In weak acids the amount of dissociation is small, so the equilibrium is shifted to the left and K_a is also small. Table 16-1 in the text shows K_a values for a few weak acids. The favorite weak acid of most instructors is acetic acid, so you should become especially familiar with its dissociation reaction. Polyprotic acids are very similar to monoprotic acids except that their dissociation occurs in steps and so is a little more complex to analyze. Usually we neglect all but one dissociation step to simplify the calculations involved.

The percent dissociation of weak acids increases as they become more dilute. However, the dilution reduces the concentration of H^+ so the more dilute solutions are less acidic even though the dissociation is higher.

16-2
The dissociation of weak bases

Strong bases are completely dissociated in water. All of the hydroxides of group IA and group IIA metals except beryllium are strong bases. Transition metal hydroxides, ammonium hydroxide (NH_4OH), and certain organic compounds are weak bases. Ammonium hydroxide is frequently used for illustrations and calculations involving weak bases, so become familiar with its dissociation. Ammonia, ammonia water, aqueous ammonia, and ammonium hydroxide are all names for the same substance: NH_3 dissolved in water. This is often a source of confusion to students in the classroom and laboratory because chemists are apt to use any or all of these names regularly. The dissociation constants of a few weak bases are listed in Table 16-3 in the text.

16-3
The dissociation of
water

Since water is such an important compound and affects the dissociation of acids and bases dissolved in it, we consider its dissociation separately. Again, the equilibrium concepts are the same but there are some new terms. Get a feeling for these terms quickly and this section will not be difficult. pH is probably the chemical term used most often by nonchemists and has very widespread applications. Remember that a pH change of one unit means that the H^+ concentration has changed tenfold. Understanding Table 16-4 is basic to learning the language of acid-base chemistry.

16-4
Hydrolysis

Hydrolysis is another special name for a special reaction, a reaction with water. Anions of weak acids and cations of weak bases undergo hydrolysis. Note how the hydrolysis constant K_h is related to K_a or K_b and K_w. Instructors often assign a problem that is easily solved by the equilibrium expression of the hydrolysis reaction, but give K_a or K_b and expect the student to recognize that K_h must be calculated before the problem can be solved. Careful reading of problems will help you recognize such tricky situations.

Hydrolysis of salts usually results in a solution that is not neutral. Consequently, salts are classified as acidic or basic. The salt of a weak acid and a strong base is basic. The stronger acid or base always determines the acid-base character of the salt.

16-5
Acid-base indicators
and titration

Certain organic compounds are one color in basic solution and a different color in acidic solutions. They are called indicators because their color indicates the acid-base character of the solution. Indicators that change colors at almost any given pH value are available. Universal indicator has several color changes through the range of pH.

An important application of indicators is determining the equivalence point of a titration. Titration is a standard laboratory technique for determining the concentration of acid or base in solutions.

Figures 16-3 and 16-4 in the text show how the pH changes during titration of a strong or weak acid. Care must be taken in selecting the correct indicator for titration of weak acids and weak bases because the pH change is gradual and the equivalence point is not at pH = 7.

16-6
Buffers

A buffer is a solution that resists changing its pH when H^+ or OH^- is added to it. It is always a combination of a weak acid or base and its salt (a conjugate acid-base pair). One compound of the buffer effectively removes H^+ as it is added; the other removes OH^-. Of course, the capacity of a buffer may be swamped by adding more acid or base than the buffer can remove.

In the case of the acetic acid/acetate ion buffer, acetic acid neutralizes OH^- and the acetate ion reacts with H^+.

The Henderson-Hasselbalch equation is a special form of the equilibrium expression for use with buffer solutions.

16-7
Simultaneous
acid-base equilibria

Handling true simultaneous equilibria invoves mathematical equations too complex to present in an introductory course. We will restrict ourselves to situations in which the dissociation constants of simultaneous equilibria are different enough in magnitude so that all but one can be neglected. In essence, we are making justified assumptions to simplify the problem to a single equilibrium expression.

KEY EQUATIONS

16-1
The dissociation of weak acids

The dissociation of weak acids can be represented by the general reaction

$$HA \rightleftharpoons H^+ + A^-$$

for which the equilibrium expression is

$$K_a = \frac{[H^+][A^-]}{[HA]}$$

16-2
The dissociation of weak bases

The dissociation of weak bases can be represented by the general reaction

$$BOH \rightleftharpoons B^+ + OH^-$$

for which the equilibrium expression is

$$K_b = \frac{[B^+][OH^-]}{[BOH]}$$

16-3
The dissociation of water

The equation for the dissociation of water is

$$H_2O \rightleftharpoons H^+ + OH^-$$

for which the equilibrium expression is

$$K_w = [H^+][OH^-] = 1.0 \times 10^{-14}$$

$[H^+]$ is measured by pH

$$pH = -\log[H^+]$$

The acid-base relationship in water is expressed by two equivalent relations

$$[H^+][OH^-] = 1.0 \times 10^{-14}$$

and

$$pH + pOH = 14$$

16-4
Hydrolysis

The hydrolysis of the anion of a weak acid is represented by the general reaction

$$A^- + H_2O \rightleftharpoons HA + OH^-$$

for which the equilibrium expression is

$$K_h = \frac{[HA][OH^-]}{[A^-]}$$

The hydrolysis of the cation of a weak acid is represented by the general reaction

$$B^+ + H_2O \rightleftharpoons BOH + H^+$$

for which the equilibrium expression is

$$K_h = \frac{[BOH][H^+]}{[B^+]}$$

K_h of an anion is related to K_a of the corresponding weak acid by

$$K_w = K_h K_a$$

K_h of a cation is related to K_b of the corresponding weak acid by

$$K_w = K_h K_b$$

In general, K_a and K_b of a conjugate acid-base pair are related by

$$K_w = K_a K_b$$

16-6
Buffers

The Henderson-Hasselbalch equation relates the pH of a buffer to its composition.

$$pH = pK_a - \log \frac{[\text{weak acid}]}{[\text{salt of weak acid}]}$$

LEARNING OBJECTIVES

As a result of studying Chap. 16 you should be able to do the following:
Write the definition and give an example illustrating the use of each key term.

16-1
The dissociation of
weak acids

1 Combine the concepts of weak electrolytes from Chap. 12 and equilibrium from Chap. 15 to understand the dissociation of weak acids and bases.
2 Identify weak acids from their dissociation constant. (Text Table 16-1)
3 Write the dissociation reaction and its equilibrium expression for weak monoprotic and diprotic acids.
4 Calculate K_a for weak acids given equilibrium concentrations of the dissociation species. (Text Probs. 16-18, 16-19) (New Skills Example 1; Self Test 7)
5 Calculate the concentration of each chemical species and the pH of a solution of a weak acid. (Text Examples 16-1, 16-3, 16-5; Text Probs. 16-10 to 16-15, 16-17, 16-49, 16-52)
6 Calculate the percent dissociation of a weak acid. (Text Examples 16-2 to 16-4; Text Prob. 16-16) (Self Test 2)

16-2
The dissociation of
weak bases

1 Identify weak bases from their dissociation constants. (Text Table 16-3)
2 Write the dissociation reaction and its equilibrium expression for weak bases.
3 Calculate the concentration of each chemical species and the pH of a solution of a weak base. (Text Example 16-6; Text Probs. 16-20 to 16-23)
4 Know the different names for a solution of ammonia in water and write the dissociation reaction in terms of NH_3 or NH_4OH.
5 Apply the common-ion effect to calculate concentrations of ions of a weak base. (Text Example 16-7; Text Prob. 16-24)

16-3
The dissociation of
water

1 Explain the dissociation of water in terms of chemical species obtained and their significance in chemistry.
2 Memorize the numerical value of K_w and use it to calculate $[H^+]$ given $[OH^-]$, and vice versa. (Text Examples 16-8, 16-9; Text Probs. 16-3, 16-7) (New Skills Example 2; Self Test 17)

3 Explain what makes a solution acidic, basic, or neutral.

4 Know the definition of pH and solve for pH given $[H^+]$, or vice versa. (Text Examples 16-10, 16-11; Text Probs. 16-1, 16-2) (New Skills Example 3; Self Test 3, 8)

5 Calculate the pH of a solution given $[OH^-]$ and vice versa. (Text Prob. 16-3) (New Skills Examples 4; Self Test 9, 18)

6 Calculate the pH and pOH of strong acids and bases. (Text Examples 16-10, 16-12; Text Probs. 16-4 to 16-7, 16-51, 16-61) (New Skills Example 5; Self Test 8, 9, 19)

16-4
Hydrolysis

1 Write chemical equations and equilibrium expressions for the hydrolysis of the anion of a weak acid and the cation of a weak base. (Text Prob. 16-25) (Self Test 5, 10)

2 Predict whether or not anions and cations hydrolyze in solution. (Text Example 16-13; Text Probs. 16-25)

3 Predict the acidic or basic character of a salt from the strengths of the acid and base from which it is derived. (Text Probs. 16-26) (Self Test 12)

4 Write an equation showing the relationship between K_h for an anion, K_a for its weak acid, and K_w. (Text Probs. 16-30, 16-31) (Self Test 11, 20)

5 Write an equation showing the relationship between K_h for a cation, K_b for its weak base, and K_w.

6 Write an equation showing the relationship between K_a, K_b, and K_w for a conjugate acid-base pair.

7 Calculate the percent hydrolysis of hydrolyzed salts. (Text Example 16-14; Text Prob. 16-29)

8 Calculate the pH of a salt whose ions hydrolyze. (Text Examples 16-14 to 16-16; Text Probs. 16-27, 16-28) (Self Test 16)

9 Calculate K_{diss} given the pH of a hydrolyzed salt. (New Skills Example 6)

16-5
Acid-base indicators and titration

1 Understand how titration is used to determine the concentration of solutions of acids and bases.

2 Understand how indicators are used to determine the equivalence point of a titration and what factors must be considered in choosing an indicator for a given titration. (Text Prob. 16-43)

3 Understand why the equivalence point for the titration of a weak acid or weak base is not necessarily at pH 7.

4 Calculate the pH at the equivalence point for an acid-base titration. (Text Examples 16-17, 16-18; Text Probs. 16-33 to 16-37) (New Skills Example 7; Self Test 13)

5 Calculate the pH at any point on the titration curve of an acid-base titration. (Text Example 16-19; Text Probs. 16-38 to 16-40) (New Skills Examples 8, 9) (Self Test 21)

6 Construct a titration curve. (Text Figs. 16-3 to 16-5; Text Prob. 16-41)

16-6
Buffers

1 Understand how buffers resist change in pH when acid or base is added. (Text Prob. 16-45) (Self Test 23)

2 Use the Henderson-Hasselbalch equation to calculate the pH of a buffer solution or the composition of a buffer of known pH. (Text Example 16-21; Text Probs. 16-44, 16-46, 16-59) (New Skills Examples 10, 11; Self Test 22, 24, 25)

3 Use the Henderson-Hasselbalch equation to determine the change in pH of a buffer solution after the addition of a given quantity of acid or base. (Text Example 16-20; Text Probs. 16-47, 16-48) (New Skills Example 12)

16-7
Simultaneous
acid-base equilibria

1 Make justified assumptions about which dissociation steps can be neglected in calculations involving simultaneous equilibria. (Text Examples 16-22, 16-24)
2 Calculate the total ion concentration of a species involved in simultaneous equilibria. (Text Example 16-23; Text Probs. 16-55 to 16-58, 16-60)
3 Understand what is meant by an acid salt and give examples.

NEW SKILLS

This chapter emphasizes solving equilibrium problems in acid-base reactions. Understanding the examples in the text is basic to solving the problems at the end of the chapter. In most equilibrium problems it is possible to make a justified assumption that will greatly simplify the mathematics and yet not affect the answer. Learn how to recognize when and where to make these assumptions by paying close attention to how they are made in the worked examples. As in previous chapters, we will work problems presenting new concepts in considerable detail the first time, then reduce the detail and discussion as we repeat similar calculations.

16-1
The dissociation of
weak acids

It should become quickly apparent that all equilibrium problems involving weak acids and weak bases are centered around setting up and solving the appropriate equilibrium expression. You should have learned the basic steps in solving equilibrium problems in Chap. 15.

1 Calculation of concentration of species in dissociation of a pure weak acid
To calculate the concentration of all species in a solution, you first need to know what species are involved. Get in the habit of writing the dissociation reaction and corresponding equilibrium expression so the chemistry of the reaction is well defined and understood before you set up the calculations. Notice how this is done in Example 16-1 in the text.

2 Calculation of concentration of species in the dissociation of a weak acid when other
 sources of ions are present (common-ion effect)
There is often another source of ions in the solution in addition to the dissociating acid. This source must also be considered in the equilibrium expression. In the case of acetic acid, $HC_2H_3O_2$, H^+ could also come from a strong acid present in solution and acetate ion could come from a dissolved salt present in addition to the acetic acid. Example 16-3 in the text illustrates the calculation of all species in a solution of acetic acid in the presence of sodium acetate. Acetate ions are common to both substances, so the compounds exhibit a common-ion effect.

Note that in Example 16-1, x represented the concentration of both H^+ and acetate ion at equilibrium, while in Example 16-3, x is only part of the equilibrium concentration of acetate ion but represents all of the H^+. It is important to fully understand the meaning of x in each problem to be able to relate its numerical value to the concentration desired.

It makes sense to always make the assumption that x can be neglected when it is subtracted from a concentration and then check the validity of the assumption by comparing the calculated value of x with the concentration from which it would have been subtracted to see if x is small enough in comparison with the concentration to justify neglecting it. It generally is.

3 Calculation of K_{diss} given the concentration of the weak acid and of the ions formed by its dissociation

Another variation on the equilibrium calculations involving weak acids is solving the equilibrium expression for K_{diss} when the concentration of all species is given or can be determined from the data given.

● **EXAMPLE 1**   **Problem:** In a 0.500 M solution of hydrofluoric acid, HF, it was found that the equilibrium concentration of H^+ was 5.5×10^{-3} M at 25°C. What is the dissociation constant for HF?

Solution: As is the case in all equilibrium calculations, first we need the chemical reaction and corresponding equilibrium expression.

$$HF \rightleftharpoons H^+ + F^-$$

$$K_{diss} = \frac{[H^+][F^-]}{[HF]}$$

According to the chemical equation, the $[F^-]$ must equal the $[H^+]$. $[HF]$ has been reduced by the amount of H^+ produced.

$$[H^+] = 5.6 \times 10^{-3}\ M$$

$$[F^-] = 5.6 \times 10^{-3}\ M$$

$$[HF] = 0.050 - (5.6 \times 10^{-3}) = 0.044\ M$$

Neglecting the amount of HF dissociated would not really simplify the calculations and it is not negligible with respect to the 0.050 M initial concentration.

Since we have equilibrium concentrations we can substitute directly into the equilibrium expression and solve for K_{diss}:

$$K_{diss} = \frac{(5.6 \times 10^{-3})^2}{0.044} = 7.1 \times 10^{-4} \ ●$$

4 Calculation of percent dissociation of a weak acid

We must be given the concentration of weak acid and its dissociation constant (Table 16-1 in the text) to make this calculation. Examples 16-2 and 16-4 in the text show this calculation and illustrate how the percent dissociation changes with concentration of the weak acid.

16-2
The dissociation of
weak bases

Calculations concerning the dissociation of weak bases are approached in exactly the same manner as those for weak acids. The same types of calculations are possible. NH_3 in aqueous solution is by far the most common weak base, and most calculations you make involving weak bases are likely to involve it. Example 16-6 in the text illustrates the method of calculating concentrations of dissolved species and Example 16-7 illustrates the common-ion effect when additional OH^- is present.

16-3
The dissociation of
water

1 Using the ion-product constant of water, K_w, in calculations

The dissociation constant, or ion-product constant, of water is a simple but powerful tool for calculating acid-base concentrations in water solutions.

$$H_2O \rightleftharpoons H^+ + OH^-$$

$$K_w = [\text{H}^+][\text{OH}^-] = 1 \times 10^{-14} \quad \text{at } 25°\text{C}$$

The product of $[\text{H}^+]$ and $[\text{OH}^-]$ is always 1×10^{-14} at $25°\text{C}$ regardless of what other chemical reactions are taking place in the solution. If $[\text{H}^+]$ is known, $[\text{OH}^-]$ can be calculated from K_w; and if $[\text{OH}^-]$ is known, $[\text{H}^+]$ can be determined.

● **EXAMPLE 2**   **Problem:** Calculate $[\text{H}^+]$ in a $0.03\ M$ solution of Sr(OH)_2.

Solution: Sr(OH)_2 is a strong base and completely dissociates in aqueous solution

$$\text{Sr(OH)}_2 \longrightarrow \text{Sr}^{2+} + 2\ \text{OH}^-$$

Since 2 mol of OH^- are obtained for each mole of Sr(OH)_2

$$[\text{OH}^-] = 2[\text{Sr(OH)}_2] = 2(0.03\ M) = 0.06\ M$$

Using K_w to find $[\text{H}^+]$

$$[\text{H}^+] = \frac{K_w}{[\text{OH}^-]} = \frac{1 \times 10^{-14}}{0.06} = 1.7 \times 10^{-13}\ M \bullet$$

Example 16-8 in the text illustrates the calculation of $[\text{OH}^-]$ in an acid solution.

2 pH calculations

pH is a measure of $[\text{H}^+]$ defined as $\text{pH} = -\log[\text{H}^+]$. $[\text{H}^+]$ can easily vary from 10^{-14} to $1\ M$. The pH scale varies from 0 to 14 over this range and is a more convenient measurement to use. Its use is so common that you must memorize the definition. Also become familiar with Table 16-4 in the text so you understand the pH scale. First we will work some simple problems to become familiar with pH. Example 16-10 in the text illustrates the basic calculation. If you are rusty on using logarithms refer to App. D-3 in the text or to any algebra text.

● **EXAMPLE 3**   **Problem:** What is the $[\text{H}^+]$ of a solution of pH 5.62?

Solution: Solve the definition of pH for $[\text{H}^+]$. Since $\text{pH} = -\log[\text{H}^+]$

$$\log[\text{H}^+] = -\text{pH}$$

$$[\text{H}^+] = \text{antilog}(-\text{pH})$$

$$[\text{H}^+] = \text{antilog}(-5.62) = \text{antilog}(+0.38 - 6) = 2.40 \times 10^{-6}\ M$$

Alternate solution:

$$\log[\text{H}^+] = -\text{pH}$$

$$[\text{H}^+] = 10^{-\text{pH}}$$

$$[\text{H}^+] = 10^{-5.62} = 2.40 \times 10^{-6}\ M$$

The first solution method is best if you use logarithmic tables; the alternate solution can be done quickly using most electronic calculators. ●

● **EXAMPLE 4**   **Problem:** Calculate $[\text{OH}^-]$ of a solution of pH 8.54.

Solution: First find the $[\text{H}^+]$ as in Example 3; then use K_w to find $[\text{OH}^-]$.

$$[H^+] = 10^{-pH} = 10^{-8.54} = 2.88 \times 10^{-9}\ M$$

$$[OH^-] = \frac{K_w}{[H^+]} = \frac{1 \times 10^{-14}}{2.88 \times 10^{-9}} = 3.47 \times 10^{-6}\ M$$

Alternate solution: Determine the pOH and find $[OH^-]$ from pOH.

$$pH + pOH = 14$$

$$pOH = 14 - pH = 14 - 8.54 = 5.46$$

$$[OH^-] = 10^{-pOH} = 10^{-5.46} = 3.47 \times 10^{-6}\ M \ \bullet$$

• **EXAMPLE 5**   **Problem**: What is the pOH of a $4.45 \times 10^{-4}\ M$ solution of HBr?

Solution: HBr is a strong acid so

$$[H^+] = [HBr] = 4.45 \times 10^{-4}\ M$$

$$pH = -\log [H^+] = -\log (4.45 \times 10^{-4}) = -(0.65 - 4) = 3.35$$

$$pOH = 14 - pH = 14 - 3.35 = 10.65$$

Alternate solution: First determine $[OH^-]$ from $[H^+]$ using K_w; then find pOH.

$$[H^+] = [HBr] = 4.45 \times 10^{-4}\ M$$

$$[OH^-] = \frac{K_w}{[H^+]} = \frac{1 \times 10^{-14}}{4.45 \times 10^{-4}} = 2.25 \times 10^{-11}\ M$$

$$pOH = -\log [OH^-] = -\log (2.25 \times 10^{-11}) = -(0.35 - 11) = 10.65 \ \bullet$$

Examples 16-8 to 16-12 in the text are problems similar to these.

16-4   *1 The pH of hydrolyzed salts*
Hydrolysis   Salts ionize when they dissolve and certain cations and anions undergo hydrolysis in solution. Anions may hydrolyze to form weak acids while cations hydrolyze to weak bases. Either of these situations will affect the pH of the solution.

NaCN is the salt of a strong base, NaOH, and a weak acid, HCN. We expect its solution to be basic, so the pH will be greater than 7. The dissociation reaction is

$$NaCN \longrightarrow Na^+ + CN^-$$

We must examine each ion formed to see if it hydrolyzes. There is no tendency for Na^+ to react with water to form $NaOH + H^+$ because NaOH is a strong base. However, the hydrolysis $H_2O + CN^- \rightleftharpoons HCN + OH^-$ occurs because HCN is a weak acid (see Table 16-1 in the text). Examples 16-14 and 16-15 in the text illustrate the calculation of the pH of a basic salt and an acidic salt which undergo hydrolysis.

2 Determination of dissociation constants from hydrolysis data
Since the dissociation constant of a weak acid or base is related to the hydrolysis constant of its salt through K_w, we can determine dissociation constants by measuring the pH of hydrolyzed salts.

● **EXAMPLE 6**   **Problem:** The pH of 0.100 M sodium hypochlorite, NaOCl, is 10.25. Calculate K_{diss} for hypochloric acid, HClO.

Solution: First we will determine K_h for the hypochlorite ion and then find K_{diss} for HClO. The dissociation reaction for the salt is

$$NaClO \longrightarrow Na^+ + OCl^-$$

The hypochlorite ion hydrolyzes according to the reaction

$$OCl^- + H_2O \rightleftharpoons HOCl + OH^-$$

The hydrolysis expression for OCl^- is

$$K_h = \frac{[HOCl][OH^-]}{[OCl^-]}$$

We can find the equilibrium concentration of OH^- from the given pH

$$[H^+] = 10^{-pH} = 10^{-10.25} = 5.62 \times 10^{-11} \, M$$

$$[OH^-] = \frac{K_w}{[H^+]} = \frac{1 \times 10^{-14}}{5.62 \times 10^{-11}} = 1.78 \times 10^{-4} \, M$$

The hydrolysis reaction for OCl^- tells us that equal numbers of moles of HOCl and OH^- are generated during hydrolysis. It also says that the original OCl^- concentration decreases by an amount equal to the OH^- generated.

$$[OH^-] = 1.78 \times 10^{-4} \, M$$

$$[HOCl] = 1.78 \times 10^{-4} \, M$$

$$[OCl^-] = 0.100 - 1.78 \times 10^{-4} = 0.100 \, M$$

Substituting these values into the hydrolysis expression gives the value of K_h

$$K_h = \frac{(1.78 \times 10^{-4})^2}{0.100} = 3.17 \times 10^{-7}$$

Now we can use the relationship between K_h, K_{diss}, and K_w to find K_{diss}

$$K_{diss} = \frac{K_w}{K_h} = \frac{1 \times 10^{-14}}{3.17 \times 10^{-7}} = 3.15 \times 10^{-8}$$

This calculated value compares well with the value tabulated in Table 16-1 in the text. ●

16-5
Acid-base indicators
and titration

In a titration procedure we want the indicator to change color at the equivalence point. Since different indicators change color at different pH values, we must predict the pH at the equivalence point before we can choose an appropriate indicator.

1 pH at the equivalence point in a titration of a strong acid with a strong base
Any neutralization of a strong acid with a strong base can be represented by the reaction

$$H^+ + OH^- \rightleftharpoons H_2O$$

The equivalence point is defined as the point during titration when equal numbers of moles of H^+ and OH^- have been added. The resulting solution must be neutral, so the pH is 7. See Example 16-17 in the text.

2 pH at the equivalence point of titrations involving weak acids or weak bases

● **EXAMPLE 7**   **Problem**: What is the pH at the equivalence point for the titration of 30.0 ml of 0.10 M NH_3 solution with 0.30 M HCl?

Solution: The reaction for the neutralization of the weak base and the strong acid is

$$NH_3 + HCl \rightleftharpoons NH_4^+ + Cl^-$$

At the equivalence point equal numbers of moles of NH_3 and HCl have been added so the solution contains NH_4^+ and Cl^- ions. NH_4^+ is the cation of a weak base so it hydrolyzes according to the reaction

$$NH_4^+ + H_2O \rightleftharpoons NH_3 + H_3O^+$$

The presence of H_3O^+ will make the solution acidic at the equivalence point. The pH will be the pH of the NH_4Cl solution.

Let us first find the concentration of NH_4Cl. The titration involved adding 0.30 M HCl to 30.0 ml of 0.10 M NH_3 until the moles of each were equal. The volume of HCl is found using the titration equation.

$$(NV)_{NH_3} = (NV)_{HCl}$$

Molarity equals normality for both HCl and NH_3, so the volume of HCl is

$$V_{HCl} = \frac{N_{NH_3}}{N_{HCl}} V_{NH_3} = \frac{0.10\ N}{0.30\ N} (30.0\ ml) = 10.0\ ml$$

The total volume after titration is 30.0 ml + 10.0 ml = 40.0 ml. There was (0.10 mol liter^{-1})(0.030 liter) = 3.0×10^{-3} mol of NH_3 originally present, and the neutralization reaction says that the number of moles of NH_4^+ produced must be equal to the number of moles of NH_3 reacted. The concentration of NH_4^+ before hydrolysis is

$$[NH_4^+]_0 = \frac{3.0 \times 10^{-3}\ mol}{0.040\ liter} = 0.075\ M$$

The only sources of H^+ at the equivalence point are the hydrolysis of NH_4^+ and water dissociation. Normally we can neglect the $[H^+]$ from water dissociation. The pH of 0.075 M NH_4Cl can be calculated by the procedure of Example 16-15 in the text.

$$K_h = \frac{K_w}{K_b} = \frac{1 \times 10^{-14}}{1.8 \times 10^{-5}} = 5.6 \times 10^{-10}$$

The value of K_b is given in Table 16-3 in the text. The hydrolysis expression for NH_4^+ is

$$K_h = \frac{[NH_3][H_3O^+]}{[NH_4^+]} = 5.6 \times 10^{-10}$$

Let x = the amount of NH_4^+ that hydrolyzes, in moles per liter. From the hydrolysis reaction we can see that $x = [NH_3] = [H_3O^+]$

$$[NH_4^+] = 0.075 - x = 0.075\ M$$

The criteria for neglecting x with respect to 0.075 are met, so we can substitute concentrations into the hydrolysis expression and solve directly for x

$$5.6 \times 10^{-10} = \frac{x^2}{0.075}$$

$$x^2 = 4.2 \times 10^{-11}$$

$$x = [H_3O^+] = 6.5 \times 10^{-6}\ M$$

Now the pH can be found

$$pH = -\log [H_3O^+] = -\log (6.5 \times 10^{-6}) = 5.2$$

As was predicted, the pH at the equivalence point is acidic rather than neutral. Example 16-18 in the text illustrates a similar calculation for the titration of a weak acid with a strong base. There the equivalence point pH is basic. ●

3 Construction of titration curves for strong acids with strong bases
The change of pH in a solution being titrated can be plotted against the amount of titrant added to give a titration curve. Figures 16-3 to 16-5 in the text show examples of titration curves. If we calculate the pH of the solution being titrated at several points during the titration we could construct a titration curve for any given titration. We will investigate the method of calculation for a strong acid-base titration first.

● **EXAMPLE 8**   **Problem:** A titration is performed in which 25.0 ml of 0.150 M NaOH is titrated with 0.150 M HCl. What is the pH of the solution after 10.0 ml of HCl have been added?

Solution: Titration of a strong acid with a strong base does not produce ions that hydrolyze so the neutralization is completely described by the reaction

$$NaOH + HCl \rightleftharpoons NaCl + H_2O$$

or the net ionic equation

$$H^+ + OH^- \rightleftharpoons H_2O$$

The number of moles of NaOH neutralized equals the number of moles of HCl added.

Moles of NaOH in initial solution = 0.150 mol liter^{-1} (0.0250 liter) = 3.75×10^{-3} mol
Moles of HCl added = 0.150 mol liter^{-1} (0.0100 liter) = 1.5×10^{-3} mol
Moles of NaOH remaining after HCl addition = 3.75×10^{-3} - 1.5×10^{-3} = 2.25×10^{-3} mol

After 10 ml of HCl is added the total volume of solution is 0.025 liter + 0.010 liter = 0.035 liter.

$$[NaOH]\ \text{after 10.0 ml HCl} = \frac{2.25 \times 10^{-3}\ \text{mol}}{0.035\ \text{liter}} = 0.0643\ M$$

Since NaOH is a strong base it is completely dissociated so

$$[OH^-] = [NaOH] = 0.0643 \, M$$

$$[H^+] = \frac{K_w}{[OH^-]} = \frac{1 \times 10^{-14}}{0.0643} = 1.56 \times 10^{-13}$$

$$pH = -\log [H^+] = -\log (1.56 \times 10^{-13}) = 12.81 \quad \bullet$$

Similar calculations could be done using several different volumes of added HCl and the results plotted to give a graph similar to Fig. 16-3 in the text.

4 Construction of a titration curve for titrations involving weak acids or weak bases
Since the salts of weak acids and weak bases give ions that hydrolyze in solution, the pH of the solution is affected by the concentrations of weak acid or weak base remaining to be titrated and of the salt formed during titration. To calculate the pH of these solutions we need to consider both the neutralization and hydrolysis reactions and their effect on the OH^- and H^+ concentrations.

● **EXAMPLE 9**   **Problem**: If 25.0 ml of 0.150 M NH_3 solution is titrated with 0.200 M HBr, what is the pH of the NH_3 solution after adding 10.0 ml of HBr?

Solution: First we will investigate the stoichiometry of the neutralization process to determine the amount of NH_3 remaining after 10.0 ml of HBr is added. The neutralization reaction is

$$NH_3 + HBr \rightleftharpoons NH_4^+ + Br^-$$

Initial moles of NH_3 = 0.150 mol liter^{-1} (0.0250 liter) = 3.75 $\times 10^{-3}$ mol
Moles HBr added = 0.200 mol liter^{-1} (0.0100 liter) = 2.00 $\times 10^{-3}$ mol
Moles NH_3 remaining after HBr addition = 3.75 $\times 10^{-3}$ - 2.00 $\times 10^{-3}$ = 1.75 $\times 10^{-3}$ mol

After the HBr addition the total volume of solution is 25.0 ml + 10.0 ml = 35.0 ml.

$$[NH_3] = \frac{1.75 \times 10^{-3} \text{ mol}}{0.0350 \text{ liter}} = 0.0500 \, M$$

The number of moles of NH_4^+ formed is equal to the number of moles of NH_3 neutralized, 2.00 $\times 10^{-3}$ mol

$$[NH_4^+]_0 = \frac{2.00 \times 10^{-3} \text{ mol}}{0.0350 \text{ liter}} = 0.0571 \, M$$

The NH_4^+ hydrolyzes according to the reaction

$$NH_4^+ + H_2O \rightleftharpoons NH_3 + H_3O^+$$

and the hydrolysis expression is

$$K_h = \frac{[NH_3][H_3O^+]}{[NH_4^+]}$$

We can find the concentrations after hydrolysis by a typical equilibrium calculation. Let x = the amount of NH_4^+ hydrolyzed in moles per liter.

	Concentration after neutralization, mol liter^{-1}	Concentration change from hydrolysis	Equilibrium concentration after hydrolysis, mol liter^{-1}
NH_4^+	0.0571	$-x$	$0.0571 - x$
NH_3	0.0500	$+x$	$0.0500 + x$
H_3O^+	0	$+x$	x

The criteria to neglect x with respect to 0.0571 and 0.0500 are met, so the hydrolysis expression becomes

$$K_h = 5.6 \times 10^{-10} = \frac{0.0500x}{0.0571}$$

$$x = [H_3O^+] = 6.4 \times 10^{-10} M$$

$$pH = -\log [H^+] = -\log (6.4 \times 10^{-10}) = 9.19 \quad \bullet$$

Values of pH could be calculated using other volumes of added HBr and the results plotted to give a titration curve similar to Fig. 16-14 in the text. Example 16-19 in the text illustrates a similar calculation for titration of a weak acid with a strong base.

16-6 Buffers

1 Calculation of the pH of a buffer of known composition
The Henderson-Hasselbalch equation is used to calculate the pH of a buffer if the concentrations of weak acid or weak base and the corresponding salt are known.

• **EXAMPLE 10**   **Problem:** What is the pH of a buffer solution made of 0.50 M $HC_2H_3O_2$ and 0.30 M $NaC_2H_3O_2$?

Solution: The Henderson-Hasselbalch equation can be written as

$$pH = pK_a - \log \frac{[\text{weak acid}]}{[\text{salt}]}$$

For this system

$$[HC_2H_3O_2] = 0.50 \, M$$

$$[NaC_2H_3O_2] = 0.30 \, M$$

$$K_a = 1.8 \times 10^{-5} \quad \text{from Text Table 16-1}$$

$$pK_a = -\log K_a = -\log (1.8 \times 10^{-5}) = 4.74$$

Substituting these values into the Henderson-Hasselbalch equation gives

$$pH = 4.74 - \log \frac{0.50}{0.30} = 4.74 - 0.22 = 4.52 \quad \bullet$$

2 Calculation of the composition of a buffer to provide a given pH
The Henderson-Hasselbalch equation can also be used to determine the amounts of weak acid or salt necessary to make a buffer of a certain pH.

- **EXAMPLE 11**   **Problem:** How many moles of NH_4Cl must be added to 500 ml of 0.500 M NH_3 to make a buffer of pH 9.50?

Solution: The Henderson-Hasselbalch equation for basic buffers is

$$pOH = pK_b - \log \frac{[\text{weak base}]}{[\text{salt}]}$$

For this buffer

$$[\text{Weak base}] = [NH_3] = 0.500\ M$$

$$K_b = 1.8 \times 10^{-5} \text{ from Text Table 16-3}$$

$$pK_b = -\log K_b = -\log (1.8 \times 10^{-5}) = 4.74$$

$$pOH = 14 - pH = 14 - 9.50 = 4.50$$

Now we can substitute these values into the Henderson-Hasselbalch equation and solve for [salt]

$$4.50 = 4.74 - \log \frac{0.500}{[\text{salt}]}$$

$$\log \frac{0.500}{[\text{salt}]} = 0.24$$

$$\frac{0.500}{[\text{salt}]} = 10^{0.24} = 1.74$$

$$[\text{salt}] = [NH_4Cl] = \frac{0.500}{1.74} = 0.288\ M$$

The number of moles of NH_4Cl needed is

$$\text{Moles } NH_4Cl = 0.288 \text{ mol liter}^{-1} \times 0.500 \text{ liter} = 0.144 \text{ mol} \bullet$$

3 Comparison of the effect of adding H^+ or OH^- to a buffer or to pure water

- **EXAMPLE 12**   **Problem:** Compare the change in pH upon adding 0.10 mol of H^+ to 1 liter of the buffer in Example 11 to the pH change when the same amount of H^+ is added to 1 liter of distilled water.

Solution: The change for the buffer system can be determined by the Henderson-Hasselbalch equation. We can determine the concentrations by the usual methods of equilibrium calculations. The 0.10 mol of H^+ converts 0.10 mol of NH_3 to 0.10 mol of NH_4^+, so the $[NH_3]$ decreases by 0.10 mol liter^{-1} and the $[NH_4^+]$ increases by 0.10 mol liter^{-1}. Substituting these values into the Henderson-Hasselbalch equation gives

$$pOH = 4.74 - \log \frac{0.500 - 0.100}{0.288 + 0.100}$$

$$= 4.74 - \log \frac{0.400}{0.388} = 4.73$$

$$pH = 14.00 - 4.73 = 9.27$$

The initial pH of the buffer (Example 10) was 9.50, so the pH change is

$$pH = 9.50 - 9.27 = 0.23$$

The pH change for pure water is found as follows: The $[H^+]$ is 0.10 mol liter^{-1}, so the pH is

$$pH = -\log [H^+] = -\log (0.10) = 1.00$$

The pH of pure water is 7.00, so the change in pH is

$$pH = 7.00 - 1.00 = 6.00$$

The pH of the pure water changed by 6.00 pH units while that of buffer changed by only 0.23 units. ●

Example 16-20 in the text is a similar calculation for a weak acid buffer.

SELF TEST

True or false ____ 1 The presence of acetate ions in a solution of acetic acid shifts the acid dissociation to the left.

____ 2 The percent dissociation of a weak acid increases as the solution is concentrated.

____ 3 A pH change of 3 means the $[H^+]$ has changed by 300.

____ 4 Anions of very weak acids tend to hydrolyze strongly.

____ 5 Anions of weak bases hydrolyze in solution to form the weak base plus OH^-.

Completion 6 Repression of dissociation of HCN molecules by the presence of _____ is called the _____ effect.

7 The $[H^+]$ of strong acids is always equal to the original concentration of _____ _____, but the concentration of H^+ of weak acids must be calculated using the _____.

8 The pH of a $1 \times 10^{-3} M$ HCl solution is _____.

9 The pH of a $1 \times 10^{-3} M$ NaOH solution is _____.

10 Hydrolysis is the reaction of the _____ of a _____ with water.

11 The relationship between K_h, K_a, and K_w may be expressed mathematically as _____.

12 The salt of a _____ plus a _____ is basic.

13 The pH at the equivalence point for the titration of a strong base and a weak acid is _____ (greater than, less than, equal to) 7.

Multiple choice 14 Adding NaOH to a solution of acetic acid
(a) increases $[H^+]$ (b) increases $[HC_2H_3O_2]$
(c) decreases $[C_2H_3O_2^-]$ (d) increases $[C_2H_3O_2^-]$

15 Which of the following will have the lowest $[H^+]$?
(a) $1.0 M$ $HC_2H_3O_2$ in $1.0 M$ $NaC_2H_3O_2$ (b) $1.0 M$ $HC_2H_3O_2$ in $1.0 M$ HCl
(c) $1.0 M$ $HC_2H_3O_2$ in $1.0 M$ KCl   (d) $1.0 M$ $HC_2H_3O_2$ in $1.0 M$ HCN

16 Given $K_h = 5.6 \times 10^{-10}$ for NH_4^+, the pH of $0.050 M$ NH_4Cl is
(a) 4.0   (b) 5.3   (c) 8.0   (d) 10.6

17 The $[OH^-]$ in 0.05 M HCl is
   (a) $2.0 \times 10^{-13} M$ (b) $5.0 \times 10^{-12} M$ (c) $2.2 \times 10^{-6} M$ (d) 0.025 M

18 The pH of 0.020 M $Ba(OH)_2$ is
   (a) 13.96   (b) 12.6   (c) 12.3   (d) 12.0

19 If the pH of a solution of $Sr(OH)_2$ is 8.00 at 25°C, then the $[OH^-]$ is
   (a) $5 \times 10^{-6} M$ (b) $2 \times 10^{-6} M$ (c) $1 \times 10^{-6} M$ (d) $1 \times 10^{-8} M$

20 K_{II} for sulfurous acid is 6.30×10^{-8}. The hydrolysis constant for the sulfite ion, SO_3^{2-}, is
   (a) 3.15×10^{-8} (b) 1.60×10^{-7} (c) 6.30×10^{-6} (d) 2.51×10^{-4}

21 When 25 ml of 0.10 M HCl reacts with 25 ml of 0.20 M NaOH, the final $[H^+]$ is
   (a) 0.1 M (b) 0.05 M (c) $10^{-7} M$ (d) $10^{-13} M$ (e) $2 \times 10^{-13} M$

22 What is the $[OH^-]$ in a solution containing 0.050 ml NH_4Cl and 0.030 mol NH_3 per liter? ($K_b = 1.8 \times 10^{-5}$)
   (a) $1.1 \times 10^{-5} M$ (b) $3.0 \times 10^{-5} M$ (c) $9.5 \times 10^{-4} M$ (d) $7.3 \times 10^{-4} M$

23 When a small amount of NaOH is added to a buffer made of $HC_2H_3O_2$ and $NaC_2H_3O_2$, the pH changes very little because
   (a) The $HC_2H_3O_2$ dissociates to compensate for the NaOH.
   (b) $NaC_2H_3O_2$ hydrolyzes to form NaOH and $HC_2H_3O_2$.
   (c) $C_2H_3O_2^-$ reacts with NaOH to form $HC_2H_3O_2$.
   (d) $HC_2H_3O_2$ dissociates to give H^+ which reacts with OH^- to form H_2O.

24 Given $K_a = 1.8 \times 10^{-5}$, a buffer made of an equal number of moles of acetic acid and sodium acetate has a pH of
   (a) 1.8   (b) 3.74   (c) 4.74   (d) 9.26

25 How many moles of NaOCl should be added to 0.100 M HCl to prepare 1 liter of a buffer with pH 6.5? ($K_a = 3.2 \times 10^{-8}$)
   (a) 0.010   (b) 0.10   (c) 1.0   (d) 10

17 AQUEOUS SOLUTIONS: SOLUBILITY AND COMPLEX-ION EQUILIBRIA

CHAPTER OVERVIEW

Chapter 17 is a continuation of the application of equilibrium concepts. We will apply these concepts to saturated solutions of slightly soluble electrolytes in water to study and predict the solubility of salts and to determine when precipitates are expected to form. We will also apply equilibrium concepts to complex ions and multicomponent systems.

17-1
The solubility of ionic solids

The equilibrium constant describing the solubility of an electrolyte is called the solubility product constant or solubility product and is designated K_{sp}. Equilibrium conditions for solution of any salt are obtained by writing the equilibrium expression for the dissociation reaction of the salt. Note that the salt itself does not appear in the expression because it is a pure substance. The dissociation reaction for the salt M_2A_3 is:

$$M_2A_3 \rightleftharpoons 2M^{3+} + 3A^{2-}$$

The solubility product expression is

$$K_{sp} = [M^{3+}]^2 [A^{2-}]^3$$

Numerical values of K_{sp} are tabulated for many salts. (See Table 17-1 and App. H in the text or any chemical handbook for a more extensive list.)

There are no new *concepts* presented in this section, only new applications of familiar equilibrium concepts. Note how the common-ion effect has a dramatic effect on the solubility of salts. Le Chatelier's principle is used to predict the results of the common-ion effect. Equilibrium calculations in this section are very similar to those of Chaps. 15 and 16.

17-2
Precipitation reactions

When the value of the ion-product or mass-action expression is less than K_{sp}, the solution is unsaturated; when it is equal to K_{sp}, the solution is saturated; when it is greater than K_{sp}, the solution is supersaturated and precipitation will generally occur unless care is taken to preserve a supersaturated solution and prevent precipitation. Comparing numerical values of the mass-action quotient (or calculated ion product) with

K_{sp} allows us to predict whether or not a precipitation will occur and what compound will precipitate from solution.

17-3
Complex-ion
equilibria

The basic terms used in complex-ion chemistry were introduced in Sec. 13-2. You may want to review some of the definitions in Chap. 13 to be sure you do not hinder your study in this section by a lack of understanding of the terms. Again, the equilibrium concepts are the same as the ones you have already used, but the terms are specific for the kinds of reactions involved.

17-4
Simultaneous
equilibria

When a given substance is involved in several different equilibria at the same time, calculating concentrations can be very difficult and may require a computer. Often, however, simplifying assumptions can be made because one equilibrium condition dominates the system making the calculation much simpler. Note how the equilibria in Examples 17-10 and 17-11 in the text are treated independently even though they occur simultaneously. Watch for these simplifying techniques when you work simultaneous equilibria problems.

LEARNING OBJECTIVES

As a result of studying Chapter 17, you should be able to do the following:
Write the definition and give an example illustrating the use of each key term.

17-1
The solubility of
ionic solids

1 Write an expression for the equilibrium condition for solution of an electrolyte. (New Skills Sec. 17-1; Self Test 7, 8, 14)
2 Calculate K_{sp} for an electrolyte given its solubility. (Text Examples 17-1, 17-2; Text Probs. 17-1 to 17-7) (New Skills Example 1; Self Test 1, 15)
3 Calculate the solubility of an electrolyte given K_{sp}. (Text Examples 17-3, 17-4; Text Probs. 17-8, 17-10, 17-12 to 17-14) (Self Test 17)
4 Calculate the solubility of an electrolyte in solution containing additional sources of ion common to the electrolyte (common-ion effect). (Text Examples 17-5, 17-6; Text Probs. 17-9, 17-11) (New Skills Example 2; Self Test 4, 9, 18, 19)

17-2
Precipitation
reactions

1 Calculate the minimum concentration of ions necessary to cause precipitation of a salt. (Text Probs. 17-15, 17-16) (New Skills Example 3; Self Test 2)
2 Predict whether or not a precipitate will form by comparing the calculated ion product with K_{sp}. (Text Example 17-7; Text Probs. 17-17, 17-18, 17-21) (New Skills Example 4)
3 Predict what salt will precipitate first from a solution containing several ions when a common ion is added. (Text Example 17-8; Text Prob. 17-19) (Self Test 4)

17-3
Complex-ion
equilibria

1 Write dissociation reactions and equilibrium expressions for complex ions. (New Skills Example 5; Self Test 11, 12)
2 Relate the relative stabilities of complex ions to the numerical values of their cumulative dissociation constants. (Self Test 5)
3 Calculate the concentration of metal ion in equilibrium with a complex ion. (Text Example 17-9; Text Probs. 17-22 to 17-25) (New Skills Example 5; Self Test 20)

4 Write chemical equations showing amphoteric behavior of a metal hydroxide. (Self Test 6, 21)

5 Write chemical equations showing amphiprotic behavior of a complex ion containing water and hydroxide as ligands.

17-4
Simultaneous
equilibria

1 Determine the order of precipitation of different salts as an electrolyte is added to a solution containing several ions. (Text Example 17-10; Text Probs. 17-26, 17-27, 17-29)

2 Calculate the amount of substance necessary to give a common-ion effect sufficient to cause or to prevent the precipitation of a salt. (Text Example 17-11; Text Probs. 17-28, 17-30, 17-32, 17-33) (New Skills Examples 6, 7; Self Test 10, 16, 22)

3 Calculate the amount of common ion necessary to separate substances by selective precipitation. (Text Example 17-12; Text Prob. 17-31) (Self Test 13, 23 to 25)

NEW SKILLS

17-1
The solubility of
ionic solids

In this section we use a special equilibrium constant called the solubility product constant. It is equal to the product of the concentrations of ions in solution, each raised to the power indicated by the stoichiometric coefficient of the dissociation equation.

For example, silver phosphate, Ag_3PO_4, is a slightly soluble salt. It dissolves in water according to the reaction

$$Ag_3PO_4(s) \rightleftharpoons 3Ag^+ + PO_4^{3-}$$

The equilibrium for a saturated solution is described by the expression

$$K_{sp} = [Ag^+]^3 [PO_4^{3-}]$$

Since Ag_3PO_4 is a pure solid, it is not included in the equilibrium expression. A saturated solution contains all the Ag^+ and PO_4^{3-} ions it can hold in equilibrium with solid Ag_3PO_4. Adding more solid Ag_3PO_4 does not change the concentration of ions in solution. As long as the solution remains saturated, the product $[Ag^+]^3 [PO_4^{3-}]$ must be constant. If additional Ag^+ is added, $[PO_4^{3-}]$ will decrease; if more PO_4^{3-} is added, $[Ag^+]$ decreases so that their product always equals K_{sp} for a saturated solution.

1 Calculation of K_{sp} from solubility data
Problems in this chapter can be solved by the general approach to equilibrium problems used in Chaps. 15 and 16. It is always a good idea to begin by writing a balanced chemical equation for the process and analyzing the stoichiometry involved.

$$Ag_3PO_4 \rightleftharpoons 3Ag^+ + PO_4^{3-}$$

Stoichiometry tells us that for every mole of Ag_3PO_4 that dissolves, 3 mol of Ag^+ and 1 mol of PO_4^{3-} are produced.

● **EXAMPLE 1**   **Problem:** A saturated solution of silver phosphate at 25°C is 1.6×10^{-5} M. Calculate K_{sp} at 25°C for Ag_3PO_4.

Solution: The balanced equation representing the solution reaction is

$$Ag_3PO_4(s) \rightleftharpoons 3Ag^+ + PO_4^{3-}$$

and the equilibrium expression is

$$K_{sp} = [Ag^+]^3 [PO_4^{3-}]$$

The concentration tells us that there is 1.6×10^{-5} mol liter^{-1} of Ag_3PO_4, so

$$[Ag^+] = 3(1.6 \times 10^{-5}) = 4.8 \times 10^{-5} \ M$$

$$[PO_4^{3-}] = 1.6 \times 10^{-5} \ M$$

Substituting these concentrations into the equilibrium expression gives the value of K_{sp}

$$K_{sp} = [Ag^+]^3 [PO_4^{3-}] = (4.8 \times 10^{-5})^3 (1.6 \times 10^{-5}) = 1.8 \times 10^{-18} \ \bullet$$

Now work through Examples 17-1 and 17-2 in the text.

2 Calculation of solubility from K_{sp}

Since values of K_{sp} are available in tables, a common problem is to calculate the concentration of ions in a saturated solution using the value of K_{sp}. Examples 17-3 and 17-4 in the text illustrate this calculation.

3 The common-ion effect on solubility

Since the product of the concentrations of ions in a saturated solution must equal K_{sp}, the presence of two salts containing a common ion in the same solution will affect the solubility of the system. Generally, the net result is to decrease the solubility of the less soluble salt.

● **EXAMPLE 2**   **Problem:** Compare the solubility of AgI in pure water and in $0.10 \ M$ $AgNO_3$ at $25°C$. K_{sp} for AgI is 8.5×10^{-17} at $25°C$.

Solution: AgI dissolves in pure water or in $0.10 \ M$ $AgNO_3$ according to the reaction

$$AgI(s) \longrightarrow Ag^+ + I^-$$

and the equilibrium is represented by

$$K_{sp} = 8.5 \times 10^{-17} = [Ag^+] [I^-]$$

In pure water $[Ag^+] = [I^-]$. Let $x = [Ag^+] = [I^-]$. Then

$$x^2 = 8.5 \times 10^{-17}$$

$$x = \text{solubility} = 9.2 \times 10^{-9} \ M$$

In $0.10 \ M$ $AgNO_3$ the concentration of Ag^+ is $0.10 \ M$. Adding AgI will increase this by about $9.2 \times 10^{-9} \ M$, which is negligible compared to 0.10. Let $x = [I^-]$. Then

$$[Ag^+] = 0.10 \qquad [I^-] = x$$

Substitute these values into the K_{sp} expression.

$$K_{sp} = 8.5 \times 10^{-17} = [Ag^+][I^-] = 0.10(x)$$

$$x = [I^-] = \frac{8.5 \times 10^{-17}}{0.10} = 8.5 \times 10^{-16} \ M$$

Even though $[Ag^+] = 0.10 \ M$, the solubility of AgI is limited to the $[I^-]$. Therefore

$$[I^-] = \text{solubility} = 8.5 \times 10^{-16} \, M$$

in $0.10 \, M$ $AgNO_3$, or about 10^7 times less than the solubility in pure water. ●

Example 17-5 in the text shows how the presence of I^- from a second source also dramatically affects the solubility of AgI. Example 17-6 in the text shows how pH has a large effect on the solubility of slightly soluble bases.

17-2 Precipitation reactions

1 Predicting when precipitation will occur

A comparison of the numerical value of the ion product or mass-action coefficient with K_{sp} will show if a solution is unsaturated, saturated, or supersaturated. A supersaturated solution can result in precipitation of the compound until its concentration is reduced to the saturated level. If Q represents the ion product:

$Q < K_{sp}$ means the solution is unsaturated
$Q = K_{sp}$ means the solution is saturated
$Q > K_{sp}$ means precipitation can occur because the solution is supersaturated

● **EXAMPLE 3**   **Problem:** Calculate the $[Ag^+]$ necessary to start precipitation of AgI from a solution that is $0.0030 \, M$ in iodide ions at $25°C$. K_{sp} for AgI at $25°C$ is 8.5×10^{-17}.

Solution: Precipitation of AgI will occur as soon as the ion product, $[Ag^+][I^-]$, exceeds K_{sp}

$$K_{sp} = [Ag^+][I^-] = 8.5 \times 10^{-17}$$

For a solution with $[I^-] = 0.0030$

$$Ag^+ = \frac{K_{sp}}{[I^-]} = \frac{8.5 \times 10^{-17}}{3.0 \times 10^{-3}} = 2.8 \times 10^{-14} \, M$$

As soon as $[Ag^+]$ exceeds $2.8 \times 10^{-14} \, M$, precipitation of AgI will occur. ●

● **EXAMPLE 4**   **Problem:** If 300 ml of $0.100 \, M$ HCl and 300 ml of $5.0 \times 10^{-3} \, M$ $Pb(NO_3)_2$ are mixed, will $PbCl_2$ precipitate? K_{sp} for $PbCl_2$ is 1.6×10^{-5}.

Solution: Precipitation will occur if the ion product for $PbCl_2$ exceeds K_{sp}.

$$PbCl_2(s) \rightleftharpoons Pb^{2+} + 2Cl^-$$

For a saturated solution

$$K_{sp} = [Pb^{2+}][Cl^-]^2 = 1.6 \times 10^{-5}$$

When the two solutions are mixed, the total volume will be 600 ml, or twice the original volumes; therefore, the ion concentrations will be one-half the original values

$$[Cl^-] = 0.100 \left(\tfrac{300}{600}\right) = 0.0500 \, M$$

$$[Pb^{2+}] = 5.00 \times 10^{-3} \left(\tfrac{300}{600}\right) = 2.50 \times 10^{-3} \, M$$

The ion-product quotient is

$$Q = [Pb^{2+}][Cl^-]^2 = (2.50 \times 10^{-3})(0.0500)^2 = 6.3 \times 10^{-6}$$

Since $Q < K_{sp}$, precipitation will not occur. ●

Example 17-7 in the text illustrates a case where precipitation will occur.

3 Predicting which compound will precipitate first
When the concentration of a mixture of ions is increased, the compound whose ion product exceeds K_{sp} first will precipitate first. Example 17-8 in the text illustrates this calculation.

17-3
Complex-ion
equilibria

Complex ions are often used to regulate the concentration of metal ions in solution during electroplating processes. A very small, but constant, concentration of metal ion gives a uniform layer of metal deposited during electroplating.

● **EXAMPLE 5**

Problem: Silver plating is done from a solution containing the complex ion $Ag(CN)_2^-$. What is the concentration of silver ions in a solution which is 0.100 M in $Ag(CN)_2^-$? $K_{formation}$ for $Ag(CN)_2^-$ is 3.0×10^{20}.

Solution: The formation reaction for $Ag(CN)_2^-$ is

$$Ag^+ + 2CN^- \rightleftharpoons Ag(CN)_2^-$$

$$K_{form} = 3.0 \times 10^{20} = \frac{[Ag(CN)_2^-]}{[Ag^+][CN^-]^2}$$

Let $x = [Ag^+]$. Then

$$2x = [CN^-]$$

$$[Ag(CN)_2^-] = 0.10 - x \cong 0.100$$

The large value of K_{form} shows that x is very small and can be neglected with respect to 0.100. Substituting these values into the expression for K_{form} gives

$$3.0 \times 10^{20} = \frac{0.100}{x(2x)^2}$$

$$x^3 = \frac{0.100}{4(3.0 \times 10^{20})} = 8.3 \times 10^{-23}$$

$$x = [Ag^+] = 4.4 \times 10^{-8} \ M \ ●$$

Example 17-9 in the text shows the calculation of metal-ion concentration in equilibrium with a complex ion using the cumulative dissociation constant. The formation and dissociation constants are related by

$$K_{diss} = \frac{1}{K_{form}}$$

17-4
Simultaneous
equilibria

Sometimes the solubility of a compound is affected by other ions in solution. When this happens it is necessary to consider the interacting equilibria simultaneously.

● **EXAMPLE 6**

Problem: Will MnS precipitate if 1×10^{-3} M $Mn(NO_3)_2$ is saturated with H_2S? A saturated H_2S solution is 0.10 M. K_{sp} for MnS is 1×10^{-16}.

Solution: The MnS and H_2S equilibria must be considered simultaneously. First let us find the concentration of S^{2-} in a saturated H_2S solution. The two-step dissociation is represented by

$$H_2S \rightleftharpoons H^+ + HS^- \quad K_1 = 1.1 \times 10^{-7}$$

$$HS^- \rightleftharpoons H^+ + S^{2-} \quad K_2 = 1 \times 10^{-14}$$

Since K_1 is much larger than K_2, nearly all the H^+ will be produced from the first dissociation step, and $[H^+]$ will be approximately equal to $[HS^-]$.

We can find $[H^+]$ as follows: Let $x = [H^+] = [HS^-]$. Then

$$[H_2S] = 0.10 - x \cong 0.10$$

$$K_1 = 1.1 \times 10^{-7} = \frac{[H^+][HS^-]}{[H_2S]} = \frac{x^2}{0.10 - x} \cong \frac{x^2}{0.10}$$

$$x^2 = 0.10(1.1 \times 10^{-7}) = 1.1 \times 10^{-8}$$

$$x = [H^+] = [HS^-] = 1.05 \times 10^{-4}$$

Now we can use K_2 to find $[S^{2-}]$.

$$K_2 = 1.0 \times 10^{-14} = \frac{[H^+][S^{2-}]}{[HS^-]} = \frac{1.05 \times 10^{-4}[S^{2-}]}{1.05 \times 10^{-4}}$$

$$[S^{2-}] = K_2 = 1.0 \times 10^{-14}$$

We can use this value for $[S^{2-}]$ to see if the ion product $[Mn^{2+}][S^{2-}]$ is greater than K_{sp}

$$[Mn^{2+}] = 1 \times 10^{-3} \quad [S^{2-}] = 1.0 \times 10^{-14}$$

$$[Mn^{2+}][S^{2-}] = 1 \times 10^{-3}(1.0 \times 10^{-14}) = 1 \times 10^{-17}$$

Since the ion product is smaller than K_{sp}, MnS will not precipitate from a saturated H_2S solution. Note, however, that if the pH were increased, the $[H^+]$ would be less, the dissociations would shift to the right to increase $[S^{2-}]$, and MnS would precipitate. ●

● **EXAMPLE 7** **Problem:** A 1.0×10^{-3} M solution of MnS is buffered at pH 7 and saturated with H_2S (0.10 M). Will MnS precipitate? (See Example 6 for equilibrium constants.)

Solution: Since $[H^+]$ is known, we can use the overall equilibrium for H_2S dissociation to find $[S^{2-}]$.

$$H_2S \rightleftharpoons 2H^+ + S^{2-}$$

$$K = K_1 K_2 = \frac{[H^+]^2[S^{2-}]}{[H_2S]} = 1.1 \times 10^{-7}(1 \times 10^{-14}) = 1.1 \times 10^{-21}$$

$$[H^+] = 10^{-pH} = 10^{-7}$$

$$[H_2S] = 0.1$$

Substituting these values in the equilibrium expression and solving for $[S^{2-}]$ gives

$$[S^{2-}] = \frac{[H_2S]K}{[H^+]^2} = \frac{0.10(1.1 \times 10^{-21})}{(10^{-7})^2} = 1.1 \times 10^{-8}$$

Now determine the ion product $[Mn^{2+}][S^{2-}]$ using this value for $[S^{2-}]$

$$[Mn^{2+}] = 1 \times 10^{-3} \qquad [S^{2-}] = 1.1 \times 10^{-8}$$

$$[Mn^{2+}][S^{2-}] = 1 \times 10^{-3}(1.1 \times 10^{-8}) = 1.1 \times 10^{-11}$$

which is considerably larger than the value of K_{sp}, 1×10^{-16}. Therefore, MnS will precipitate from a saturated H_2S solution at pH 7. ●

Text Examples 17-10 to 17-12 give additional illustrations of simultaneous equilibria.

SELF TEST

True or false ____ 1 K_{sp} is the solubility of a compound.
____ 2 K_{sp} values apply only to saturated solutions of slightly soluble compounds.
____ 3 K_{sp} for AgCl is 1.7×10^{-10} and K_{sp} for $CaSO_4$ is 2.4×10^{-5}; therefore, $CaSO_4$ is more soluble than AgCl.
____ 4 Mixing solutions of $AgNO_3$ and NaCl will always result in a precipitate of AgCl.
____ 5 Cumulative dissociation constants are a measure of the stability of complex ions.
____ 6 Amphoteric substances can behave as either acids or bases.

Completion 7 The ion product for CaF_2 can be expressed as _____ .
8 The solubility product expression for $Ca(OH)_2$ is _____
_____ .
9 The presence of NaCl in a solution of Ag^+ will _____ (increase, decrease) $[Ag^+]$.
10 The presence of H^+ will _____ (increase, decrease) the solubility of $Mg(OH)_2$.
11 The expression for the formation constant of the complex ion $Co(NH_3)_6^{3+}$ is _____ .
12 The cumulative dissociation reaction for the complex ion $Cu(NH_3)_4^{2+}$ is _____
_____ .
13 Metal sulfides can be separated by selective precipitation from a saturated H_2S solution by controlling the _____ of the solution.
14 The equation $H_2S \rightleftharpoons 2H^+ + S^{2-}$ _____ (does, does not) represent an equilibrium.

Multiple choice 15 The solubility of silver carbonate, Ag_2CO_3, is 0.032 g liter^{-2} at 20°C. K_{sp} for Ag_2CO_3 at 20°C is
(a) 6.2×10^{-12} (b) 1.6×10^{-12} (c) 2.7×10^{-8} (d) 1.3×10^{-4}
16 In a saturated solution of $Fe(OH)_3$, the pH was found to be 5.13. What is the solubility of $Fe(OH)_3$?
(a) 2.47×10^{-6}
(b) 1.35×10^{-9}
(c) 4.50×10^{-10}
(d) insufficient information to determine

17 The solubility, M, of $Pb(IO_3)_2$ is related to K_{sp} by
  (a) $K_{sp} = 4M^3$ (b) $K_{sp} = M$ (c) $K_{sp} = 2M^3$ (d) $K_{sp} = 2M^2$

18 Addition of $AgNO_3$ to a saturated solution of AgI will
  (a) lower K_{sp} for AgI
  (b) lower $[Ag^+]$
  (c) lower the ion product of AgI
  (d) lower $[I^-]$

19 K_{sp} for AgI is 8.5×10^{-17}. The solubility of AgI in 0.028 M NaI is
  (a) $1.1 \times 10^{-13} M$ (b) $1.5 \times 10^{-15} M$
  (c) $3.0 \times 10^{-15} M$ (d) $2.4 \times 10^{-18} M$

20 K_{diss} for $Ag(NH_3)_2^+$ is 5.9×10^{-8}. The concentration of Ag^+ ion in 1.0 liter of solution containing 0.10 mol of $AgNO_3$ and 0.50 mol of NH_3 is
  (a) 1.2×10^{-8} (b) 2.4×10^{-8} (c) 6.6×10^{-8} (d) 1.2×10^{-9}

21 An amphoteric substance
  (a) forms a complex ion when it dissolves
  (b) is soluble in acid or base but not in pure water
  (c) acts as either an Arrhenius acid or an Arrhenius base
  (d) all of the above

22 What is the minimum concentration of chloride ions necessary to precipitate $PbCl_2$ from a solution which is $0.010 M$ in $Pb(NO_3)_2$? K_{sp} for $PbCl_2$ is 1.6×10^{-5}.
  (a) $1.6 \times 10^{-2} M$ (b) $4.0 \times 10^{-2} M$
  (c) $8.0 \times 10^{-2} M$ (d) $1.6 \times 10^{-3} M$

23 What is the pH of a saturated solution of $Fe(OH)_3$? K_{sp} for $Fe(OH)_3$ is 1.1×10^{-36}.
  (a) 5.1   (b) 5.4   (c) 8.9   (d) 9.4

24 What concentration of NH_4^+ is necessary to prevent the precipitation of $Fe(OH)_2$ in a solution that is $0.020 M$ in Fe^{2+} and $0.050 M$ in NH_3? K_{sp} for $Fe(OH)_2$ is 2×10^{-15}.
  (a) $2.9 M$ (b) $2.5 M$ (c) $8.9 \times 10^{-4} M$ (d) $3.2 \times 10^{-7} M$

25 A solution that is $5 \times 10^{-3} M$ in Sn^{2+} and $0.050 M$ in H^+ is saturated with H_2S $(0.10 M)$. What concentration of Sn^{2+} remains in solution after SnS has precipitated? K_{sp} for SnS is 1×10^{-26}; $K_I = 1.1 \times 10^{-7}$, and $K_{II} = 1 \times 10^{-14}$ for H_2S.
  (a) $9.1 \times 10^{-5} M$ (b) $4.5 \times 10^{-6} M$
  (c) $2.3 \times 10^{-7} M$ (d) $1.0 \times 10^{-13} M$

18 CHEMICAL THERMODYNAMICS

CHAPTER OVERVIEW

One of the most powerful tools for understanding why and how chemical reactions occur is through the analysis of energy changes accompanying chemical and physical changes. The study of energy and work changes is called thermodynamics. In this chapter you will learn the three fundamental laws of thermodynamics and use them to help you better understand chemistry.

You learned to write and balance chemical reactions in Chaps. 3 and 13, but even a balanced chemical equation does not tell whether the reaction will actually take place. An understanding of thermodynamics will allow you to predict, with confidence, when a reaction can take place, or better, when it is thermodynamically allowed. Chapter 18 will show you how to apply the laws of thermodynamics to determine whether a chemical reaction is spontaneous or nonspontaneous.

18-1
The first law

A reaction that is allowed in a thermodynamic sense is called a spontaneous reaction. In a nonscientific sense a spontaneous reaction is one that starts or ignites by itself. To a chemist, however, a spontaneous change is one capable of doing work. A thermodynamically spontaneous reaction may not be self-starting, and energy may even be consumed, but the capability of doing work is present and that is the necessary condition for spontaneity.

The reverse of a change capable of doing work is a change requiring an input of work. Likewise, the reverse of a spontaneous change, a nonspontaneous change, can be accomplished only by the input of work into the system by some external source. This is an important concept to understand about spontaneity: namely, that nonspontaneous changes or unnatural changes can be accomplished only by doing work on the system. Often there is no practical way to get work into the system and, therefore, many nonspontaneous changes will not occur at all.

You will study three fundamental laws of thermodynamics and see applications of each law. The first law is commonly called the law of conservation of energy. It simply says that energy cannot be created or destroyed. Energy can manifest itself in several different forms, such as heat or work, and the first law permits calculations of the effects of energy as it is changed from one form to another. The amount of energy in any isolated system is constant or, in other words, energy is conserved in isolated systems. You will see how the concept of conservation of energy allows calculation of relationships between heat and work in many systems. One important example is the decrease in energy of a gas as it expands and does work against a constant resisting force such as the atmosphere.

18-2 Enthalpy and heat capacity	The concept of energy changes and accompanying pressure-volume changes is so basic to chemistry that a new variable, enthalpy (H), was defined to include both effects, $H = E + PV$. It is important to remember that $\Delta E = q_V$, the energy change is equal to the heat change for a constant-volume process, and also the parallel relationship, $\Delta H = q_P$, the change in enthalpy is equal to the heat change at constant pressure.

A very important variable in connection with energy or enthalpy calculations is the molar heat capacity, C_P. You will work several problems where the key to determining energy or enthalpy changes is through the molar heat capacity. Many text problems use the simple relationship $\Delta H = q_P = nC_P\Delta T$, where q_P is the heat exchanged under conditions of constant pressure, n is the number of moles of substance in the system, and ΔT is the temperature change taking place in the system.

18-3 Thermochemistry	Application of the first law of thermodynamics to chemistry leads to the field of thermochemistry and involves calculations of energy changes during chemical reactions. Sometimes the most important product in a chemical reaction is heat. You should be able to think of at least two common reactions where this is so. These changes are usually calculated in terms of enthalpy changes; hence the variable enthalpy is of paramount importance in Chap. 18.

Hess's law allows calculation of enthalpy changes that cannot be measured experimentally. You will work some problems illustrating this.

For any reaction at standard conditions ΔH can be calculated from tabulated values of standard enthalpies of formation in Table 18-2 of the text using Hess's law in the form

$$\Delta H^\circ_{\text{reaction}} = \Sigma(\Delta H^\circ_f)_{\text{products}} - \Sigma(\Delta H^\circ_f)_{\text{reactants}}$$

18-4 The second law	Understanding the second law of thermodynamics depends on understanding two variables connected with it: entropy and free energy. Your first introduction to thermodynamics may seem difficult because it deals with variables and concepts that are abstract. Even energy, a term we use almost daily, is difficult to comprehend in a thermodynamic sense. Terms like enthalpy, entropy, and free energy may seem difficult at first so you must allow time to read and study their definitions and uses several times if necessary. Be sure you understand these terms and how they relate to each other. The second law points to an additional abstract concept, entropy, a continually increasing variable in natural changes. You may be accustomed to dealing with physical variables that are conserved such as energy, but probably not with a variable like entropy that tends to increase as a natural reaction takes place. Concentrating on relating entropy to disorder will help you get by this hurdle.

18-5 Entropy and free-energy changes	The equation $\Delta G = \Delta H - T\Delta S$ relates the three most important variables in Chap. 18 and so is important to understand. The following definitions may help you understand the relationship among these variables.

$$\Delta G \quad = \quad \Delta H \quad - \quad T\Delta S$$

Energy	Total	Energy not available
available to	energy	to do work outside
do useful work	change	of the system

Now we finally get back to what we started out to do in this chapter: predict spontaneous changes. Remember that reactions tending towards lowest energy and maximum increased entropy tend to be spontaneous. Both of these tendencies are combined in the concept of free energy in the equation

$$\Delta G = \Delta H - T\Delta S$$

Study the table in the text relating the signs of ΔG, ΔH, and ΔS to spontaneity of change to see the relationship between energy and randomness in determining whether or not a chemical change is thermodynamically allowed.

18-6
Thermodynamics
and equilibrium

Entropy is the only thermodynamic variable for which we can calculate an absolute value. The third law allows us to do this from absolute entropy values such as those in Table 18-3 in the text.

Chapters 18 and 15 are united by the equation $\Delta G° = -2.303RT \log K_P$. This relationship allows us to convert thermodynamic data to equilibrium data and vice versa. You will work some problems showing how equilibrium constants can be calculated from tabulated thermodynamic values.

KEY EQUATIONS

18-1
The first law

1 The first law

$$\Delta E = q - w$$

where ΔE = energy change of a system
   q = heat gained by a system from its surroundings
   w = work done by a system on its surroundings

2 Work of expansion

$$w = P_{ext}\, \Delta V$$

where P_{ext} = external pressure acting on a system
   ΔV = change in volume of the system (gas)

18-2
Enthalpy and heat
capacity

1 Enthalpy definition

$$H = E + PV$$

$$\Delta H = \Delta E + P\,\Delta V \quad \text{at constant pressure}$$

2 Heat change at constant pressure

$$\Delta H_P = q_P$$

where ΔH_P = enthalpy change of a system at constant pressure
   q_P = heat gained by a system at constant pressure

3 Heat change at constant volume

$$\Delta E = q_V$$

where ΔE = energy change of a system at constant volume

q_V = heat gained by a system at constant volume

4 Use of heat capacity to calculate enthalpy changes

a For a constant-pressure process

$$\Delta H = q_P = nC_P\,\Delta t$$

where n = moles of substance

C_P = molar heat capacity at constant pressure, J mol^{-1} °C^{-1}

Δt = temperature change, K or °C

b For a constant-volume process

$$\Delta E = q_V = nC_V\,\Delta t$$

where C_V = molar heat capacity at constant volume, J mol^{-1} K^{-1} or J mol^{-1} °C^{-1}

18-3
Thermochemistry

1 Calculation of enthalpy of reaction from tabulated values of standard enthalpy of formation (Hess's law)

$$\Delta H^{\circ}_{\text{reaction}} = \Sigma(\Delta H^{\circ}_f)_{\text{products}} - \Sigma(\Delta H^{\circ}_f)_{\text{reactants}}$$

where $\Delta H^{\circ}_{\text{reaction}}$ = standard enthalpy or heat of reaction

ΔH°_f = standard enthalpy or heat of formation of a substance (Text Table 18-2)

18-4
The second law

1 The second law

$$\Delta S > 0 \qquad \text{for spontaneous change in an isolated system}$$

where ΔS = entropy change of a system, J mol^{-1} K^{-1}

2 Free-energy change for an isothermal system

$$\Delta G = \Delta H - T\,\Delta S$$

where ΔG = free-energy change, or energy available to do work

3 Calculation of free-energy change of a reaction from tabulated values of free energy of formation

$$\Delta G^{\circ}_{\text{reaction}} = \Sigma(\Delta G^{\circ}_f)_{\text{products}} - \Sigma(\Delta G^{\circ}_f)_{\text{reactants}}$$

where ΔG°_f = standard free energy of formation (Text Table 18-4)

4 Entropy change for a phase change

$$\Delta S_{\text{fus}} = \frac{\Delta H_{\text{fus}}}{T_m}$$

where ΔS_{fus} = entropy of fusion

ΔH_{fus} = enthalpy or heat of fusion

T_m = melting temperature, K

A similar equation applies to the entropy of vaporization.

5 Calculation of absolute entropy of a reaction

$$\Delta S^{\circ} = \Sigma S^{\circ}_{\text{products}} - \Sigma S^{\circ}_{\text{reactants}}$$

where S° = absolute entropy of a substance (see Text Table 18-3)

18-6
Thermodynamics and equilibrium

1 Relationship between free energy and equilibrium constant

$$\Delta G° = -2.303RT \log K_P$$

LEARNING OBJECTIVES

As a result of studying Chap. 18 you should be able to do the following:
Write the definition and give an example illustrating the use of each key term.

18-1
The first law

1 Clearly distinguish between spontaneous and nonspontaneous changes in a thermodynamic sense. (Self Test 6)
2 Calculate the work done by a gas as it expands against a constant force. (Text Example 18-1; Text Probs. 18-1, 18-2, 18-7 to 18-9, 18-14, 18-15, 18-59) (New Skills Example 1)
3 Write a word statement and mathematical equation of the first law of thermodynamics. (Text Prob. 18-3) (Self Test 1, 3)
4 Use the first law to calculate heat, work, and ΔE changes associated with the expansion of an ideal gas. (Text Example 18-2; Text Probs. 18-2, 18-5, 18-10 to 18-15, 18-59) (New Skills Example 2; Self Test 1, 7, 12, 13, 17)

18-2
Enthalpy and heat capacity

1 Write equations relating enthalpy to (a) energy, (b) heat change at constant pressure, and (c) molar heat capacity at constant pressure. (Self Test 8)
2 Calculate ΔH for a system given ΔE, and vice versa. (Text Example 18-3; Text Probs. 18-14 to 18-18, 18-59)
3 Use heat capacities to calculate temperature changes in a system given the heat change and to calculate the heat necessary to give a certain temperature change. (Text Example 18-4; Text Probs. 18-27 to 18-29) (New Skills Example 3; Self Test 15, 16)

18-3
Enthalpy changes in chemical reactions

1 Use Hess's law to calculate ΔH of reaction from tabulated values of $\Delta H_f°$. (Text Table 18-2; Text Examples 18-5, 18-6; Text Probs. 18-19 to 18-25) (New Skills Example 4; Self Test 19)

18-4
The second law

1 Write a word statement and mathematical expression for the second law of thermodynamics. (Self Test 9)
2 Predict the sign of entropy changes for physical and chemical processes. (Text Probs. 18-32, 18-41) (New Skills Example 5; Self Test 9)
3 Relate entropy to disorder and probability. (Text Probs. 18-33, 18-34, 18-38) (Self Test 4)

18-5
Entropy and free-energy changes

1 Clearly distinguish between the entropy change of a system and the entropy change of the surroundings. (Text Prob. 18-40) (Self Test 14)
2 Explain why free energy is a reliable criterion for predicting spontaneity of reactions based on its relationship to enthalpy and entropy. (Text Prob. 18-45)
3 Use the algebraic sign of ΔG to predict whether a reaction is spontaneous or nonspontaneous. (Text Prob. 18-51) (Self Test 5)
4 Use the algebraic sign of ΔH and ΔS to predict the effects of temperature on the

spontaneity of a reaction. (Text Probs. 18-46, 18-47, 18-52, 18-53) (New Skills Sec. 18-5:1; New Skills Example 9; Self Test 2, 10, 24)

5 Calculate entropy change of a phase transition. (Text Example 18-7; Text Probs. 18-35 to 18-37, 18-64) (New Skills Example 6; Self Test 20)

6 Calculate entropy changes from tabulated third law entropy values or from tabulated values of enthalpy and free energy. (Text Example 18-8; Text Probs. 18-42 to 18-44) (Self Test 21)

7 Calculate free-energy changes from tabulated values of standard enthalpy of formation and absolute entropies. (Text Tables 18-2, 18-3; Text Example 18-9; Text Probs. 18-52, 18-53)

8 Calculate free-energy changes from tabulated values of free energy of formation. (Text Table 18-4; Text Example 18-10; Text Probs. 18-48 to 18-50) (New Skills Example 7; Self Test 22)

18-6
Thermodynamics
and equilibrium

1 Explain the changes in free energy and entropy of a system as it approaches equilibrium. (Text Fig. 18-4)

2 Calculate equilibrium constants from tabulated thermodynamic data. (Text Example 18-11; Text Probs. 18-54 to 18-56) (New Skills Example 8; Self Test 25)

3 Calculate free-energy changes from equilibrium data. (Text Probs. 18-58, 18-61, 18-62)

4 Calculate the temperature at which a reaction is at equilibrium. (Text Prob. 18-53) (New Skills Example 9; Self Test 11)

NEW SKILLS

18-1
The first law

Years of observation have shown that energy is neither created nor destroyed during physical or chemical changes but that it often changes forms. A bunsen burner converts the chemical energy of fuel and oxidizer into heat energy, an automobile engine converts it to mechanical energy, and a power plant converts it to electrical energy. The first law of thermodynamics says that this energy is not destroyed but merely changes form. The total energy of an isolated system before a chemical reaction takes place is the same as the total energy after the reaction. Energy is conserved. The first law expresses this conservation of energy in terms of heat added and work done on a system. The increase in energy of a system is equal to heat added plus the work done on the system. The sign conventions for q and w are easy to remember if you think of an engine. You add heat to an engine and it does work. Heat into the engine is positive and work done by the engine is positive. The engine is representative of any system.

$$q(+) \longrightarrow \boxed{\text{Engine}} \longrightarrow w(+)$$

It follows that work done *on* the system will be negative. The first law becomes

$$\Delta E = q - w$$

Quite often the heat and work effects are calculated separately, then combined to give the energy change.

1 Work of expansion

When a gas expands against a resisting force it does work. If the gas is the system, the work of the system is a positive quantity. Example 18-1 in the text illustrates this calculation. For a compression process V_{final} is less than $V_{initial}$, so ΔV is negative and w is negative. P_{ext} is the pressure exerted to compress the gas.

● **EXAMPLE 1**   **Problem**: Calculate the work done on a gas to compress 1.0 mol from 50 to 30 liters by a force exerting a pressure of 2.0 atm on the gas.

Solution:

$$w = P_{ext} \, \Delta V$$

$$P_{ext} = 2.0 \text{ atm}; \quad V_{initial} = 50 \text{ liters}; \quad V_{final} = 30 \text{ liters}$$

$$w = P_{ext}(V_{final} - V_{initial}) = 2.0 \text{ atm } (30 \text{ liters} - 50 \text{ liters}) = -40 \text{ liter atm}$$

$$-40 \text{ liter atm} \times 0.101 \text{ kJ (liter atm)}^{-1} = -4.0 \text{ kJ} \ \bullet$$

2 Calculation of ΔE, q, or w using the first law

The first law can be used to calculate $\Delta E, q$, or w if two of these quantities are known. Text Example 18-2 illustrates this calculation.

● **EXAMPLE 2**   **Problem**: If 2 mol of an ideal gas expand isothermally (at constant temperature) from 10.0 to 60.0 liters against a resisting pressure of 0.500 atm, calculate ΔE, q, and w for the expansion process.

Solution: The energy of an ideal gas is a function of its temperature only. If the temperature remains constant so does the energy. Therefore, for any constant-temperature expansion of an ideal gas

$$\Delta E = 0$$

From the first law

$$\Delta E = 0 = q - w$$

$$q = w$$

The heat added to an ideal gas during an isothermal expansion is equal to the work of expansion done by the gas.

$$w = P_{ext} \, \Delta V = 0.500 \text{ atm } (60.0 \text{ liters} - 10.0 \text{ liters}) = 25.0 \text{ liter atm}$$

$$25.0 \text{ liter atm} \times 0.101 \text{ kJ (liter atm)}^{-1} = 2.53 \text{ kJ}$$

$$q = w = 2.53 \text{ kJ} \ \bullet$$

18-2
Enthalpy and heat
capacity

1 Calculation of enthalpy changes

The enthalpy change of a substance undergoing a physical change may be calculated by several different techniques. When the energy change is known, it is convenient to use the definition of enthalpy, $\Delta H = \Delta E + \Delta(PV)$. The $\Delta(PV)$ term is usually small unless a gas is involved, so ΔH and ΔE normally have very similar values in condensed systems. For processes taking place at constant pressure, the relationship $\Delta H = q_P = nC_P \, \Delta t$ can be used. Text Example 18-3 illustrates this calculation.

2 Heat capacity calculations

Heat changes accompanying physical changes are calculated using heat capacities.

● **EXAMPLE 3**   **Problem**: A piece of aluminum weighing 10.0 g is heated in boiling water so its temperature is 100°C. It is quickly dried and placed in a beaker containing 70.0 g of cold water whose initial temperature is 15.0°C. Assuming no heat is lost to the surroundings, what is the final temperature of the beaker of water?

Solution: The system in this problem includes the aluminum plus the cold water. The boiling water is not part of the system. After the aluminum is added to the cold water there is no heat gained or lost from the system so the net heat change is zero. The aluminum gives up heat to the cold water until both are at the same final temperature. A heat balance on the system gives

$$\text{Net heat change} = 0 = \text{heat lost by Al} + \text{heat gained by } H_2O$$

or

$$-\text{Heat lost by Al} = \text{heat gained by } H_2O$$

Using the relationship $q = nC_P \, \Delta t$

$$-(nC_P \, \Delta t)_{Al} = (nC_P \, \Delta t)_{H_2O}$$

$$-n_{Al}(C_P)_{Al}(t_f - t_i)_{Al} = n_{H_2O}(C_P)_{H_2O} \, \Delta t_{H_2O}$$

where t_f = final temperature and t_i = initial temperature.

From Table 18-1 in the text we see that

$$(C_P)_{Al} = 24.3 \text{ J }°C^{-1} \text{ mol}^{-1} \qquad (C_P)_{H_2O} = 75.3 \text{ J }°C^{-1} \text{ mol}^{-1}$$

Substituting appropriate values into the heat-balance equation gives

$$-(10.0 \text{ g Al}) \left(\frac{1 \text{ mol Al}}{27.0 \text{ g Al}} \right) (24.3 \text{ J mol}^{-1} \, °C^{-1}) [(t_f)_{Al} - 100°C] =$$

$$70.0 \text{ g } H_2O \left(\frac{1 \text{ mol } H_2O}{18 \text{ g } H_2O} \right) (75.3 \text{ J mol}^{-1} \, °C^{-1}) (t_{f(H_2O)} - 15°C)$$

and since $(t_f)_{Al} = (t_f)_{H_2O}$

$$-9.00 \, t_f + 900 = 292.8 \, t_f - 4392$$

$$t_f = \frac{4392 + 900}{292.8 + 9.00} = \frac{5292}{301.8} = 17.5°C \quad ●$$

Example 18-4 in the text illustrates the calculation of enthalpy changes using heat capacities.

18-3
Enthalpy changes in
chemical reactions

Enthalpy changes accompanying chemical changes are often measured experimentally, but they are also calculated using Hess's law. There are many chemical reactions for which the enthalpy change cannot be measured directly, so Hess's law is used.

● **EXAMPLE 4**   **Problem**: When carbon is burned with just enough oxygen to form carbon monoxide the actual products are a mixture of carbon dioxide and unburned carbon, so the ΔH_f°

of carbon monoxide cannot be determined experimentally. It can be determined from readily available experimental data by application of Hess's law. Use Hess's law to calculate ΔH_f° of CO given the heats of combustion of C and CO. The heats of combustion of carbon and carbon monoxide can be determined experimentally.

$$C(s) + O_2(g) \longrightarrow CO_2(g) \qquad \Delta H = -393.5 \text{ kJ}$$

$$CO(g) + \tfrac{1}{2} O_2(g) \longrightarrow CO_2(g) \qquad \Delta H = -283.0 \text{ kJ}$$

Solution: The chemical reaction for the formation of CO from its elements can be obtained from the given reactions by reversing the reaction for combustion of CO and adding it to the combustion reaction for carbon.

$$CO_2(g) \longrightarrow CO(g) + \tfrac{1}{2} O_2(g) \qquad\qquad \Delta H = +283.0 \text{ kJ}$$

$$C(s) + O_2(g) \longrightarrow CO_2(g) \qquad\qquad \Delta H = -393.5 \text{ kJ}$$

$$\overline{CO_2(g) + C(s) + O_2(g) \longrightarrow CO(g) + \tfrac{1}{2} O_2(g) + CO_2(g) \quad \Delta H = -110.5 \text{ kJ}}$$

If 1 CO_2 and $\tfrac{1}{2} O_2$ are subtracted from both sides of this equation, the desired equation for the heat of formation of CO is obtained.

$$C(s) + \tfrac{1}{2} O_2(g) \longrightarrow CO(g) \qquad \Delta H_f^\circ = -110.5 \text{ kJ}$$

The ΔH for the overall reaction is found by treating the ΔH values for the given reactions in the same manner. Simply add the ΔH values of the elementary reactions to get ΔH of the overall reaction.

$$(\Delta H_f^\circ)_{CO} = 283.0 - 393.5 = -110.5 \text{ kJ}$$

Thus ΔH_f° for CO has been determined from available experimental data by application of Hess's law. ●

Example 18-5 in the text is a similar problem.

In general, the application of Hess's law becomes:

$$\Delta H_{reaction}^\circ = \Sigma (\Delta H_f^\circ)_{products} - \Sigma (\Delta H_f^\circ)_{reactants}$$

from which the ΔH° of any reaction may be calculated from tabulated values of the standard enthalpy of formation. Example 18-6 in the text shows the application of Hess's law to calculate the heat of combustion of methyl alcohol.

18-4
The second law

Entropy changes

As a system moves from an ordered state to a disordered state, the entropy increases. The entropy of a gas is higher than that of a liquid or solid. A solution has higher entropy than its unmixed components. Chemical or physical changes that cause disorder or mixing, generate gases, or substantially increase the number of moles will have a positive ΔS.

● **EXAMPLE 5**

Problem: Predict the sign of the entropy change for each of the following processes: (a) melting of ice   (b) shuffling of a new deck of cards   (c) conversion of amorphous sulfur to crystalline sulfur   (d) burning of carbon monoxide to carbon dioxide   (e) $2Fe(s) + \tfrac{3}{2} O_2(g) \longrightarrow Fe_2O_3(s)$

Solution: (a) H_2O goes from an ordered solid state to a disordered liquid state. ΔS is positive.

(b) The cards go from an ordered state to a random distribution. ΔS is positive.

(c) The sulfur goes from a disordered amorphous state to an ordered crystalline state. ΔS is negative.

(d) $CO(g) + \frac{1}{2} O_2(g) \longrightarrow CO_2(g)$ The number of moles of gas decreases from $1\frac{1}{2}$ to 1, so the system becomes more ordered. ΔS is negative. Note that Δn_{gas} equals the number of moles of gaseous products minus the number of moles of gaseous reactants so $\Delta n_{gas} = 1 - 1.5 = -0.5$. ΔS always has the same sign as Δn_{gas}.

(e) $\Delta n_{gas} = 0 - 1.5 = -1.5$ ΔS is negative. •

18-5 Entropy and free-energy changes

1 ΔG, ΔH, ΔS, and spontaneity

Free energy is a measure of the ability or capacity of a system to do work. The free energy of a system decreases during a spontaneous change so it loses its ability to do work. When all of the capacity to do work has been used, the system is at equilibrium and the free energy cannot decrease further. Another way of saying this is ΔG is negative for a spontaneous process and $\Delta G = 0$ at equilibrium. Since $\Delta G = \Delta H - T\Delta S$, either ΔH or ΔS can determine the sign of ΔG depending on the relative magnitude of ΔH and $T\Delta S$. Usually ΔH is larger than $T\Delta S$ so enthalpy (heat) considerations govern the sign of ΔG and determine whether or not a reaction or process is spontaneous. Occasionally ΔH is small and $T\Delta S$ may determine the sign of ΔG, so molecular ordering becomes the most important factor in deciding whether or not a reaction can proceed. If the temperature is high enough, the $T\Delta S$ term will become the deciding factor. When $\Delta H = T\Delta S$, the energy and molecular ordering exactly balance and $\Delta G = 0$. The system is at equilibrium.

2 Entropy of phase changes

Entropy and enthalpy of phase changes are related by the expressions

$$\Delta S_{fus} = \frac{\Delta H_{fus}}{T_m} \quad \text{and} \quad \Delta S_{vap} = \frac{\Delta H_{vap}}{T_b}$$

• **EXAMPLE 6**   **Problem:** Calculate the entropy change for the condensation of 1 mol of water at 100°C. $\Delta H_{vap} = 40.7$ kJ mol^{-1}.

Solution: The enthalpy of condensation is the negative of ΔH_{vap}.

$$\Delta S_{cond} = \frac{\Delta H_{cond}}{T_b} = \frac{-40.7 \text{ kJ mol}^{-1}}{373 \text{ K}} = -0.109 \text{ kJ K}^{-1} \text{ mol}^{-1} \quad \bullet$$

Example 18-7 in the text is a similar problem.

3 Free-energy calculations

Hess's law applies to free-energy changes in the same manner as we have seen for enthalpy changes. This can be illustrated by the following example.

• **EXAMPLE 7**   **Problem:** Calculate the standard free energy for the conversion of graphite to diamond.

$$(\Delta G_f^\circ)_{graphite} = 0$$

$$(\Delta G_f^\circ)_{diamond} = +2.91 \text{ kJ mol}^{-1}$$

Solution: The reaction for the process is

$$C_{\text{(graphite)}} \longrightarrow C_{\text{(diamond)}}$$

Applying Hess's law to the free-energy change for the reaction gives

$$\Delta G^\circ_{\text{reaction}} = \Sigma(\Delta G^\circ_f)_{\text{products}} - \Sigma(\Delta G^\circ_f)_{\text{reactants}}$$

$$= (\Delta G^\circ_f)_{\text{diamond}} - (\Delta G^\circ_f)_{\text{graphite}} = +2.91 \text{ kJ} - 0 = 2.91 \text{ kJ}$$

Since ΔG is positive the reaction is nonspontaneous. This is one explanation why many years and much effort were expended before a way to accomplish the conversion was found. Note that since the forward reaction is nonspontaneous, the reverse action (decomposition of diamond to graphite) is spontaneous! Do not worry about your diamond ring decomposing though; thermodynamics only predicts the possibility of a reaction occurring. It says nothing about the rate of reaction. Decomposition of diamond to graphite *is* spontaneous, but the reaction is extremely slow. •

Free energy of reaction can be calculated from tabulated values of free energy of formation. Example 18-10 in the text shows this calculation and Example 18-8 applies the Hess's law technique to calculation of absolute entropy.

18-6
Thermodynamics
and equilibrium

1 Calculation of equilibrium constants from free-energy values
The concepts of equilibrium and thermodynamics are joined by the equation

$$\Delta G^\circ = -2.303RT \log K_P$$

You need to be able to calculate equilibrium constants from tabulated values of standard free energy of formation. This is illustrated by the following example.

• **EXAMPLE 8**   **Problem:** Calculate the equilibrium constant at 298 K for the reaction

$$CaCO_3(s) \rightleftharpoons CaO(s) + CO_2(g)$$

given $(\Delta G^\circ_f)_{CaCO_3(s)} = -1129 \text{ kJ mol}^{-1}$
$(\Delta G^\circ_f)_{CaO(s)} = -604.2 \text{ kJ mol}^{-1}$
$(\Delta G^\circ_f)_{CO_2(g)} = -394.4 \text{ kJ mol}^{-1}$

Solution: ΔG° for the reaction is found by Hess's law

$$\Delta G^\circ_{\text{reaction}} = \Sigma(\Delta G^\circ_f)_{\text{products}} - \Sigma(\Delta G^\circ_f)_{\text{reactants}}$$

$$= (\Delta G^\circ_f)_{CO_2} + (\Delta G^\circ_f)_{CaO} - (\Delta G^\circ_f)_{CaCO_3}$$

$$= -394.4 \text{ kJ} + (-604.2 \text{ kJ}) - (-1129 \text{ kJ}) = +130 \text{ kJ}$$

Note that since ΔG is positive the reaction is nonspontaneous. The equilibrium constant can be calculated from the relationship

$$\Delta G^\circ = -2.303RT \log K_P$$

First put this in the form

$$\log K_P = \frac{-\Delta G^\circ}{2.303RT} = \frac{-(+130,000 \text{ J mol}^{-1})}{2.303(8.314 \text{ J mol}^{-1} \text{ K}^{-1})(298 \text{ K})} = -22.8$$

$$K_P = 10^{-22.8} = 1.6 \times 10^{-23}$$

The equilibrium expression for this reaction is $K_P = P_{CO_2}$. Therefore, the pressure of CO_2 in equilibrium with $CaCO_3$ (limestone) at standard conditions is 1.6×10^{-23} atm. ●

Thus we see that another interpretation of a nonspontaneous reaction is $K_P < 1.0$ so that the equilibrium concentrations strongly favor the reactants over the products.

2 Free energy and the position of equilibrium

What happens to the equilibrium constant in the foregoing example as the temperature increases? One would expect $CaCO_3$ to decompose if the temperature is high enough. In fact, this is the very process used to make lime (CaO) from limestone ($CaCO_3$) in a lime kiln.

● **EXAMPLE 9**   **Problem**: Calculate the temperature at which the decomposition of $CaCO_3$ becomes spontaneous at 1 atm pressure. $(\Delta H_f^\circ)_{CaCO_3} = -1207$ kJ mol^{-1}, $(\Delta H_f^\circ)_{CaO} = -635.5$ kJ mol^{-1}, and $(\Delta H_f^\circ)_{CO_2} = -393.5$ kJ mol^{-1}.

Solution: To solve this problem we need to find how ΔG° for the reaction varies with temperature. Using the relationship

$$\Delta G^\circ = \Delta H^\circ - T \Delta S^\circ$$

we can take advantage of the fact that ΔH° and ΔS° are essentially constant over a fairly wide temperature range. We can determine their values at 298 K from tabulated data and assume these values hold constant over the temperature range of interest.

First we find ΔH° from Hess's law

$$\Delta H^\circ = \Sigma(\Delta H_f^\circ)_{products} - \Sigma(\Delta H_f^\circ)_{reactants}$$

$$= (\Delta H_f^\circ)_{CaO} + (\Delta H_f^\circ)_{CO_2} - (\Delta H_f^\circ)_{CaCO_3}$$

$$= (-393.5 \text{ kJ}) + (-635.5 \text{ kJ}) - (-1207 \text{ kJ}) = +178 \text{ kJ}$$

Now we can determine ΔS° using the value of ΔG° from Example 8.

$$\Delta S^\circ = \frac{\Delta H^\circ - \Delta G^\circ}{T} = \frac{178 \text{ kJ} - 130 \text{ kJ}}{298 \text{ K}} = 0.161 \text{ kJ K}^{-1}$$

We can substitute the values for ΔH° and ΔS° into the equation for ΔG° to get an expression relating ΔG° to temperature.

$$\Delta G^\circ = 178 - 0.161T$$

Since both ΔH° and ΔS° are positive, ΔG° will become more negative as the temperature is increased. (See the table in Sec. 18-5 of the text.) If the temperature is high enough ΔG will become negative and the reaction will be spontaneous.

At some temperature, ΔG° will equal 0 and the reaction will be at equilibrium. In this case, you can see that equilibrium signifies $K_P = 1$, since when $\Delta G^\circ = 0 = -2.303RT \log K_P$, $\log K_P = 0$ and $K_P = 1$. At any temperature above that which gives $\Delta G^\circ = 0$, the reaction will be spontaneous because ΔG° will be negative.

If we set $\Delta G^\circ = 0$ in the expression relating ΔG° to temperature, we find

$$\Delta G^\circ = 0 = 178 - 0.161T$$

$$T = \frac{178}{0.161} = 1100 \text{ K} \quad \text{or} \quad \text{about } 830°C$$

Therefore, at any temperature above $830°C$, $CaCO_3$ will decompose to CaO and CO_2 with an equilibrium pressure of CO_2 greater than 1 atm. •

   In general, we can say that the temperature at which a reaction is at equilibrium is given by

$$\Delta G° = 0 = \Delta H° - T \Delta S°$$

$$T_{\Delta G° \to 0} = \frac{\Delta H°}{\Delta S°}$$

If $\Delta H°$ and $\Delta S°$ have the same algebraic sign, equilibrium will occur at some finite temperature.

SELF TEST

True or false   ____ 1 When a system does work its energy decreases.

____ 2 Exothermic reactions are capable of doing work and therefore are spontaneous.

____ 3 The total quantity of energy available in an isolated system is constant.

____ 4 The most probable state of an isolated system left to itself is the most disordered state.

____ 5 A spontaneous change results in a decrease in free energy of the system.

Completion   6 In order to cause a nonspontaneous change, _____ must be done on the system.

7 If a system absorbs heat from its surroundings and has work done on it by the surroundings, the sign of ΔE is _____ .

8 The heat necessary to increase the temperature of one mole of a substance by one degree Celsius is called _____ .

9 In an isolated system the sign of ΔS for a spontaneous change must be _____ _____ .

10 A reaction for which both ΔH and ΔS are positive will be _____ at high temperatures.

11 When $\Delta G = 0$, the system is _____ .

Multiple choice   12 If a system absorbs heat from its surroundings and its energy remains constant, it must

(a) do work on the surroundings   (b) be compressed

(c) expand into a vacuum

(d) violate the first law of thermodynamics since energy cannot be conserved if heat is absorbed

13 One mole of ideal gas is allowed to expand into a vacuum. During the expansion, the temperature of the gas remains constant (an isothermal expansion). Which of the following statements is true?

(a) $q = 0$; ΔE and w are positive numbers

(b) $\Delta E = w = 0$; q is a positive number

(c) $\Delta E = 0$; w and q are positive numbers

(d) $\Delta E = w = q = 0$

14 In the process of photosynthesis, small molecules such as CO_2 and H_2O are combined to form large, ordered biological molecules in living plants. Which of the following statements is true?

(a) This is an example of violation of the second law of thermodynamics since the entropy of the universe is decreasing as the plant grows.

(b) The second law is not violated but thermodynamics does not apply in this case.

(c) The second law is not violated because the entropy of the surroundings is increased.

(d) The second law is not violated because the entropy of the universe remains constant.

15 If 5 g of ice at $0°C$ is added to 100 g of water at $25.0°C$, what is ΔH for the overall process? Heat of fusion of ice = 335 J g^{-1}; specific heat of water = 4.18 J g^{-1} K^{-1}.

    (a) -3350 J   **(b)** 3350 J   **(c)** 1675 J   **(d)** 0

16 What is the final temperature of the water in Prob. 15 after the ice has melted if no heat is lost from the system?

    (a) $25.0°C$ **(b)** $21.0°C$ **(c)** $21.2°C$

    (d) cannot be determined without additional data to define the system

17 What is ΔE for the evaporation of 1 mol of water at its normal boiling point? The molar heat of vaporization is 40.7 kJ mol^{-1}.

    (a) 40.7 kJ   **(b)** -40.7 kJ   **(c)** 37.6 kJ   **(d)** 0

18 Given the enthalpy of the following reactions at $25°C$ and 1 atm pressure:

$$S(s) + O_2(g) \longrightarrow SO_2(g) \qquad \Delta H° = -296.8 \text{ kJ mol}^{-1}$$

$$SO_2 + \tfrac{1}{2} O_2 \longrightarrow SO_3(g) \qquad \Delta H° = -98.9 \text{ kJ mol}^{-1}$$

What is the standard enthalpy of formation of SO_3?

    (a) -395.7 kJ   **(b)** -197.9 kJ   **(c)** +197.9 kJ

    (d) cannot be determined from the data given

19 What is the standard heat of reaction for the combustion of ethylene

$$C_2H_4(g) + 3 O_2(g) \longrightarrow 2CO_2(g) + 2H_2O(l)$$

given these standard heats of formation (see Table 18-2 of the text):

$(\Delta H_f°)_{C_2H_4(g)} = +52.3 \text{ kJ}, (\Delta H_f°)_{CO_2(g)} = -393.5 \text{ kJ}, \text{and } (\Delta H_f°)_{H_2O(l)} = -285.8 \text{ kJ}.$

    (a) -1411 kJ   **(b)** +1411 kJ   **(c)** -627 kJ   **(d)** -731.6 kJ

20 What is the entropy change when 1 mol of liquid water at $100°C$ is converted to vapor? The molar heat of vaporization is 40.7 kJ mol^{-1} K^{-1} mol^{-1}.

    (a) 149 J mol^{-1} K^{-1} **(b)** -109 J mol^{-1} K^{-1} **(c)** 109 J mol^{-1} K^{-1}

    (d) 407 J mol^{-1} K^{-1}

21 What is the standard entropy change for formation of 1 mol of ammonia from its elements?

$$N_2(g) + 3H_2(g) \longrightarrow 2NH_3(g)$$

The third law entropies at 298 K are $S°_{N_2(g)} = 191.5$ J mol^{-1} K^{-1}, $S°_{H_2(g)} = 130.6$ J mol^{-1} K^{-1}, and $S°_{NH_3(g)} = 192.3$ J mol^{-1} K^{-1}.

    (a) 0   **(b)** -129.8 J mol^{-1} K^{-1} **(c)** -198.7 J mol^{-1} K^{-1}

    (d) -99.4 J mol^{-1} K^{-1}

22 If the reaction

$$CO(g) + NO(g) \longrightarrow CO_2(g) + \tfrac{1}{2} N_2(g)$$

were spontaneous, it might solve the problem of automobile exhaust emissions. It would remove two troublesome pollutants, CO and NO, by converting them to harmless CO_2 and N_2. What is the value of ΔG for this reaction at standard conditions?

$(\Delta G_f^\circ)_{CO} = -137.2$ kJ mol^{-1}, $(\Delta G_f^\circ)_{CO_2} = -394.4$ kJ mol^{-1}, and $(\Delta G_f^\circ)_{NO} = +86.6$ kJ mol^{-1}.

(a) +445 kJ   (b) –445 kJ   (c) –343.8 kJ   (d) +343.8 kJ

23 Above what temperature will Ag_2O decompose to silver and oxygen at 1 atm pressure? For Ag_2O, $\Delta H_f^\circ = -30.5$ kJ and $\Delta G_f^\circ = -10.9$ kJ.

(a) 463°C   (b) 190°C   (c) 165°C

(d) not enough data given for calculation

24 Consider the following possible combinations of ΔH° and ΔS°. Which of these processes might be spontaneous at some temperature at 1 atm?

Process	ΔH°	ΔS°
1	–	+
2	+	–
3	–	–
4	+	+

(a) 1 and 2 are always spontaneous; 3 and 4 are uncertain.

(b) 3 and 4 are always spontaneous; 1 and 2 are uncertain.

(c) 1 is always spontaneous; 2 is always nonspontaneous; 3 and 4 are uncertain.

(d) 3 is always spontaneous; 4 is always nonspontaneous; 1 and 2 are uncertain.

25 What is the equilibrium constant at 25°C for the decomposition reaction given in problem 23?

(a) –1.91   (b) 1.2×10^{-2} (c) 1.7×10^{-23} (d) 4.5×10^{-6}

19
ELECTROCHEMISTRY

CHAPTER OVERVIEW

This chapter discusses the relationship between chemical and electrical energies. We will learn the terms associated with electrodes and electrochemical cells and study their stoichiometry. The operation and applications of some practical cells are described.

19-1
Galvanic cells

Galvanic cells use a spontaneous chemical reaction to generate electricity. Theoretically, any spontaneous redox reaction could be used to generate electricity, but design problems have limited the number of practical galvanic cells to a few types. These are covered in Sec. 19-6. This section discusses the theory of their operation.

To make a galvanic cell from any spontaneous redox reaction we simply physically separate the oxidation and reduction half-reactions into separate compartments and connect them electrically. This is shown for a zinc-copper cell in text Fig. 19-2. Study Fig. 19-2 to see how this electrical connection is made and how the electrons get from the oxidation half-cell to the reduction half-cell. Note how a salt bridge or porous plate is used to allow ions to migrate so electrical neutrality is preserved in the electrolyte solutions.

The voltage of a chemical cell is about 2 V or less. We will see how this voltage can be calculated very accurately depending on the cell components and concentrations.

Cell diagrams are shorthand notations showing how the cell is constructed. Practice writing cell reactions from cell diagrams, and vice versa.

Electrodes are devices for providing electrical contact between the reacting ions in solution and the external circuit. Each cell has two electrodes and chemical reactions occur at the electrode surfaces. The type of electrode used depends on the state of the chemical species in the reaction, but they all serve the same purpose: to transfer electrons between the reacting chemical and the external circuit. Remember that oxidation always occurs at the anode and anions always flow toward the anode. A voltmeter in the external circuit measures the cell voltage. Galvanic cells always have a positive cell potential.

19-2
Electrolytic cells

An electrolytic cell uses electrical energy to force a nonspontaneous reaction to occur. Electrical energy (voltage) is used to overcome the negative ΔG for the reaction. Theoretically, any nonspontaneous redox reaction could be made to occur in an electrolytic cell, but from a practical standpoint we cannot always figure out how to get the electrical energy into the separate reduction and oxidation half-reactions. Many successful chemical reactions are carried out by electrolysis on a commercial basis, and the text discusses electrolysis of HCl and NaCl solutions and molten NaCl. Compare these systems so you can see how the products are formed and understand the electron-transfer processes. The cell potential of an electrolytic cell is always negative.

Faraday's laws are used to relate the amount of chemical reacting to the quantity of electricity (coulombs) flowing through the cell.

19-3
Standard electrode potentials

The sum of the half-cell potentials for the reduction and oxidation half-reactions gives the cell potential. Half-cell potentials for reduction half-reactions are given in Table 19-1 in the text. These values are relative to the standard hydrogen electrode. To determine the voltage of a cell, read the reduction half-cell potential directly from Table 19-1. Since oxidation half-cell reactions are found by reversing reduction half-cell reactions, the oxidation potential is the reduction potential times −1. Simply change the sign of the value given in Table 19-1 to get the oxidation half-cell potential. The cell potential or voltage is the sum of the oxidation and reduction half-cell potentials. Remember that cell voltages do not depend on amounts of material reacting, so Table 19-1 values are never multiplied or divided by stoichiometric coefficients.

Pay attention to the hints in the text on predicting spontaneity of reaction and strengths of oxidizing and reducing agents from the relative position of the reactants in Table 19-1. It may save you some time in working problems on exams. It is well worthwhile to become familiar with Table 19-1.

19-4
Free energy,
cell voltage,
and equilibrium

Thermodynamics and electrochemistry are related by

$$\Delta G = -n\mathcal{F}\mathcal{E}$$

The table in the text shows how the algebraic sign of $\mathcal{E}$ can predict spontaneity just as ΔG does. Note the opposite signs of the variables, however.

The Nernst equation is used to calculate cell voltages for cells where concentrations are not 1 M. Temperature effects are also included in this equation.

Since $\Delta G°$ is related to both K and $\mathcal{E}°$, we have a powerful relationship between thermodynamics, equilibrium, and electrochemistry. You will be expected to work problems relating the basic constants of these three fields of study.

19-5
The electrochemical
measurement of pH

The Nernst equation relates cell potential to the concentration of electrolyte. If the electrolyte is H^+, we can determine its concentration by measuring the cell potential with a voltmeter. Electrodes responding specifically to H^+ ions have been developed for use in pH meters. The same technique is employed using ion-specific electrodes for measuring the concentration of a wide variety of ionic species.

19-6
Commercial galvanic
cells

The most important commercial galvanic cells (batteries) are the Leclanche dry cell, the lead storage cell, and the NiCad (nickel-cadmium) cell. Study text Figs. 19-9 and 19-10 and the corresponding chemical reactions so you are familiar with their operation.

A fuel cell is simply a galvanic cell designed so the reactants can be supplied and the products removed to give continuous operation.

The H_2-O_2 cell shown in Fig. 19-11 is typical of fuel cells. The use of fuel cells involves a dilemma: those with high efficiencies require very expensive catalysts and fuel, while those operating on less expensive fuels or catalysts show poor operating characteristics. If design and development problems can be overcome, fuel cells offer great promise for power generation.

KEY EQUATIONS

19-2
Electrolytic cells

Faraday's laws:

$$1 \text{ faraday} = 9.65 \times 10^4 \text{ C}$$

$$\text{Coulombs} = \text{amperes} \times \text{seconds}$$

$$\text{No. of equivalents reacting} = \text{No. of faradays of electricity} = \frac{\text{amps} \times \text{seconds}}{9.65 \times 10^4 \text{ C } \mathscr{F}^{-1}}$$

19-3
Standard electrode potentials

$$\mathscr{E}^\circ_{cell} = \mathscr{E}^\circ_{oxidation} + \mathscr{E}^\circ_{reduction}$$

19-4
Free energy, cell voltage, and equilibrium

$$\Delta G = -n\mathscr{F}\mathscr{E}$$

The Nernst equation (at 25°C): $\mathscr{E} = \mathscr{E}^\circ - \dfrac{0.0592}{n} \log Q$

Equilibrium constant: $\mathscr{E}^\circ = \dfrac{0.0592}{n} \log K$

LEARNING OBJECTIVES

As a result of studying Chap. 19, you should be able to do the following:
Write the definition and give an example illustrating the use of each key term.

19-1
Galvanic cells

1 Tell how a galvanic cell differs from an electrolytic cell with respect to sign of ΔG of the cell reaction, sign of $\mathscr{E}^\circ_{cell}$, and relationship between chemical and electrical energy. (Text Prob. 19-1)

2 Give an example showing how a redox reaction can be divided into two half-cell reactions.

3 Assign oxidation and reduction half-reactions to the correct electrode. (Text Probs. 19-2, 19-3) (Self Test 1, 9)

4 List three functions of a salt bridge. (Text Probs. 19-5, 19-23) (Self Test 15)

5 Write a cell diagram for the Daniell cell. (Self Test 7, 8, 17)

6 List two functions of electrodes.

7 Give examples of a metal–metal ion electrode, a gas-ion electrode, and a metal–insoluble salt-anion electrode.

8   Relate the voltage of a cell to the spontaneity of the cell reaction. (Text Example 19-7; Text Prob. 19-20) (Self Test 3)

9   Write cell diagrams given the cell reaction. (Text Prob. 19-20) (New Skills Example 3; Self Test 2, 14, 16)

10   Make a drawing of the cell compartments given the cell reaction. Show the anode, cathode, and direction of electron flow and give the half-cell reactions. (Text Probs. 19-3, 19-4) (New Skills Example 4; Self Test 13)

19-2
Electrolytic cells

1   Show what must be done to convert a galvanic cell into an electrolytic cell and list the consequences of the change. (Text Prob. 19-1)

2   Explain the function of the electrolyte in an electrochemical cell. (Text Prob. 19-7)

3   Write the chemical reactions for the electrolysis of aqueous HCl, aqueous NaCl, and molten NaCl. (Text Probs. 19-8, 19-10) (Self Test 10)

4   Use Faraday's laws to calculate the amounts of chemicals reacting when a given quantity of electricity passes through a cell, and vice versa. (Text Examples 19-1, 19-2; Text Probs. 19-11 to 19-19) (New Skills Example 1, 2; Self Test 4, 11, 18 to 20)

19-3
Standard electrode
potentials

1   Use Table 19-1 in the text to find the standard electrode potentials of oxidation and reduction half-reactions. (Text Prob. 19-28) (New Skills Example 3)

2   Calculate cell potentials given the cell reaction or cell diagram and Table 19-1 in the text. (Text Examples 19-5, 19-6; Text Probs. 19-29, 19-33) (New Skills Example 4; Self Test 22)

3   Relate the strength of oxidizing and reducing agents to their position in Table 19-1 in the text. (Text Example 19-8; Text Probs. 19-31, 19-32) (Self Test 5, 12, 21)

19-4
Free energy,
cell voltage,
and equilibrium

1   Calculate ΔG from ε and vice versa. (Text Example 19-9; Text Probs. 19-44 to 19-48, 19-51, 19-52) (New Skills Example 5; Self Test 23)

2   Use the Nernst equation to calculate the cell potential of cells not at standard state. (Text Example 19-10; Text Probs. 19-34 to 19-41, 19-52) (New Skills Example 6; Self Test 24)

3   Calculate K from $\varepsilon°$, and vice versa. (Text Example 19-11; Text Probs. 19-49, 19-50, 19-54) (New Skills Example 7; Self Test 25)

19-5
The electrochemical
measurement of pH

1   Explain how the Nernst equation is used to determine concentrations of ions from cell-potential measurements.

2   Describe how a hydrogen electrode or a glass electrode can be combined with a calomel reference electrode to form a cell used to measure pH.

3   Calculate the pH of a solution given the voltage measured by a glass electrode or a hydrogen electrode with a calomel reference electrode. (Text Example 19-12; Text Probs. 19-42, 19-43)

19-6
Commercial galvanic
cells

1   Make sketches showing the operation and construction of the Leclanche cell, the lead storage cell, the nickel-cadmium cell, and the H_2–O_2 fuel cell. Identify the anode and cathode and show the direction of electron flow in each sketch. (Text Figs. 19-9 to 19-11; Text Probs. 19-24, 19-27)

2 Write the half-cell and cell reactions for the cells in Learning Objective 19-6:1. (Text Probs. 19-25, 19-26)

NEW SKILLS

This chapter presents the basic concepts involved in electrochemical cells. It is essential that you know the new terms used to describe the cells so you can concentrate on understanding how the cells work.

19-1
Galvanic cells

Study the cell diagram for the Daniell cell in conjunction with Fig. 19-2 in the text until you understand how the cell diagram conveys the same information about the cell as the figure. Become familiar with the order of terms in the cell diagram. You should be able to identify the anode, the anode reaction, where electrons leave the cell (anode), what kind of cell junction is used, what kind of electrodes are present, and the overall cell reaction by inspecting the cell diagram. Reread the text discussion on cell diagrams until you see how they present all this information.

Do not worry too much about the "sign" of the electrode. If you understand the operation of the cell you should be able to assign the "sign" according to the convention used by your instructor.

19-2
Electrolytic cells

The terms and symbols used in galvanic cells also apply to electrolytic cells. In electrolytic cells a voltage is applied which forces the electrons to flow in the reverse direction (compared to galvanic cells). As the text shows, this reverses the nature of the redox reactions and the electrodes.

Calculations involving Faraday's laws.
Faraday's laws can be stated mathematically by the relationship

$$\text{Faradays} = \text{No. of equivalents of chemical reacting} = \frac{\text{Coulombs}}{9.65 \times 10^4 \text{ C } \mathcal{F}^{-1}}$$

$$= \frac{\text{amps} \times \text{seconds}}{9.65 \times 10^4 \text{ C } \mathcal{F}^{-1}}$$

● **EXAMPLE 1**

Problem: An electrical current of 10 amps passes through an electrochemical cell for 3 hours. How many moles of electrons pass through the cell?

Solution: One mole of electrons is a faraday. Faradays are related to coulombs by

$$\text{Faradays} = \frac{C}{9.65 \times 10^4 \text{ C } \mathcal{F}^{-1}}$$

Since one coulomb is one ampere-second

$$C = A \times s$$

$$\text{Faradays} = \frac{A \times s}{9.65 \times 10^4 \text{ C } \mathcal{F}^{-1}}$$

$$\text{Moles of electrons} = \text{faradays} = \frac{10.0 \text{ A } (3 \text{ h}) (3600 \text{ s h}^{-1})}{9.65 \times 10^4 \text{ C } \mathcal{F}^{-1}} = 1.12 \text{ mol } e^- \quad ●$$

● EXAMPLE 2   **Problem**: What length of time is required to deposit 0.100 g Cu from a $Cu(NO_3)_2$ solution using a current of 0.300 A?

Solution: The half-cell reaction for the reduction of Cu^{2+} at the cathode is

$$Cu^{2+} + 2e^- \longrightarrow Cu$$

Thus the equivalent weight of Cu is

$$\text{Equiv wt} = \frac{\text{atomic wt}}{\text{No. of } e^- \text{ transferred}} = \frac{63.5}{2} = 31.8 \text{ g equiv}^{-1}$$

The number of equivalents of Cu is

$$\text{Equiv of Cu} = \frac{\text{g Cu}}{\text{equiv wt}} = \frac{0.100 \text{ g Cu}}{31.8 \text{ g Cu equiv}^{-1}} = 3.14 \times 10^{-3} \text{ equiv}$$

Now we use Faraday's laws to find the time required.

$$\text{Equiv} = \frac{\text{A} \times \text{s}}{9.65 \times 10^4 \text{ C} \mathcal{F}^{-1}}$$

$$\text{s} = \frac{9.65 \times 10^4 \text{ C} \mathcal{F}^{-1}}{\text{A}} = \frac{9.65 \times 10^4 \text{ C} \mathcal{F}^{-1} (3.14 \times 10^{-3} \text{ equiv})}{0.300 \text{ A}}$$

$$= 1010 \text{ s} \quad \text{or} \quad 16.8 \text{ min} \; ●$$

Examples 19-1 and 19-2 in the text give further illustrations of the use of Faraday's laws in calculations involving electrochemical cells.

19-3
Standard electrode
potentials

1 Cell diagrams
The structure and operation of electrochemical cells is conveniently represented in shorthand notation by a cell diagram. Cell diagrams are written so the anode reaction (oxidation) is on the left and the cathode reaction (reduction) is on the right. Boundaries between different phases are indicated by a single vertical line and a salt bridge is represented by double vertical lines. Concentrations of reacting substances or pressures of gases are shown in parentheses after the chemical formulas. The electrodes are always written first for the anode and last for the cathode so they appear as the first and last items in the cell diagram.

For the Daniell cell operating at standard conditions where the concentrations of dissolved chemical species are 1.0 M, the anode reaction is $Zn \longrightarrow Zn^{2+} (1 \, M) + 2e^-$ and is represented in a cell diagram as $Zn \mid Zn^{2+} (1 \, M)$ where the vertical line represents the phase boundary between the solid Zn electrode and the Zn^{2+} electrolyte in solution. The cathode reaction is $Cu^{2+} (1 \, M) + 2e^- \longrightarrow Cu$ and is represented as $Cu^{2+} (1 \, M) \mid Cu$. The cell diagram is written with the anode on the left and the cathode on the right separated by a salt bridge.

$$Zn \mid Zn^{2+} (1 \, M) \| Cu^{2+} (1 \, M) \mid Cu$$

● EXAMPLE 3   **Problem**: Write a cell diagram for an electrolytic cell in which an iron electrode is in contact with a 1.50 M solution of $FeCl_2$ in the anode compartment and 0.30 M HCl is reduced to H_2 at 2.0 atm at a platinum electrode in the cathode compartment. The anode and cathode compartments are connected through a salt bridge.

Solution: The anode reaction is represented on the left of the cell diagram with the electrode written first.

Anode: $Fe \,|\, Fe^{2+}\ (1.50\ M)$

The cathode reaction is represented in the order: reactant, product, electrode as

Cathode: $H^+\ (0.30\ M) \,|\, H_2\ (2.0\ atm) \,|\, Pt$

The two half cells are separated by a salt bridge, so the cell diagram is

$$Fe \,|\, Fe^{2+}\ (1.50\ M) \,\|\, H^+\ (0.30\ M) \,|\, H_2\ (2.0\ atm) \,|\, Pt \ \bullet$$

2 Using text Table 19-1 to determine cell potentials

Table 19-1 in the text can be used to find the standard cell potential of any cell composed of some combination of half-cell reactions included in the table.

● **EXAMPLE 4**   **Problem**: Write the anode and cathode half-reactions and the cell reaction, and use Table 19-1 to determine the standard cell potential for the electrolytic cell in Example 3.

Solution: Oxidation always occurs at the anode. In this case Fe is oxidized to Fe^{2+} so the anode half-reaction is

$$Fe \longrightarrow Fe^{2+}\ (1.50\ M) + 2e^- \qquad \mathscr{E}^{\circ}_{ox} = +0.44\ V$$

In Table 19-1 we find only cathode, or reduction, half-reactions. We must change the sign of the standard reduction potential found in the table to have it apply to an oxidation half-reaction. The numerical value is unchanged; only the sign is changed.

At the platinum cathode hydrogen ions are reduced to H_2, so the reaction is

$$2H^+\ (0.30\ M) + 2e^- \longrightarrow H_2\ (2.0\ atm) \qquad \mathscr{E}^{\circ}_{red} = 0\ V$$

The standard potential for a hydrogen half-cell is zero.

The cell reaction is found by adding the oxidation and reduction half-reactions, and the cell potential is found by adding the oxidation and reduction half-cell potentials.

$$\mathscr{E}^{\circ}_{cell} = \mathscr{E}^{\circ}_{ox} + \mathscr{E}^{\circ}_{red}$$

Care must be taken to be sure the number of electrons lost in oxidation is equal to the number gained in reduction.

Anode (oxidation):	$Fe \longrightarrow Fe^{2+}\ (1.50\ M) + 2e^-$	$\mathscr{E}^{\circ}_{ox} = +0.44\ V$
Cathode (reduction):	$2H^+\ (0.30\ M) + 2e^- \longrightarrow H_2\ (2.0\ atm)$	$\mathscr{E}^{\circ}_{red} = \ \ 0\ V$
Cell reaction:	$Fe + 2H^+\ (0.30\ M) \longrightarrow Fe^{2+}\ (1.50\ M) + H_2\ (2.0\ atm)$	$\mathscr{E}^{\circ}_{cell} = +0.44\ V \ \bullet$

Examples 19-5 and 19-6 in the text give additional illustrations of the use of Table 19-1 to find cell potentials.

19-4
Free energy,
cell voltage,
and equilibrium

This section presents some simple equations that relate thermodynamics, electrochemistry, and equilibrium. We will learn how the basic constants of these fields are closely related, and we will use the Nernst equation to calculate cell potentials of cells not at standard state.

1 Relationship between free energy and cell potential

The relationship between thermodynamics and electrochemistry is given by the simple equation

$$\Delta G^\circ = -n\mathcal{F}\mathcal{E}^\circ$$

where ΔG° = standard Gibbs free energy

n = moles of electrons transferred

$\mathcal{F}$ = Faraday's constant = 9.65×10^4 C $\mathcal{F}^{-1}$

$\mathcal{E}^\circ$ = standard cell potential

The relationship also applies when the system is not at standard state.

● **EXAMPLE 5**   **Problem:** For the reaction

$$2Fe(s) + 3Cu^{2+}(aq) \rightleftharpoons 2Fe^{3+}(aq) + 3Cu(s)$$

the standard free energy is -218 kJ. What is the standard cell potential for this reaction?

Solution: We need to determine the value of n for the reaction. First separate the reaction into half-cell reactions. These are

Oxidation: $2Fe(s) \longrightarrow 2Fe^{3+}(aq) + 6e^-$

Reduction: $3Cu^{2+}(aq) + 6e^- \longrightarrow 3Cu(s)$

There are six electrons transferred in the reaction so $n = 6\,\mathcal{F}$ or 6 mol of electrons.

$$\mathcal{E}^\circ = \frac{-\Delta G^\circ}{n\mathcal{F}} = \frac{-(-218{,}000 \text{ J})}{(6\mathcal{F})(9.65 \times 10^4 \text{ C } \mathcal{F}^{-1})} = 0.377 \text{ J C}^{-1} \quad \text{or} \quad 0.377 \text{ V} ●$$

Text Example 19-9 shows the calculation of ΔG° from tabulated standard reduction potentials.

2 The Nernst equation: calculating the effect of concentration on cell voltage

The voltage of a cell is a function of the logarithm of the concentrations of reactants and products. This dependence is given quantitatively by the Nernst equation,

$$\mathcal{E} = \mathcal{E}^\circ - \frac{0.0592}{n} \log Q \quad \text{at } 25^\circ C.$$

where $\mathcal{E}$ = cell voltage at conditions given

$\mathcal{E}^\circ$ = cell voltage at standard conditions

n = moles of electrons transferred

Q = mass-action quotient

Review Sec. 15-2 if you do not remember the meaning of the mass-action quotient.

Table 19-1 in the text can be used to determine $\mathcal{E}^\circ$, the cell potential at standard conditions where all concentrations are 1 M and all gases are present at 1 atm partial pressure. At other concentrations the Nernst equation is used to determine $\mathcal{E}$, the cell potential when the system is not at standard conditions.

● **EXAMPLE 6**   **Problem:** Calculate the voltage at $25^\circ C$ for the reaction

$$2H^+(aq) + Zn(s) \longrightarrow H_2(g) + Zn^{2+}(aq)$$

when $[H^+] = 3.0 \times 10^{-3}$ M, $[Zn^{2+}] = 0.50$ M, and the H_2 partial pressure is 0.75 atm.

Solution: First use the half-cell potentials in text Table 19-1 to determine the standard cell potential. The half-cell reactions are:

Oxidation: $Zn(s) \longrightarrow Zn^{2+}(aq) + 2e^-$ $\mathcal{E}^\circ_{ox} = +0.76 \text{ V}$

Reduction: $2H^+(aq) + 2e^- \longrightarrow H_2(g)$ $\mathcal{E}^\circ_{red} = 0$

Cell: $2H^+(aq) + Zn(s) \longrightarrow H_2(g) + Zn^{2+}(aq)$ $\mathcal{E}^\circ_{cell} = +0.76 \text{ V}$

We see that $n = 2$ for the reaction, so the Nernst equation becomes

$$\mathcal{E} = \mathcal{E}^\circ - \frac{0.0592}{n} \log \frac{P_{H_2}[Zn^{2+}]}{[H^+]^2}$$

$$= 0.76 - \frac{0.0592}{2} \log \frac{0.75\,(0.50)}{(3.0 \times 10^{-3})^2} = 0.76 - \frac{0.0592}{2} \log (4.2 \times 10^4)$$

$$= 0.76 - \frac{0.0592}{2}\,(4.62) = 0.76 - 0.14 = 0.62 \text{ V}$$

The cell potential is reduced 0.14 V compared to the standard state potential. ●

Example 19-10 in the text is a similar problem.

3 Determination of equilibrium constants from standard cell potentials
The relationship between the equilibrium constant of a reaction and its standard cell potential is given by the expression

$$\mathcal{E}^\circ = \frac{0.0592}{n} \log K$$

where K is the type of equilibrium constant appropriate to the chemical reaction considered.

● **EXAMPLE 7**   **Problem:** Calculate the solubility product constant for AgCl at 25°C.

Solution: The K_{sp} of AgCl is the equilibrium constant for the reaction

$$AgCl(s) \rightleftharpoons Ag^+ + Cl^-$$

The cell potential for this reaction is related to K_{sp} by the equation

$$\mathcal{E}^\circ_{cell} = \frac{0.0592}{n} \log K_{sp}$$

The cell diagram for the solubility equilibrium would be

$$Ag(s)\,|\,Ag^+(aq)\,\|\,Cl^-\,|\,AgCl(s)\,|\,Ag(s)$$

which is a silver–silver ion electrode in the anode compartment connected to a silver–silver chloride electrode in the cathode compartment. The half-cell reactions and potentials are

Oxidation: $Ag(s) \longrightarrow Ag^+(aq) + e^-$ $\mathcal{E}^\circ_{ox} = -0.80 \text{ V}$

Reduction: $AgCl(s) + e^- \longrightarrow Ag(s) + Cl^-(aq)$ $\mathcal{E}^\circ_{red} = +0.22 \text{ V}$

Cell: $AgCl(s) \longrightarrow Ag^+(aq) + Cl^-(aq)$ $\mathcal{E}^\circ_{cell} = -0.58 \text{ V}$

The standard potential for the silver–silver ion electrode is given in text Table 19-1. The potential for the silver–silver chloride electrode is in text App. I. The equation for K_{sp} becomes

$$-0.58 = \frac{0.0592}{1} \log K_{sp}$$

$$\log K_{sp} = \frac{-0.58}{0.0592} = -9.80$$

$$K_{sp} = 1.6 \times 10^{-10}$$

This compares favorably with the value of 1.7×10^{-10} given in Table 17-1. ●

Example 19-11 in the text is an additional example of using electrochemical data to calculate equilibrium constant values.

SELF TEST

True or false   _____ 1 Oxidation takes place at the anode in any kind of electrochemical cell.

_____ 2 Cell diagrams generally give the cathode first.

_____ 3 The overall reaction in a galvanic cell is always spontaneous.

_____ 4 In the electrolysis of $CuSO_4$, one faraday of electricity is required to produce one mole of copper.

_____ 5 Na^+ lies above Mg^{2+} in the table of standard reduction potentials. This means that Na^+ will reduce Mg^{2+} to Mg.

_____ 6 Galvanic cells can be used in rechargeable batteries only when the overall cell reaction is reversible.

Completion   7 The cell diagram for the Daniell cell is _____.

8 In the Daniell cell, _____ is the anode, _____ is the cathode, and electrons leave the cell at the _____ electrode.

9 _____ charged ions are attracted to the anode where they are _____ in an electrolytic cell.

10 The electrolysis of molten NaCl yields _____ at the cathode.

11 The quantity of substance produced by electrolysis is proportional to _____.

12 The best reducing agents are at the _____ (left, right) of the half-cell reactions at the _____ (top, bottom) of a table of standard reduction potentials.

Multiple choice   13 In a galvanic cell, the electrons flow
(a) from anode to cathode   (b) through the salt bridge
(c) from cathode to anode   (d) from the battery to the cathode

14 The cell diagram for the reaction

$$2Ag^+(aq) + H_2(g) \longrightarrow 2Ag(s) + 2H^+(aq)$$

is
(a) $H_2 \,|\, Ag^+ \,\|\, Ag \,|\, H^+$ (b) $Pt \,|\, H_2 \,|\, H^+ \,\|\, Ag^+ \,|\, Ag$
(c) $H_2 \,|\, H^+ \,\|\, Ag^+ \,|\, Ag$ (d) $|\, Ag \,|\, H_2 \,\|\, Ag^+ \,|\, H^+$

15 The salt bridge in the cell in Prob. 14 preserves electrical neutrality in the cell by permitting
    (a) electrons to flow from the anode to the cathode
    (b) cations to migrate from the cathode to the anode compartment
    (c) anions to migrate from the anode to the cathode compartment
    (d) cations to migrate from the anode to the cathode compartment

16 For the cell

$$Al(s)\,|\,AlCl_3\,(aq)\,|\,Cl_2\,(g)\,|\,Pt$$

the cell reaction is
    (a) $3Pt + 2AlCl_3 \longrightarrow 3PtCl_2 + 2Al$
    (b) $2AlCl_3 + PtCl_2 \longrightarrow 2Al + Pt + 4Cl_2$
    (c) $2Al + 3Cl_2 \longrightarrow 2AlCl_3$
    (d) No reaction is possible because there is no salt bridge.

17 In the Daniell cell, cations
    (a) move toward the Zn electrode
    (b) move toward the Cu electrode
    (c) are formed in the $ZnSO_4$ solution
    (d) are removed from the $CuSO_4$ solution

18 9.65×10^4 coulombs
    (a) will oxidize 1 mol of Na^+ to Na   (b) will reduce 1 mol of Cl_2 to Cl^-
    (c) will reduce 1 equiv of CO_2 to C   (d) is 1 A flowing for 1 h

19 How many grams of Fe^{3+} will be reduced to Fe by one faraday?
    (a) 19   (b) 28   (c) 56   (d) 168

20 How many amperes would be needed to reduce 1.0 g of Ni^{2+} to Ni in 20 min?
    (a) 0.045   (b) 2.7   (c) 5.4   (d) 162

21 Na^+ is above Zn^{2+} in the table of standard reduction potentials. This means that
    (a) Na^+ is a better reducing agent than Zn^{2+} (b) Na will reduce Zn
    (c) Na is a better reducing agent than Zn   (d) Na^+ will reduce Zn^{2+}

22 The standard reduction potentials of Fe^{2+} and Cu^{2+} are -0.44 and +0.34 V, respectively. The cell potential for a galvanic cell containing these two ions would be
    (a) -0.10 V   (b) +0.10 V   (c) -0.78 V   (d) +0.78 V

23 For the reaction

$$8H^+ + 2NO_3^- + 3Cu \longrightarrow 2NO + 3Cu^{2+} + 4H_2O$$

the value of n in the equation $\Delta G = -n\mathcal{F}\mathscr{E}$ is
    (a) 1   (b) 2   (c) 6   (d) 8

24 The standard reduction potential of Zn is -0.76 V. The potential of the following cell

$$Zn\,|\,Zn^{2+}\,(0.50\,M)\,\|\,H^+\,(0.020\,M)\,|\,H_2\,(0.30\,atm)\,|\,Pt$$

at 25°C is
    (a) 0.68 V   (b) 0.73 V   (c) 0.76 V   (d) -0.84 V

25 The equilibrium constant for the cell reaction in Prob. 24 is
    (a) 3.1×10^{11} (b) 6.9×10^{12} (c) 9.4×10^{22} (d) 4.7×10^{25}

20 THE NONMETALS

CHAPTER OVERVIEW

If you have been progressing through the text chapter by chapter, you will note a dramatic change in the nature and presentation of material beginning with this chapter. We leave the area where basic principles are emphasized and enter a study (known as descriptive chemistry) of the properties and reactions of substances. The approach will be less mathematical, but still requires an intensive effort to master the large amount of material presented. Your instructor should guide you about the extent of memorization work expected. The *Study Guide* is designed to help you organize the material and recognize the important correlations and trends.

This chapter is mainly concerned with the properties and chemistry of ten nonmetallic elements. First we proceed to a systematic study of nomenclature in inorganic compounds.

**20-1
Inorganic
nomenclature**

Naming inorganic compounds is largely a matter of attaching the correct prefix and suffix to the root name. The prefix tells the number of atoms per molecule and the suffix indicates the oxidation state. It is obvious that you must learn the meaning of the prefixes and suffixes before you can use them fluently. The prefixes are very straightforward and are given in the text, so you should have no problem learning them. There are two different systems of suffixes for cations: the *ous–ic* system and the Stock or roman numeral system. Since both are widely used you need to learn both systems. Oxidation states of anions are indicated by the *-ide*, *-ite*, and *-ate* suffixes. The text examples for the oxoanions of chlorine illustrate the use of these suffixes. Oxoanions of bromine and iodine are named in the same way. It will be well worthwhile to memorize the names and formulas of the polyatomic ions in Table 20-6 in the text. Learning inorganic nomenclature is essential so the names do not become a stumbling block as you study the chemistry of these compounds in the remaining chapters. Be sure to refer to App. C-2 in the text for helpful hints and examples of inorganic nomenclature.

**20-2
Hydrogen**

Hydrogen is present in more compounds than any other element, but most of it is combined with oxygen as water. Hydrogen gas is prepared by the electrolytic or chemical reduction of water. It is usually found in the +1 oxidation state. The hydride ion, H^-, exists only in compounds with very reactive metals.

**20-3
Oxygen**

Oxygen is the most abundant element on earth. It occurs combined with metals and nonmetals or uncombined as O_2 or O_3. O_2 is prepared by the distillation of air or electrolytic or chemical reduction of oxygen-containing compounds. Important compounds of oxygen in the −2 oxidation state include metal and nonmetal oxides, hydroxides, oxoacids, and oxosalts. Peroxides contain oxygen in the −1 oxidation state, while superoxides contain the superoxide ion, O_2^-, where the oxidation state is $-\frac{1}{2}$. Positive oxidation states are found only in compounds containing fluorine.

**20-4
Water**

Water molecules combine with many salts to form hydrates.

**20-5
The halogens**

In this section you will study the group VIIA elements, or halogens. Their chemistry is very similar and follows the periodic behavior and trends discussed in Chap. 7. As you proceed down the group from fluorine to iodine the atomic radius increases so the ionization potential decreases and the elements become progressively more metallic. Fluorine differs from the other halogens in several ways because of its small size and high electronegativity.

The text discusses the preparation, chemical properties, and compounds of each oxidation state for F, Cl, Br, and I. Interhalogen compounds are also possible.

Since the halogens show a strong tendency to follow predicted periodic behavior, we can expect their compounds to follow the same trends. As you study the compounds, notice how the expected periodic trends gradually change the properties and reactions as you proceed through the halogens.

**20-6
The chalcogens,
especially sulfur**

The group VIA elements show a strong periodic trend from nonmetallic to metallic, as one proceeds from top to bottom in the group. This trend is much stronger than in the halogens so the chemical properties are not as similar among the chalcogens as they are among the halogens. Oxygen is quite different from the other elements in group VIA in physical and chemical properties. It is the only element of the group which is a gas under normal conditions. It is found mostly in the −2 oxidation state as the oxide of many elements in nature. Selenium and tellurium show considerable metallic behavior and are usually classed as metalloids. Sulfur shows several stable oxidation states from −2 to +6, and much of sulfur chemistry is not shared by other members of the group. For these reasons it is not as convenient to study the chalcogens as a group as it was for the halogens. This section focuses mainly on sulfur. The text discusses the Frasch method for mining sulfur, its several allotropic forms, and the chemistry of its different oxidation states. Like the halogens, sulfur can form numerous oxoacids and oxosalts.

**20-7
The group-VA
nonmetals: nitrogen
and phosphorus**

The trend from nonmetallic to metallic behavior as one proceeds from top to bottom of group VA is very pronounced. The elements As, Sb, and Bi show metallic behavior not observed for N and P. Nitrogen is the smallest element in the group and (like fluorine and oxygen) has physical and chemical properties unique among its group.

Nitrogen is the only gaseous element in group **VA**. In spite of its high electronegativity, it is relatively inert, but shows a wide variety of oxidation states when combined.

The text discusses the reactions and properties of nitrogen in several oxidation states. The most important compounds of nitrogen are ammonia and nitric acid. Pay close attention to the chemistry and properties of these two compounds. Nitric acid usually acts as an oxidizing agent in reactions rather than showing usual acid behavior. The typical reactions with Cu and Zn given in the text show how different products can be formed when nitric acid is reduced, depending on the reaction conditions.

Phosphorus does not show the metallic behavior of As, Sb, and Bi, but is much more chemically active than nitrogen. The main reactions include preparation of elemental phosphorus, reaction with oxygen to produce phosphorous oxides, and further reaction with water to produce a family of oxoacids.

20-8
Carbon

Carbon is the smallest member of group IVA and shows properties different from the other members of the group because of this size difference. It is the only nonmetallic member of the group. It has the unique capability of bonding with itself to form long chains; this property gives rise to the field of organic chemistry to be discussed in Chap. 23. This section is concerned with the element and its inorganic compounds.

20-9
The noble gases

Before 1962, it was generally believed that the noble gases were chemically inert. The chemistry presented in this section was not known until the generalities associated with group behavior of the noble-gas elements were disregarded by those doing basic research.

Classifying chemicals according to group behavior is an aid to understanding present knowledge, but can be a barrier to developing new ideas.

LEARNING OBJECTIVES

As a result of studying Chap. 20 you should be able to do the following:
Write the definition and give an example illustrating the use of each key term:

20-1
Inorganic
nomenclature

1 Write the prefixes used to represent one through eight atoms of a given type in a molecule. (Text App. C-2; Text Probs. 20-1, 20-4)

2 Write the names of common cations in the *ous–ic* and the Stock systems. (Text Tables 20-1, 20-2; Text App. C-2; Text Prob. 20-2) (Self Test 1, 18)

3 Use the suffixes *-ide*, *-ite*, and *-ate* in naming anions. (Text App. C-2; Text Probs. 20-3, 20-8)

4 Write the names of the oxohalide ions. (Text Table 20-6; Text App. C-2; Text Probs. 20-4, 20-8) (Self Test 21)

5 Write the names of salts and binary acids. (Text Table 20-3; Text App. C-2; Text Probs. 20-5, 20-6, 20-10) (Self Test 2, 8)

6 Write the names and formulas of common polyatomic ions. (Text Table 20-6; Text App. C-2; Text Prob. 20-9) (Self Test 8)

7 Write the names of common oxoacids. (Text Table 20-5; Text App. C-2; Text Prob. 20-7) (Self Test 8)

8 Write the chemical formula of salts and oxoacids given the name. (Text Tables 20-3 to 20-6; Text App. C-2; Text Prob. 20-11) (Self Test 9)

20-2 **Hydrogen**	1 Name and give properties for the isotopes of hydrogen. (Text Table 20-7; Text Probs. 20-12 to 20-14, 20-16)
	2 Write chemical equations for the preparation of H_2. (Text Probs. 20-15, 20-17, 20-18) (Self Test 19)
20-3 **Oxygen**	1 Compare the VB and MO explanations of bonding in O_2 and related compounds. (Text Table 20-9; Text Fig. 9-39; Text Probs. 20-20, 20-21, 20-25, 20-26) (Self Test 20)
	2 Explain the differences between ionic oxides and molecular oxides. (Text Prob. 20-23)
	3 Write the chemical equations for the preparation of O_2 and its reactions to form oxides. (Text Prob. 20-29)
20-4 **Water**	1 Explain the differences and similarities between the structures of liquid and solid water. (Text Fig. 20-2; Text Prob. 20-30) (Self Test 4)
	2 Explain how clathrates are formed. (Text Prob. 20-31)
20-5 **The halogens**	1 Apply the periodic law to explain trends in physical and chemical properties of the halogen compounds. (Text Prob. 10-37) (Self Test 3, 11, 12)
	2 Use the VSEPR theory to predict the shape of oxohalogen and interhalogen compounds. (Text Probs. 20-41, 20-44)
	3 Write chemical equations for reactions of halogens and halogen compounds. (Text Probs. 20-45 to 20-47) (Self Test 13)
20-6 **The chalcogens,** **especially sulfur**	1 Describe the changes in physical properties and chemical structure that take place as sulfur is heated. (Text Prob. 20-48)
	2 Write Lewis structures for various oxosulfur compounds and ions. (Text Prob. 20-51)
	3 Write chemical equations for the production of H_2SO_4. (Text Prob. 20-52) (Self Test 14)
	4 Use the VSEPR theory to predict bonding and geometry in covalent sulfur compounds. (Text Prob. 20-53)
	5 Write chemical equations for reactions of compounds containing sulfur. (Text Prob. 20-56) (Self Test 22, 23)
20-7 **The group-VA** **nonmetals: nitrogen** **and phosphorus**	1 Use the principles of chemical equilibrium of Chap. 15 to predict optimum conditions of temperature and pressure for the Haber and Ostwald processes. (Text Prob. 20-57) (Self Test 16)
	2 Draw Lewis structures for the nitrogen oxides. (Text Prob. 20-61)
	3 Explain how the formation of N_2O_4 affects properties of NO_2 at low temperatures (Text Prob. 20-62)
	4 Explain why reduction of nitric acid gives nitrogen products of lower oxidation state when more dilute acid is used. (Text Prob. 20-63) (Self Test 6)
	5 Account for the presence of a strong triple bond in N_2 but not in phosphorus on the basis of orbital overlap in second-period but not in third-period elements. (Text Prob. 20-65)
	6 List the properties of the allotropes of phosphorus. (Text Prob. 20-66)

7 Write chemical equations for the formation and hydrolysis of phosphorus oxides. (Text Probs. 20-69, 20-75) (Self Test 7, 17)

8 Write chemical equations showing reactions of nitrogen compounds. (Text Prob. 20-74) (Self Test 5, 15)

9 Write chemical equations showing reactions of salts containing phosphorus. (Text Prob. 20-75)

20-8 Carbon

1 Compare the properties and structures of allotropes of carbon. (Text Probs. 20-76), 20-78) (Self Test 25)

2 Write equations showing equilibria in the CO_2–HCO_3^-–CO_3^{2-} system. (Text Probs. 20-79, 20-81)

3 Draw Lewis structures for inorganic carbon compounds. (Text Prob. 20-80)

4 Explain the effect of hydrogen bonding in HCN. (Text Prob. 20-82)

5 Write chemical equations for reactions of inorganic carbon compounds. (Text Prob. 20-83)

20-9 The noble gases

1 Predict the structure of xenon compounds using the VSEPR theory. (Text Prob. 20-85)

SELF TEST

True or false

____ 1 Another name for the Sn(II) ion is stannic.

____ 2 BiOCl is bismuth hypochlorite.

____ 3 HF, HCl, and HBr are all strong acids.

____ 4 Hydrogen bonding in H_2O and H_2S are responsible for their relatively high boiling points.

____ 5 NH_4NO_2 can be heated carefully to produce NO_2.

____ 6 Concentrated nitric acid is a powerful oxidizing agent.

____ 7 H_3PO_3 is a diprotic acid.

Completion

8 The formula is

_____ for copper(II) sulfate

_____ for nitrous acid

_____ for sodium bromate

_____ for calcium carbide

_____ for bromous acid

_____ for the permanganate ion

_____ for aluminum bisulfate

_____ for silver carbonate

9 The Stock name is _____ for CuI, _____ for $Pb(OCl)_2$, _____ for $CoPO_4$, and _____ for $Sn(NO_2)_4$.

10 The net reaction for the disproportionation of H_2O_2 is _____.

11 The most easily oxidized halide ion is _____.

12 The strongest of all acids is _____.

13 _____ is the only halogen that cannot be prepared by chemical oxidation of the halide.

14 The chemical reactions in the contact process are _____
_____.

15 NH_4NO_3 can be heated carefully to produce _____.
16 The first step in the Ostwald process is the oxidation of _____.
17 Elemental phosphorus is obtained by heating _____ with _____
and _____ in an electric furnace.

Multiple choice

18 What is an acceptable alternate name for iron(II) hypochlorite?
   (a) iron(II) oxide chloride   (b) ferrous oxide chloride
   (c) ferrous dihypochlorite   (d) ferrous hypochlorite

19 Which of the following metals is least effective in reducing water?
   (a) Zn   (b) Ca   (c) K   (d) Rb

20 Which of the following gives the best interpretation of the structure and properties of O_2?
   (a) valence-bond theory   (b) Lewis structure
   (c) atomic-orbital theory   (d) molecular-orbital theory

21 An aqueous solution of chlorine contains all of the following except
   (a) Cl^- (b) ClO_2^- (c) ClO^- (d) Cl_2

22 Which of the following does not apply to sulfuric acid?
   (a) strong acid   (b) dehydrating agent
   (c) reducing agent   (d) anhydride of sulfur trioxide

23 Which of the following is not a common oxidation state of sulfur in its compounds?
   (a) -2   (b) +2   (c) +4   (d) +6

24 Which of the following is a property of nitrous acid?
   (a) weak acid   (b) stable compound
   (c) good solvent for metals   (d) nontoxic

25 Which of the following is a property of graphite?
   (a) carbon with sp^3 hybridization   (b) semimetallic luster
   (c) equal carbon-carbon bonds   (d) good lubricant in vacuum systems

21 THE REPRESENTATIVE METALS AND METALLOIDS

CHAPTER OVERVIEW

There are less than 20 nonmetal elements and over 80 metals and semimetals. This chapter presents the representative metals (A-group metals). Review the properties of metals in Sec. 10-5 and note how elements that show strong metallic behavior in a chemical sense are not necessarily the common and familiar metals. From a chemical standpoint, metals are elements that lose electrons to become positive ions. The group IA elements (alkali metals) have the lowest first-ionization energies and therefore show strong metallic behavior. In general, metallic behavior decreases from left to right across the periodic table and the metalloids represent the transition from metallic to nonmetallic behavior.

21-1
The alkali metals

The group IA, or alkali, metals all show strong metallic behavior. They have high electrical conductivity and crystallize in body-centered-cubic structures. They are strong reducing agents and so are readily oxidized to the +1 state. Periodic trends are very pronounced in the alkali metals, so you can observe a gradual increase in metallic behavior from top to bottom in the group. Lithium is the smallest alkali metal and shows the deviation from group behavior expected for second-period elements.

The text discusses historical aspects of the metals; methods of preparation; their reactions with H_2O, O_2, and N_2; and properties and uses of their compounds.

21-2
The alkaline-earth metals

The group IIA, or alkaline-earth, metals show only the +2 oxidation state in compounds. They are less reactive than the alkali metals but are still strong reducing agents. Periodic trends are very pronounced in the group and metallic behavior decreases from bottom to top in the group to the extent that beryllium forms mostly covalent bonds and shows less reactivity than other members of the group. The text explains why only the +2 oxidation state is observed and discusses the preparation, reactions, and properties of some compounds.

The Ca^{2+}, Mg^{2+}, and Fe^{3+} ions are responsible for hardness in water. They form deposits in water lines, appliances, heat exchangers, and boilers. Temporary hardness results when HCO_3^- ions are present. This is a troublesome problem in industrial and home water heaters because heating results in precipitation of $CaCO_3$ or $MgCO_3$. Permanent water hardness is generally removed by the lime-soda method in industrial applications or by ion-exchange water softeners for domestic uses.

21-3
The group-IIIA metals

In group IIIA we have moved far enough across the periodic chart so that metallic behavior is much less pronounced than in groups IA and IIA. The smallest member of the group shows considerable nonmetallic behavior and forms only covalent bonds. It is classed as a metalloid. Thallium has a stable +1 oxidation state in addition to the +3 oxidation state common for the group. Aluminum is by far the most important metal in group IIIA. It is the most abundant metal in the earth's crust and is extracted from the mineral bauxite by the Bayer process and reduced to the metal electrolytically by the Hall process.

Aluminum is a highly reactive element and finds widespread use as a metal only because it forms a dense protective layer of Al_2O_3 on its surface which prevents further oxidation. Reactions and uses of aluminim are discussed in the text.

21-4
Other representative metals

The representative metals in groups IVA and VA are tin, lead, and bismuth. These metals are far to the right in the periodic table and have high electronegativities for metals. They form either ionic or covalent bonds. Tin has three stable allotropes, only one of which has the metallic properties commonly associated with tin. Tin exists in the +2 and +4 states in compounds and its reactions are discussed in the text.

Lead occurs only in the +2 oxidation state in reactions with acids, and most common compounds contain lead in the +2 state. PbO_2, in which lead has a +4 oxidation state, is important for its use in lead storage cells. Reactions and uses of lead and its compounds are discussed in the text.

Bismuth is a hard, brittle metal whose main use is in low-melting alloys. It exists in the +3 or +5 oxidation states in compounds, with the +3 state being more common.

21-5
The metalloids

Metalloids show either metallic or nonmetallic behavior depending on their chemical environment. They are located on a diagonal to the left of the center of the periodic table as shown in text Fig. 21-4. The most important metalloids from a chemical standpoint are boron and silicon. The chemistry of boron halides, borates, and boranes is discussed in the text. The chemistry of silicon is quite complex, but you should note that many common minerals are silicates.

Arsenic and antimony resemble phosphorus and bismuth in chemical behavior. They each form a series of oxides and oxoanions.

Selenium and tellurium resemble sulfur in chemical reactions and form similar compounds.

LEARNING OBJECTIVES

As a result of studying Chap. 21 you should be able to do the following:
Write the definition and give an example illustrating the use of each key term.

21-1
The alkali metals

1 Write equations showing the preparation of the alkali-metal elements. (Text Prob. 21-3)
2 Write equations showing the different reactions of the alkali metals with O_2. (Text Prob. 21-8) (Self Test 3, 18)

3   Recognize the similarities and differences in properties and reactions within the group. (Text Probs. 21-2, 21-10) (Self Test 1, 2, 4, 17)

4   Write equations for reactions of the alkali metals and their compounds. (Text Probs. 21-6, 21-9)

21-2
The alkaline-earth
metals

1   Compare the chemical properties and reactions of alkaline-earth and alkali metals. (Text Prob. 21-12) (Self Test 19)

2   Explain the similarities and differences in chemical properties and reactions among members of the group. (Text Probs. 21-16, 21-19, 21-20) (Self Test 5, 9)

3   Write equations for reactions of the alkaline-earth metals and their compounds. (Text Probs. 21-13, 21-17, 21-21)

4   Explain what causes hard water and some of its effects. Describe the different types of hard water and how each type can be removed. (Text Probs. 21-22 to 21-25) (Self Test 10, 11, 20, 21)

21-3
The group-IIIA
metals

1   Write reactions for the Bayer and Hall processes for production of aluminum. (Text Probs. 21-27, 21-29, 21-34) (Self Text 12, 13, 22)

2   Explain the trends in chemical properties and reactions among members of the group. (Text Prob. 21-26)

3   Describe the properties and characteristics of aluminum and its compounds. (Text Probs. 21-28, 21-30) (Self Test 14, 23)

4   Explain the covalent nature of many aluminum compounds. (Text Probs. 21-31, 21-32)

5   Write equations for the reactions of group IIIA metals and their compounds. (Text Prob. 21-33)

21-4
Other representative
metals

1   Relate the allotropic forms of tin to tin disease. (Text Prob. 21-36)

2   Explain the amphoteric behavior of group IVA and VA metal hydroxides. (Text Probs. 21-37, 21-41)

3   Show the effect of complex ions containing lead on the chemistry of lead compounds. (Text Probs. 21-38, 21-39)

4   Write equations showing reactions for Sn, Pb, and Bi and their compounds. (Text Probs. 21-35, 21-42)

21-5
The metalloids

1   Draw Lewis structures for boranes and BF_3 and interpret the results in terms of electronic bonding in these compounds. (Text Probs. 21-43 to 21-47) (Self Test 15)

2   Compare the allotropes of boron nitride to the allotropes of carbon. (Text Prob. 21-48)

3   Draw structures showing discrete and extended silicate ions. (Text Probs. 21-49 to 21-53) (Self Test 25)

4   Use the VSEPR theory to predict the structure of covalent silicon compounds. (Text Prob. 21-54)

5   Explain the differences and similarities in chemical properties and reactions among group IVA, VA, and VIA metalloids on the basis of periodic trends. (Text Probs. 21-55 to 21-57)

6   Write equations for reactions of compounds of the metalloids. (Text Prob. 21-58)

SELF TEST

True or false   _____ 1 Lithium ions have a stronger tendency to undergo hydrolysis than potassium ions.

_____ 2 Lithium has the highest ionization energy and yet is the easiest to oxidize of the alkali metals.

_____ 3 Alkali metals react with oxygen to form oxides.

_____ 4 Lithium compounds are generally less soluble than sodium compounds.

_____ 5 Beryllium usually forms covalent bonds in its compounds.

_____ 6 The most stable oxidation states of the group IVA metals is +4.

_____ 7 The most important metalloids are boron and silicon.

Completion   8 Three characteristics of metallic elements are _____, _____, and _____.

9 Except for _____, the alkaline-earth metals form ionic compounds.

10 Ions responsible for hard water include _____, _____, and _____.

11 The lime-soda method for softening water consists of adding _____ to remove temporary hardness and _____ to remove permanent hardness.

12 In the Bayer process, impure _____ is dissolved in _____ from which _____ precipitates and is heated to form pure _____.

13 In the Hall process _____ is produced at the iron cathode while _____ and _____ are produced at the graphite anode.

14 Aluminum is oxidized easily, but _____ protects it against attack by O_2.

15 Boranes are _____ compounds that form _____ bonds.

Multiple choice   16 Chemical properties of metals are related to
(a) high density of solid state   (b) ease of removal of electrons
(c) low chemical reactivity   (d) body-centered-cubic structures

17 Alkali metals have which of the following properties?
(a) high densities   (b) low conductivity
(c) soft metals   (d) good oxidizing ability

18 The only alkali metal that forms the oxide on reaction with O_2 is
(a) Li   (b) Na   (c) K   (d) Be

19 Alkaline-earth metals do not show +1 ions because
(a) they have two electrons in the valence shell
(b) the first ionization energy is too high
(c) the +1 ion does not interact with anions or water molecules as strongly as the +2 ion with its higher charge density
(d) the first and second ionization energies are about equal so both electrons come off in a cascade effect

20 Temporary water hardness
(a) can be removed by NaCl
(b) occurs only when SO_4^{2-} ions are present
(c) can be removed by allowing the water to stand quietly in the presence of CO_2
(d) can be removed by lime

21 Which of the following will remove permanent hardness from water?
   (a) adding $Ca(OH)_2$
   (b) adding NaCl
   (c) adding washing soda
   (d) permanent hardness cannot be removed; that is why it is called permanent

22 The Bayer process is used to
   (a) obtain aluminum from cryolite by electrolytic reduction
   (b) make aspirin
   (c) obtain magnesium from seawater
   (d) purify bauxite

23 Cleansers containing lye (NaOH) dissolve or pit aluminum pans because
   (a) the aluminum is anodized
   (b) the soluble aluminate ion is formed
   (c) the small aluminum ion hydrolyzes extensively in base
   (d) the cleansers also contain chlorine bleach which forms soluble $AlCl_3$

24 Which of the following does not apply to boron?
   (a) is found in vitamin B_{12} (b) is found in Pyrex dishes
   (c) occurs in nature as borax   (d) forms compounds deficient in electrons

25 Silicates containing some three-bridge oxygens and some two-bridge oxygens form a series of minerals which includes
   (a) talc   (b) mica   (c) asbestos   (d) sand

22 THE TRANSITION METALS

CHAPTER OVERVIEW

The elements between groups IIA and IIIA in the periodic table, along with the lanthanoids and actinoids, comprise the transition metals. These metals have several unique properties and characteristics and many similarities. Their ionization energies, electronegativities, and ionic radii show very little variation throughout the series. The availability of d orbitals allows complex hybridization which leads to a wide variety of geometries in the complex ions formed. We will investigate the nature of bonding and geometry in these compounds and see how the electronic structure is related to geometry and to the intense colors observed.

22-1
Electronic
configuration

Recall from Secs. 6-1 and 7-3 how d electrons are added to build transition metals in the Aufbau process. Note the irregular structures of chromium and copper associated with half-filled or filled d shells. This irregularity also occurs in fifth- and sixth-period elements and in the f shell of the lanthanoids and actinoids.

22-2
General properties

The transition metals have properties generally associated with metals. Their hardness, density, conductivity, and chemical reactivity vary greatly and they show a wide range of oxidation states (Table 22-3 in the text). Note the Added Comment in the text explaining why the $4s$ electrons are ionized first even through the $3d$ electrons are added last in the Aufbau process.

22-3
Complex ions:
general structure
and nomenclature

The concepts and terms involved in the study of complex ions were introduced in Secs. 13-2 and 17-3 and it would be a good idea to review those sections now. The geometry of coordination numbers 2, 4, and 8 will be studied in conjunction with bonding and structure. Become familiar with the nomenclature rules so the names become an aid to your study rather than a stumbling block. Considerable help with nomenclature can be found in App. C-2 in the text.

22-4
Complex ions:
bonding

There are three theories that describe the bonding in complex ions.

1 Valence-bond theory
Review Sec. 9-3 to recall how atomic orbitals combine to form an equal number of equivalent hybrid orbitals. The geometry of the compound depends on the type of

hybridization (see text Table 9-4). Valence-bond theory successfully predicts the geometry of complex ions but fails to predict whether an inner-orbital or outer-orbital complex will result in certain cases. This difference determines the spectral and magnetic properties of many complex ions, so the valence-bond theory is inadequate for explaining the color and magnetic properties of some complex ions.

2 Ligand-field theory

Ligand-field theory is the direct application of molecular-orbital theory to complex ions. Molecular orbitals are formed by the combination of hybridized orbitals on the central ion with ligand orbitals. A bonding and an antibonding orbital result from each combination of orbitals on the central ion with orbitals of a ligand. The d orbitals on the central ion that are not engaged in bonding have no change in energy and are nonbonding orbitals. Energy levels and electron distributions in these orbitals are shown in Fig. 22-3 in the text. The t_{2g} orbitals are the nonbonding d_{xy}, d_{xz}, and d_{yz} orbitals, and the e_g or e_g^* orbitals are the higher energy d_{z^2} and $d_{x^2-y^2}$ orbitals.

Ligand-field theory leads to the same geometric prediction as the valence-bond theory and is quite successful in predicting magnetic properties, but it is unable to explain color differences caused by different ligands on a central ion.

3 Crystal-field theory

Crystal-field theory uses the same molecular orbital approach as the ligand-field theory but extends the approach by considering electrostatic attractions between the ligands and the central ion that split the energies of the d orbitals. The e_g orbitals thus have higher energies than the t_{2g}. The energy difference between e_g and t_{2g} orbitals is called the ligand-field splitting energy and denoted by Δ_o or Δ_t. The nature of d-orbital splitting is shown in Fig. 22-4 in the text for octahedral geometry and in Fig. 22-6 for tetrahedral geometry. Note that in octahedral geometry e_g orbitals have higher energies than t_{2g}, but in tetrahedral geometry the reverse is true.

The type of ligand determines the strength of the ligand field which fixes the magnitude of Δ. For weak-field ligands, the d-orbital splitting is small and electrons occupy any d orbital so there is maximum unpairing and the complex is of high electron spin. Strong-field ligands cause more d-orbital splitting, so electrons pair in lower energy orbitals to give low-spin complexes. The magnitude of Δ is also correlated with the wavelengths of the colors observed in complex ions.

Crystal-field theory successfully predicts the geometry, magnetic properties, and color of complex ions.

The spectrochemical series arranges ligands in order of their ability to cause splitting of d orbitals on the central metal ion.

22-5
Complex ions:
stereochemistry

Square-planar complex ions with at least two different ligands can form cis-trans isomers, or stereoisomers. In cis isomers identical ligands are adjacent or next to each other, while in trans isomers they are opposite or across the ion from each other.

Tetrahedral complex ions with four different ligands can exist in two structures which are mirror images of each other. These are called optical isomers or enantiomers. Examine Fig. 22-9 in the text closely to see how these isomers are different.

Cis-trans isomers for octahedral complexes having the general formula MA_4B_2 are shown in text Fig. 22-11a. Isomers of octahedral complexes of type MA_3B_3 are shown in Fig. 22-11b.

The presence of chelating agents can result in optical isomers of octahedral complexes as shown in text Fig. 22-13.

22-6 Descriptive chemistry of selected transition metals

The maximum oxidation number for groups IIIB to VIIB is the same as the group number. Most of the elements in these groups have several oxidation numbers and all elements in the first transition series except Sc have a +2 oxidation number. For Ti and V the maximum oxidation number is also the most stable state, but lower oxidation states become more stable moving from left to right across the series. Most of the first-series transition metals are strong and hard and resist corrosion, so they find important uses in alloys. The many oxidation states allow them to serve as oxidizing and reducing agents, and the ease with which electrons can be promoted to higher energy levels makes them important catalysts.

Unlike the representative elements, similarities among members of horizontal periods in the transition elements are more noticeable than similarities in the vertical groups.

Some important aspects of the descriptive chemistry you should study include the redox reactions of chromium and manganese, especially $Cr_2O_7{}^{2-}$ and $MnO_4{}^-$; the chemical reactions occurring in blast furnaces in steel metallurgy; the mechanism and prevention of iron corrosion; and the complex ions of iron, cobalt, and nickel.

The platinum metals have very similar properties and are chemically quite unreactive. Copper, silver, and gold all have the same outer electronic configuration but have different stable oxidation states: Cu^{2+}, Ag^+, and Au^{3+}. They are excellent electrical conductors and quite unreactive chemically. The chemical reactions of silver in photography should be understood.

Zinc, cadmium, and mercury have +2 oxidation states; +1 is also common for mercury. These elements are quite reactive chemically compared to the group IB metals. Zinc and cadmium have very similar physical and chemical properties and both are used as coatings to prevent oxidation of iron.

Mercury is the only transition metal which is liquid at ordinary temperatures. It dissolves other metals to form alloys called amalgams. Dimethyl mercury and Hg^{2+} compounds are very toxic, making mercury a serious contaminant in the environment.

LEARNING OBJECTIVES

As a result of studying Chap. 22 you should be able to do the following:
Write the definition and give an example illustrating the use of each key term.

22-1 Electronic configuration

1 Tell what is distinctive about the electronic configuration of the transition metals compared to the representative elements. (Text Probs. 22-1 to 22-3)
2 Give the electronic configurations of the first-series transition metals and explain the irregularities in the Aufbau process for chromium and copper. (Text Prob. 22-7) (Self Test 19)

22-2 General properties

1 List the chemical and physical properties that are similar for the transition metals and those that are not. (Self Test 2)

    2 List the common and the maximum oxidation states for the first-series transition metals. (Text Table 22-3; Text Prob. 22-9) (Self Test 8)

22-3
Complex ions:
general structure
and nomenclature

1 List the geometries possible for coordination numbers 2, 4, and 6. (Text Prob. 22-20) (Self Test 9)

2 Use the rules for writing formulas and names of complex ions. (Text App. C-2; Text Prob. 22-28) (Self Test 3, 10, 11)

22-4
Complex ions:
bonding

1 Describe bonding in complex ions according to the valence-bond theory.

2 Describe the formation of molecular orbitals in complex ions according to ligand-field theory. (Text Figs. 22-1, 22-2; Text Probs. 22-11, 22-21)

3 Describe the splitting of d orbitals into e_g and t_{2g} orbitals with different energies as ligands approach the central ion. (Text Figs. 22-4 to 22-6; Text Probs. 22-13, 22-14, 22-17 to 22-19) (Self Test 13)

4 Apportion the ligand and central-ion electrons in bonding, nonbonding, and anti-bonding orbitals for complex ions of the first-series transition metals and identify the unpaired electrons. (Text Fig. 22-7; Text Probs. 22-15, 22-16, 22-45) (Self Test 22 to 24)

5 Correlate weak-field ligands and strong-field ligands of the spectrochemical series with their ability to split the d electrons on the central ion and the resulting magnitude of Δ. (Self Test 5, 6)

6 Explain how the magnitude of Δ correlates with high-spin or low-spin complexes and with the color of complex ions. (Self Test 23, 24)

7 List the electron configurations of elements for which high- and low-electron-spin configurations are possible. (Self Test 7)

8 Correlate paramagnetic measurements with a high- or low-spin configuration and classify the ligands involved as strong- or weak-field ligands. (Text Example 22-1)

9 List the advantages of the crystal-field theory over the ligand-field and valence-bond theories. (Text Prob. 22-12) (Self Test 4, 21)

22-5
Complex ions:
stereochemistry

1 List the types of isomers possible in square-planar, tetrahedral, and octahedral geometries. (Text Probs. 22-22, 22-23) (Self Test 15, 25)

2 Sketch cis-trans isomers in square-planar structures. (Text Prob. 22-25)

3 Sketch structures showing cis-trans and optical isomerism in octahedral complexes. (Text Figs. 22-11 to 22-13; Text Probs. 22-26, 22-46)

22-6
Descriptive
chemistry of
selected transition
metals

1 Explain what is meant by the lanthanoid contraction and list its effects on the properties of the second- and third-series transition metals. (Text Prob. 22-4)

2 List the highest, lowest, and most stable oxidation states of each of the first-series transition metals. (Text Prob. 22-30)

3 Write equations showing the use of $Cr_2O_7^{2-}$ and MnO_4^- in oxidation-reduction reactions. (Text Probs. 22-31e, 22-35c, h, 22-37) (Self Test 26, 27)

4 Write equations for the reactions occurring in a blast furnace. (Text Prob. 22-36) (Self Test 28)

5 Write electrochemical equations showing the corrosion of iron. (Text Prob. 22-31f) (Self Test 29)

6 List ways of preventing the corrosion of transition metals, especially iron. (Text Prob. 22-32)

7 List the groups of transition metals whose reactions and properties are very similar. (Text Prob. 22-39)

8 Describe the use and chemical reactions of silver in photography. (Text Prob. 22-43) (Self Test 30)

9 Be familiar with the properties and reactions of transition metals. (Text Probs. 22-31, 22-33, 22-35, 22-40, 22-47)

10 Write reactions showing the formation and decomposition of complex ions of first-series transition metals. (Text Probs. 22-35d, e, 22-41, 22-42)

11 Explain what is meant by ferromagnetism and list the elements that are ferromagnetic. (Text Prob. 22-38) (Self Test 18)

SELF TEST

True or false

_____ 1 The d electrons added last to transition metals in the Aufbau process are the first to ionize.

_____ 2 The stable oxidation state gradually increases from left to right in a transition series.

_____ 3 Ligands may be either neutral molecules or charged ions.

_____ 4 The ligand-field theory successfully predicts the color variations of complex ions.

_____ 5 Weak-field ligands cause less splitting of d orbitals on the central atom.

_____ 6 F^- is a strong-field ligand because it strongly repels the d electrons of the central atom.

_____ 7 High- and low-spin configurations are possible for all first-series transition metals.

Completion

8 All first-series transition elements except scandium are known in the _____ oxidation state.

9 A coordination number of 6 gives _____ geometry and has _____ or _____ hybridization.

10 The correct name for $[Co(NH_3)_2Cl_4]^-$ is _____.

11 The formula for diamminediaquodibromochromium(III) is _____.

12 The coordination number of Co in $[CoCl_2(H_2O)en]^+$ is _____.

13 In crystal-field theory, nonbonding d orbitals are designated _____.

14 The energy difference between the d-orbital subsets is called the _____ and designated by _____.

15 The square-planar compound MA_2B_2 has _____ isomers, while the tetrahedral configuration of the same formula has _____ isomers.

16 When _____ different ligands are bonded to the central atom, the central atom is said to be _____ and the structure is said to be _____. The structures are called _____ or _____.

17 Ligands that bond to the central metal ion at more than one point are called _____ or _____.

18 Transition elements that are ferromagnetic are _____.

Multiple choice

19 Which of the following transition elements has only one valence electron?
(a) Sc   (b) La   (c) Fe   (d) Cu

20 The hybridization involved in $CoCl_3(NH_3)_3$ is

(a) sp^3 (b) d^2sp (c) d^2sp^3

(d) no hybridization is involved since it is a neutral compound and not a complex ion

21 The valence-bond model of bonding in complex ions

(a) correctly predicts the geometry of all complex ions

(b) is combined with MO theory to give the crystal-field theory

(c) correctly predicts the geometry and spectral properties of complex ions

(d) divides the d-orbitals into t_{2g} and e_g subsets

22 Electrons from the central ion occupy

(a) nonbonding or t_{2g} orbitals   (b) antibonding or e_g orbitals

(c) empty hybrid orbitals   (d) orbitals shared with the ligand electrons

23 The number of unpaired electrons when Cr^{2+} is combined in a strong-field ligand complex is

(a) 1   (b) 2   (c) 3   (d) 4

24 The number of unpaired electrons when Cr^{2+} is combined in a weak-field ligand complex is

(a) 1   (b) 2   (c) 3   (d) 4

25 The number of possible isomers of $[NiCl_4(NH_3)_2]^{2-}$ is

(a) 1   (b) 2   (c) 3   (d) 4

26 The dichromate ion

(a) is the dimer of $HCrO_4^-$

(b) reduces H_2O_2 in acidic solution, but oxidizes it in basic solution

(c) is used in glass-cleaning solutions

(d) all of the above

27 When MnO_4^- is used as an oxidizing agent

(a) the reducing agent is added to the MnO_4^-

(b) MnO_4^- is added to the reducing agent

(c) the reducing agent is added to acidified MnO_4^-

(d) the order of addition of reagents does not matter if the solution is basic

28 The reduction of iron ore in a blast furnace can be best represented by the reaction

(a) $2C + Fe_3O_4 \longrightarrow 3Fe + 2CO_2$

(b) $4CO + Fe_3O_4 \longrightarrow 3Fe + 4CO_2$

(c) $4H_2 + Fe_3O_4 \longrightarrow 3Fe + 4H_2O$

(d) $4Ca + Fe_3O_4 \longrightarrow 3Fe + 4CaO$

29 The cathode reaction in the rusting of iron may be represented as

(a) $Fe \longrightarrow Fe^{2+} + 2e^-$

(b) $Fe \longrightarrow Fe^{3+} + 3e^-$

(c) $O_2 + 4H^+ + 4e^- \longrightarrow 2H_2O$

(d) $2Fe^{3+} + 3H_2O \longrightarrow Fe_2O_3 + 6H^+$

30 Silver is widely used in photography because

(a) its complex ions are highly colored

(b) the amount of silver oxidized is proportional to the intensity of light striking the film

(c) the reduced silver is easily dissolved by hypo, or $Na_2S_2O_3$

(d) Ag^+ has a low reduction potential and forms soluble complex ions

23
ORGANIC CHEMISTRY

CHAPTER OVERVIEW

In Chaps. 20 and 21 we saw how the first member of each group of representative elements has properties and reactivity different from the remaining members of the group. Carbon shows this departure from group behavior most strongly. It has a strong tendency to form covalent bonds with other carbon atoms to form compounds with chains of carbon atoms in various configurations.

This chapter concerns organic chemistry, which is the chemistry of compounds containing carbon, hydrogen, and other elements, most commonly oxygen and nitrogen. The study of organic chemistry has been organized and simplified by classifying compounds into groups that depend on the functional group attached to the carbon chain. A functional group is an atom or group of atoms that gives special chemical properties to the organic compound. The common functional groups are listed in Table 23-6 in the text, and it is essential that you learn their names and structures.

The many different structures in Tables 23-1 to 23-5 show the need for a systematic system of nomenclature in organic chemistry. The text discusses the nomenclature of each functional group and this may be the most important material to learn to help you organize the large amount of material presented in the chapter.

The IUPAC names are designed to describe the exact structure of a molecule, so once you learn the terms used, you should be able to construct the chemical formula of complicated organic molecules from the name and devise correct names when the structural formula is given. Appendix C-3 in the text gives many examples of the nomenclature of organic compounds.

The type of bonding and hybridization on carbon determines the structure and many properties of organic compounds. You should review Sec. 9-3 on hybrid orbitals and observe how the orientation of hybrid orbitals determines the shapes of molecules and leads to the occurrence of different types of isomers.

**23-1
Saturated
hydrocarbons**

Keep in mind that carbon forms four covalent bonds in organic compounds. In saturated hydrocarbons the carbon skeleton is saturated with hydrogen atoms so that each carbon has four single bonds either to other carbon atoms or to hydrogen. Saturated hydrocarbons are called alkanes, or cycloalkanes if the carbon chain forms a closed ring.   The names of the first ten straight-chain or normal hydrocarbons should be learned (Table 23-1 in the text).   Names of cycloalkanes follow automatically from those of the normal alkanes.   Short carbon chains are often attached to, or branch from, longer chains.   These branching groups are called alkyl groups.   The names of short-chain alkyl groups, especially those with one, two, or three carbon atoms, are often used in chemical nomenclature.   You need to recognize these groups and their names.

Notice the different kinds of structural formulas that are used in organic chemistry. Figure 23-1 in the text shows structural formulas and three-dimensional models of simple alkanes.   Compare the information conveyed by three-dimensional models, full structural formulas, condensed structural formulas, and carbon skeleton formulas. Chemists tend to use as many shortcuts as possible in structures so carbon skeleton formulas are very common, but you should be aware that they do not show the complete structure.

When using the IUPAC nomenclature system be careful to identify the longest carbon chain.   Often a structure is not written to appear as a "straight" chain.   The locator numbers and chain orientation may be arranged in several different ways on paper and still represent the same spatial configuration.   Note especially the example of 2-methylbutane (Examples 23-1 to 23-3 in the text) in this respect.

Molecules with four or more carbon atoms have more than one way of bonding the carbon atoms together and thus form isomers.   The best way to visualize the spatial arrangement of carbon chains and the formation of isomers is by using ball-and-stick models.   Styrofoam balls or marshmallows and toothpicks can be used to make models if you do not have access to a molecular model kit.   You will find these models a valuable aid in visualizing organic bonding and structures.

The properties and reactions of alkanes are discussed in this section.

**23-2
Unsaturated
hydrocarbons**

Hydrocarbons with at least one double bond are called alkenes.   If they have at least one triple bond they are called alkynes.   Suffixes -*ane*, -*ene*, and -*yne* are used to indicate alkanes, alkenes, and alkynes, respectively.

Cis-trans or geometrical isomerism is possible in alkenes.   Study Table 23-4 in the text to see a comparison of cis-trans isomers and their names.   The cis isomer has identical groups on the same side of the double bond while the trans isomer has identical groups on opposite sides (across) the double bond.

Become familiar with the names and structures of the simple alkenes and alkynes in Table 23-4 and 23-5 in the text.

Reactions and properties of unsaturated hydrocarbons are discussed in this section.

**23-3
Aromatic
hydrocarbons**

The chemistry of aromatic hydrocarbons is the chemistry of benzene and its related compounds.   Become familiar with the peculiarities of the structure of benzene shown in Fig. 23-3 in the text and with its shorthand structural formula.   The delocalized electrons and bond angles give it special stability and it forms the basic structure of most other aromatic compounds.

**23-4
Functional groups**

Learn the structures and names of the functional groups in Table 23-6 in the text.

**23-5
Alcohols**

Alcohols contain the —OH functional group.   Both IUPAC and common names of alcohols (listed in Table 23-7 in the text) are used frequently.

Become familiar with the preparation, properties, and reactions of the low-molecular-weight alcohols and with the use and meaning of the terms primary, secondary, and tertiary in alcohol nomenclature. The most important reactions of alcohols are dehydration and oxidation.

**23-6
Ethers**

Ethers contain the functional group —O— and have the general formula ROR'. Become familiar with the common names and structures of the ethers given in Table 23-9 in the text. Ethers are generally quite unreactive.

**23-7
Aldehydes**

Aldehydes are prepared by the oxidation of primary alcohols. They contain the func-

$$\underset{\displaystyle \parallel}{\overset{\displaystyle O}{}}$$

tional group —C—H and can be easily oxidized to carboxylic acids. Become familiar with the IUPAC and common names and the structures of the aldehydes listed in Table 23-10 in the text.

**23-8
Ketones**

Ketones are closely related to aldehydes. They are prepared by the oxidation of secondary alcohols, so the double-bonded oxygen is not on a carbon atom at the end of the chain as it is for aldehydes. Become familiar with the IUPAC and common names and the structures of the simple ketones listed in Table 23-11 in the text.

**23-9
Carboxylic acids**

Carboxylic acids contain the functional group $-C\overset{\displaystyle O}{\underset{\displaystyle OH}{}}$. This functional group may appear to be a combination of an alcohol and an aldehyde, but its properties and reactions are very different from them. The names and formulas of some common carboxylic acids are given in Table 23-12. You should become familiar with them. They participate in typical acid-base reactions.

**23-10
Esters**

Esters contain the functional group $-C\overset{\displaystyle O}{\underset{\displaystyle O-C-}{}}$ and are prepared by the reaction of carboxylic acids and alcohols. Know the names and structures of the esters in Table 23-13 in the text. You should be able to give the name and structure of the carboxylic acid and alcohol from which each ester is derived.

Note the unique properties and varied uses of esters. The most important reaction of esters is their hydrolysis (splitting into the parent acid and alcohol).

**23-11
Amines**

Amines result when hydrogen atoms in NH_3 are replaced by an organic group. They are sometimes called organic bases, and they react with acids in a manner similar to ammonia. The names and structures of some simple amines are given in Table 23-14 in the text.

**23-12
Synthetic organic polymers**

Polymers are very large molecules made by the combination of many small monomers. Addition polymers are formed when the monomers add to each other. The addition reaction is usually catalyzed by a free radical such as an organic peroxide. Some examples of addition polymers and their monomers are shown in Table 23-15 in the text. Condensation polymers are formed when different types of monomer molecules combine by splitting out an H_2O or HCl molecule and forming a link between the monomers. Nylons, polyamides, and polyesters are examples of condensation polymers.

23-13
Optical isomerism in
organic compounds

Carbon atoms bonded to four different groups are called asymmetric. Compounds with asymmetric carbon atoms form isomers which are mirror images; these are called enantiomers. These isomers rotate a beam of polarized light as it passes through them. Fischer projections are used to show the configuration of the D and L forms of the enantiomers.

23-14
Carbohydrates
and proteins

Carbohyhdrates are aldehydes or ketones which also contain several alcohol groups. D-Glucose and D-fructose are common examples of simple carbohydrates called monosaccharides or simple sugars. D-Glucose and D-fructose can link together to form a disaccharide called sucrose (common table sugar). Many monosaccharide units can link together to form polysaccharides called starch or cellulose depending on how the monosaccharides are linked. Human beings can break the starch linkages and thus can digest starch, but cannot break the cellulose linkages.

Proteins are polymers of amino acids. Amino acids are molecules having both carboxylic acid and amine functional groups. The link between amino acids is called a peptide link, so small proteins are often called peptides. Hemoglobin, insulin, hormones, and many enzymes are naturally occurring proteins.

LEARNING OBJECTIVES

As a result of studying Chap. 23, you should be able to do the following:
Write the definition and give an example illustrating the use of each key term.

23-1
Saturated
hydrocarbons

1 Apply the hybridization concepts of Sec. 9-3 to predict the bonding and geometry of simple hydrocarbons. (Text Fig. 23-2; Text Probs. 23-3, 23-5, 23-15, 23-16, 23-20, 23-22, 23-26) (Self Test 3, 22)
2 Draw Lewis structures for simple organic compounds. (Text Prob. 23-5)
3 Give the IUPAC names for hydrocarbons whose parent compounds have up to six carbon atoms when given the structural formula, and draw structural formulas when given the names. (Text Tables 23-1 to 23-3; Text App. C-3; Text Examples 23-1 to 23-3; Text Probs. 23-6, 23-11, 23-12) (Self Test 2, 10, 25)
4 Draw structural formulas for all the isomers of butane, pentane, and hexane. (Text Example 23-4; Text Probs. 23-7, 23-8, 23-10) (Self Test 13, 23, 24)
5 Write equations for ring-opening reactions of cycloalkanes and substitution reactions of alkanes. (Text Probs. 23-13, 23-14)

23-2
Unsaturated
hydrocarbons

1 Give the IUPAC name for all alkenes and alkynes through hexene and hexyne when given the structural formula, and draw the structural formula when given the names. (Text Tables 23-4, 23-5; Text App. C-3; Text Example 23-5; Text Probs. 23-17 to 23-20) (Self Test 11, 12)
2 Write equations for addition of hydrogen halides to double or triple carbon bonds. (Text Prob. 23-21) (Self Test 14)

23-3
Aromatic
hydrocarbons

1 Use Fig. 23-3 in the text to explain the bonding in benzene according to MO theory and draw Lewis structures to explain resonance in benzene and related compounds. (Text Probs. 23-23, 23-25) (Self Test 4)
2 Write IUPAC names of benzene derivatives given a structural formula or the ortho-

meta-para system name. Draw the structural formula given the name in either system. (Text Probs. 23-24, 23-27) (Self Test 15, 16)

3 Draw structural formulas of isomers of the alkylbenzenes. (Text Prob. 23-24) (Self Test 5)

23-4
Functional groups

1 Write the names and structures of the functional groups in Table 23-6 in the text.

23-5
Alcohols

1 Write the IUPAC and common names of simple alcohols and draw the structural formulas when given the names. (Text Table 23-7; Text Probs. 23-28, 23-32**b**, **g**) (Self Test 6, 17)

2 Write equations for the preparation and oxidation of simple primary and secondary alcohols. (Text Probs. 23-29, 23-33) (Self Test 7)

3 Explain the different solubilities and boiling points of simple alcohols on the basis of hydrogen bonding. (Text Table 23-8; Text Prob. 23-37)

23-6
Ethers

1 Write the common names of simple ethers and draw the structural formulas when given the names. (Text Table 23-9; Text Prob 23-31)

23-7
Aldehydes

1 Give the IUPAC and common names of simple aldehydes and draw the structural formulas when given the names. (Text Table 23-10; Text Prob. 23-32**i**)

2 Write a chemical equation showing the oxidation of primary alcohols to aldehydes. (Text Prob. 23-30)

23-8
Ketones

1 Write the IUPAC and common names of simple ketones and draw the structural formulas when given the names. (Text Table 23-11; Text Prob. 23-32**a**, **e**, **h**) (Self Test 8)

2 Write a chemical reaction showing the oxidation of secondary alcohols to ketones.

23-9
Carboxylic acids

1 Write the IUPAC and common names for simple carboxylic acids and draw the structural formulas when given the names. (Text Table 23-12; Text Prob. 23-32**d**, **j**)

2 Relate the strength of carboxylic acids to their structure. (Text Table 23-12; Text Probs. 23-39, 23-40, 23-44)

3 Write chemical equations for reactions of carboxylic acids with inorganic bases and alcohols. (Text Prob. 23-34) (Self Test 18)

23-10
Esters

1 Write the IUPAC and common names for simple esters and draw structural formulas when given the names. (Text Table 23-13); Text Prob. 23-32**f**)

2 Know the general properties and uses of simple esters.

23-11
Amines

1 Write the common names of simple amines and draw structural formulas when given the names. (Text Table 23-14; Text Prob. 23-32**c**, **k**)

2 Classify amines as primary, secondary, or tertiary. (Text Prob. 23-43) (Self Test 19)

23-12
Synthetic organic polymers

1 Write equations showing how the addition polymer, polyethylene, is formed, and show how other addition polymers are formed by the same mechanism. (Text Probs. 23-45, 23-47) (Self Test 28)

2 Write equations showing how the condensation polymer, nylon 66, is formed, and

show how other condensation polymers are formed by the same mechanism. (Text Prob. 23-45)

3 Relate the structure of a polymer to the structure of its monomer. (Text Table 23-15; Text Prob 23-48)

23-13
Optical isomerism in
organic compounds

1 Draw structures that show how optical isomerism arises in compounds with asymmetric carbon atoms. (Text Probs. 23-50, 23-51, 23-53) (Self Test 9, 20, 29)

23-14
Carbohydrates
and proteins

1 Draw the acyclic structure of a simple sugar. (Text Prob. 23-56)

2 Show the relation between mono-, di-, and polysaccharides.

3 Explain the differences between cellulose and starch. (Text Prob. 23-57) (Self Test 30)

4 Name the functional groups present in amino acids and explain the special properties resulting from a basic and an acidic site in the same molecule. (Text Prob. 23-60)

5 Describe the peptide link that joins amino acids to form peptides and proteins. (Text Probs. 23-61, 23-63) (Self Test 21)

SELF TEST

True or false

___ 1 Carbon always bonds to four other atoms in organic compounds.

___ 2 Propane and isopropane are isomers.

___ 3 Rotation about a carbon-carbon double bond is not possible.

___ 4 The π electrons in benzene are localized between two adjacent carbon atoms to form a system of alternating double and single bonds.

___ 5 There are three isomers of dimethylbenzene.

___ 6 Isopropyl alcohol is a primary alcohol.

___ 7 Primary alcohols cannot be oxidized to ketones.

___ 8 Acetone is the ketone of acetic acid.

___ 9 An asymmetric carbon atom always gives two enantiomers which have chiral centers and rotate polarized light in opposite directions.

Completion

10 The IUPAC name for isobutane is _____.

11 The structural formula for 3,5-dimethyl-4-ethyl-3-isopropyl-1-hexyne is _____ _____ .

12 The IUPAC name for

$$CH_3 - CH = CH$$
$$|$$
$$CH_3 - CH_2 - CH - CH_2 - CH_3$$

is _____ .

13 There are _____ isomers of dichlorobutane.

14 The product of addition of HCl to propene is _____.

15 Another name for methylbenzene is _____ .

16 The IUPAC name for m-dimethylbenzene is _____ .

17 The IUPAC name for a secondary alcohol with four carbon atoms is _____.

18 The IUPAC name of the product of the reaction between acetic acid and n-propyl alcohol is _____ .

Its common name is _____.

19 Isopropyl amine is a _____ (primary, secondary, tertiary) amine.

20 Enantiomers arise in compounds that have an _____ carbon atom.

21 Proteins contain _____ links.

Multiple choice   **22** The class of hydrocarbons that has bonding involving sp^2 hybridization on carbon is the

(a) alkanes   (b) alkenes   (c) alkynes   (d) cycloalkanes

23 Which of the following is not an isomer of the others?

(a) $CH_3-CH-CH_2-CH_3$ (b) $CH_3-CH_2-CH_2-CH_2-CH_3$
            |
            CH_3

            CH_3
            |
(c) CH_3-C-CH_3 (d) $CH_2-CH-CH_3$
            | | |
            CH_3 CH_2-CH_2

24 The number of possible isomers of $C_5H_{11}Cl$ is

(a) 3   (b) 5   (c) 7   (d) 8

25 The IUPAC name for $CH_3-CH_2-CH_2-CH-CH_2-CH_3$ is
                                            |
                                           CH_3

(a) 4-ethylpentane   (b) 4-methylhexane

(c) 3-methylhexane   (d) all of the above are correct

26 The ether which is an isomer of ethanol is

(a) methyl ether   (b) methyl ethyl ether

(c) ethyl ether   (d) ethers are not isomers of alcohols

27 Which of the following can exist as cis-trans isomers?

(a) 1-butene   (b) 2-methyl-1-butene

(c) 2,3-dimethyl-2-butene   (d) 2-methyl-2-butene

28 The polymer Teflon has the formula $(-CF_2-CF_2-)_n$. The monomer which polymerizes to produce Teflon is

(a) $-CF_2-$ (b) CF_2-CF_2

(c) $CF_2=CF_2$ (d) $CF=CF$
                             | |
                             H   H

29 Which of the following has a chiral center?

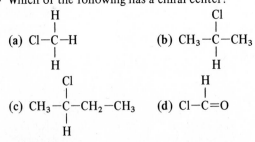

30 A starch is

(a) an enantiomer of cellulose   (b) the cyclic form of sucrose

(c) invert sugar   (d) a polymer of D-glucose units.

24 NUCLEAR PROCESSES

CHAPTER OVERVIEW

Up to this point we have studied reactions involving the electrons in outer orbitals around the nuclei of atoms. The nucleus of an atom is not affected by these chemical interactions, but it is capable of undergoing changes called nuclear reactions or nuclear transformations in processes quite different from ordinary chemical reactions.

We have already covered considerable information about the nucleus and its properties in our study of atomic structure. Recall the properties of subatomic particles found in the nuclei and the types of radioactivity emanating from atoms discussed in Sec. 5-1. In Sec. 5-2 we found that isotopes are atoms of the same element that have different numbers of neutrons in the nucleus and we used atomic symbols to distinguish those isotopes. In this chapter we will enlarge upon these concepts and consider the important aspects of nuclear processes.

**24-1
Radioactivity**

Recall from Sec. 5-1 our discussion of types of radioactivity: the alpha, beta, and gamma rays. All three types of radioactivity emanate from nuclei of atoms undergoing nuclear disintegration. These processes can be described by equations much like chemical equations. The isotope symbols showing mass number and atomic number (see Sec. 5-2) are used in equations for nuclear processes. There are two distinct types of radioactivity: natural and artificial. This section deals only with natural radioactivity; artificial radioactivity is discussed in Sec. 24-3.

The most common type of natural radioactivity is the ordered decay of naturally occurring, unstable nuclei called the radioactive decay series. Three different natural decay series are known. One of these starts with $^{238}_{92}U$ and is shown in Fig. 24-2 in the text. Each step in this series is represented by a nuclear equation. You should be able to write equations of this type given sufficient information about the decay process.

**24-2
The kinetics of
nuclear decay**

All radioactive decay processes follow first-order kinetics. The first-order equations developed in Sec. 14-2 apply directly to nuclear processes and can be used to calculate the time necessary for a given amount of decay to occur or the amount of material remaining after a given time.

Each radioactive isotope has a characteristic half-life, and decay rates of different processes are often compared through values of half-lives of the isotopes. Half-lives vary from a fraction of a second to billions of years. The kinetics of decay of natural radioactive isotopes can be used to determine the age of substances containing the isotope. Uranium dating is used for minerals and carbon dating for artifacts containing carbon.

24-3
Nuclear reactions

Artificial or induced radioactivity results from the bombardment of nuclei with subatomic particles. The products of these bombardment processes are usually radioactive and undergo nuclear decay. Figure 24-3 in the text shows a diagram of a cyclotron used to bombard target nuclei with protons. All the elements with atomic numbers greater than 92 (beyond uranium) are artificial. They were produced by bombardment techniques and are all radioactive.

24-4
Nuclear stability

Figure 24-4 in the text can be used to determine whether or not a given isotope is radioactive. If the isotope lies outside the belt of stability it will decay spontaneously toward the stable region. Note how the neutron/proton ratio for stable nuclei increases as the atomic number increases.

24-5
Fission, fusion,
and nuclear
binding energy

Mass is not conserved in nuclear reactions. Spontaneous nuclear reactions always involve the loss of mass and the production of large amounts of energy. The decrease in mass can be determined by the difference between the mass of products and the mass of reactants, and the energy equivalent of this mass loss can be determined by Einstein's equation: $E = mc^2$.

The mass of an atomic nucleus is always less than the mass of the constituent neutrons and protons. The energy equivalent of this mass defect or mass loss is called the binding energy of the nucleus. The highest binding energies per nucleon are found in elements of intermediate atomic number, as shown in Fig. 24-6 in the text. Moving toward the center from either end of this plot results in the formation of more stable nuclei accompanied by the release of energy. Therefore, the fusion of light nuclei into heavier ones and the fission of heavy nuclei into lighter ones both result in the release of energy. Nuclear fission, used in present nuclear reactors, is based on moving to the left on this plot. Nuclear fusion is based on moving to the right.

When a $^{235}_{92}U$ nucleus is bombarded by a neutron with the right kinetic energy, it undergoes fission to form two lighter nuclei, free neutrons, and energy. The free neutrons cause other $^{235}_{92}U$ atoms to fission, resulting in a chain reaction.

Uncontrolled chain reactions produce nuclear explosions or atomic bombs, but by controlling the concentration of fissionable $^{235}_{92}U$ and absorbing excess neutrons, the rate of the fission process is slowed and energy is released under controlled conditions. Figure 24-7 in the text shows a diagram of a nuclear reactor which uses this process. In the uncontrolled process the fission fragments produce radioactive fallout from the explosion; in the controlled process they form highly radioactive waste materials.

Fusion of ^3_1H and ^2_1H has been proposed as an almost unlimited source of energy without the serious waste-disposal problems associated with fission-type reactors. The technological problems of developing fusion power are not solved and practical use of nuclear fusion is still many years in the future.

24-6
Applications of radioactivity

We have already discussed the use of radioactivity for determining the age of minerals and objects containing carbon and for power generation. This section mentions other uses in chemical research, in medicine, and as tracers for following changes in almost any kind of process.

KEY EQUATIONS

24-2
The kinetics of nuclear decay

The decay of a radioactive isotope is given by

$$\log \frac{N}{N_0} = -\frac{kt}{2.303}$$

where N = number of parent nuclei at time t
     N_0 = number of parent nuclei at time $t = 0$
     k = first-order rate constant
     t = time since initial concentration N_0 was observed

The half-life is related to the rate constant by

$$t_{1/2} = \frac{0.693}{k}$$

where $t_{1/2}$ = half-life of the isotope
     k = first-order rate constant

24-5
Fission, fusion, and nuclear binding energy

The Einstein relationship gives the energy equivalent of a quantity of mass

$$E = mc^2$$

where E = energy, J
     m = mass, kg
     c = speed of light = 2.998×10^8 m s^{-1}

LEARNING OBJECTIVES

As a result of studying Chap. 24 you should be able to do the following.
     Write the definition and give an example illustrating the use of each key term.

24-1
Radioactivity

1 List the three main types of radioactivity and give their symbols. (Text Probs. 24-2, 24-16)
2 Write nuclear equations for natural radioactive decay by alpha or beta emission. (Text Example 24-1; Text Probs. 24-10 to 24-12, 24-17, 24-18) (New Skills Examples 1, 2; Self Test 2, 10, 14, 15, 20)
3 Identify the type of radioactive decay given the parent and daughter isotopes. (Text Example 24-2; Text Prob. 24-9) (Self Test 1, 17)
4 Describe three methods for detecting radioactivity.

24-2
The kinetics of nuclear decay

1 Calculate the amount of a radioactive isotope remaining after a given time or the time required for a given amount to decay given the rate constant for decay or the half-life. (Text Examples 24-3, 24-4; Text Probs. 24-19, 24-21) (New Skills Example 3; Self Test 18)

2 Use uranium, potassium-argon, and carbon dating calculations to determine the age of an object. (Text Examples 24-5, 24-6; Text Probs. 24-23 to 24-25) (Self Test 3, 19)

<table>
<tr><td>24-3
Nuclear reactions</td><td>1 Write nuclear equations for the transmutation of elements by nuclear bombardment. (Text Prob. 24-15) (Self Test 4, 15)</td></tr>
<tr><td>24-4
Nuclear stability</td><td>1 Write nuclear equations for radioactive decay by neutron or positron emission and for electron capture. (Text Probs. 24-5, 24-7, 24-13, 24-14) (Self Test 7, 11, 21)
2 Use the belt of stability in Fig. 24-4 in the text to predict whether or not a nucleus is unstable and the type of decay likely for unstable nuclei. (Text Probs. 24-26 to 24-28) (Self Test 5, 8, 9, 22, 23)
3 Write nuclear reactions typical of the fission process for $^{235}_{92}U$ (Text Prob. 24-29)</td></tr>
<tr><td>24-5
Fission, fusion, and nuclear binding energy</td><td>1 Calculate the binding energy of a given isotope. (Text Prob. 24-30) (New Skills Example 4; Self Test 12, 25)
2 Describe the $^{235}_{92}U$ chain reaction and construction of an atomic bomb and a nuclear power plant and list the basic differences in their construction and energy release. (Text Prob. 24-34) (Self Test 13)
3 List some problems that have not yet been solved in the development of controlled fusion reactions. (Text Prob. 24-35)
4 Calculate the energy released in nuclear processes. (Text Prob. 24-36) (New Skills Example 5; Self Test 24, 25)</td></tr>
<tr><td>24-6
Applications of radioactivity</td><td>1 Describe four uses of radioactivity or radioactive isotopes. (Text Probs. 24-37 to 24-40)</td></tr>
</table>

NEW SKILLS

24-1
Radioactivity

Nuclear equations

We can write equations for nuclear processes in the same general manner as for chemical reactions. The isotope symbol is always used in nuclear equations and care must be taken to balance the total mass numbers and atomic numbers for products and reactants.

● EXAMPLE 1

Problem: Write a nuclear equation for the decay of cobalt 60 by beta emission to nickel 60.

Solution: The isotope symbols for the particles are: cobalt 60, $^{60}_{27}Co$; nickel 60, $^{60}_{28}Ni$; and a beta particle, $^{0}_{-1}e$. The nuclear equation is

$$^{60}_{27}Co \longrightarrow ^{0}_{-1}e + ^{60}_{28}Ni ●$$

● EXAMPLE 2

Problem: Write an equation for the alpha decay of radium 226.

Solution: The daughter isotope produced by the decay is not identified, but we can determine its mass number and atomic number from the information given because the totals of the mass numbers and atomic numbers remain constant during any nuclear process. The nuclear equation is

$$^{226}_{88}\text{Ra} \longrightarrow {}^4_2\text{He} + ?$$

The mass numbers of the helium nucleus and the daughter isotope must total 226 and their atomic numbers must total 88. Therefore, the daughter isotope has mass number 226 − 4 = 222 and atomic number 88 − 2 = 86, so it must be $^{222}_{86}\text{Rn}$. The completed equation is

$$^{226}_{88}\text{Ra} \longrightarrow {}^4_2\text{He} + {}^{222}_{86}\text{Rn} \quad \bullet$$

Examples 24-1 and 24-2 in the text are similar problems.

24-2
The kinetics of
nuclear decay

Actually there are no *new* skills in this section, only the application of familiar first-order kinetics to nuclear decay processes. We will work two examples illustrating these applications.

1 Using the first-order rate law to determine the amount of a radioactive species remaining after a given time

● **EXAMPLE 3**   **Problem**: Sodium 24 is injected into the bloodstream of patients suspected of having an obstruction in their circulatory system. The amount of radioactivity detected in parts of the body affected by the obstruction indicates the quantity of blood reaching that area and helps locate the obstruction. Sodium 24 undergoes beta decay with a half-life of 15.0 h. How long could a hospital keep a sample of sodium 24 before it loses 90 percent of its radioactivity?

Solution: Ten percent of the sodium 24 will be left after this time. The first-order decay rate gives the fraction of radioactive isotope left as a function of time

$$\log \frac{N}{N_0} = -\frac{kt}{2.303}$$

where $\dfrac{N}{N_0}$ = fraction of $^{24}_{11}\text{Na}$ remaining = 0.10

$$k = \text{rate constant} = \frac{0.693}{t_{1/2}} = \frac{0.693}{15.0 \text{ h}} = 4.62 \times 10^{-2} \text{ h}^{-1}$$

t = time for 90% of $^{24}_{11}\text{Na}$ to decay

Substituting these values into the rate equation gives

$$\log 0.10 = -\frac{(4.62 \times 10^{-2})t}{2.303}$$

$$t = 49.8 \text{ h} \quad \bullet$$

Example 24-3 in the text illustrates the calculation of the amount of a nuclide remaining after a given time period of decay.

2 Use of radioactivity in determining the age of artifacts
There are several methods for determining the age of an artifact by radioactivity. The best known of these is carbon dating or radiocarbon dating. Carbon 14 is radioactive

and exists in a constant ratio with the more abundant isotope, carbon 12, in all living plants or animals. After death there is no more input of carbon so the carbon 14 decays and the $^{14}_{6}C/^{12}_{6}C$ ratio decreases. Measurements of this ratio can be used in the first-order decay rate equation to determine the time elapsed since the artifact was living.

Example 24-5 in the text illustrates the use of the $^{238}_{92}U/^{206}_{82}Pb$ ratio in dating and Example 24-6 shows an application of radiocarbon dating.

24-5
Fission, fusion, and nuclear binding energy

1 Calculation of binding energy
The mass of a nucleus is always less than the mass of the protons and neutrons in that nucleus. This difference in mass is called the mass loss or mass defect of the nuclide. Its energy equivalent is the binding energy of the nucleus.

● **EXAMPLE 4**

Problem: Calculate the nuclear binding energy of a helium-4 nucleus. The mass of a helium-4 nucleus is 4.00150 amu, of a proton 1.00728 amu, and of a neutron 1.00867 amu.

Solution: Helium 4 contains two protons and two neutrons. We would expect its mass to be

$$\text{Mass of 2 protons} = 2(1.00728 \text{ amu}) = 2.01456 \text{ amu}$$

$$\text{Mass of 2 neutrons} = 2(1.00867 \text{ amu}) = 2.01734 \text{ amu}$$

$$\text{Total mass of nucleons} \qquad\qquad = 4.03190 \text{ amu}$$

The actual mass of the nucleus, 4.00150 amu, is less than the mass of the nucleons.

Mass of nucleons	4.03190 amu
Mass of nucleus	4.00150 amu
Mass loss	0.03040 amu

We use the Einstein relationship to calculate the energy equivalent to this mass loss

$$E = mc^2$$

where E = energy, J
  m = mass, kg
  c = speed of light = 2.998×10^8 m s^{-1}
It is most convenient to convert the mass loss to kilograms before substituting into the Einstein relationship.

$$\text{Mass loss} = 0.03040 \text{ amu} \ \frac{1 \text{ g}}{6.023 \times 10^{23} \text{ amu}} \ \frac{10^{-3} \text{ kg}}{\text{g}} = 5.047 \times 10^{-29} \text{ kg}$$

The Einstein relationship becomes

$$E = (5.047 \times 10^{-29} \text{ kg})(2.998 \times 10^8 \text{ m s}^{-1})^2 = 4.536 \times 10^{-12} \text{ kg m}^2 \text{ s}^{-2}$$

$$\text{or} \quad 4.536 \times 10^{-12} \text{ J}$$

Binding energies are usually expressed per nucleon. There are four nucleons in a helium-4 nucleus, so the binding energy per nucleon is

$$\frac{4.536 \times 10^{-12} \text{ J}}{4 \text{ nucleons}} = 1.134 \times 10^{-12} \text{ J nucleon}^{-1} \quad \bullet$$

Figure 24-6 in the text shows how nuclear binding energy varies for the elements. The highest binding energies are found in elements with intermediate atomic numbers and these are the most stable nuclei.

2 Calculation of energy released in fission or fusion processes

• **EXAMPLE 5**   **Problem**: A fusion reaction that has been producing energy since the dawn of time remains virtually untapped to this day. The sun releases energy according to the overall process

$$4\,{}^{1}_{1}\text{H} \longrightarrow {}^{4}_{2}\text{He} + 2\,{}^{0}_{1}e$$

Calculate the energy released when 1 mol of helium nuclei is formed by this process. The mass of a proton is 1.00728 amu, of an alpha particle 4.00150 amu, and of a positron 0.000549 amu.

Solution: The energy released is the energy equivalent of the mass loss for the reaction. We can determine this mass loss as follows.

$$\text{Mass of } 4\,{}^{1}_{1}\text{H} = 4(1.00728) = 4.02912 \text{ amu}$$

$$\text{Mass of } {}^{4}_{2}\text{He} + 2\,{}^{0}_{1}e = 4.00150 + 2(0.000549) = 4.01248$$

$$\text{Mass loss} = 4.02912 - 4.01248 = 0.01664 \text{ amu}$$

The energy equivalent of this mass loss is

$$E = mc^2 = 0.01664 \text{ amu} \frac{1 \text{ g}}{6.023 \times 10^{23} \text{ amu}} \frac{10^{-3} \text{ kg}}{\text{g}} (2.998 \times 10^8 \text{ m s}^{-1})^2$$

$$= 2.483 \times 10^{-12} \text{ J per He nucleus}$$

$$2.483 \times 10^{-12} \text{ J (He nucleus)}^{-1} (6.023 \times 10^{23} \text{ He nuclei mol}^{-1})$$

$$= 1.500 \times 10^{12} \text{ J mol}^{-1} \quad \bullet$$

The text works an example showing the calculation of the energy released in a fission process.

SELF TEST

True or false   ____ 1 Lead 210 decays to bismuth 210 by alpha emission.
____ 2 Beta emission leaves the mass number of a nucleus unchanged.
____ 3 The ratio of carbon to uranium can be used to determine the age of ancient relics.
____ 4 Transuranium elements can be produced only by bombardment techniques.
____ 5 The most common method of decay for nuclei that have a high neutron/proton ratio is neutron emission.

Completion

6 The rate constant for the decay of ^{110}Sn is 0.173 h^{-1}; its half-life is _____.

7 A positron is a particle which has the same _____ as an electron but has a _____ charge.

8 When the number of neutrons is plotted against the number of protons for non-radioactive nuclei a region called the _____ is formed.

9 The neutron/proton ratio is approximately _____ for light nuclei and gradually _____ (increases, decreases) for heavier nuclei.

10 Beta decay _____ (increases, decreases) the atomic number and _____ (increases, decreases) the neutron/proton ratio.

11 _____ can be induced when a $^{235}_{92}$U nucleus captures a _____ .

12 The difference between the mass of a nucleus and the mass of the _____ plus _____ contained in the nucleus is the _____ . The energy equivalent of this mass difference is called the _____ .

13 The quantity of fissionable material capable of sustaining a chain reaction is called a _____ .

Multiple choice

14 Which of the following isotopes results from the beta decay of $^{234}_{90}$Th?
(a) $^{234}_{91}$Pa   (b) $^{234}_{89}$Ac   (c) $^{235}_{90}$Th   (d) $^{233}_{90}$Th

15 Which of the following nuclear equations is not balanced correctly?
(a) $^{238}_{92}$U $\longrightarrow$ $^{234}_{90}$Th + $^{4}_{2}$He
(b) $^{76}_{36}$Kr + $^{0}_{-1}e$ $\longrightarrow$ $^{76}_{35}$Br
(c) $^{209}_{83}$Bi + $^{2}_{1}$H $\longrightarrow$ $^{210}_{84}$Po + $^{1}_{0}n$
(d) $^{30}_{14}$Si $\longrightarrow$ $^{30}_{15}$P + $^{0}_{1}e$

16 The type of decay involved when $^{65}_{35}$Br decays into $^{65}_{34}$Se is
(a) alpha decay   (b) beta decay   (c) positron decay   (d) neutron emission

17 The natural radioactive decay series for $^{226}_{88}$Ra is by successive emission of five alpha particles and four beta particles. At the end of this series the nucleus has mass and atomic numbers of
(a) 216, 79   (b) 206, 72   (c) 210, 83   (d) 206, 82

18 The half-life of cobalt 60 is 5.0 years. How much of a 1.00-g sample of this nuclide will remain after 7 years?
(a) 0.0063 g   (b) 0.286 g   (c) 0.378 g   (d) 0.422 g

19 A scroll of parchment is claimed to be a Dead Sea Scroll, but archaeologists suspect that it is not authentic. Radiocarbon data shows the parchment to have a $^{14}_{6}$C/$^{12}_{6}$C ratio of 0.950. How old is the parchment? $t_{1/2}$ for $^{14}_{6}$C is 5670 years.
(a) 420 years   (b) 1890 years   (c) 8110 years   (d) 24,500 years

20 When a nucleus undergoes alpha decay the mass number
(a) does not change   (b) decreases by 1
(c) decreases by 2   (d) decreases by 4

21 When a nucleus undergoes neutron emission it
(a) does not change atomic number   (b) increases its atomic number by 1
(c) decreases its atomic number by 1   (d) splits into different fragments

22 Nuclei with neutron/proton ratios laying above the belt of stability undergo
(a) alpha decay   (b) beta decay
(c) positron emission   (d) electron capture

23 Nuclei with neutron/proton ratios lying below the belt of stability undergo
(a) alpha decay   (b) beta decay
(c) neutron emission   (d) positron emission

24 What is the loss in mass during the formation of a $^{12}_{6}C$ nucleus? (Mass of $^{12}_{6}C$ = 11.99671 amu, mass of neutron = 1.00867 amu, and mass of a proton = 1.00728 amu.)

(a) 0.00834 amu   (b) 0.09899 amu

(c) 1.643×10^{-22} kg   (d) none of the above

25 What is the binding energy of a $^{12}_{6}C$ nucleus? (Use the data in problem 24; the speed of light is 2.998×10^8 m s^{-1}.)

(a) 1.231×10^{-12} J nucleon^{-1} (b) 1.037×10^{-13} J nucleon^{-1}

(c) 4.926×10^{-20} J nucleon^{-1} (d) 4.151×10^{-21} J nucleon^{-1}

ANSWERS TO
SELF TESTS

Chapter 1   **1** False: Science terms often have several meanings. Some may be ambiguous. It takes considerable effort to learn these terms.   **2** True: This will soon become apparent.   **3** True   **4** False: Units must be consistent in applying unit factors. Grams cannot be converted to grams/volume.   **5** False: The last zero is significant. **6** True   **7** False: You are entitled to four significant figures in your answer. 1.928 is correct.   **8** Hypothesis   **9** Theory   **10** Mixture   **11** Compound   **12** 3.70×10^{-4} **13** 1.5×10^{13} **14** 4.0×10^{-10} **15** 1 liter/10^3 ml   **16** 10^3 g/1 kg **17 (c)**   **18 (d)** This is a physical change.   **19 (d)**   **20 (c)** Watch those significant figures.   **21 (a)**   **22 (c)** It has the correct number of significant figures and correct round off. The answer is in kilograms.

$$125 \text{ lb} \times \frac{454}{1 \text{ lb}} \times \frac{1 \text{ kg}}{1000 \text{ g}} = 56.8 \text{ kg}$$

23 (c) $1 \text{ km} \times \dfrac{1000 \text{ m}}{1 \text{ km}} \times \dfrac{100 \text{ cm}}{1 \text{ m}} \times \dfrac{1 \text{ in}}{2.54 \text{ cm}} \times \dfrac{1 \text{ ft}}{12 \text{ in}} \times \dfrac{1 \text{ mi}}{5280 \text{ ft}} = 0.621 \text{ mi}$

24 (d) $30 \text{ globs} \times \dfrac{10 \text{ chunks}}{1 \text{ glob}} = 300 \text{ chunks}$

25 (c) $55 \dfrac{\text{mi}}{\text{h}} \times \dfrac{1 \text{ km}}{0.621 \text{ mi}} = 88 \dfrac{\text{km}}{\text{h}}$

Chapter 2   **1** True: Not the conventional units but still a measure of mass per unit volume. **2** False: It may be "pure" in the sense that there are no harmful bacteria, but there are several chemical compounds present, making it a mixture.   **3** False: Na and Cl are chemical symbols for sodium and chlorine, but NaCl is the chemical formula for sodium chloride.   **4** True: The law of conservation of mass.   **5** False: The physical appearance of the egg changes, but the chemical compounds also are changed. This is a chemical change.   **6** False: For instance, it takes more heat to raise 100 g of water 1°C, than to raise 1 g of water 1°C.   **7** True   **8** Homogeneous   **9** Molecule   **10** Atoms   **11** Work   **12** Heat   **13** Joule   **14** −273°C   **15** Potential energy   **16** Kinetic energy   **17 (c)**   **18 (d)** Combustion of natural gas is a chemical change.   **19 (c)** The sugar simply dissolves; it does not change its chemical composition.   **20 (d)** Kinetic energy is energy of motion.

21 (b) Density $= \dfrac{mass}{volume} = \dfrac{655 \text{ g}}{85.0 \text{ cm}^3} = 7.71 \text{ g cm}^{-3}$

22 (c) Volume $= 35.0 \text{ g} \times \dfrac{1 \text{ cm}^3}{2.70 \text{ g}} = 13.0 \text{ cm}^3$

23 (a) % potassium $= \dfrac{\text{g potassium}}{\text{g potassium chloride}} \times 100 = \dfrac{39.3 \text{ g}}{39.3 \text{ g} + 35.7 \text{ g}} \times 100 = 52.4\%$

24 (d) $50 \text{ g carbon} \times \dfrac{72.7 \text{ g oxygen}}{27.3 \text{ g carbon}} = 133 \text{ g oxygen}$

25 (a) $^{\circ}\text{C} = \frac{5}{9} (^{\circ}\text{F} - 32) = \frac{5}{9} (98.6 - 32) = 37.0^{\circ}\text{C}$
$\qquad \text{K} = {}^{\circ}\text{C} + 273 = 37.0 + 273 = 310 \text{ K}$

Chapter 3   1 True   2 False: The term "mole" means two things. It signifies Avogadro's number of particles and it also represents the amount of mass contained in that number of particles of the substance.   3 False: The moles of individual elements must balance, but not necessarily the total moles of compounds.   4 True   5 True
6   12

7 Atoms of O $= 32 \text{ g O}_2 \times \dfrac{2 \text{ mol O}}{32 \text{ g O}_2} \times \dfrac{6.02 \times 10^{23} \text{ atoms of O}}{1 \text{ mol O}}$

$\qquad = 1.2 \times 10^{24} \text{ atoms of O}$

8 Mol $\text{O}_2 = 16 \text{ g O}_2 \times \dfrac{1 \text{ mol O}_2}{32 \text{ g O}_2} = 0.5 \text{ mol O}_2$

9 $3(137.3) + 2(31.0) + 8(16.0) = 602 \text{ g mol}^{-1}$

10 $3.01 \times 10^{23} \text{ molecules CH}_4 \times \dfrac{1 \text{ mol CH}_4}{6.02 \times 10^{23} \text{ molecules CH}_4} \times \dfrac{16.0 \text{ g CH}_4}{1 \text{ mol CH}_4} = 8.00 \text{ g}$

11 $5.00 \text{ mol ZnO} \times \dfrac{81.4 \text{ g ZnO}}{1 \text{ mol ZnO}} = 407 \text{ g}$

12 g $\text{NH}_3 = 1.20 \times 10^{25} \text{ molecules} \times \dfrac{1 \text{ mol}}{6.02 \times 10^{23} \text{ molecules}} \times \dfrac{17.0 \text{ g}}{1 \text{ mol}} = 339 \text{ g}$

13 $2.16 \text{ g B} \times \dfrac{1 \text{ mol B}}{10.8 \text{ g B}} \times \dfrac{1 \text{ mol Na}_2\text{B}_4\text{O}_7}{4 \text{ mol B}} = 0.050 \text{ mol Na}_2\text{B}_4\text{O}_7$

14 Basis for calculations: 1 mol NaBr

$\qquad\qquad \% \text{ Br} = \dfrac{79.9 \text{ g Br}}{(23.0 + 79.9) \text{ g NaBr}} \times 100 = 77.6\% \text{ Br}$

15 $1.0 + 2(12.0) + 3.0 + 2(16.0) = 60.0 \text{ g mol}^{-1}$ 16 limiting reagent   17 (c)
18 (c)   19 (c)   20 (a) Use 1 mol SO_2 as basis for calculation

$\qquad\qquad \% \text{ O} = \dfrac{32 \text{ g O}}{64 \text{ g SO}_2} \times 100 = 50.0\%$

21 (d) g $\text{Ca} = 4.00 \text{ mol CaCO}_3 \times \dfrac{1 \text{ mol Ca}}{1 \text{ mol CaCO}_3} \times \dfrac{40.1 \text{ g Ca}}{1 \text{ mol Ca}} = 160 \text{ g}$

22 (d) Atomic weights of X and Y are needed to determine the empirical formula.

23 (b) g $\text{Ca} = 2 \text{ mol Ca}_3(\text{PO}_4)_2 \times \dfrac{3 \text{ mol Ca}}{1 \text{ mol Ca}_3(\text{PO}_4)_2} \times \dfrac{40.1 \text{ g Ca}}{1 \text{ mol Ca}} = 241 \text{ g}$

24 (c)   25 (d) Let the basis for the calculations be 100 g of compound.

$\qquad\qquad \text{mol Mn} = \dfrac{56.3 \text{ g Mn}}{54.9 \text{ g Mn mol}^{-1}} = 1.03 \text{ mol Mn}$

$$\text{mol S} = \frac{43.7 \text{ g S}}{32.0 \text{ g S mol}^{-1}} = 1.37 \text{ mol S}$$

Normalize the moles

$$\text{mol Mn} = \frac{1.03}{1.03} = 1.00$$

$$\text{mol S} = \frac{1.37}{1.03} = 1.33$$

This gives a whole-number ratio of 3 mol Mn to 4 mol S, or Mn_3S_4.

Chapter 4   **1** False: PV = constant only if the temperature remains unchanged.   **2** False: The number of molecules or moles does not change as the pressure changes.   **3** True: This is Charles' law.   **4** True: from Dalton's law.   **5** True: Gay-Lussac's law of combining volumes.   **6** True: Graham's law says the gas with the lower molecular weight diffuses faster.   **7** Unit area   **8** Kelvin   **9** 273   **10** Increase   **11** Decrease   **12** Less   **13** Partial pressure   **14** Molecular weights or densities   **15** 0.0821 liter atm mol^{-1} K^{-1} **16** (a) 5.0 liters $\times \frac{380}{760}$ = 2.5 liters   **17** (c) 5.0 liters $\times \frac{546}{273}$ = 10.0 liters   **18** (d) The gas increases in temperature so the volume will increase and the temperature ratio must be greater than 1 and expressed in kelvins, 473/373.   The gas decreases in pressure so the volume will increase and the pressure ratio must also be greater than 1, 760/400.   **19** (b) Final volume changes by $\frac{1}{2}$ for pressure change and 3 for temperature change.   Net change is $\frac{1}{2} \times 3 = \frac{3}{2}$ increase.   **20** (c) The temperature and mass of gas do not change, but the volume increases by a factor of 3 because of the pressure change. Since density = mass per unit volume, the density must decrease by a factor of 3 as the volume increases.

21 (c) Density at STP = $\dfrac{\text{molecular weight in g mol}^{-1}}{22.4 \text{ liters mol}^{-1}}$

22 (d) mol H_2 = 2000 lb $NH_3 \times \dfrac{454 \text{ g}}{\text{lb}} \times \dfrac{1 \text{ mol } NH_3}{17.0 \text{ g } NH_3} \times \dfrac{3 \text{ mol } H_2}{2 \text{ mol } NH_3}$

$$= 8.01 \times 10^4 \text{ mol } H_2$$

liters H_2 = 8.01×10^4 mol $\times$ 22.4 liters mol^{-1} = 1.79×10^6 liters

23 (c) The densities of the possible gases at STP are

$H_2:$ $\dfrac{2 \text{ g mol}^{-1}}{22.4 \text{ liters mol}^{-1}} = 0.089$ $O_2:$ $\dfrac{32 \text{ g mol}^{-1}}{22.4 \text{ liters mol}^{-1}} = 1.43$

$CH_4:$ $\dfrac{16 \text{ g mol}^{-1}}{22.4 \text{ liters mol}^{-1}} = 0.714$ $SO_2:$ $\dfrac{64 \text{ g mol}^{-1}}{22.4 \text{ liters mol}^{-1}} = 2.86$

O_2 has a density very near the 1.43 g $liter^{-1}$ of the unidentified gas and is the best choice.
24 (b) Using Graham's law of effusion

$$\frac{\text{Rate}_{He}}{\text{Rate}_g} = \frac{\sqrt{MW_g}}{\sqrt{MW_{He}}}$$

Since the rate for He is 2 times the rate of the unidentified gas

$$\frac{2}{1} = \frac{\sqrt{MW_g}}{\sqrt{4}}$$

$$\sqrt{MW_g} = 2 \times 2 = 4$$

$$MW_g = 16$$

The molecular weight is close to that of CH_4 **25 (c)** The balanced reaction is

$$CH_4 + 2O_2 \longrightarrow CO_2 + 2H_2O$$

Since the gases are measured under the same conditions

$$\text{liters } O_2 = 12 \text{ liters } CH_4 \times \frac{2 \text{ liters } O_2}{1 \text{ liter } CH_4} = 24 \text{ liters } O_2$$

Chapter 5   **1** False: Dalton proposed that different elements have different properties because their atoms are different.   **2** True: This shows that electrons carry a negative charge. **3** True   **4** True: Removal of an electron leaves an excess of positive charge on the atom.   **5** True   **6** False: Isotopes are atoms of the same element having different numbers of neutrons and therefore different masses.   **7** Electrons   **8** Negative **9** Nucleus, electrons   **10** Mass number   **11** Mass spectrometry   **12** Cycles per second   **13** Quantized   **14** Bohr atom   **15** Line   **16 (c)**   **17 (c)** Thomson measured the charge-to-mass ratio.   **18 (a)**   **19 (b)** According to classical physics, both the stationary atom and the planetary atom would collapse.   **20 (a)** 27.185 MHz = 2.7185×10^7 Hz

$$\lambda = \frac{c}{\nu} = \frac{3.00 \times 10^8 \text{ m s}^{-1}}{2.7185 \times 10^7 \text{ s}^{-1}} = 11.0 \text{ m}$$

21 (d) ^{14}N has mass number 14, which is the highest.   **22 (b)** Both have six neutrons.   **23 (c)** ^{10}B and ^{11}B are isotopes of boron.   **24 (a)** There is 55 percent ^{79}Br and 45 percent ^{81}Br. The weight of Br is the sum of the contributions from ^{79}Br and ^{81}Br.

$$\text{Contribution of } ^{79}Br = 0.55 (79.0) = 43.45$$

$$\text{Contribution of } ^{81}Br = 0.45 (81.0) = \underline{36.45}$$

$$\text{Total weight of Br} = 79.90$$

$$\text{Atomic weight of Br} = 79.9$$

25 (d) The Rydberg equation is used to calculate the wavelength.

$$\frac{1}{\lambda} = 1.10 \times 10^{-2} \text{ nm}^{-1} \left(\frac{1}{n_1^2} - \frac{1}{n_2^2} \right)$$

$$\frac{1}{\lambda} = 1.10 \times 10^{-2} \text{ nm}^{-1} \left(\frac{1}{2^2} - \frac{1}{5^2} \right)$$

$$= 1.10 \times 10^{-2} \text{ nm}^{-1} (0.25 - 0.04) = 2.30 \times 10^{-3} \text{ nm}^{-1}$$

$$\lambda = \frac{1}{2.30 \times 10^{-3}} \text{ nm} = 433 \text{ nm}$$

Chapter 6   **1** False: Read the first paragraph of the text chapter again if you missed this question. **2** True: Two electrons are the maximum allowed in any orbital.   **3** False: Paired electrons have antiparallel spins.   **4** False: The energy of sublevels can shift depending on the number of electrons present. Half-filled or filled f subshells can alter the order of filling. See Table 6-2 in the text, expecially elements Cr, Nb, Pd, and Gd.   **5** True: See Fig. 6-8 in the text.   **6** True: There are one $3s$, three $3p$, and five $3d$ orbitals in the third energy level, for a total of nine orbitals. Each orbital holds two electrons.

7 4, 16. (Subshells are 4s, 4p, 4d, and 4f. There are one 4s, three 4p, five 4d, and seven 4f orbitals.)   **8** Magnetic   **9** 2, 2, 1, 3   **10** $1s^2 2s^2 2p^6 3s^2 3p^6 3d^5 4s^1$ or [Ar] $3d^5 4s^1$ **11** 4 (Minimum value of l is 3, so $n - 1 = 3$ or $n = 4$ is the minimum value of n.)   **12** One   **13** 13. ($n = 3$ designates the third shell; $l = 1$ designates a p orbital; $m_l = -1$ designates the first p orbital; and $m_s = -\frac{1}{2}$ designates the first electron in the orbital, so the last electron was $3p_x$.)   **14** Spins   **15** One. (See Table 6-4 in the text.)   **16** Seven. ($l = 3$ refers to f orbitals.)   **17** (d) $2n^2 = 2(5)^2 = 50$ **18** (d) Cr has five $3d$ and one $4s$ electrons that are unpaired.   **19** (b) Filling order is $4s$, then $3d$.   **20** (c)   **21** (c) $_{17}$P has electronic configuration [Ne] $3s^2 3p^3$.   **22** (c) In the Aufbau procedure the $5s$ subshell fills first.   **23** (c) For $l = 2$, the possible values of m_l are -2, -1, 0, 1, and 2, for a total of five values.   **24** (c) One electron in $4s$ and three electrons in $3d$ is not a ground-state configuration. (d) contains a half-filled $3d$ subshell, so the filling order is altered. This is the configuration of $_{24}$Cr.   **25** (a) The mass of a proton in SI units is

$$m = 1 \text{ amu} \times \frac{1 \text{ g}}{6.02 \times 10^{23} \text{ amu}} \times \frac{1 \text{ kg}}{10^3 \text{ g}} = 1.66 \times 10^{-27} \text{ kg}$$

The velocity of the proton is

$$v = 3.00 \times \frac{10^8 \text{ m s}^{-1}}{100} = 3.00 \times 10^6 \text{ m s}^{-1}$$

$$\lambda = \frac{h}{mv} = \frac{6.63 \times 10^{-34} \text{ kg m}^2 \text{ s}^{-1}}{1.66 \times 10^{-27} \text{ kg} (3.00 \times 10^6 \text{ m s}^{-1})} = 1.33 \times 10^{-13} \text{ m}$$

Chapter 7   **1** True   **2** True   **3** False: The atomic radius increases from top to bottom in a group.   **4** False: Both chemical and physical properties follow the periodic law.   **5** True   **6** Groups or columns   **7** Electron affinity   **8** Transition metals   **9** Less   **10** Smaller   **11** Group number   **12** Cerium   **13** Metalloids or semi-metals   **14** (b)   **15** (c)   **16** (c) Atoms are largest at the left of a given period and sizes increase going down a group.   **17** (b) Ionization energy is highest at the left of a given period and at the top of a group.   **18** (b) Electron affinity shows the same trend as ionization energy in Prob. 17.   **19** (c)   **20** (c)   **21** (d)   **22** (b) Br is in the same group.   **23** (c) Ca is in the same group.   **24** (a) N is in the same group; V has only two valence electrons.   **25** (c) Electron affinity is highest in the upper left corner of the periodic table, except for the inert gases which have a completed valence shell.

Chapter 8   **1** False: They occupy orbitals of one atom only and are not engaged in bonding.   **2** True   **3** False: (See Prob. 8-15 in the text.) Electron affinity is the energy released when an isolated atom gains another electron. Electronegativity is the tendency of a bonded atom to gain another electron.   **4** True   **5** True
6 Al $\longrightarrow$ Al^{3+} + 3e^-
We know it loses three electrons because it is in group IIIA.   **7** X$_3$Y$_2$; X has +2 charge; Y has -3 charge.   **8** [Na]$^+$[Cl]$^-$

9
$$\text{H}\overset{\displaystyle\text{H}}{\underset{\displaystyle:\overset{..}{\text{Cl}}:}{:\text{C}:\overset{..}{\text{Cl}}:}}$$

10 $\left[:\overset{..}{\underset{..}{\text{O}}}:\overset{..}{\underset{..}{\text{S}}}:\overset{..}{\underset{..}{\text{O}}}:\right]^{2-}$

11 Electronegativity   **12** Polar covalent bond   **13** +6. (Use rules 4, 3, and 2 to find oxidation numbers of K, H, and O. Then use rule 5c to find the oxidation number of S.)   **14** +3. (Since chlorine is more electronegative, it is assigned its normal oxidation number of $^-1$. Rule 5d then gives +3 for I.)   **15 (b)   16 (c) 17 (d)** Do not forget the two electrons for the ionic charge.   **18 (d)** There are two double bonds.   **19 (a)   20 (c)** Cs and F have the greatest difference in electronegativities.   **21 (b)** In calculating formal charges S has four electrons as its share of four shared pairs. Formal charge = 6 − 4 = +2.   **22 (d)** Rule 4 gives an oxidation number of +1 for K; rule 2 gives an oxidation number of −2 for O; Rule 5c gives an oxidation number of +7 for Cl.

$$x + 1 + 4(-2) = 0$$

$$x = +7$$

23 (d) Rule 3 gives an oxidation number of +1 for H; rule 5c gives an oxidation number of $^-4$ for C.

$$x + 4(1) = 0$$

$$x = {}^-4$$

24 (c) Rule 2 gives an oxidation number of −2 for O; rule 5c gives an oxidation number of $+2\frac{2}{3}$ for Pb.

$$3x + 4(-2) = 0$$

$$x = +\frac{8}{3} = +2\frac{2}{3}$$

25 (c) Structure C obeys the octet rule, but the formal charge on oxygen is +2 which is not consistent with a group VIA element so the structure is not allowed. Note also that oxygen has four bonds in structure C.

Chapter 9   1 False: It is the total number of bonds plus lone pairs on the central atom.   **2** True   **3** False: One or more of the lobes of the tetrahedron may be occupied by lone pairs, so the overall geometry is not tetrahedral.   **4** False: The relative energies of σ_{2p} and Π_{2p} depends on the total number of valence electrons and charges between N_2 and O_2.   **5** True: The greater the overlap, the stronger the bond. **6** Sigma   **7** Pi   **8** sp^2 **9** Tetrahedron   **10** Bonding   **11** Sigma   **12** Three (CO has 10 electrons and so is isoelectronic with N_2 and has the same configuration and bond order.)   **13** Unstable or does not exist   **14** Antibonding   **15 (d)** Repulsion between bonding pairs is weak and can be neglected.   **16 (d)** NH_3 is the only one that has a plane dividing the center of positive and negative charge. **17 (a)** O has four pairs of valence electrons which gives sp^3 hybridization (Table 9-1). **18 (b)** P has four pairs: three are bonded and one is a lone pair. According to Table 9-2, this gives trigonal pyramidal geometry.   **19 (d)** SiH_4 is analagous to CH_4, H_2O is bent, NH_3 is pyramidal, and C_2H_2 is linear.   **20 (d)** The Lewis structure for 22 valence electrons is

$$:\!\overset{..}{\underset{..}{F}}\!:\overset{..}{\underset{..}{Xe}}\!:\!\overset{..}{\underset{..}{F}}\!:$$

where Xe has 10 electrons in its valence shell. There are two bonding pairs and three nonbonding pairs on Xe, so the steric number is 5.   **21 (c)** There are eight total valence electrons

$$H\!:\!\overset{..}{\underset{..}{Se}}\!:\!H$$

giving two lone pairs on Se.   **22 (b)** NO^+ has 10 valence electrons, is isoelectronic with N_2, and has the same configuration (see Table 9-5). There are two antibonding and eight bonding electrons.   **23 (b)** There is one sigma bond between each pair of bonded atoms. There are also two pi bonds between the carbon atoms.   **24 (d)** The configurations and bond orders are: NF (same as O_2 in Table 9-5), BN (same as C_2 in Table 9-5), BeC (same as B_2 in Table 9-5), and He_2^+ $(\sigma_{1s})^2$ $(\sigma_{1s}*)^1$. The bond order is $\frac{1}{2}$.

25 (b)

	Bonding e^-	Antibonding e^-	Bond order
O_2	8	4	2
O_2^+	8	3	$2\frac{1}{2}$
O_2^-	8	5	$1\frac{1}{2}$
O_2^{2-}	8	6	1

The highest bond order gives the shortest and strongest bond.

Chapter 10   **1** True   **2** True: One particle at each of eight corners belongs to eight different cells, so each cell has one net particle for the corners. There is also one particle in each of six faces that belongs to two unit cells, so each cell has three net particles in the faces. The total is four particles per cell.   **3** True   **4** True   **5** False: Van der Waals forces are much weaker than electrostatic attractions in ionic bonds.   **6** False: Melting points and freezing points are identical temperatures.   **7** Amorphous solids or supercooled liquids   **8** Spacing of planes of atoms   **9** Unit cell   **10** Packing efficiency   **11** Ionic, molecular, covalent, and metallic   **12** Dipole-dipole forces and London or dispersion forces   **13** Poor   **14** Low   **15 (b)** One-eighth of each of eight corner atoms plus one body-center atom gives two atoms per cell.   **16 (d)** See Fig. 10-17b in the text.   **17 (b)** The Bragg relation gives

$$n\lambda = 2d \sin \theta$$

Since $n = 1$, $\lambda = 1.54$ nm, and $\sin \theta = \sin 25°30' = 0.43$

$$d = \frac{n\lambda}{2 \sin \theta} = \frac{1(1.54 \text{ nm})}{2(0.43)} = 1.79 \text{ nm}$$

18 (c) There are twice as many tetrahedral holes as spheres in the unit cell of a close-packed structure.

19 (b)   Mass of unit cell $= \dfrac{\text{atomic wt}}{N_{\text{Avogadro}}} \times$ atoms (unit cell)$^{-1}$

$$= \frac{184 \text{ g mol}^{-1}}{6.02 \times 10^{23} \text{ atoms mol}^{-1}} \times \frac{2 \text{ atoms}}{\text{unit cell}}$$

$$= 6.11 \times 10^{-22} \text{ g (unit cell)}^{-1}$$

Volume of unit cell $=$ g (unit cell)$^{-1}$ $\dfrac{1}{\text{g cm}^{-3}} = \dfrac{\text{cm}^3}{\text{unit cell}}$

$$= 6.11 \times 10^{-22} \text{ g (unit cell)}^{-1} \frac{1}{19.3 \text{ g cm}^{-3}}$$

$$= 3.16 \times 10^{-23} \text{ cm}^3$$

$$3.16 \times 10^{-23} \text{ cm}^3 \left(\frac{10^7 \text{ nm}}{1 \text{ cm}}\right)^3 = 3.16 \times 10^{-2} \text{ nm}^3$$

20 (b) The length of an edge of the unit cell is

$$l = (0.0316 \text{ nm}^3)^{1/3} = 0.316 \text{ nm}$$

In a body-centered structure atoms touch along the diagonal of the cell through the body-centered atom (see Fig. 10-15b in the text). The cell diagonal forms a right triangle with an edge of the cell and the diagonal of the face of the cell. The cell diagonal forms the hypotenuse of this triangle so

$$(\overline{CD})^2 = l^2 + d^2$$

where $\overline{CD}$ = length of cell diagonal
$\quad\quad d$ = length of face diagonal
$\quad\quad l$ = length of cell edge
We have already shown in Example 2 in the *Study Guide* that

$$d^2 = 2l^2$$

so

$$(\overline{CD})^2 = l^2 + 2l^2 = 3l^2$$

In the body-centered cell $\overline{CD} = 4r$ where r is the radius of the atoms touching along the cell diagonal

$$(4r)^2 = 3l^2$$

$$r = \frac{\sqrt{3}}{4}\, l = \frac{\sqrt{3}}{4}\,(0.316 \text{ nm}) = 0.137 \text{ nm}$$

21 (b) Some metallic solids have low melting points, but all molecular solids do. Weak van der Waals forces result in low melting points.

22 (a) $\Delta H_{lat} = \Delta H_{form} - (\Delta H_{subl} + \Delta H_{ion} + \Delta H_{diss}/2 + \Delta H_{e.a.})$
$$= -612 - (155 + 520 + 79/2 - 333) = -994 \text{ kJ mol}^{-1}$$
See *Study Guide* Example 5.

23 (d) This is the basic relation of the Clausius-Clapeyron equation.

24 (c) $\log\dfrac{P_1}{P_2} = \dfrac{-\Delta H_{vap}}{2.303R}\left(\dfrac{1}{T_1} - \dfrac{1}{T_2}\right)$

$$P_1 = 760 \text{ mmHg}$$

$$P_2 = ?$$

$$T_1 = 273 - 42.1°C = 231 \text{ K}$$

$$T_2 = 273 + 25°C = 298 \text{ K}$$

$$\Delta H_{vap} = 11{,}200 \text{ J mol}^{-1}$$

$$R = 8.31 \text{ J mol}^{-1} \text{ K}^{-1}$$

$$\log\frac{760 \text{ mmHg}}{P_2} = \frac{-11{,}200 \text{ J mol}^{-1}}{2.303(8.31 \text{ J mol}^{-1}\text{ K}^{-1})}\left(\frac{1}{231 \text{ K}} - \frac{1}{298 \text{ K}}\right)$$

$$\log\frac{760}{P_2} = -0.570$$

$$\frac{760}{P_2} = 10^{-0.570} = 0.269$$

$$P_2 = \frac{760}{0.269} = 2820 \text{ mmHg}$$

$$\frac{2820 \text{ mmHg}}{760 \text{ mmHg atm}^{-1}} = 3.71 \text{ atm}$$

25 (a) $\log\dfrac{P_1}{P_2} = \dfrac{-\Delta H_{vap}}{2.303R}\left(\dfrac{1}{T_1} - \dfrac{1}{T_2}\right)$

$$P_1 = 760 \text{ mmHg}$$

$$P_2 = 1820 \text{ mmHg}$$

$$T_1 = ?$$

$$T_2 = 273 + 25°C = 298 \text{ K}$$

$$\Delta H_{vap} = 21{,}000 \text{ J mol}^{-1}$$

$$R = 8.31 \text{ J mol}^{-1} \text{ K}^{-1}$$

$$\log \frac{760 \text{ mmHg}}{1820 \text{ mmHg}} = \frac{-21{,}000 \text{ J mol}^{-1}}{2.303(8.31 \text{ J mol}^{-1} \text{ K}^{-1})} \left(\frac{1}{T_1} - \frac{1}{298 \text{ K}} \right)$$

$$-0.379 = -1.10 \times 10^3 \left(\frac{1}{T_1} - 3.356 \times 10^{-3} \right)$$

$$\frac{1}{T_1} = \frac{-0.379}{-1.10 \times 10^3} + 3.356 \times 10^{-3} = 3.70 \times 10^{-3}$$

$$T_1 = 270 \text{ K} \quad \text{or} \quad -3°C$$

Chapter 11 **1** True   **2** True: Hydrogen and helium are important exceptions.   **3** True: Crystals react faster and grow faster along dislocations. Metal crystals free from dislocations are much stronger than ordinary crystals.   **4** True   **5** True: Electron-rich impurities form n-type semiconductors, impurities with fewer electrons per atom than the crystal make p-type semiconductors.   **6** True   **7** False: If the pressure is low enough, the gas phase is stable below the triple-point temperature.   **8** Inversion **9** Boiling chips   **10** Supercooled   **11** Edge dislocations and screw dislocations **12** Interstitial   **13** Increases   **14** Liquid   **15** Decreases   **16** Polymorphic **17** (d)   **18** (b)   **19** (b)   **20** (c)   **21** (b)   **22** (d)   **23** (a)   **24** (b)

25 (b) $P = \dfrac{nRT}{V - nb} - \dfrac{n^2 a}{V^2}$

$$P = \frac{2.00 \text{ mol} (0.082 \text{ liter atm mol}^{-1} \text{ K}^{-1})(298 \text{ K})}{1.00 \text{ liter} - (2.00 \text{ mol})(0.0371 \text{ liter mol}^{-1})}$$

$$- \frac{(2.00 \text{ mol})^2 (4.17 \text{ liter}^2 \text{ atm mol}^{-2})}{(1.00 \text{ liter})^2}$$

$$= 36.1 \text{ atm}$$

Chapter 12 **1** False: The percent by mass is 50 percent but the mole fractions are different because there are different numbers of moles of each.   **2** True: Where the volume of solute is negligible.   **3** True: $\Delta H_{soln} = \Delta H_{hyd} - \Delta H_{lat}$. ΔH_{hyd} is negative, while ΔH_{lat} is positive, so if $\Delta H_{hyd} > \Delta H_{lat}$, ΔH_{soln} will be negative.   **4** False: ΔH_{soln} must be positive for solubility to increase with temperature.   **5** False: The solubility of gases increases as temperature decreases, so the solution becomes unsaturated. **6** True: The strong interactions between unlike molecules reduces their escaping tendency and hence their vapor pressure is below that predicted by Raoult's law for ideal behavior.   **7** True   **8** Mole fraction   **9** Solute-solvent, solvent-solvent, solute-solute   **10** Moles, kilogram   **11** Fractional distillation   **12** Vapor-pressure lowering, freezing-point depression, boiling-point elevation, and osmotic pressure   **13** 70   **14** 100.52   **15** Salts or strong electrolytes   **16** H_3O^+

17 (a) $n_{CaCl_2} = \dfrac{16.0 \text{ g}}{111 \text{ g mol}^{-1}} = 0.144 \text{ mol}$

$$n_{H_2O} = 27.8 \text{ mol}$$

$$X_{CaCl_2} = \frac{0.144 \text{ mol}}{0.144 \text{ mol} + 27.8 \text{ mol}} = 0.00515$$

18 (a) mol % = $X_{CaCl_2}(100) = 0.00515\,(100) = 0.515\%$

19 (d) $m = \dfrac{\text{mol } CaCl_2}{\text{kg } H_2O} = \dfrac{0.144 \text{ mol}}{0.5 \text{ kg}} = 0.288 \ m$

20 (c) $V = \dfrac{g}{\text{density}} = \dfrac{500 \text{ g} + 16 \text{ g}}{1.010 \text{ g cm}^{-3}} = 511 \text{ cm}^3$ or   511 ml

$$M = \frac{\text{mol}}{\text{liter}} = \frac{0.144 \text{ mol}}{0.511 \text{ liter}} = 0.282 \ M$$

21 (b) Total weight of solution = 100 ml $(1.10 \text{ g cm}^{-3}) = 110$ g

wt $H_2O = 110$ g $-$ 18.0 g $= 92$ g

$$m = \frac{18.0 \text{ g NaCl}}{0.092 \text{ kg } H_2O} \times \frac{1 \text{ mol NaCl}}{58.5 \text{ g NaCl}} = 3.34 \ m$$

22 (b) $V_{conc} = V_{dil} \dfrac{M_{dil}}{M_{conc}} = 1.00 \text{ liter} \dfrac{0.350 \ M}{6.00 \ M} = 0.0583$ liter or 58.3 ml

23 (a) $X_{O_2} = K_{O_2}P_{O_2} = 2.58 \times 10^{-5} \text{ atm}^{-1}\,(2.00 \text{ atm}) = 5.16 \times 10^{-5}$

$$X_{O_2} = \frac{n_{O_2}}{n_{O_2} + n_{H_2O}} = \frac{n_{O_2}}{n_{O_2} + (1000 \text{ g}/18 \text{ g mol}^{-1})}$$

$\dfrac{n_{O_2}}{n_{O_2} + 55.6} = 5.16 \times 10^{-5}$

$n_{O_2} = 2.87 \times 10^{-3}$ mol

g $O_2 = n_{O_2}(32 \text{ g mol}^{-1}) = 2.87 \times 10^{-3} \text{ mol}(32 \text{ g mol}^{-1}) = 0.0918$ g

24 (c) $m = 3.000$ molal $= \dfrac{3.000 \text{ mol solute}}{1 \text{ kg } H_2O}$

$$X_{H_2O} = \frac{1000 \text{ g}/18 \text{ g mol}^{-1}}{3.000 \text{ mol} + (1000 \text{ g}/18 \text{ g mol}^{-1})} = 0.9488$$

$P_{soln} = X_{H_2O}P^{\circ}_{H_2O} = 0.9488\,(42.18 \text{ mmHg}) = 40.02 \text{ mmHg}$

25 (b) $m_{\text{total ions}} = 2m_{NaCl} = 0.2 \ m$

$$\Delta T_b = K_b m = 0.512^{\circ}C \ m^{-1}\,(0.2 \ m) = 0.10^{\circ}C$$

26 (c) $m_{\text{toluene}} = \dfrac{8.90 \text{ g}/92 \text{ g mol}^{-1}}{0.200 \text{ kg benzene}} = 0.484 \ m$

$\Delta T_f = -K_f m = -(5.12^{\circ}C \ m^{-1})\,(0.484 \ m) = -2.48^{\circ}C$

$T_f = 5.50 - 2.48 = 3.02^{\circ}C$

27 (d) The osmotic pressure required is

$$100 \text{ m } H_2O \times \frac{10^3 \text{ mm}}{1 \text{ m}} \times \frac{1 \text{ mmHg}}{13.55 \text{ mmH}_2O} \times \frac{1 \text{ atm}}{760 \text{ mmHg}} = 9.71 \text{ atm}$$

$$M = \frac{\Pi}{RT} = \frac{9.71 \text{ atm}}{(0.082 \text{ liter atm mol}^{-1} \text{ K}^{-1})(298 \text{ K})} = 0.397\, M$$

28 (d) $m = \dfrac{-\Delta T_f}{K_f} = \dfrac{-(-0.415°C)}{1.855°C\, m^{-1}} = 0.224\, m$

Moles $= m(\text{kg solvent}) = 0.224 \text{ mol kg}^{-1} (0.200 \text{ kg}) = 0.0448 \text{ mol}$

$$\text{MW} = \text{g mol}^{-1} = \frac{2.50 \text{ g}}{0.0448 \text{ mol}} = 55.8 \text{ g mol}^{-1}$$

29 (c) $n_2 = \dfrac{\Pi V}{RT} = \dfrac{2.30 \text{ mmHg } (1 \text{ atm}/760 \text{ mmHg})(1 \text{ liter})}{(0.082 \text{ liter atm mol}^{-1} \text{ K}^{-1})(298 \text{ K})} = 1.24 \times 10^{-4} \text{ mol}$

$$\text{MW} = \text{g mol}^{-1} = \frac{5.00 \text{ g}}{1.24 \times 10^{-4} \text{ mol}} = 40,400 \text{ g mol}^{-1}$$

30 (c) The freezing point of undissociated acetic acid would be

$$\Delta T_f = -K_f m = -(1.855°C\, m^{-1})(0.150\, m) = -0.278°C$$

$$\frac{m_{\text{diss}}}{m_{\text{undiss}}} = \frac{(\Delta T_f)_{\text{diss}}}{(\Delta T_f)_{\text{undiss}}} = \frac{-0.308}{-0.278} = 1.11$$

The acid is 11 percent dissociated. (See Prob. 12-55 in the text.)

Chapter 13   **1** True   **2** False: Acids are electron-pair acceptors.   **3** True: The protonated solvent is the strongest acid possible in any solvent system   **4** False: The salt formed may hydrolyze and make the solution acidic or basic.   **5** True   **6** Aqueous   **7** Autodissociation   **8** Loses, increases   **9** Reduction   **10** Will ($SrCO_3$ is insoluble)   **11** Three   **12** 0.600 N **13** 1.80 N **14** (d)   **15** (b)   **16** (b)   **17** (b)   **18** (d) The coefficients are 2, 1, 3, 1, 6, 2, 8.   **19** (d) The coefficients are $6H^+$, 10, 2, 5, 2, $8H_2O$.   **20** (c)

21 (c) $N_{\text{Ca(OH)}_2} = 0.100\, M \dfrac{2 \text{ equiv}}{1 \text{ mol}} = 0.200\, N$

$N_{\text{HNO}_3} = M_{\text{HNO}_3} = 0.250\, N$

$V_{\text{Ca(OH)}_2} = V_{\text{HNO}_3} \dfrac{N_{\text{HNO}_3}}{N_{\text{Ca(OH)}_2}} = 30.0 \text{ ml} \dfrac{0.250\, N}{0.200\, N} = 37.5 \text{ ml}$

22 (d) equiv $= 4.0 \text{ mol} \times \dfrac{2 \text{ equiv}}{\text{mol}} = 8.0 \text{ equiv}$

23 (d) N in HNO_3 changes oxidation state from +5 to +2

$$N = 3M = 3(3.00\, M) = 9.00\, N$$

24 (c) In this reaction 1 mol Na_2CO_3 = 1 equiv Na_2CO_3, so

$$\text{equivalent weight} = \text{molecular weight} = 106 \text{ g equiv}^{-1}$$

25 (c) $V_{\text{KMnO}_4} = V_{\text{AsH}_3} \dfrac{N_{\text{AsH}_3}}{N_{\text{KMnO}_4}} = 20.0 \text{ ml} \dfrac{0.250\, N}{0.150\, N} = 33.3 \text{ ml}$

Answers to redox equation balancing problems

Answers are the numerical coefficients of substances in the same order as they appear in the given equation. Required H^+, OH^-, and H_2O are indicated.

1 6, 10, 3, 10, 5   **2** 5, 2, 6, 5, 2, 2, 8   **3** 1, 2, 2, 1, 1   **4** 1, 10, 1, 3, 10, 5   **5** 2, 3, 24, 6, 1, 4, 15   **6** 5, 2, 16, 10, 2, 8   **7** 10, 8, 2, 5, 1, 2, 8   **8** 3, 8, 6, 1   **9** 3, 3, 6, 1   **10** 1, 4, 12, 2, 5, 1   **11** $8H^+$, 5, 1, 5, 1, $4H_2O$ **12** $4H^+$, 1, 2, 1, 1, $2H_2O$ **13** $10H^+$, 4, 1, 4, 1, $3H_2O$ **14** $3H_2O$, 6, 1, 1, 6, $6H^+$ **15** $6H^+$, 1, 2, 2, 2, $4H_2O$ **16** $6H^+$, 1, 6, 1, 3, $3H_2O$ **17** $6H^+$, 2, 5, 2, 5, $8H_2O$ **18** $6\,OH^-$, 3, 5, 1, $3H_2O$ **19** $10\,OH^-$, 2, 3, 6, 2, $8H_2O$ **20** $3H_2O$, $3\,OH^-$, 1, 3, 1   **21** OH^-, 1, 1, 2, 1, H_2O **22** 2, 3, 3, 2, $3H_2O$

Chapter 14   **1** False: It can, since the rate of production of products is related stoichiometrically to the rate of disappearance of reactants, even though the rate is not a function of product concentration. See New Skills 14-1:2.   **2** True   **3** False: A plot of the logarithm of concentration versus time would be linear.   **4** False: Only true for the elementary processes in a reaction mechanism.   **5** True: See Added Comment in Sec. 14-1 of the text.   **6** False: A plot of $\log k$ versus $1/T$ is linear.   **7** Instantaneous rate   **8** $M\ s^{-1}$ or mol liter^{-1} s^{-1} **9** Arrhenius   **10** Activated complex   **11** Activation energy   **12** Homogeneous catalyst   **13** Alters   **14** (c)   **15** (b)   **16** (b)   **17** (a)   **18** (c)

19 (a) Rate $= k[A]^2$

$$k = \frac{\text{rate}}{[A]^2} = \frac{3 \times 10^{-3}\ M\ s^{-1}}{(0.030\ M)^2} = 3.33\ M^{-1}\ s^{-1}$$

Rate $= 3.33\ M^{-1}\ s^{-1}(0.015\ M)^2 = 7.5 \times 10^{-4}\ M\ s^{-1}$

20 (c) $t_{1/2} = \dfrac{0.693}{k} = \dfrac{0.693}{3.0 \times 10^{-3}\ s^{-1}} = 231\ s$

21 (c) $\log [A] = \dfrac{-kt}{2.303} + \log [A]_0$

$$k = \frac{2.303}{t} \log \frac{[A]_0}{[A]} = \frac{2.303}{30\ \text{min}} \log \frac{0.55}{0.15} = 0.0433\ \text{min}^{-1}$$

$$t = \frac{2.303}{k} \log \frac{[A]_0}{[A]} = \frac{2.303}{0.0433\ \text{min}^{-1}} \log \frac{0.35}{0.15} = 19.6\ \text{min}$$

22 (b) $k = 0.0433\ \text{min}^{-1}$

$$\log [A] = \frac{-kt}{2.303} + \log [A]_0$$

$$= \frac{-(0.0433\ \text{min}^{-1})\,(60\ \text{min}/1\ \text{h})\,(1\ \text{h})}{2.303} + \log 0.75$$

$$= -1.128 + (-0.125) = -1.253$$

$$[A] = 0.0558\ M$$

23 (a)

24 (d) $\log \dfrac{k_2}{k_1} = \dfrac{E}{2.303R} \left(\dfrac{1}{T_1} - \dfrac{1}{T_2} \right)$

$$\log \frac{k_2}{0.033 \text{ s}^{-1}} = \frac{125,000 \text{ J mol}^{-1}}{2.303(8.31 \text{ J mol}^{-1} \text{ K}^{-1})} \left(\frac{1}{328} - \frac{1}{373}\right) = 2.40$$

$$\frac{k_2}{0.033 \text{ s}^{-1}} = 10^{2.40} = 251$$

$$k_2 = 251(0.033 \text{ s}^{-1}) = 8.3 \text{ s}^{-1}$$

25 (b) $E = \dfrac{2.303R \log (k_2/k_1)}{(1/T_1) - (1/T_2)}$

$$= \frac{2.303(8.31 \text{ J mol}^{-1} \text{ K}^{-1}) \log (7.35 \times 10^{-2} \text{ s}^{-1}/4.27 \times 10^{-3} \text{ s}^{-1})}{(1/298) - (1/353)}$$

$$= 45,200 \text{ J mol}^{-1}$$

Chapter 15   1 True: This is the law of chemical equilibrium.   2 False: It shifts to the right until Q becomes as large as K.   3 False: They apply to any system.   4 True   5 False: True for an endothermic reaction.   6 Right   7 Left   8 Right   9 Left   10 Zero

11 3.4 $K_c = \dfrac{[C]^3}{[A][B]^2} = \dfrac{3^3}{2(2)^2} = 3.4$

12 1.25 $K_c = \dfrac{[C]^2}{[A][B]}$ $[A] = \dfrac{[C]^2}{K_c[B]} = \dfrac{5^2}{8(2.5)} = 1.25$

13 (c)   14 (c) $\Delta n = 0$ so $K_P = K_c$

15 (b) $Q = \dfrac{[C]^2}{[A][B]} = \dfrac{(1.5)^2}{2(4)} = 0.28$

Since $Q < K$, the reaction will shift to the right.   16 (b)   17 (d)   18 (c)

19 (a) $\log \dfrac{2.0}{(K_P)_2} = -\dfrac{(-100,000)}{2.303(8.31)} \left(\dfrac{1}{298} - \dfrac{1}{373}\right)$

$$(K_P)_2 = 5.96 \times 10^{-4}$$

20 (b) $K_c = \dfrac{[C]^2}{[A]^2[B]} = \dfrac{(0.210)^2}{(0.250)^2(0.300)} = 2.35$

21 (c) $K_P = P_{CO_2} = 0.061 \text{ atm}$

22 (c) $K_c = \dfrac{[A][B]}{[C]^2}$

Let $x = [A] = [B]$

Then $2.50 = \dfrac{x^2}{3.00^2}$

$$x = [2.50(3.00)^2]^{1/2} = 4.74$$

23 (a) $K_P = \dfrac{1}{P_a P_b}$

$$P_a = \frac{1}{K_P P_b} = \frac{1}{4.00(0.50)} = 0.50$$

24 (c) $K_c = \dfrac{[C]^2}{[A][B]}$

Let x = the amounts of A and B produced during the reaction in moles per liter.

	Initial concentration mol liter^{-1}	Change	Equilibrium concentration
A	0	x	x
B	0	x	x
C	2	$-2x$	$2 - 2x$

$$49 = \frac{(2 - 2x)^2}{x^2}$$

Take the square root of each side

$$7 = \frac{2 - 2x}{x}$$

$$x = 0.22$$

$$[C] = 2 - 2x = 2 - 2(0.22) = 1.56\ M$$

25 (b) $K_c = \dfrac{[C]}{[A][B]}$

Let x = the amount of C generated during the reaction in moles per liter.

	Initial concentration, mol liter^{-1}	Change	Equilibrium concentration
A	1.00	$-x$	$1.00 - x \cong 1.00$
B	2.00	$-x$	$2.00 - x \cong 2.00$
C	0	$+x$	x

$$1 \times 10^{-5} = \frac{x}{1.00(2.00)}$$

$$x = [C] = 2 \times 10^{-5}$$

Chapter 16   **1** True: This is an example of the common-ion effect.   **2** False: The percent dissociation decreases as the solution is concentrated.   **3** False: The $[H^+]$ has changed by 10^3 or 1000.   **4** True   **5** False: They form the weak base plus H^+. **6** A cyanide salt, common ion   **7** The acid, the equilibrium condition or expression **8** 3   **9** 11   **10** Anion or cation, weak acid or weak base   **11** $K_w = K_h K_a$ **12** Weak acid, strong base   **13** greater than   **14** (d)   **15** (a) **16 (b)** See Example 16-15 in the text

$$NH_4^+ + H_2O \rightleftharpoons NH_3 + H_3O^+ \qquad K_h = \frac{[NH_3][H_3O^+]}{[NH_4^+]}$$

Let x = the amount of NH_4^+ hydrolyzed in moles per liter.

	Initial concentration, mol liter^{-1}	Change	Equilibrium concentration
NH_4^+	0.05	$-x$	$0.05 - x \cong 0.05$
NH_3	0	$+x$	x
H_3O^+	0	$+x$	x

$$5.6 \times 10^{-10} = \frac{x^2}{0.05}$$

$$x = [H_3O^+] = 5.3 \times 10^{-6}$$

$$pH = -\log (5.3 \times 10^{-6}) = 5.3$$

17 (a) $[OH^-] = \dfrac{K_w}{[H^+]} = \dfrac{1 \times 10^{-14}}{0.05} = 2.0 \times 10^{-13} \, M$

18 (b) $[OH^-] = 2[Ba(OH)_2] = 2(0.020) = 0.040$

$$[H^+] = \frac{K_w}{[OH^-]} = \frac{1 \times 10^{-14}}{(0.040)} = 2.5 \times 10^{-13}$$

$$pH = -\log [H^+] = -\log (2.5 \times 10^{-13}) = 12.6$$

19 (c)   pOH = 14.00 − 8.00 = 6.00

$$[OH^-] = 10^{-pOH} = 10^{-6} \, M$$

20 (b) $K_h = \dfrac{K_w}{K_{II}} = \dfrac{1 \times 10^{-14}}{6.30 \times 10^{-8}} = 1.60 \times 10^{-7}$

21 (e) $[OH^-] = \dfrac{(0.025)(0.20) - (0.025)(0.10)}{0.025 + 0.025} = 0.050 \, M$

$$[H^+] = \frac{1 \times 10^{-14}}{0.05} = 2 \times 10^{-13} \, M$$

22 (a) $NH_3 + H_2O \rightleftharpoons NH_4^+ + OH^-$ $K_b = \dfrac{[NH_4^+][OH^-]}{[NH_3]}$

Let x = the amount of NH_3 dissociated in moles per liter.

	Initial concentration, mol liter^{-1}	Change	Equilibrium concentration, mol liter^{-1}
NH_3	0.03	$-x$	$0.03 - x$
NH_4^+	0.05	$+x$	$0.05 - x$
OH^-	0	$+x$	x

Neglecting x with respect to 0.03 and 0.05, and substituting into the dissociation expression, we obtain

$$1.8 \times 10^{-5} = \frac{(0.05)x}{0.03}$$

$$x = [OH^-] = 1.1 \times 10^{-5} \, M$$

23 (d)

24 (c) $pH = pK_a - \log \dfrac{[\text{acetic acid}]}{[\text{sodium acetate}]}$

$= -\log(1.8 \times 10^{-5}) - 0 = 4.74$

25 (a) $pH = pK_a - \log \dfrac{[\text{HOCl}]}{[\text{NaOCl}]}$

$pK_a = -\log(3.2 \times 10^{-8}) = 7.5$

$6.5 = 7.5 - \log \dfrac{0.100}{\text{NaOCl}}$

$\log \dfrac{0.100}{\text{NaOCl}} = 1.0$

$[\text{NaOCl}] = \dfrac{0.1}{10} = 0.01$

Chapter 17   **1** False: K_{sp} is the solubility product constant. It is the product of the concentrations of ions in solution raised to the proper power. The solubility of a compound is the number of moles per liter needed to make a saturated solution.   **2** True   **3** True
4 False: Only if the ion product exceeds K_{sp} **5** True   **6** True
7 $[\text{Ca}^{2+}][\text{F}^-]^2$ **8** $K_{sp} = [\text{Ca}^{2+}][\text{OH}^-]^2$ **9** Decrease   **10** Increase
11 $K_f = \dfrac{[\text{Co(NH}_3)_6{}^{3+}]}{[\text{Co}^{3+}][\text{NH}_3]^6}$
12 $\text{Cu(NH}_3)_4{}^{2+} \rightleftharpoons \text{Cu}^{2+} + 4\text{NH}_3$
13 pH   **14** Does not (See Added Comment at the end of the chapter in the text.)

15 (a) $\text{Ag}_2\text{CO}_3(s) \rightleftharpoons 2\text{Ag}^+ + \text{CO}_3{}^{2-}$

$K_{sp} = [\text{Ag}^+]^2[\text{CO}_3{}^{2-}]$

$[\text{Ag}_2\text{CO}_3(aq)] = \dfrac{0.032 \text{ g liter}^{-1}}{276 \text{ g mol}^{-1}} = 1.16 \times 10^{-4} \ M$

$[\text{Ag}^+] = 2(1.16 \times 10^{-4} \ M) = 2.32 \times 10^{-4} \ M$

$[\text{CO}_3{}^{2-}] = 1.16 \times 10^{-4} \ M$

$K_{sp} = (2.32 \times 10^{-4})^2 (1.16 \times 10^{-4}) = 6.2 \times 10^{-12}$

16 (c) $pOH = 14 - pH = 14 - 5.13 = 8.87$

$[\text{OH}^-] = 10^{-pOH} = 10^{-8.87} = 1.35 \times 10^{-9} \ M$

$[\text{Fe(OH)}_3] = \dfrac{[\text{OH}^-]}{3} = \dfrac{1.35 \times 10^{-9}}{3} = 4.5 \times 10^{-10} \ M$

17 (a) $\text{Pb(IO}_3)_2 \rightleftharpoons \text{Pb}^{2+} + 2\text{IO}_3{}^-$

$K_{sp} = [\text{Pb}^{2+}][\text{IO}_3{}^-]^2$

$[\text{Pb}^{2+}] = M \qquad [\text{IO}_3{}^-] = 2M$

$K_{sp} = M(2M)^2 = 4M^3$

18 (d) See Table 17-2 in the text.
19 (c) $\text{AgI} \rightleftharpoons \text{Ag}^+ + \text{I}^-$

$K_{sp} = [\text{Ag}^+][\text{I}^-]$

$[\text{I}^-] = 0.028 \ M$

$$[Ag^+] = \frac{K_{sp}}{[I^-]} = \frac{8.5 \times 10^{-17}}{0.028} = 3.0 \times 10^{-15}$$

$$\text{Solubility} = [Ag^+] = 3.0 \times 10^{-15}$$

20 (c) $Ag(NH_3)_2^+ \rightleftharpoons Ag^+ + 2NH_3$

Let $x = [Ag^+]$. Then

$$[Ag(NH_3)_2^+] = 0.10 - x \cong 0.10$$

$$[NH_3] = 0.50 - 2[Ag(NH_3)_2^+] = 0.50 - 2(0.10) = 0.30$$

$$K_{diss} = \frac{[Ag^+][NH_3]^2}{[Ag(NH_3)_2^+]}$$

$$[Ag^+] = \frac{K_{diss}[Ag(NH_3)_2^+]}{[NH_3]^2} = \frac{5.9 \times 10^{-8}(0.10)}{(0.30)^2} = 6.6 \times 10^{-8}$$

21 (d)

22 (b) $PbCl_2 \rightleftharpoons Pb^{2+} + 2Cl^-$

$$K_{sp} = [Pb^{2+}][Cl^-]^2$$

$$[Pb^{2+}] = 0.010\,M$$

$$[Cl^-] = \left(\frac{K_{sp}}{[Pb^{2+}]}\right)^{1/2} = \left(\frac{1.6 \times 10^{-5}}{0.01}\right)^{1/2} = 4.0 \times 10^{-2}\,M$$

23 (a) $Fe(OH)_3 \rightleftharpoons Fe^{3+} + 3OH^-$

$$K_{sp} = [Fe^{3+}][OH^-]^3$$

Let $x = [Fe^{3+}]$. Then

$$3x = [OH^-]$$

$$1.1 \times 10^{-36} = x(3x)^3$$

$$x^4 = \frac{1.1 \times 10^{-36}}{27} = 4.07 \times 10^{-38}$$

$$x = 4.5 \times 10^{-10}$$

$$[OH^-] = 3x = 3(4.5 \times 10^{-10}) = 1.35 \times 10^{-9}$$

$$[H^+] = \frac{K_w}{[OH^-]} = \frac{10^{-14}}{1.35 \times 10^{-9}} = 7.4 \times 10^{-6}$$

$$pH = -\log[H^+] = -\log(7.4 \times 10^{-6}) = 5.1$$

24 (a) $Fe(OH)^2 \rightleftharpoons Fe^{2+} + 2OH^-$

$$K_{sp} = [Fe^{2+}][OH^-]^2$$

$$[OH^-] = \left(\frac{K_{sp}}{[Fe^{2+}]}\right)^{1/2} = \left(\frac{2 \times 10^{-15}}{0.020}\right)^{1/2} = 3.2 \times 10^{-7}\,M$$

Enough NH_4^+ must be added to repress the dissociation of NH_3 so $[OH^-]$ is less than $3.2 \times 10^{-7}\,M$.

$$NH_3 + H_2O \rightleftharpoons NH_4^+ + OH^-$$

$$K_b = \frac{[NH_4^+][OH^-]}{[NH_3]} = 1.8 \times 10^{-5}$$

$$[NH_4^+] = \frac{K_b[NH_3]}{[OH^-]} = \frac{1.8 \times 10^{-5}(0.050)}{3.2 \times 10^{-7}} = 2.9 \ M$$

25 (c) $H_2S \rightleftharpoons 2H^+ + S^{2-}$

$$K = K_I K_{II} = \frac{[H^+]^2[S^{2-}]}{[H_2S]} = 1.1 \times 10^{-7} \ (1 \times 10^{-14}) = 1.1 \times 10^{-21}$$

$$[S^{2-}] = \frac{K[H_2S]}{[H^+]^2} = \frac{1.1 \times 10^{-21}(0.10)}{(0.050)^2} = 4.4 \times 10^{-20} \ M$$

$$SnS \rightleftharpoons Sn^{2+} + S^{2-}$$

$$K_{sp} = [Sn^{2+}][S^{2-}] = 1 \times 10^{-26}$$

$$[Sn^{2+}] = \frac{K_{sp}}{[S^{2-}]} = \frac{1 \times 10^{-26}}{4.4 \times 10^{-20}} = 2.3 \times 10^{-7} \ M$$

Chapter 18 **1** True: w is defined so that work done on the system is positive.   **2** False: The sign of ΔH is not a reliable indicator of spontaneity. Entropy changes may determine the sign of ΔG in certain cases.   **3** True: For instance, in the universe.   **4** True: Highest entropy state is most probable and most disordered.   **5** True: The spontaneous change will continue until the available free energy has been removed and the system is no longer able to do work. At this point the system is at equilibrium.   **6** Work   **7** Positive   **8** The molar heat capacity   **9** Positive   **10** Spontaneous   **11** At equilibrium   **12** (a) Since $\Delta E = 0$, $q = w$ and the system must lose the acquired heat energy by doing an equal amount of work to maintain constant energy. (b) and (c) are incorrect because compressing the system or expanding into a vacuum would not dissipate the heat energy. (d) is incorrect because energy is conserved by balancing heat and work for the system.   **13** (d) Since the expansion is into a vacuum where $P_{ext} = 0$, $w = p_{ext}\Delta_V = 0$. Since the expansion is also at constant temperature, $\Delta E = C_V \Delta T = 0$ and $q = \Delta E + w = 0$, and only (d) can be correct. Answers (a) and (b) are not consistent with the first law.   **14** (c) The second law says the entropy of the universe must increase for any irreversible change, so (d) is incorrect. ΔS for the system (the growing plant) is negative since the reaction products (the plant) are more ordered than the reactants.

$$\Delta S_{universe} = \Delta S_{system} + \Delta S_{surroundings} > 0$$

must hold, so $\Delta S_{surroundings}$ must have a large enough positive value to make $\Delta S_{universe} > 0$.

15 (d) ΔH gained by ice = 5.00 g $(335 \ J \ g^{-1})$ = 1675 J

ΔH lost by water = $-\Delta H$ gained by ice = -1675 J

ΔH net = ΔH gained by ice + ΔH lost by water = $1675 - 1675 = 0$

16 (c) From Prob. 15, ΔH lost by the water (including water from the melted ice) is -1675 J

$$\Delta t = \frac{\Delta H}{mC_P} = \frac{-1675 \ J}{105 \ g(4.18 \ J \ g^{-1} \ K^{-1})} = -3.82 \ K$$

$$t_{final} = 25.0°C - 3.8°C = 21.2°C$$

Answer (b) is obtained if you forgot to include the melted ice in the total mass of water.   17 (c) Since the water absorbs its molar heat of vaporization during this process, $q = 40.7$ kJ mol^{-1}. Work involved in expanding the vapor against the atmosphere is

$$w = P \, \Delta V = P(V_{\text{vapor}} - V_{\text{liquid}} \cong PV_{\text{vapor}}$$

$$V_{\text{vapor}} = \frac{nRT}{P} = \frac{1.00 \text{ mol}(0.0821 \text{ liter atm mol}^{-1} \text{ K}^{-1})(373 \text{ K})}{1 \text{ atm}} = 30.6 \text{ liters}$$

$$w = 1.00 \text{ atm}(30.6 \text{ liters}) \times 101.2 \text{ J (liter atm)}^{-1} = 3100 \text{ J}$$

$$\Delta E = q - w = 40.7 \text{ kJ} - 3.1 \text{ kJ} = 37.6 \text{ kJ}$$

18 (a) The formation reaction for SO_3 is

$$S(s) + \tfrac{3}{2} O_2(g) \longrightarrow SO_3(g)$$

This can be obtained from the given equations by algebraically adding them as follows:

$S(s) + O_2(g) \longrightarrow SO_2(g)$	$\Delta H = -296.8$ kJ mol^{-1}
$SO_2(g) + \tfrac{1}{2} O_2(g) \longrightarrow SO_3(g)$	$\Delta H = -98.9$ kJ mol^{-1}
$S(s) + SO_2(g) + \tfrac{3}{2} O_2(g) \longrightarrow SO_2(g) + SO_3(g)$	$\Delta H = -395.7$ kJ mol^{-1}

The net result is $S(s) + \tfrac{3}{2} O_2(g) \longrightarrow SO_3(g)$. Hess's law says that adding the ΔH's of the given reactions in the same manner as the reactions themselves will give ΔH for the net reaction.

19 (a) $\Delta H^{\circ}_{\text{reaction}} = \Sigma(\Delta H^{\circ}_f)_{\text{products}} - \Sigma(\Delta H^{\circ}_f)_{\text{reactants}}$
$= [2(\Delta H^{\circ}_f)_{CO_2} + 2(\Delta H^{\circ}_f)_{H_2O}] - [(\Delta H^{\circ}_f)_{C_2H_4} + 3(\Delta H^{\circ}_f)_{O_2}]$
$= [2(-393.5 \text{ kJ}) + 2(-285.8 \text{ kJ})] - [52.3 \text{ kJ} + 3(0 \text{ kJ})]$
$= -1359 \text{ kJ} - 52.3 \text{ kJ} = -1411 \text{ kJ}$

If your answer was (c) or (d) you forgot to multiply the standard enthalpies of formation by the number of moles of each component indicated by the stoichiometric coefficients. Be sure you keep the signs straight.

20 (c) $\Delta S = \dfrac{\Delta H_{\text{vap}}}{T} = \dfrac{40,700 \text{ J mol}^{-1}}{(273 + 100)\text{K}} = 109$ J mol^{-1} K^{-1}

This calculation on entropy applies to any phase change.

21 (d) $\Delta S^{\circ} = \Sigma S^{\circ}_{\text{products}} - \Sigma S^{\circ}_{\text{reactants}} = 2S^{\circ}_{NH_3} - S^{\circ}_{N_2} - 3S^{\circ}_{H_2}$

$= [2 \text{ mol}(192.3 \text{ J mol}^{-1} \text{ K}^{-1}) - [1 \text{ mol}(191.5 \text{ J mol}^{-1} \text{ K}^{-1})$

$\quad + 3 \text{ mol}(130.6 \text{ J mol}^{-1} \text{ K}^{-1})] = -384.6 \text{ J K}^{-1} - 583.3 \text{ J K}^{-1}$

$= -198.7 \text{ J K}^{-1}$

Since the reaction is written for 2 mol of NH_3, ΔS°_f per mole of NH_3 is

$$\Delta S^{\circ}_f = \frac{-198.7 \text{ J K}^{-1}}{2 \text{ mol NH}_3} = -99.4 \text{ J mol}^{-1} \text{ K}^{-1}$$

The negative value of ΔS°_f means the products are more ordered than the reactants. Can you explain why from a molecular point of view? Note that ΔG°_f and ΔH°_f of N_2 and H_2 are 0, while S° for the elements has a finite value. Why is this so?
22 (c) For the reaction

$$\Delta G^{\circ} = \Sigma(\Delta G^{\circ}_f)_{\text{products}} - \Sigma(\Delta G^{\circ}_f)_{\text{reactants}}$$

$$\Delta G^\circ = (\Delta G_f^\circ)_{CO_2} + \tfrac{1}{2}(\Delta G_f^\circ)_{N_2} - (\Delta G_f^\circ)_{CO} - (\Delta G_f^\circ)_{NO}$$

$$= -394.4 \text{ kJ} + 0 - (-137.2 \text{kJ}) - (86.6 \text{ kJ}) = -343.8 \text{ kJ}$$

Since ΔG is negative, the reaction is thermodynamically spontaneous. Many environmental problems might be solved with this reaction if the right catalyst were found to initiate it.

23 (b) The chemical reaction is $Ag_2O(s) \longrightarrow 2Ag(s) + \tfrac{1}{2}O_2(g)$ for which $\Delta G^\circ = +10.9$ kJ and $\Delta H^\circ = +30.5$ kJ.

$$\Delta S^\circ = \frac{\Delta H^\circ - \Delta G^\circ}{T} = \frac{30.5 - 10.9}{298} = 0.0658 \text{ kJ K}^{-1}$$

$$T_{\Delta G = 0} = \frac{\Delta H^\circ}{\Delta S^\circ} = \frac{30.5}{0.0658} = 463 \text{ K} \quad \text{or} \quad 190^\circ \text{C}$$

This low temperature of decomposition explains why silver is not found in nature as the oxide.

24 (c) $\Delta G = \Delta H - T\,\Delta S$. Since T is always positive:

    1 If ΔH° is negative and ΔS° is positive, ΔG° is always negative so the process is always spontaneous.

    2 If ΔH° is positive and ΔS° is negative, ΔG° is always positive so the process is always nonspontaneous.

    3 and 4 If ΔH° and ΔS° are both positive or both negative, the sign of ΔG° depends on their relative values and the temperature.

25 (b) $Ag_2O(s) \longrightarrow 2Ag(s) + \tfrac{1}{2} O_2(g)$

$$\Delta G^\circ = +10.9 \text{ kJ}$$

$$\log K_P = \frac{-\Delta G^\circ}{2.303RT} = \frac{-10,900 \text{ J mol}^{-1}}{2.303(8.314 \text{ J mol}^{-1} \text{ K}^{-1})(298 \text{ K})} = -1.91$$

$$K_P = 1.2 \times 10^{-2}$$

If your answer was (c) you forgot to use the absolute temperature.

Chapter 19   1 True   2 False: The anode is given first.   3 True   4 False: $CuSO_4 \rightleftharpoons$ $Cu^{2+} + SO_4^{2-}$ There are 2 equiv of Cu per mole, so 2 $\mathcal{F}$ are required per mole of Cu. 5 False: The reducing agent is Na not Na^+. (Reducing agents are on the right side of the equation.) Na^+ has already lost its valence electron so cannot act as a reducing agent. Na will reduce Mg^{2+} to Mg.   6 True   7 $Zn(s)|ZnSO_4(aq)\|CuSO_4(aq)|Cu(s)$ 8 Zn, Cu, Zn   9 Negatively, oxidized   10 Sodium   11 The quantity of electricity used   12 Right, top   13 (a)   14 (b)   15 (d)   16 (c)   17 (a) 18 (c)
19 (a) $Fe^{3+} + 3e^- \longrightarrow Fe$

Since 1 mol of Fe is 3 equiv, the equivalent weight is $56/3 = 19$.

20 (b) $Ni^{2+} + 2e^- \longrightarrow Ni$

$$\text{Equiv Ni} = \frac{1.0 \text{ g}(2 \text{ equiv mol}^{-1})}{59 \text{ g mol}^{-1}} = 0.034 \text{ equiv}$$

$$A = \frac{\text{equiv}}{s}(9.65 \times 10^4) = \frac{0.034(9.65 \times 10^4)}{20 \text{ min }(60 \text{ s min}^{-1})} = 2.7 \text{ A}$$

21 (c)

22 (d) $\mathcal{E}_{cell} = -(-0.44) + 0.34 = 0.78$

23 (c) The half-reactions are

$$6e^- + 2NO_3^- + 8H^+ \longrightarrow 2NO + 4H_2O$$

$$3Cu \longrightarrow 3Cu^{2+} + 6e^-$$

24 (a) The half-reactions are

$$
\begin{array}{lll}
Zn \longrightarrow Zn^{2+} + 2e^- & \mathcal{E}_{ox} = +0.76 \text{ V} \\
\underline{2H^+ + 2e^- \longrightarrow H_2} & \underline{\mathcal{E}_{red} = \ \ 0 \text{ V}} \\
2H^+ + Zn \longrightarrow Zn^{2+} + H_2 & \mathcal{E}_{cell} = \ \ 0.76 \text{ V}
\end{array}
$$

The Nernst equation is

$$\mathcal{E} = \mathcal{E}° - \frac{0.0592}{2} \log \frac{[Zn^{2+}]\, P_{H_2}}{[H^+]^2}$$

$$= 0.76 - \frac{0.0592}{2} \log \frac{0.50\,(0.30)}{(0.020)^2} = 0.68 \text{ V}$$

25 (d) $\log K = \dfrac{n\mathcal{E}°}{0.0592} = \dfrac{2(0.76)}{0.0592} = 25.7$

$$K = 10^{25.7} = 4.7 \times 10^{25}$$

Chapter 20   **1** False   **2** False: Bismuth oxide chloride. Bismuth hypochlorite would be $Bi(OCl)_3$.
3 False: HF is a weak acid.   **4** False: There is very little hydrogen bonding in H_2S
so it has a low boiling point.   **5** False: Thermal decomposition of NH_4NO_2 gives N_2.
6 True   **7** True   **8** $CuSO_4$, HNO_2, $NaBrO_3$, CaC_2, $HBrO_2$, MnO_4^-, $Al(HSO_4)_3$,
Ag_2CO_3 **9** Copper(I) iodide, lead(II) hypochlorite, cobalt(III) phosphate, tin(IV)
nitrite   **10** $H_2O_2 \longrightarrow H_2O + \frac{1}{2} O_2$ **11** I^- **12** $HClO_4$ **13** F_2
14 $S + O_2 \longrightarrow SO_2$

$$SO_2 + \tfrac{1}{2} O_2 \longrightarrow SO_3$$

$$SO_3 + H_2SO_4 \longrightarrow H_2S_2O_7$$

$$H_2S_2O_7 + H_2O \longrightarrow 2H_2SO_4$$

15 N_2O **16** NH_3 **17** Phosphate rock, $Ca_3(PO_4)_2$; coke; and sand   **18** (d)
19 (a)   **20** (d)   **21** (b)   **22** (c)   **23** (b)   **24** (a)   **25** (b)

Chapter 21   **1** True: The small size of Li^+ causes strong hydrolysis.   **2** True: See text for an
explanation of this paradox.   **3** False: Only Li forms the oxide. Na forms the
peroxide. K, Rb, and Cs form superoxides.   **4** True   **5** True   **6** False: +2 is
a more stable state.   **7** True   **8** Luster, good conductor, easily oxidized   **9**
Beryllium   **10** Ca^{2+}, Mg^{2+}, Fe^{2+} **11** $Ca(OH)_2$, Na_2CO_3 **12** Al_2O_3, NaOH,
$Al(OH)_3$, Al_2O_3 **13** Al, O_2, and F_2 **14** A tough layer of Al_2O_3 **15** Electron-
deficient, three-center   **16** (b)   **17** (c)   **18** (a)   **19** (c)   **20** (d)   **21** (c)
22 (d)   **23** (b)   **24** (a)   **25** (c)

Chapter 22   **1** False: The ns^2 electrons are lost first in ionization.   **2** False: It increases to
the center of the series and then decreases.   **3** True   **4** False: Crystal-field
theory does.   **5** True   **6** False: F^- is a weak-field ligand.   **7** False: Only for
d^4, d^5, d^6, and d^7 ions.   **8** +2   **9** Octahedral, d^2sp^3 or sp^3d^2 **10** Diam-
minetetrachlorocobaltate(III) ion   **11** $[CrBr_2(H_2O)_2(NH_3)_2]^+$ **12** 6   **13** t_{2g}
14 Ligand-field splitting energy, Δ **15** 2, 1   **16** 4, asymmetric, chiral, optical

isomers or enantiomers   **17** Polydentate or chelating agents   **18** Fe, Co, Ni
19 (d)   **20** (c)   **21** (a)   **22** (a)   **23** (b) Cr^{2+} has d^4 configuration.   The
strong-field d-orbital energy diagram is

$$-- \; e_g$$
$$\underline{\text{⥮ ↑ ↑}} \; t_{2g}$$

24 (d) Cr^{2+} has d^4 configuration.   The weak-field d-orbital energy configuration is

$$\underline{\text{↑}} \; _- \; e_g$$
$$\underline{\text{↑ ↑ ↑}} \; t_{2g}$$

25 (b) As trans forms.   **26** (d)   **27** (b)   **28** (b)   **29** (c)   **30** (d)

Chapter 23   **1** False: Carbon always forms four bonds in organic compounds, but if double or
triple bonds are formed it will bond to fewer than four atoms.   **2** False: There is
no such compound as isopropane.   **3** True   **4** False: The Π electrons are delocalized.   **5** True   **6** False: It is a secondary alcohol.   **7** True: They give aldehydes.   **8** False: It is the ketone of propane.   **9** True   **10** 2-Methylpropane

$$
\begin{array}{c}
CH_3-CH_2-CH_3 \\
| \\
\mathbf{11}\ CH{\equiv}C-C\!-\!\!-\!\!-CH-CH-CH_3 \\
||| \\
CH_3\ CH_2\ CH_3 \\
| \\
CH_3
\end{array}
$$

12 4-Ethyl-2-hexene (The double bond is given the lower number.)   **13** Nine
14 2-Chloropropane (Why not 1-chloropropane?)   **15** Toluene   **16** 1-3-Di-
methylbenzene   **17** 2-Butanol   **18** Propyl ethanoate, n-propyl acetate
19 Primary   **20** Asymmetric   **21** Peptide   **22** (b)   **23** (d)   **24** (d)
25 (c)   **26** (a)   **27** (d)   **28** (c)   **29** (c)   **30** (d)

Chapter 24   **1** False: Alpha emission would reduce the mass number by 4 and the atomic number
by 2.   **2** True   **3** False: $^{238}_{92}U/^{206}_{82}Pb$ and $^{14}_{6}C/^{12}_{6}C$ ratios are used.   **4** True
5 False: Neutron emission is rare.   These nuclei decay by beta emission.   **6** 4 h
7 Mass, positive   **8** Belt of stability   **9** One, increases   **10** Increases, decreases
11 Fission, slow or thermal neutron   **12** Neutrons plus protons, loss in mass or mass
defect, nuclear binding energy   **13** Critical mass   **14** (a)   **15** (d)   **16** (c)
17 (d)

18 (c) $k = \dfrac{0.693}{t_{1/2}} = \dfrac{0.693}{5.0 \text{ years}} = 0.139 \text{ year}^{-1}$

$\log \dfrac{x}{1} = -\dfrac{0.139 \text{ year}^{-1}\ (7.0 \text{ years})}{2.303} = -0.422$

$x = 10^{-0.422} = 0.378$

19 (a) $k = \dfrac{0.693}{t_{1/2}} = \dfrac{0.693}{5670 \text{ years}} = 1.22 \times 10^{-4} \text{ year}^{-1}$

$\log 0.950 = \dfrac{-(1.22 \times 10^{-4} \text{ year}^{-1})\, t}{2.303}$

$$t = 420 \text{ years}$$

20 (d)   **21** (a)   **22** (b)   **23** (d)

24 (b) Mass of 6 neutrons = 6(1.00867) = 6.05202 amu
Mass of 6 protons = 6(1.00728) = 6.04368 amu

$$12.09570 \text{ amu}$$

$$\text{Mass loss} = 12.09570 - 11.99671 = 0.09899 \text{ amu}$$

25 (a) $0.09899 \text{ amu} \dfrac{1 \text{ g}}{6.023 \times 10^{23} \text{ amu}} \dfrac{10^{-3} \text{ kg}}{\text{g}} = 1.643 \times 10^{-28} \text{ kg}$

$$E = mc^2 = 1.643 \times 10^{-28} \text{ kg} \ (2.998 \times 10^8 \text{ m s}^{-1})^2 = 1.477 \times 10^{-11} \text{ J}$$

$$\frac{1.477 \times 10^{-11} \text{ J}}{12 \text{ nucleons}} = 1.231 \times 10^{-12} \text{ J nucleon}^{-1}$$